Experimental Economics

Experimental Economics

Rethinking the Rules

Nicholas Bardsley

Robin Cubitt

Graham Loomes

Peter Moffatt

Chris Starmer

Robert Sugden

Princeton University Press

Princeton and Oxford

Copyright © 2010 by Princeton University Press

Published by Princeton University Press,
41 William Street, Princeton, New Jersey 08540

In the United Kingdom: Princeton University Press,
6 Oxford Street, Woodstock, Oxfordshire OX20 1TW

All Rights Reserved

ISBN: 978-0-691-12479-7 (alk. paper)

Library of Congress Control Number: 2009932364

British Library Cataloging-in-Publication Data is available

This book has been composed in LucidaBright using TEX
Typeset and copyedited by T&T Productions Ltd, London
Printed on acid-free paper. ∞

press.princeton.edu

Printed in the United States of America

10 9 8 7 6 5 4 3 2 1

Contents

Preface

This book is a coauthored work of six economists with wide-ranging experience of experimental economics and a long history of collaboration with each other stretching over several decades. It is the culmination of a research project that we began in 2002, funded by the Leverhulme Trust, and entitled "The Role of Experimental Methods in Economics." That project was motivated by two striking facts about the evolving landscape of contemporary economics research. One was the remarkable explosion in the use of experimental methods, a trend that has continued over recent years. The other was the extent of the controversy that accompanied this development: many in our profession continue to regard experimental results with skepticism; and, even among advocates of experimental methods, there are sharp disputes regarding how and where they should be used, and what can be learned from them.

On reflection, it may be no great surprise that the rise of experimental economics should provoke a degree of methodological controversy. The experimental turn in economics marks a clear departure from earlier received methodological wisdom and has happened very fast. The purpose of this book is to give a frank and informed assessment of the role, scope, output to date, and future potential of experimental research in economics. While, inevitably, it fell to individual coauthors to produce first drafts of different components of the text, the broad themes and issues were agreed in advance and the material evolved over many discussions and iterations before it reached its final form. The result is a jointly authored book to which we all subscribe.

We hope the book will be of interest and value to a variety of audiences. One important target group consists of experimental economists, including established practitioners and new or potential users. We hope the book will also be useful to other economists, particularly those who need to evaluate data, theory, or policy advice that draws support from experimental economics. More generally, we hope the work will be of value to those interested in the philosophy and history of science, be they economists, other social scientists, or professional philosophers with an interest in the methods of economics.

With this relatively wide audience in mind, we have aimed to construct a text that will be both stimulating for specialists and accessible to nonspecialists. We do not presume that readers have detailed prior knowledge of experimental economics, nor do we assume specialist knowledge of the philosophical literature on which we sometimes draw. In several chapters, we have placed parts of the text in shaded boxes. These are used to provide compact summaries of particular arguments or techniques. We urge readers not to skip the boxes, even if the box title sounds familiar, because boxed text does not merely state definitions or report received views. We use boxes to comment on, or set out, specific positions in relation to topics, as well as to provide convenient cross-references to the initial discussion of concepts that arise repeatedly within and between chapters.

We would like to thank Princeton University Press, and especially Richard Baggaley, for support and encouragement with this project. Three anonymous reviewers, commissioned by the Press, provided very helpful input. We are grateful to them, as well as to Sam Clark and Elizabeth Peters of T&T Productions Ltd for their careful and sympathetic copy-editing. We thank the Leverhulme Trust (award F/00204/K) and the Economic and Social Research Council (award RES 051 27 0146) for financial support.

In the development of the book, an important role was played by an interdisciplinary workshop that we organized at the University of Nottingham in 2003. It brought together an international group of academics with expertise covering experimental economics, economic theory, psychology, and philosophy of science. Some of the results of that workshop can be found in special issues of *Journal of Economic Methodology* (June 2005) and *Experimental Economics* (December 2005). After the workshop, we were able to identify more clearly the issues on which to focus when developing the assessment of experimental economics that we present in this book. We owe a special debt of gratitude to the participants. We would like to thank Francesco Guala for numerous discussions spread over many years. We also thank the very large number of people— including colleagues at the University of East Anglia, the University of Nottingham (particularly members of the CeDEx group), and elsewhere; participants at many conferences and workshops; other experimenters; methodologists; and several cohorts of graduate students—with whom the six of us have, over many years, discussed the various issues that arise in this book. While those who have shaped our thinking are too numerous to identify individually, their collective impact has been crucial. The reader must judge whether our influences have been effective at steering us down the right path. If not, the fault naturally rests entirely with us. Finally, we thank our loved ones for supporting us with their encouragement and, above all, their patience.

1
Introduction

1.1 Experiments in Economics

Over the last thirty years, there has been a revolutionary change in the methods of economics. For most of the twentieth century, reports of experiments were almost unknown in the literature. Economics—as viewed by economists, and as viewed by professional methodologists— was generally taken to be a nonexperimental science. This understanding of economics is encapsulated in an incidental remark in Milton Friedman's famous essay on the methodology of positive economics—an essay that deeply influenced economists' methodological self-perceptions for at least three decades. Friedman says:

> Unfortunately, we can seldom test particular predictions in the social sciences by experiments explicitly designed to eliminate what are judged to be the most important disturbing influences. Generally, we must rely on evidence cast up by the "experiments" that happen to occur.
>
> Friedman (1953, p. 10)

The implication is that the methods of economics, like those of astronomy (in the philosophy of science, the traditional example of a non-experimental science), are an adaptation to the practical impossibility of controlled experiments. But, from the 1980s onwards, there has been an explosive growth in the use of experimental methods in economics. In terms of most obvious signals, these methods are now accepted as part of the discipline. Experimental research is carried out by many economists around the world. Its results are routinely reported in the major journals. In 2002, Daniel Kahneman and Vernon Smith were awarded the Nobel memorial prize in recognition of their work as pioneers of experimental economics.

Even so, it would be a mistake to think that experimental methods are no longer controversial in economics. Most economists do not conduct experiments and many remain unconvinced of their usefulness, as experimentalists still often discover when invited to present research papers to general economics audiences. Perhaps more significantly, the apparent consensus that experiments have a legitimate role in economics hides major disagreements about what that role is. Experimental economics is not a unified research program. Indeed, the two Nobel memorial prize winners represent two very different lines of research: Smith is an economist who has developed novel experimental techniques to investigate traditional economic questions about the workings of markets; Kahneman is a psychologist who has used the well-established experimental methods of his discipline to challenge economists' conventional assumptions about the rationality of economic agents. Some commentators have seen these two styles of research as so different that they have reserved the term "experimental economics" for Smith's program, in distinction to the *behavioral economics* of Kahneman's program.[1] We find it more natural to define all forms of experimental research in economics as "experimental economics" and to use the term "behavioral economics" to refer to work, whether experimental or not, that uses psychological hypotheses to explain economic behavior. But whatever terminology one uses, it is undeniable that the research programs pursued by Smith and Kahneman began with different presuppositions and methodologies.

Economists can and do use experimental methods in their own work while rejecting the different methods used by other experimenters. They can and do recognize the value of some programs of experimental research while expressing skepticism about, or even hostility toward, others. There are ongoing disputes about what economics should learn from experimental results, about whether (or in what sense) economic theory can be tested in laboratory experiments, and about how far traditional theory needs to be adapted in the light of experimental results.

Given the speed with which experimental methods have been taken up, and the absence of a tradition of experimental research in economics, the existence of such controversies is hardly surprising. Perhaps for the same reasons, it is not always easy to discern exactly what the disputants are arguing about. In part, these controversies can be seen as normal scientific disagreements about how to interpret new findings. In part, they reflect disagreements about particular features of experimental method. In some cases, however, opponents may be arguing

---

[1] For example, Loewenstein (1999) criticizes some features of "experimental economics" (by which he means work in Smith's program) "from the vantage-point of behavioral economics."

at cross purposes, failing to appreciate that different types of experiments have different purposes and potentially different methodologies. In other cases, apparent disagreements about experimental method may be the surface indications of much deeper differences between rival understandings of what economics is and how its claims to knowledge are grounded. Because widespread use of experimental methods is so new to the discipline, professional methodologists have only just begun to revise their accounts of the methods of economics to take account of the change. Among the profession generally, there is no recognized set of general methodological principles that can be used to structure these controversies.

This book is the result of our sense that economics needs a methodological assessment of the claims to knowledge that can be derived from the various kinds of experiments that are now being used. Our aim is to offer such an assessment—to describe, appraise, and, where possible, adjudicate between different positions on how experiments do or do not help us to understand the real economic world. In doing so, we hope to enrich the practice and understanding of experimental economics.

We hope to interest at least three kinds of reader: *practicing experimental economists* engaged in these controversies at first hand; *nonexperimental economists* trying to decide how to interpret (or whether to take any notice of) experimental results and the claims that experimentalists make about them; and *philosophers of science* who want to examine the status of the knowledge claims made in economics, or are curious about how a scientific community that once disclaimed experimental methods adapts to their introduction. Clearly, these groups of readers will come to the book with different background knowledge. In the rest of this chapter we provide some basic orientation for our varied readers. In section 1.2, we take a brief look at the history of experiments in economics and ask why economics saw itself for so long as a nonexperimental science. This leads into a discussion of some of the reservations that economists continue to express about experiments, and that feature in ongoing methodological controversies. In section 1.3, we provide outline descriptions of eight experiments, chosen from across the range of experimental economics, broadly interpreted. Our aim here is to give readers who are not familiar with experimental economics a preliminary sense of what this form of research is, and the kinds of claims that its practitioners make. In section 1.4, we use these examples to illustrate the main issues that will be addressed in the rest of the book. Finally, in section 1.5, we explain the stance that we take as authors, as practicing experimental economists writing about the methodology of our own branch of our discipline.

1.2   Does Economics Need Experiments?

Perhaps surprisingly, given the general perceptions among economists, the idea that controlled experiments can contribute to economics has a long history.

In an account of the history of experimental economics, Alvin Roth (1995a) uses as his earliest example the work of Daniel and Nicholas Bernoulli on the "St. Petersburg paradox" Bernoulli (1738). The St. Petersburg paradox is a hypothetical problem of decision under risk, in which most people's ideas about reasonable choice contravene the principle of maximizing expected monetary value. In an informal use of experimental methods, Nicholas Bernoulli tried out this decision problem on a famous mathematician to check his own intuitions about it.

We suggest that David Hume is another candidate for the experimental economists' Hall of Fame. Hume's *A Treatise of Human Nature* (1739-40) is now generally regarded as one of the canonical texts of philosophy, but it can also be read as a pioneering work in experimental psychology and decision and game theory. Significantly, the subtitle of Hume's book is: *Being an Attempt to Introduce the Experimental Method of Reasoning Into Moral Subjects.* In the preface, Hume describes his work as a study of "the extent and force of human understanding, . . . the nature of the ideas we employ, and of the operations we perform in our reasonings." He undertakes to use the methodology of the natural sciences, investigating the workings of the human mind by "careful and exact experiments, and the observation of those particular effects, which result from its different circumstances and situations" (Hume 1739-40 pp. xv-xvii).[2] In the course of the book, he describes the designs of a series of psychological experiments, and invites his readers to try these out on themselves. Among the results he finds are phenomena that were rediscovered (as so-called anomalies of decision-making behavior) by experimental psychologists and experimental economists in the late twentieth century.[3]

It is particularly significant that neoclassical economics—the orthodox approach to the subject for most of the twentieth century—was, in the first years of its existence, based on experimental research. The pioneers of neoclassical economics were strongly influenced by what were then recent findings of experimental psychology. In launching the "marginal revolution" in economic theory, Stanley Jevons (1871) and Francis Edgeworth (1881) based their analyses of diminishing marginal

---

[2] Page numbers are from the 1978 edition.
[3] This interpretation of Hume is defended by Sugden (1986, 2006).

utility on psychological findings about the relationship between stimuli and sensations. These authors were well aware of the work of psychophysicists such as Gustav Fechner and Wilhelm Wundt, which they saw as providing the scientific underpinning for the theory of demand. It was only from the beginning of the twentieth century that neoclassical economics separated itself off from experimental psychology, in a self-conscious process initiated by Vilfredo Pareto (1906).[4] Intriguingly, Jevons (1870) may have been the first person to report the results of a controlled economic experiment in a scientific journal. This report, in the second volume of *Nature*, is of a series of experiments carried out by Jevons himself, investigating the relationship between fatigue and the effectiveness of human muscular effort. This was a matter of real economic importance at a time when major civil engineering works were being constructed by men with spades and wheelbarrows. Jevons (1871, pp. 213–16)[5] tells us that he ran these experiments to illustrate "the mode in which some of the laws forming the physical basis of economics might be ascertained." As one might expect of a pioneer of neoclassical economics, Jevons was interested in such maximization problems as determining the optimal size of spade for shifting different materials, and the optimal rate of marching for an army.[6]

Nevertheless, for much of the twentieth century, experimentation was a marginal activity in economics, barely impinging on the consciousness of most economists. With hindsight, it is possible to pick out landmark contributions to experimental economics, some even published in major economics journals; but it is striking that, for many years, very little was done to build on these isolated pieces of work. It seems that they were seen as having curiosity value, rather than as being part of the real business of economics.

For example, an experiment by Louis Thurstone (1931) is now seen as a classic. Thurstone, who was based at the University of Chicago, was one of the leading psychophysicists of his time. Through conversations with his colleague Henry Schultz, an economist doing pathbreaking work on the statistical estimation of demand functions, Thurstone had become aware that the concept of an indifference curve in economic theory had no direct empirical grounding. His experiment attempted to elicit individuals' indifference curves from responses to binary choice problems.

---

[4] For more on this episode in the history of economics, see Maas (2005) and Bruni and Sugden (2007).

[5] Page numbers are from the 1970 edition.

[6] This early exercise in experimental economics was pointed out to us by Harro Maas. The historical and methodological significance of these experiments is discussed in Maas (2005).

Over the following three decades, the project of investigating whether the preferences postulated in theory can be elicited from actual choice behavior was pursued by only a tiny number of economists and decision theorists (see, for example, Mosteller and Nogee 1951; Allais 1953; Davidson et al. 1957; Davidson and Marschak 1959). Maurice Allais's discovery, in the early 1950s, of a systematic divergence between theory and behavior (that we describe in chapter 2) did not much trouble economists for another twenty years.

Similarly, Edward Chamberlin's (1948) investigation of price-determination in an experimental market would appear on any present-day list of great experiments in economics. Chamberlin was a leading industrial economist, famous for his theory of monopolistic competition. His experiment (described in chapter 4) was motivated by his awareness that price theory, despite its formal sophistication, provided no real explanation of how equilibrium is reached in real markets. His results seemed to confirm his hunch that equilibrium would *not* be reached under conditions typical of real-world markets. His paper was published in the *Journal of Political Economy*, but little further work was done for more than a decade. Systematic research on experimental markets was getting under way from the end of the 1950s (see, for example, Sauermann and Selten 1959; Siegel and Fouraker 1960; Smith 1962), but it remained very much a minority taste.[7] It seems that most economists did not think that price theory was in need of experimental support.

Notwithstanding the existence of a few studies now seen as landmarks, it is probable that the large majority of economists saw their subject as fundamentally nonexperimental at least until the last two decades of the twentieth century. For many trained in the third quarter of the century, Friedman's 1953 essay would be their sole excursion into the subject's methodological literature; and echoes of its incidental remark on experiments could also be found in introductory textbooks of the time. For example, consider the following quotation from the 1979 edition[8] of Richard Lipsey's classic textbook:

> Experimental sciences, such as chemistry and some branches of psychology, have an advantage because it is possible to produce relevant

---

[7] The psychologist Sidney Siegel (1916–61) played an important part in early experimental investigations both of individual decision making (following what would now be called a behavioral approach) and of oligopolistic markets. Innocenti (2008) appraises Siegel's contribution to experimental economics and the loss caused by his premature death.

[8] By 1979, both Vernon Smith and Daniel Kahneman, later to become Nobel laureates of experimental economics, had already completed some of what is now their most famous work.

evidence through controlled laboratory experiments. Other sciences, such as astronomy and economics, cannot do this.[9]

Lipsey (1979, p. 8)

Even now, one occasionally finds serious writers who echo Friedman's remark. For example, in the abstract of a paper on the methodology of economics published in a recent issue of *Philosophy of Science*, Marcel Boumans (2003, p. 308) asserts: "In the social sciences we hardly can create laboratory conditions, we only can try to find out which kinds of experiments Nature has carried out." Boumans's paper is an extended discussion of the question of how, given the supposed infeasibility of controlled experiments, economics can discover lawlike relationships within its domain of investigation.

Why did economists accept for so long the idea that their discipline was nonexperimental? It is sometimes suggested that the widespread use of experimental methods in economics has become possible only as a result of developments in information technology. It is certainly true that many experimental designs that are now used routinely would have been simply infeasible a few decades ago. The availability of generic software for economics experiments, such as the widely used z-Tree package designed by Urs Fischbacher (2007), has greatly reduced the investment in skills necessary to run computerized experiments. But, as our historical sketch has illustrated, there was no shortage of feasible and potentially informative experimental designs in the first three quarters of the twentieth century—just very little interest in using them. Even in the 1980s—the decade in which experimental methods began to be accepted in economics—many of the most significant experiments used pencil-and-paper technology. What has to be explained is why economists believed for so long that the information that such experiments would produce would not be useful.

Recall that Friedman's comment was that social scientists can seldom test particular predictions in controlled experiments. Since controlled experiments with human subjects are clearly possible, it seems that Friedman must be interpreted as saying that *the kinds of experiments that are possible* cannot be used to test *the kinds of predictions that economics makes.* Lipsey's use of the qualifier "relevant" suggests

---

[9] As an aside, it is interesting to note that Lipsey draws a sharp distinction between economics and psychology that would now seem harder to defend. But the relationship between experimental economics and experimental psychology has been hotly debated; some, such as Hertwig and Ortmann (2001), point to supposed advantages of economists' techniques; others, such as Loewenstein (1999), argue that experimental economics (of a certain kind) has low external validity, compared with experiments closer to traditions in psychology.

a similar view. Such claims should be understood in relation to two features of mid-twentieth-century economics. First, the domain in which economics was expected to make predictions was, by modern standards, narrow. As is suggested by the then-common use of the term "price theory" as a synonym for "microeconomics," the main focus of microeconomics was on explaining and predicting the values of statistics of aggregate market behavior—in particular, prices and total quantities traded. Macroeconomics worked at an even higher level of aggregation. Thus, the *useful* predictions of economics operated at a level at which, it was thought, direct experimental tests would be enormously costly and perhaps even unethical. The second feature was a prevailing conviction—a conviction for which Friedman (1953) argued strongly—that the "assumptions" of a theory are not claims about how the world is, but merely "as-if" propositions that happen to be useful in deriving predictions. Although price theory was derived from apparently restrictive assumptions about individuals' preferences, those assumptions were not to be interpreted as empirical hypotheses to which the theory was committed. Thus, experiments that purported to "test" the assumptions would be pointless.

A further source of resistance to experiments came from skepticism about whether people's behavior in laboratory or classroom experiments is indicative of their behavior in "real" economic environments—or, as experimentalists now more often say, *in the field*. Friedman again provides an example. As a young economist, he was the coauthor (with Allen Wallis) of a paper on Thurstone's indifference-curve experiment. Wallis and Friedman argue that this experiment is too "artificial" for its results to be reliably transferable to an "economic situation," claiming that "[f]or a satisfactory experiment it is essential that the subject give actual reactions to actual stimuli" (Wallis and Friedman 1942, pp. 179–80).[10]

Friedman seems to have thought that neoclassical price theory, when applied to the "economic situations" for which it was intended, would generally yield successful predictions. But it is surprisingly common for economists to claim that the core theories of their discipline are useful despite being *disconfirmed* by the evidence. This maneuver can be seen in the common idea that theories based on idealized assumptions— for example, the theory of perfect competition, or classical game theory with its assumption of unlimited rationality—provide "benchmarks" for

---

[10] Viewed from the perspective of modern experimental economics, this involves a non sequitur. A key step in the development of experimental economics has been acceptance of the view, promoted for example by Smith (1982a), that subjects can face and respond to actual economic stimuli even in artificial situations.

understanding the real world. The idea is that we can organize our knowledge of the real world by cataloging its "imperfections" relative to the theory. If one sees a theory in this light, the whole idea of testing it may seem misplaced.

Although probably few economists today would openly dismiss experimental methods out of hand, these (and other) arguments against the validity or usefulness of experiments continue to have resonance in the discipline. Indeed, they are often expressed by experimenters themselves, particularly when criticizing other people's research programs. To illustrate how fundamental questions about the appropriateness of experimental methods remain matters of debate in economics, we look at four recent papers written by well-known economists with experience of experimental research.

In the first paper, Ken Binmore (1999) echoes Wallis and Friedman's reservations about the significance of laboratory results. Binmore's criticisms are directed particularly at the experimental program exemplified by Kahneman's work. Characterizing the main thrust of this program as "denying the validity of orthodox economic reasoning," Binmore urges economists not to be "led by the nose" into accepting its conclusions (pp. F16, F19). He accepts that the behavior of individuals in laboratory experiments is often systematically different from that of the rational agents of economic theory, but rejects the conclusion that the theory has thereby been disconfirmed. Economic theory, he argues, can reasonably be expected to apply only under particular conditions (for example, that decision makers have incentives to deliberate and have had opportunities to learn by experience). Binmore argues that these conditions are not satisfied in the experiments he criticizes. Thus, he concludes, to use the results of such experiments as evidence against economic theory is like claiming to refute chemistry by experiments in which reagents are mixed in dirty test tubes (p. F23).

In the second paper, Steven Levitt and John List (2007) offer guidelines for judging whether laboratory results can be extrapolated to behavior in the field. While Binmore's main concern is with whether the laboratory environment satisfies the conditions presupposed by economic theory, Levitt and List frame their inquiry in terms of how far laboratory experiments capture relevant features of the settings in which economic decisions are made in the field. Their particular concern is with experiments that appear to show that economic agents act on "social preferences" (such as preferences for actions that are construed as fair or trustworthy, or that punish people who have been unfair or untrustworthy). While not proposing the wholesale rejection of any particular class of experiments,

Levitt and List identify various ways in which the "artificiality" of the laboratory might produce results that would not transfer to the field. For
example, they argue that laboratory subjects are normally conscious of
acting under the scrutiny of experimenters and that, as a result, they may
be more inclined to follow moral norms than their counterparts in the
field. Echoing an argument used by Friedman (1953), Levitt and List point
out that, in many of the environments studied by economists, decision
makers are not a representative sample of the population. Instead, people *become* decision makers through processes of selection (for example,
to continue in business as a stock-market trader, one has to make profits on one's dealings). These processes might systematically eliminate
individuals who act on social preferences. Conversely, standard methods of recruiting volunteers to participate in experiments may select
individuals who are predisposed to be cooperative or to seek social
approval.

Our third example illustrates a different kind of reservation about
experiments. Ariel Rubinstein (2001) writes as a "pure theorist" who has
returned from a "short detour" into experimental research. Focusing on
decision and game theory, he argues that it is "hopeless and, more importantly, pointless to test the predictions of models in economic theory"
(p. 618). For Rubinstein, theoretical models do not generate concrete
predictions about behavior in any particular situations. Rather, a model
represents, in an abstract form, some "consideration" or "type of argument" that decision makers *might* (not *do*) use. The test of the realism
of a model is its intuitive appeal: "[O]ur intuition provides the test. If
a phenomenon is robust, we intuitively recognize it as such. It strikes
a chord upon us. If we are honest with ourselves, we can feel that it is
true" (p. 616). Rubinstein says that, before his detour, he believed that
theorists could safely rely on their own intuitions, and so experiments
were unnecessary. He now acknowledges that there is a role for experiments as a means of testing whether the theorist's intuitions "ring true"
or "make sense" for other people, but *not* as a way of testing theoretical
predictions. And, by the end of the paper, he is not completely sure even
about that: he leaves it as an open question whether experiments are
more reliable than the theorist's "gut feelings" (p. 627).

One of Rubinstein's reasons for thinking this an open question is that
"the significance of experimental work relies so heavily on our honesty,"
with the apparently intended implication that this cannot be relied on
(Rubinstein 2001, p. 627). More explicitly, he claims that experimental economics fails to respect certain rules of good scientific method.
As one example, he asserts that many experimental economists follow
the "problematic practice" of selecting a research question only after

"sifting results ex post: namely, after the results have been gathered" (p. 626). This criticism seems to presuppose a principle that some experimentalists may reject: namely, that the function of experiments is only to *test* hypotheses and intuitions, not to *generate* them. (The latter, presumably, is the role of the theorist.) Here, we suggest, a criticism of the scientific standards of experimental work may conceal a much more fundamental disagreement about how knowledge claims can be grounded.

Our final example is a paper with the provocative title "Experimental economics: science or what?" written by Ken Binmore and Avner Shaked (2007). As in Binmore's 1999 paper, criticism is directed at the inferences that behavioral economists have drawn from experimental results. In this case, however, the criticism is directed not at particular types of experimental designs, but at what Binmore and Shaked argue are inflated claims made on behalf of particular theories. The charge is that some experimental economists use "cherry-picking" methods to appraise their favored theories—in particular, not prespecifying a theory's domain of application before testing it, citing as supporting evidence only those tests that the theory passes, and allowing parameters of the theory to take different values when fitted to different experimental data sets. Whatever one makes of Binmore and Shaked's view of particular theories in behavioral economics, their paper draws attention to important and unresolved methodological questions for experimental economics. When experimental evidence reveals systematic deviations from previously received theory, how should economists go about incorporating those findings into new theories? How far can one legitimately generalize from narrowly defined classes of experiment to the whole range of cases to which economic theories are expected to apply?

For the purposes of this introductory chapter, it is sufficient to recognize that the role of experimental methods in economics remains controversial. These controversies provide the context and raison d'être for our book.

1.3   The Practice of Experimental Economics

Before commencing a discussion of experimental economics, it is important to have some picture of what it involves. Since we do not presume that all readers will be familiar with the field, we start by illustrating some of the things that experimenters do. Since the literature is now vast, we cannot sensibly attempt a review of experimental economics in the round.[11] Instead, our strategy is to describe a few published papers that exemplify some of the main genres of experimental research. We aim to illustrate the sorts of questions that have motivated experimenters in economics and the methods they have used to tackle them; we will describe some of the main results reported in these papers and note broader claims made by the authors. In this section, our aim is strictly descriptive; we wish to give a compact account of what various researchers did, found, and wrote, while (for the moment) avoiding any evaluation of it.

Many of the things that experimental economists now do have close parallels with work that has older roots in the traditions of experimental psychology. With this in mind, we begin with two illustrations of research conducted by psychologists. The first of these, due to Amos Tversky and Daniel Kahneman (1981), is a laboratory experiment investigating individual decision making with a particular focus on decisions involving risk.

Illustration 1 (Tversky and Kahneman (1981), "The framing of decisions and psychology of choice," *Science***).** Tversky and Kahneman present the results of experiments investigating whether small changes in the description of the alternatives available in a decision problem, which apparently leave the logical structure of the decision problem unchanged, might nevertheless affect what is chosen. They find that seemingly inconsequential changes in the "framing" of decision problems can have a substantial impact on choices. Here is one example. They compare the behavior of two groups of subjects. One group of 152 subjects was confronted with the following choice problem:

> Imagine that the United States is preparing for the outbreak of an unusual Asian disease, which is expected to kill 600 people. Two alternative programs to combat the disease have been proposed. Assume that the exact scientific estimate of the consequences of the programs are as follows.
>
> If Program A is adopted, 200 people will be saved.
>
> If Program B is adopted, there is 1/3 probability that 600 people will be saved, and 2/3 probability that no people will be saved.
>
> Which of the two programs would you favor?

---

[11] The eight chapters of Kagel and Roth (1995) provide heroically comprehensive guides to the main areas of experimental economics as they existed up to the mid 1990s. But, as the bibliographies of many of the chapters ran to several pages then and the subsequent literature has grown very rapidly, a similarly comprehensive record of the whole of experimental economics would now require several volumes. For example, Camerer (2003), which runs to over five hundred pages, surveys the experimental literature on games, a topic that occupied just three of the chapters of Kagel and Roth (1995).

A second group of 155 subjects were presented with the identical scenario except that the outcomes of the two alternatives were described as numbers of lives lost (out of 600) instead of lives saved. Hence, the two alternatives presented to the second group were:

> If Program C is adopted 400 people will die.
>
> If Program D is adopted there is 1/3 probability that nobody will die, and 2/3 probability that 600 people will die.

Placed side by side, it is easy to see that the choices offered to the two groups are logically equivalent. Nevertheless, Tversky and Kahneman report very different behavior across the groups: in the first group, the majority (72 %) preferred Program A; while in the second group, the majority (78 %) preferred Program D.

The decision makers facing these tasks were students at either Stanford University or the University of British Columbia and the decisions were presented as questionnaires conducted in classrooms. While the example just described was presented to the students as a purely hypothetical choice, other choices made by subjects in their studies involved the possibility of real monetary payoffs. Tversky and Kahneman (1981, p. 453) interpret their evidence as, on the one hand, demonstrating violations of principles of coherence implicit in rational-choice theory, and, on the other, as providing clues to "psychological principles that govern the perception of decision problems and the evaluation of options."

Our second illustration, due to James Bryan and Mary Ann Test (1967), reports a set of experiments designed to explore whether individuals are more likely to engage in altruistic behavior when they see examples of other people doing so.

Illustration 2 (Bryan and Test (1967), "Models and helping: naturalistic studies in aiding behavior," *Journal of Personality and Social Psychology***).** This paper reports four experiments. One of them compared two conditions that we will call the "baseline" and the "treatment." In the baseline condition, a young female undergraduate was commissioned to stand by a car (a 1964 Mustang) with a flat tire in a residential area of Los Angeles. The setting was staged so as to make it easy for other passing drivers to see the woman, the flat tire, and the presence of an inflated tire leaning against the car. This baseline treatment was run on two successive Saturday afternoons, across a time interval long enough to allow exactly 1,000 cars to pass on each day, and the experimenters recorded how many drivers stopped to offer help. The treatment condition was exactly the same except that a second car (an Oldsmobile) with a flat tire and a young woman standing by it was positioned $\frac{1}{4}$ of a mile upstream of the traffic flow. This car, however, was already raised on a jack and a man was changing the tire as the woman watched. The order of the two conditions was reversed across the two Saturdays to "counterbalance" the design. Bryan and Test report that significantly more vehicles stopped in the treatment condition (58 out of 2,000, compared with 35 out of 2,000 in the control condition).

Bryan and Test's other three experiments involved collections for the Salvation Army on busy shopping streets. In one of these experiments, a person wearing a Salvation Army uniform stood with a collection box (or "kettle") outside the main entrance of a large department store in Princeton, New Jersey. The collector could ring a bell to signal their presence, but they were instructed to make no verbal appeals for donations and to make no responses to actual donations. Against this backdrop, the experimenters then simulated altruistic acts in the following way: every sixty seconds, a second person in the employ of the experimenters (dressed as a white-collar worker) would approach the collector from within the store, deposit 5 cents, and then head away. Observations were collected for a total of 365 such minutes. Bryan and Test hypothesized that people passing in the vicinity of the collection point when the experimental stooge made a donation would be more likely to donate themselves. To test this hypothesis, they compared the frequency of donations occurring in the twenty-second "window" immediately following the stooge's donation with those occurring in the subsequent twenty-second window. They recorded a total of sixty-nine donations occurring in the first window and only forty-three in the second. The difference is strongly statistically significant.

Bryan and Test interpret their findings as providing support for the hypothesis that "observation of altruistic activity will increase such behavior among observers" (Bryan and Test 1967, p. 403). A feature of all four of their experiments is that the participants whose decisions were being observed were simply passers-by who, it was intended, should have no knowledge of their participation in an experiment at the point they took their decision to help (or not).

Our third illustration also investigates individual decision making, but this case provides an example of a more recent study, designed and run by economists. This experiment gathers data on individual risk preferences using two quite standard approaches: individuals are asked to make straight choices between pairs of gambles; they also state selling prices for various gambles. Data of this sort has been gathered for a number of purposes. In some cases, interest centers on measurement of preference parameters in particular theories; in other cases, preference data are gathered with a view to testing particular preference theories.[12] In our third illustration, however, the primary purpose was to test the reliability of what had been a widely used experimental incentive mechanism: the *binary lottery procedure.*

The binary lottery procedure works in the following way. Suppose subjects taking part in an experiment earn points as a consequence of completing specific tasks: those tasks might, for example, be participation in strategic games, and the points would be the payoffs resulting from the strategy combinations of the players. One way to incentivize such tasks is to translate the points won by a subject into a money payment at some exchange rate. However, the binary lottery procedure instead translates points into a probability of winning a known prize in a binary lottery (i.e., one in which the subject either wins or receives nothing). The attraction of this approach is that if individuals' preferences satisfy certain conditions, subjects in an experiment implementing this procedure should make risk-neutral decisions. The ability to control preferences, by screening out attitudes to risk, could be very useful, if it works. An experiment reported by Reinhard Selten et al. (1999) was designed to test whether it does. It provides an example of how experiments can be used to investigate the properties of devices used by other experiments. This genre has a counterpart in the natural sciences, where experiments are sometimes used, for example, to test the reliability of measuring instruments.

Illustration 3 (Selten et al. (1999), "Money does not induce risk neutral behavior, but binary lotteries do even worse," *Theory and Decision*). In this experiment, each subject made a series of thirty-six pairwise choices between two lotteries. They also stated minimum selling prices for fourteen lotteries and the experimenter then generated a random offer to determine whether the subject kept or sold this lottery. Subjects were randomly allocated across two treatments, one of which involved a binary lottery procedure. In both treatments, after every pair of tasks—called a "round"—subjects received a payoff in points determined by their decisions and the resolution of lotteries from that round. In the binary lottery group the point payoff from the round then determined a probability used to play a "grand" lottery for a fixed prize. Subjects in the other condition simply had their point payoff from each round converted to a money payoff using an exchange rate designed to

---

[12] Holt and Laury (2002) is an example of the first case and Camerer (1989) of the second. Camerer (1995) and Starmer (2000) provide surveys.

equalize expected earnings across the groups. A subset of subjects facing each of these conditions also had access to computerized calculators which would report, on request, measures including a gamble's expected value.

A total of 144 subjects, recruited from the student population at the University of Bonn, took part. Sessions lasted about ninety minutes and subjects earned (on average) between DM15.50 and DM39.50 in this time. To analyze the data, the authors constructed a measure of the extent to which each individual's decisions depart from expected value maximization. Their primary conclusion was that subjects in the treatment using the binary lottery procedure departed from expected value maximization significantly more than those subjects who received direct money payments. Hence they concluded that "the use of payoffs in binary lottery tickets in experiments is counterproductive" (Selten et al. 1999, p. 225).

Another major line of enquiry in experimental economics focuses on strategic behavior in stylized games. We have three illustrations of work in this genre. The first, due to Jacob Goeree and Charles Holt (2001), reports behavior across a range of games and concludes that predictions based on Nash equilibrium work well in some cases but not in others.

Illustration 4 (Goeree and Holt (2001), "Ten little treasures of game theory, and ten intuitive contradictions," *American Economic Review***).** This paper examines behavior in twenty two-player games, consisting of ten matched pairs of games: in each such pair, there is one game where observed play corresponds well with Nash equilibrium predictions (these are the ten "treasures" of the paper's title) and another game for which the researchers predict (and find) that behavior deviates markedly from such predictions (these are the "intuitive contradictions").

Participants were undergraduate students recruited from economics classes at the University of Virginia. Subjects took part in sessions involving ten people. Prior to making decisions in the games reported in the paper, the subjects played a repeated two-person game with random matching. This was intended partly to familiarize participants with general features of the task environment, but in a different game from the subsequent one-shot tasks. After this, subjects responded to a set of one-shot games: these were a subset of the pairs of treasure/contradiction treatments reported in the paper as a whole. Sessions lasted two hours and subjects were paid an average of $35 (including a flat fee of $6 for turning up).

Here is one example from the study based on the "traveler's dilemma" game due to Basu (1994). In this game, two players simultaneously select an integer in the range 180–300. The payoffs are then determined in the following way: both players receive the lower of the two values, but, in addition, a "transfer" amount $T > 0$ is added to the payoff of the player who set the lower amount, and subtracted from the payoff of the player who set the higher amount. With $T > 0$, a player would maximize their own payoff if they managed to state a number just one less than their opponent. So if I am playing the game and I expect the other player to play 300, I should play 299. But if they expect me to play 299, then they should play 298. As Goeree and Holt explain, this type of reasoning implies that the game has a unique Nash equilibrium, in which both players select the number 180. While this equilibrium prediction does not depend on the value of T (provided $T > 0$), the authors suggest that behavior might depend on T because, since T is the cost of being underbid, Nash equilibrium predictions might work better when this cost is relatively high. They test this conjecture by observing play across two implementations of the game with T set either High ($T = 180$) or Low ($T = 5$). They report data based on the decisions of fifty subjects who were paired to make decisions in both the "High-T" and "Low-T" versions (the two games were presented in random order and separated by having subjects make decisions for other pairs of treasure/contradiction games reported in the paper). The authors report very high conformity with Nash predictions in the High-T condition (around 80% of subjects state 180) and very low conformity with Nash in the Low-T condition. In the latter case, only around 20% play the Nash strategy; moreover, relative to the Nash prediction, the majority of subjects chose values at the opposite end of the strategy space.

Our next example is an investigation of contributions to public goods. Like many experiments on this issue, the design is built around a device known as the voluntary-contributions mechanism. In an experiment that uses this mechanism, each subject in a group has to divide an endowment between a private good and a public good. Payments to each subject are determined by the decisions of all group members in such a way that, for a subject who seeks to maximize their own monetary payoff, it is a dominant strategy to allocate their whole endowment to the private good, even though all group members would be better off if all contributed their whole endowment to the public good (see box 2.3 (p. 58) for more detail). Typical findings from the many studies that have used this device are that, in a finitely repeated game, many subjects begin by contributing around half of their endowment to the public good, but that average contributions decline toward zero with repetition. The study by Ernst Fehr and Simon Gächter (2000) is set against this backdrop. It investigates whether the opportunity for players to punish each other affects contributions in a public-goods game.

Illustration 5 (Fehr and Gächter (2000), "Cooperation and punishment in public goods experiments," *American Economic Review***).** In this experiment, subjects played repeated rounds in groups of four, selected from a larger pool of participants. Some groups played under a "strangers" protocol, meaning that groups were selected at random from the larger pool separately for each round; others played under a "partners" protocol meaning that, although selected at random initially, the groupings stayed the same across rounds. (See box 2.8 (p. 88) and section 2.7 for further discussion of these protocols.) Subjects were told which of these conditions applied but, under both conditions, they interacted anonymously via computer terminals. Subjects knew that they would receive a money payoff at the end of the experiment determined by their final holdings of "tokens" from all rounds.

The main innovation of Fehr and Gächter's design was to introduce the possibility of punishment. Subjects in both protocols played ten rounds without punishment opportunities and ten rounds with them (the order of these conditions was varied, to control for order effects). When punishment opportunities were not available, in a given round, subjects played a voluntary-contributions game of the kind described above. But, when punishment opportunities were available, the voluntary-contributions stage was followed by a further stage in which, after being informed of contributions made to the public good by their fellow group members, subjects could award "punishment points" to them. Each punishment point reduced the payoff of the punished subject for that round by 10%, but punishing was also costly to subjects awarding it. Because of the latter feature, a standard game-theoretic argument implies that, if subjects care only about their own money payoffs, punishment points will never be assigned and, therefore, the opportunity to assign them will have no effect on contributions to the public good.

The no-punishment conditions replicated well-known findings of experiments using the voluntary-contributions mechanism: significant contributions were observed in early periods, but these decayed across rounds and approached full free-riding by round ten. This serves as a baseline against which to compare behavior in the punishment conditions. Although punishing was costly, punishing was observed, even in the strangers condition. The opportunity to punish had a significant impact on contributions behavior, with differences between strangers and partners conditions: in the strangers treatment with punishment, contributions no longer converged toward free-riding, but there was considerable variation in behavior and "no stable behavioral regularity regarding individual contributions" (Fehr and Gächter 2000, p. 986) emerged. In the partners condition with punishment, behavior appeared to converge toward the Pareto-efficient (full contribution) outcome.

Our third "games" example, a study by John Morgan et al. (2006), straddles the literature on games and markets. The experiment tests the predictions of a particular game-theoretic model: a "clearinghouse" model of pricing behavior among oligopolistic firms.

Illustration 6 (Morgan et al. (2006), "An experimental study of price dispersion," *Games and Economic Behavior***).** The paper begins by setting out a simple clearinghouse model; a variant of that due to Varian (1980). In this model, n identical firms (facing constant marginal costs) engage in price competition to sell a homogenous product. On the demand side there are two types of consumers: a fraction λ of "informed" consumers are assumed to buy from the firm setting the lowest price; the remaining consumers are "loyal" in the sense that their demand is equally distributed among all firms who offer prices below a critical reservation value. Morgan et al. show that when firms are risk-neutral profit maximizers, the game has a unique symmetric mixed strategy equilibrium. They also highlight two comparative static implications of the model that are key to their tests: increasing λ is predicted to reduce the prices faced by both types of consumers; whereas increasing n is predicted to impact differentially for the two types, *reducing* prices for informed consumers and *increasing* those for loyal consumers.

The experiment was run as a series of sessions, each involving subjects from the student population at the University of Nottingham. In each session, subjects sat at computer terminals and participated in experimental markets structured to mimic various features of the theoretical model. The participants played the role of sellers in these markets and their task was to set their firm's price in each of ninety market periods. The number of sellers in each market was held constant within a session, but varied between sessions (half the sessions had two sellers per market, the rest had four). At the start of each period, sellers were randomly grouped into markets (of either two or four sellers depending on session). They then simultaneously set their "prices" by selecting a number ranging from 0 to 100. The demand side of the market was simulated using computerized consumers. Sellers knew that in every period there were six consumers who would buy twelve units each; a known fraction of these consumers, being "informed" in the sense of the model, would buy from the seller with the lowest price, while the demand of the others was allocated evenly across sellers regardless of their prices. At the end of each period, each player learned the prices set by competing sellers and the resulting pattern of sales. They earned a number of points equal to their own sales level times their price. The ninety periods were divided into three phases of thirty periods and the number of informed buyers was varied across phases: for the first and last phase, half of the buyers were informed; for the intermediate phase, five out of six were informed. Sessions lasted about ninety minutes and subjects were paid a flat fee for attending plus a money reward that increased by a penny for every 100 points earned in the experiment.

The authors report mixed success for the predictions of the theoretical model. On the negative side, there are significant discrepancies between the predicted and observed price distributions: relative to theoretical predictions, observed prices are too high in two-seller treatments and too dispersed in four-seller treatments. In contrast, the comparative static predictions relating to changes in both the number of sellers and the proportion of informed consumers are broadly supported in the data.

In our next illustration, due to Smith et al. (1988), the researchers created and observed trading in an experimental asset market, with a view to studying the incidence of speculative bubbles. In economics, there has been much debate about the extent to which volatility in financial markets reflects speculation-fueled bubbles, i.e., deviations from "fundamental" asset values. An obstacle to reaching clear conclusions in these debates through the analysis of field data is the fact that some fundamentals are typically unobserved in such data. The following study came at the problem by creating a market setting in which fundamentals were controlled (and so known) by the experimenter. Consequently, the experimenters hoped to observe the extent and persistence of any deviations between prices and fundamental values.

Illustration 7 (Smith et al. (1988), "Bubbles, crashes and endogenous expectations in experimental spot asset markets," *Econometrica***).** This paper reports twenty-seven experiments investigating experimental markets in which participants had the opportunity to trade "assets." While many details vary across the different experiments, several structural features are common across them and for the most part we focus on those.

At the beginning of an experiment, participants were each endowed with experimental "assets" and "cash." They then took part in a series of (usually fifteen) market periods in which they had opportunities to buy assets for cash or to sell them and receive cash in return. The markets were organized as computerized *double auctions*. At any moment during a market period, individual participants could submit offers to buy a unit (by stating a price they were willing to pay) or to sell a unit (by stating a price they were willing to accept). All bids were subject to an improvement rule: any new bid to buy (sell) must be higher (lower) than the current best offer on the market. An asset would be traded when one participant accepted a standing offer (to buy or to sell) posted by another trader. At the end of each market period, every asset generated a dividend payoff to its current owner, which was added to their cash balance. The value of this dividend was determined randomly from a known probability distribution over dividends, the parameters of which were fixed across rounds. At the end of the experiment, subjects received a real dollar payment based on their final cash balance (incorporating all payments and income from trades, plus cumulative dividend payments.)

Earlier research had investigated some aspects of asset trading in experimental markets, but the setup of this study featured two main departures from previous designs. First, the assets were "long-lived" in the sense of generating a stream of dividends across multiple market periods; second, the expected dividend was held constant across traders. The second feature meant that if traders were risk neutral (or had a common risk attitude), and acted on the basis of rational expectations, then there would be no incentives for any asset trading to occur. That the design allowed trade across an extended number of periods was intended to permit examination of the dynamics of trade volumes and prices, should there be significant levels of trade contrary to the theoretical prediction. Variations across the experiments explored various issues, including the extent to which the "experience" level of the traders affected the conformity of market behavior with predictions.

Smith et al. report not just that trade occurred but also that it was common for their markets to exhibit "bubbles": that is, sustained periods during which assets traded at prices significantly above their expected returns. Such bubbles were typically followed by crashes, with prices and volumes of trade collapsing, near the final period. They also report that trader experience had some tendency to attenuate bubbling phenomena.

Our final illustration, due to Sheryl Ball et al. (2001), also concerns an experimental market. In this case, the interest is in examining whether the status of market participants influences the distribution of surplus in a market constructed to have multiple price-equilibria.

Illustration 8 (Ball et al. (2001), "Status in markets," *Quarterly Journal of Economics*). This paper reports the results from some experimental markets. Each market involved between ten and sixteen participants divided randomly between the roles of buyer and seller. In each market period, each seller was endowed with two units of an experimental good, they were each given a "private cost" and could make money in the experiment by selling their units at prices above their own costs. Individual buyers were each given a reservation value and knew that they could make money by buying units at prices below their reserve. Each subject knew only their own cost or reserve, but in fact in a given market the cost was the same for all sellers and the reserve was the same for all buyers. Since the cost was set below the reserve, any buyer–seller pair could, in principle, undertake a mutually profitable trade at any price in the cost–reserve interval. Markets were run for eleven periods, each by an auctioneer who alternated between inviting a randomly selected buyer to bid and inviting a randomly selected seller to state an ask. The first period was a practice but the returns to trade in the remaining ten periods contributed toward the subject's final payoff (subjects earned an average of around $17 including a $5 turn-up fee).

The primary objective of the research was to test the hypothesis that "In markets where sellers have higher status, the distribution of equilibrium prices will be higher than in markets where buyers have higher status" (p. 165). To this end, the researchers compared matched pairs of markets, identical in terms of costs and reserves, in which participants had been exposed to a prior manipulation intended to induce differential statuses. Two procedures were used for this. One, the "awarded" status procedure, required subjects to participate in a quiz with obscure answers. The experimenters awarded gold stars to half of the subjects (the "high-status" group) while the other (the "low-status" group) were required to observe and applaud. It was intended that, from the subjects' point of view, it should appear that those getting the stars had earned them through success in the quiz, though in fact stars were assigned randomly (via cover of an opaque scoring system for the quiz). Consequently, awarded status should not have been correlated with personal characteristics such as knowledge or intelligence. The second method for determining status, the "random" status procedure, similarly selected half of the subjects for the public award of stars, but in this case using a procedure intended to make the randomness of the status assignment transparent to subjects.

Ball et al. report behavior in markets under four conditions: in roughly half of the markets, the buyers (respectively sellers) were the high-status group; and for each of these conditions, there were matched pairs of markets which varied according to whether status had been determined by the awarded or random procedures. They report that, in the aggregate, mean earnings tended to be significantly higher for the high-status side of the market. Moreover, the effect appeared to operate even when status was awarded in a transparently random fashion. In the conclusion to the paper, the authors comment that:

> Our results show that in a competitive market environment, status can have an effect on price and the allocation of resources. That a status treatment that is so obviously superficial could have such an effect on behavior strengthens our belief that status plays an important role in real-world interactions.
>
> Ball et al. (2000, p. 181)

1.4   The Illustrations and the Structure of the Book

The experiments presented in section 1.3 illustrate many of the activities that experimental economists undertake and allow us to introduce the main issues that we discuss in later chapters. A central theme of the book will be a distinction between two ways of viewing experiments: as providing tests of theories and as investigating empirical regularities. As we will explain, these categories are not mutually exclusive, nor are they exhaustive; but, nevertheless, they play a useful organizing role.

In chapters 2 and 3, we consider the classic role of experiments in science: namely, *testing theories*. Among our examples, Morgan et al. (2006) and Goeree and Holt (2001) most clearly present the main objective of their study as being to test a theory. In several other cases, theory testing is one way of reading the results, though, as we will discuss later, it is not the only way. For example, Tversky and Kahneman's (1981) investigation of framing effects can be seen as a test of the principle, embedded in consequentialist theories of choice, that logically equivalent redescription of a decision problem will not affect behavior; Fehr and Gächter's (2000) study can be seen as a test of a game-theoretic prediction that subjects will neither contribute nor punish in their setup; and Smith et al.'s (1988) study can be seen as testing a theory that predicts the absence of trade in their laboratory asset markets.

Notwithstanding the prominent place of theory testing in accounts of scientific method, the theory-testing function of economics experiments is not straightforward. Perhaps the most basic reason for this is that the relationship between economic theorizing and empirical claims is itself indirect. Most of the explicit activity of economic theorists is deductive and involves the manipulation or analysis of formal models and definitions. One way in which theorists present their research is by stating assumptions and deriving conclusions from them, using mathematical or logical arguments. Conclusions are then presented as theorems, with the form of conditional statements to the effect that *if* the assumptions held in the world, *then* the conclusions would also hold. However, it is perhaps now more common for theorists to proceed in a different way, by postulating or building a model world populated by entities defined in formal terms and then deriving theorems that make *unconditional* statements about the *model world.* There are differences between these two ways of presenting theory but the important thing about them, for present purposes, is something that they share. For both presentations, if one sees the assertions made by the theory as consisting *only* of the theorems, then there is no scope for testing the theory, where this is conceived as an activity that involves empirical observation. For the first presentation, this is because the theorems only assert that the conclusions hold if the assumptions do. That the conclusions follow from the assumptions is (provided the theorist has not slipped up in the formal argument) a matter of logic. For the second presentation, it is because the theorems state properties of the model world, not the actual world.

However, we take it that most of our readers and most theorists would, like us, not be content with a view of economic theory that immunizes it not just from experimental testing but also from *all* empirical testing. Our starting point is, therefore, a view of economic theory that does not see its assertions as limited only to theorems whose truth can be established by nonempirical methods. Even though deductions made within particular formal models are not themselves subject to empirical test, if the models are to assist economics as a science, there must be some empirical claims associated with them. *These* claims are ones with which an enterprise of theory testing can sensibly be concerned; they stem not from formal theorems alone but from applications of the models whose properties those theorems establish.

For example, the study by Morgan et al. (2006) concerns a particular game-theoretic model. In that model, the game can be described in formal terms, using an abstract set of players, abstract sets of strategies for the players, and payoff functions defined on the Cartesian product of the strategy sets. Given this formal description, it is a theorem that the game has a unique Nash equilibrium and that this equilibrium has a certain form, consisting of particular mixed (i.e., random) strategies. An application of the model, sufficient to render testable claims, must associate the "players" of the model with some real agents and the "strategies" with certain options open to those agents; and it must endorse as a prediction some solution concept for the game. If this solution concept is the mixed strategy Nash equilibrium, then it is necessary to specify what observations would be taken as conforming, or not conforming, to mixed strategy equilibrium play. The application implicitly made by

Morgan et al. associates players with subjects, strategies with numbers representing prices, and takes the distribution across players of "prices" chosen as indicative or otherwise of mixed strategy Nash equilibrium play.[13]

The need for a theory to be applicable before it can be tested gives rise to many of the questions we discuss in the book, starting with those in chapters 2 and 3. Put loosely, the questions considered by these chapters are, respectively, *where* and *how* the theory should be applied.

Chapter 2 considers whether laboratories provide appropriate testing grounds for economic theories; and, if so, whether certain design features are mandated by particular views about the theory. Each of these questions can be motivated with reference to a particular aspect of the instrumentalist methodology espoused by Friedman (1953). Friedman contended that a theory should be judged by the success of its predictions *within the domain in which they are intended to apply*. For Friedman, it does not matter if, say, the theory of the profit-maximizing firm does not fit well with discussions in firms in which managers take more note of average costs than they do of marginal costs, as long as the theory predicts accurately how market prices respond to changing conditions. It is the latter, not the content of boardroom discussion, which is the intended domain of the theory. An observer sympathetic to this view might question the testing of economic theories in the laboratory. For example, Morgan et al. (2006) purport to test a theory of price dispersion, presumably intended to apply to markets made up of real firms and their customers. The observer might ask, Is it legitimate to test the theory in a laboratory environment with students playing the role of firms and the demand side of the market simulated by computer?

The questions addressed by chapter 2 are similar to this one, though couched in a more general form. The first issue is whether the domain of the theory excludes the laboratory, as suggested by the traditional mid-twentieth-century view of economics as nonexperimental. The second is whether, even if economic theory can legitimately be tested in the laboratory, as is now widely accepted, the nature of its domain requires particular types of experimental designs to be used. To motivate this question, consider again Binmore's (1999) discussion of the research of Kahneman and Tversky. Binmore argues that economics experiments

---

[13] An alternative application of mixed strategy Nash equilibria would specify that, over repeat play, *each* player's observed behavior is consistent with *that* player randomizing over their pure strategies, using the probabilities specified by the equilibrium mixed strategies. Morgan et al. (2006, pp. 150–51) consider this, but the majority of their analysis focuses on conformity of the distribution of play *across* players with the equilibrium mixed strategies.

ought to conform to certain design principles involving task simplicity, incentives, and learning opportunities. In support of this, he writes that "there is no point in testing economic propositions in circumstances to which they should not reasonably be expected to apply" (Binmore 1999, p. F23), a sentiment which, to the extent of restricting tests of economic theory to a particular domain, is reminiscent of Friedman, even if casting such a sentiment as a restriction on appropriate experimental designs is different. A related question to that of whether certain design features are required for tests of the theory is what one should conclude about the theory if its performance in the laboratory depends in systematic ways on such features. This question has been considered by another prominent experimental economist, Charles Plott, in formulating the *discovered preference hypothesis* (Plott 1996). Plott's view suggests similar boundaries for the domain of the theory to those envisaged by Binmore. Chapter 2 offers a framework for the assessment of such positions.

Chapter 3 turns to the implications for experimental economics of one of the fundamental problems of empirical science: the *Duhem–Quine problem* (Duhem 1906; Quine 1951, 1953). The problem is that, since theories must be applied before they can be tested, single theoretical hypotheses can never be tested in isolation. Supplementary assumptions are always involved in bringing a particular theoretical hypothesis into confrontation with data. As a result, if the data seem unfavorable to the hypothesis, it is never completely clear whether the hypothesis itself is at fault or whether some of the supplementary assumptions were invalid. For example, Smith et al.'s (1988) experiment can be seen as testing a hypothesis, derived from the theory of asset markets, that agents who have the same endowments of, information about, and preferences over particular assets will not trade. The observation that trade occurred in its asset markets certainly tells against the proposition that there would be no trade in them. But does it falsify the theoretical hypothesis? Or might subjects have varied in their reasons for holding the assets, perhaps because of differing attitudes to risk or differing beliefs about the likely trading behavior of other subjects? Or did some subjects just trade for fun? Or vary in their views about the truthfulness of the experimenter's reports of the assets' returns? Or, as a result of integrating experimental endowments with nonlaboratory wealth, differ in their endowments? To raise these questions is not to criticize Smith et al.; it is simply to illustrate how, even in a well-controlled experiment, there is more than one conceivable interpretation of given observations.

Chapter 3 discusses the implications of this fact for the view of experiments as tests of theories, especially where those theories are core principles deeply embedded in economic models. As an example of the latter kind, consider the treatments with punishment opportunities in Fehr and Gächter's (2000) experiment. If individual subjects want only to accumulate money for themselves, then, in a game-theoretic model of the setup created by these treatments, the unique subgame-perfect equilibrium precludes both punishment and contribution to the public good. If, as was the case, contribution and punishment are observed, does this tell against the game-theoretic concept of subgame perfection, against a particular assumption about players' objectives, or against some other assumption involved in applying a game-theoretic model to a specific situation? As such questions are unlikely to be answered by a single experiment, we require principles for the conduct and evaluation of research programs. Chapter 3 discusses precisely this form of response to the Duhem–Quine problem.

Chapter 4 broadens the perspective of the book by introducing a view of experiments that allows them to be something other than theory-testing devices. As noted earlier, an alternative interpretation sees experiments as contributing to the investigation of *empirical regularities*. Such investigation may involve attempts to "sharpen" the regularities, as well as to contribute to a search for explanations of them. Among our examples, the studies that fit this reading most immediately may be Bryan and Test (1967) and Ball et al. (2001). These studies concern supposed relationships between social experience and charitable behavior and between status and market outcomes, respectively. Several of the studies that we discussed in the role of theory tests can also be seen as investigations of empirical regularities (and, in some cases, it is this reading that the authors stress). For example, Fehr and Gächter (2000) can be read as an investigation of the part punishment opportunities play in supporting social norms of cooperation; Tversky and Kahneman (1981) as an investigation of the effects of descriptions on perceptions; and Smith et al. (1988) as studying the determinants of asset price bubbles. Subsequent research motivated by these studies has followed both readings. For example, Fehr and Gächter (2000), together with many other reports of experiments involving public-goods problems and other games, has spawned an extensive theoretical literature that develops models of social preferences.[14] But there has also been a major program of experimental research (surveyed in Camerer (2003, chapter 2)) that investigates the robustness of the behavioral regularities to changes in cultural context, design features, and other factors. Some of this research can also be seen as a follow-up to Tversky and Kahneman (1981), since

---

[14] For surveys, see Bolton (1998), Fehr and Fischbacher (2002), Fehr and Schmidt (2003), Camerer (2003, section 2.8), Bardsley and Sugden (2006), and Sugden (forthcoming).

it considers the effects of task framing on behavior in collective choice problems.

The existence of sustained programs of experimental research into particular regularities in the behavior of subjects brings out an important point about experiments, when read as investigations of empirical regularities. They are not blind searches, conducted in the hope of stumbling on regularities. For example, Smith et al. could reasonably have conjectured that bubbles might form in their laboratory asset markets because of the widespread perception that they do form in nonlaboratory markets in which shares and real estate are traded; and Bryan and Test could have conjectured, for example from the use of auctions as fund-raising devices by charities, that positive examples stimulate contributions. But such conjectures are notoriously difficult to confirm in field research, because there are so many potentially confounding factors.[15] Hence the potential role for experiments to refine the understanding of what regularities in behavior there are. In view of our claim that experiments, read as contributions to investigation of empirical regularities, are not (or at least should not be) blind searches, we prefer to think of this reading of experiments as postulating a role of *regularity refinement* or *regularity confirmation* rather than haphazard regularity hunting.[16]

When experiments are used in this way, they can take on roles that would otherwise be played by theoretical models. For example, suppose an economist is asked how prices and quantities traded in some market would be affected by some exogenous change in circumstances. The traditional response would be to build a theoretical model of the market, using components from some received economic theory (such as the Marshallian or Walrasian theory of market equilibrium), and to manipulate the model in ways that correspond with the relevant exogenous changes. But if it is known that certain types of experimental market designs reliably generate patterns of behavior that are similar to those observed in real-world markets, another strategy of investigation is possible. The real-world question that the economist is trying to answer can be represented not by a manipulation of a theoretical model but by alternative treatments in an experimental design; the answer can be arrived at not by interpreting a mathematical theorem but by interpreting an experimental finding. To put this in another way, an experiment is being

---

[15] One example is the debate about whether famous early "bubbles" really were bubbles. For example, compare Kindleberger (1996) with Garber (2000). See also the "Symposium on Bubbles" in the Spring 1990 issue of *Journal of Economic Perspectives*.

[16] Roth (1995a, p. 22) discusses "searching for facts" as a role for experiments and, like us, stresses the systematic nature of the activity, when fruitfully conducted. He sees part of its value as being to make possible the formulation of theories.

used *as a model.* The work of Ball et al. (2001) can be thought of in this way. The research question, one might say, is whether status differences affect the terms of trade in markets. Ball et al. try to answer this question by setting up an experimental market, using components that are standard in experimental research, but adding new design features that are intended to model status.

One important application of this research strategy uses experiments as "test beds" or "wind tunnels" for investigating the likely properties of new market institutions, prior to their being introduced for real.[17] The starting point for this strategy is the claim that, when certain general design principles are followed, behavior in experimental markets tends to be similar to behavior in their real-world counterparts. If this claim is supported by experience, the performance of an experimental model of a new market institution can reasonably be treated as informative about the likely performance of the institution itself. This test-bed strategy will be discussed in chapter 4.

More generally, chapter 4 discusses experiments as contributors to *inductive* reasoning in economics. One issue that immediately arises is the relationship between the theory testing and regularity-refining reading of experiments outlined above. Is it, for example, coherent to suggest, as we did earlier, that the same experiments can be read either way? Are the rules of theory testing and regularity-refining different? Indeed, what are appropriate methodological rules for regularity-refining in economics? And what is the relationship between regularity-refining and the identification of causal mechanisms or explanations? These are not idle questions, as most of the methodological reflection of economists has concentrated on theory testing.

Despite this, there is a long tradition in economics of constructing theories to explain nonexperimental empirical regularities that are perceived to be robust, often termed "stylized facts." A classic example is the postwar development of theories of aggregate consumption expenditure to explain the stylized fact that the marginal propensity to consume is greater in the long run than in the short run; a more recent example is the development of real business cycle models to explain generalizations about postwar economic fluctuations, such as the failure of employment levels and real wage rates to vary inversely together over the cycle.[18]

---

[17] A prominent recent discussion of this type of experimental research is provided by part II of Smith (2008).

[18] The consumption function puzzle has been a textbook standard for motivating permanent income and life cycle theories of aggregate consumption for much the postwar period. For its continuing use in this role, see, for example, Mankiw (2007, chapter 16). For surveys of real business cycle theory, see, for example, Plosser (1989), Stadler (1994), and King and Rebelo (1999).

Typically, theories constructed to explain stylized facts have implications that go beyond formal representation of those facts themselves. (There is an important tradition in the philosophy of science that *requires* this, if the explanation is to be judged a good one, as we discuss in chapter 3.) The role of experiments in *testing* such implications raises the same issues as the experimental testing of theories constructed in other ways, so that our discussion in chapters 2–3 also applies to testing theories that are constructed to explain stylized facts. But chapters 4 and 5 discuss a further question about experiments, arising specifically in relation to the formulation of theories to explain stylized facts. This question is whether the laboratory can provide stylized facts worth explaining.

On the one hand, the control that experiments offer seems to lend them well to a task of regularity-refinement. This may be hard to achieve with field data, where there can be a surprising degree of ambiguity, not always initially apparent, about what the stylized facts actually are.[19] But, conversely, just as a skeptic might suspect that experiments are too remote from the intended domain of theories to provide a useful testing ground for them, she might also suspect that experiments are too artificial to generate stylized facts that can be expected to hold outside the laboratory.

Concerns about whether experimental findings are reliable guides to what may happen outside the laboratory are sometimes expressed as doubts about their *external validity*. The question of whether conclusions reached on the basis of observations in one sphere are informative about what may happen in another sphere is not specific to experiments. It is a potential concern for any empirical research. But the artificiality of the laboratory arguably sharpens the question for experimental research.

Chapter 5 considers different senses in which the laboratory might be taken to be artificial and discusses their implications for external validity, in the contexts of both theory testing and regularity-refinement. The illustrative experiments described in section 1.3 vary considerably in how far the issue of artificiality seems prima facie to arise. For example, Bryan and Test did not conduct the experiments reported in their 1967 paper in a laboratory at all, if the latter is construed as a physical location dedicated to the experimenter's purpose. They went to considerable lengths to conceal from participants the fact that they were the subjects

---

[19] The cases of the consumption function puzzle and the cyclical properties of real wage rates illustrate this. See Stock (1988) on the consumption function puzzle and Abraham and Haltiwanger (1995) on the difficulties of measuring cyclical properties of real wage rates.

of an experiment, by intervening in a disguised way in a naturally occurring environment. This is an example of what, much later, Harrison and List (2004, p. 1,014) would describe as a "natural field experiment." While experiments of this naturalistic kind may mitigate concerns about artificiality, they may also give rise to other concerns. For example, Bryan and Test conducted their flat tire experiment in the street in Los Angeles, an environment in which it would not have been possible for them to hold constant everything except the treatment.[20] In contrast, Ball et al.'s (2001) investigation of the effect of status on the distribution of gains from trade in market transactions was conducted in laboratory conditions and may have a stronger claim to have held everything constant across treatments, other than the treatment manipulations themselves, because (as is normal in laboratory experiments) they assigned subjects to treatments at random. However, some, such as Bardsley (2005), have questioned whether their treatment manipulations really confer status, in the same sense as agents in the field may have it. A possible view of the comparison between Bryan and Test (1967) and Ball et al. (2001) is that it exemplifies a trade-off between naturalism and external validity, on which Bryan and Test score highly, and control, which Ball et al. (2001) have to a greater degree.[21] Early economic experimenters emphasized the virtues of control but the recent wave of field experiments in economics may reflect an increasing premium now put by some on external validity (see, for example, Levitt and List 2007). Chapter 5 considers the nature and implications of any such trade-off.

Chapter 5 also focuses on a common practice in experimental economics: namely, that of using designs that closely implement the assumptions of particular theoretical models. Among our examples there is considerable variation in how far this practice is followed. On the one hand, Bryan and Test (1967) make no attempt to implement a model; on the other hand, Goeree and Holt (2001) have subjects play games which, if they were motivated to maximize their own monetary payoffs,

---

[20] It is, nevertheless, remarkable how much control Bryan and Test were able to achieve. For example, a possible source of uncontrolled variation is how much of a hurry drivers were in, as that might vary over the course of the day. As noted earlier, Bryan and Test attempted to eliminate any effect of this on their results by repeating the experiment on another Saturday, with the timings of the two treatments reversed. But this clever idea still cannot counteract completely the possibility that, for reasons unrelated to the experiment, drivers became more hurried through the day on one Saturday and less hurried through the day on the other.

[21] The suggestion that there is a trade-off should not be taken as implying that a given increase in naturalism is always associated with a corresponding loss of control. We have already commented favorably on how much control Bryan and Test (1967) were able to achieve; it would certainly have been possible to design equally naturalistic, but much less well controlled, experiments.

would resemble certain abstract games of game theory, not just in their structure but also their presentation; and Morgan et al. (2006) go to considerable lengths to create a setup which, except for the use of human subjects in place of firms, matches the structure of the clearing-house model of price setting.

In a theory-testing context, some might argue that a theoretical model can only legitimately be tested in a laboratory experiment that closely implements its assumptions. This position is an assertion about the domain of the theory and, for that reason, chapter 5 applies and builds on the framework presented in chapter 2 in discussing it. However, the question of whether designs should implement the assumptions of models also arises in the context of regularity-refinement. Here, it takes on a slightly different hue: if an experiment closely implements the assumptions of some theoretical model of a particular real-world phenomenon, would it be legitimate to read its findings as establishing stylized facts about that phenomenon? This is a question of external validity and, once again, it connects with a type of artificiality of the laboratory. Because of the abstraction used in economic models, it is often the case that the more closely a design implements a formal model, the more artificial the experimental environment defined by it seems.

In chapters 6 and 7, we turn to two issues of everyday concern to experimenters: incentives, and interpretation of data in the light of stochastic variation. We suggest that experimental economists have been too prone to lapse, in the first case, into unreflective conformism, and, in the second case, into unreflective diversity. (Of course, we do not make either charge against all experimental economists. To name just two papers concerned with these topics, Camerer and Hogarth (1999) discuss incentives and Hey and Orme (1994) stochastic modeling of data from choice experiments.)

The issue of incentives is sometimes seen as dividing experimental economics from experimental psychology (Hertwig and Ortmann 2001). Reflecting this view, all those experiments among our examples that were conducted by economists presented subjects with a situation in which they could receive a sum of money determined by their own task responses in conjunction with those of other subjects and/or with chance, according to preset rules devised by the experimenter. Thus, for economists, it seems that creating rules to determine task-related monetary payoffs is a core part of experimental design; it is part of the process of creating a controlled laboratory environment. In contrast, the psychologists Tversky and Kahneman make no attempt to restrict their investigations of framing to cases where real outcomes hang on their choices. In the Asian disease problem from Tversky and Kahneman (1981), subjects were simply asked to say which option they would "favor" in an imaginary scenario. For the unconscious subjects of the experiments reported in Bryan and Test (1967), real consequences hung on their actions (either they changed the tire or they did not; either they put money in the collection box or they did not) but the experimenters simply relied on whatever incentives the naturalistic setting provided.

However, the differences between the designs used by economists and psychologists may not always be as great as it might seem. In any experiment, subjects arrive with whatever motivations they arrive with and face the decision problems set up by the experimenter. In general terms, the fact that, even when the experimenter seeks to induce certain preferences on the part of subjects, they may still have traces of "homemade" preferences, is a reflection of the Duhem–Quine problem discussed in chapter 3; and whether economic theory should only be expected to apply in situations where substantial sums of money are at stake or the profit motive holds sway is part of the question of the domain of the theory discussed in chapter 2. But chapter 6 goes beyond these earlier discussions to look in more detail at certain issues.

One set of questions concerns whether, or maybe better, when or at what level, task-related incentives are required by good practice. A second set of questions, on which the answers to the first set may partly depend, is what effect task-related incentives actually have on subjects' behavior in the laboratory and why. We have already seen from our examples that there are differences between disciplines on whether task-related incentives are viewed as required, but, even within experimental economics, there are also differences of opinion about their level and about whether (or, perhaps again better, when) behavior is sensitive to this. More fundamentally, why do incentives affect behavior in the laboratory? A natural first thought for economists is that stronger incentives stimulate greater effort and so better performance by subjects. But, as chapter 6 discusses, this view, though fruitful, still raises a number of issues and is, in any case, only one among several perspectives on why incentives might matter for experimental economics.

A further set of questions, considered in the second half of chapter 6, arises because certain tasks that experimenters have wanted to present to subjects are not straightforward to incentivize. Does this mean that such tasks should be avoided? A related, but perhaps more common, issue in experimental economics arises because, for many tasks, it is straightforward to link subjects' rewards to what happens in the experiment in some way or other, but the more obvious ways of doing so do not satisfy orthodox economic theory. The question is then whether *incentive compatibility* in the eyes of orthodox theory should be seen as a requirement.

To motivate this issue, consider the study reported in Selten et al. (1999) concerning the binary lottery incentive system. As noted earlier, this device is sometimes used by experimenters who wish to investigate game play, while excluding the possibility that the behavior they observe is due to risk aversion. At first sight, it may seem easy to implement, say, the payoff matrix of a particular game by paying subjects sums of money proportional to the payoffs specified by the matrix for the particular combination of choices that they have made. However, formal game theory typically works with descriptions of games in which payoffs are utilities, in the sense of Von Neumann and Morgenstern, not sums of money. These utilities are supposed to capture players' attitudes to risk; and expected utility theory specifies that they are only linear in money when the agent is risk neutral for monetary risks. So, according to orthodox theory, paying monetary amounts proportional to the payoffs of a given payoff matrix does *not* implement the relevant game if, in fact, subjects are risk loving or risk averse. The binary lottery system is an attempt to circumvent this problem, motivated by the fact that, according to expected utility theory, a subject's expected utility is linear in *chances of winning* some given sum of money, even when it is not linear in *money* itself. But the findings of Selten et al. (1999) cast doubt on whether this technique works in practice. They provide an early example of one of the themes of chapter 6; namely that incentive systems that "work" according to conventional economic theory may have unexpected effects in practice. This does not mean that such systems should never be used—for example, in testing a theory it is legitimate to use an incentive system that is valid according to that theory, even if the theory turns out to fail—but it does raise the question of how high a premium should be set on incentive compatibility, in the sense that economists have usually conceived it, and suggest that questions about the structure of incentives for an experiment cannot be settled in the abstract. They depend on the purpose at hand.

Finally, all of the example studies that we have presented have one thing in common: they draw conclusions from experimental data. The question therefore arises of how to assess the reliability of such conclusions. In a broad sense, almost the whole of this book is concerned with some aspect of this question. However, there is a further issue which, although related to the themes of chapters 2–6, is not their main focus, and yet is likely to occur to many nonexperimental applied economists. This is the issue of stochastic specification; we consider it in chapter 7.

In nonexperimental empirical economics, issues of stochastic specification and model selection loom large, but this is less common in experimental papers. This may reflect a tendency for experimenters to think that, given a well-controlled experimental design, the data will speak for themselves. But is this always correct? Or might it be argued that, just as many mid-twentieth-century economists were wrong to think that the methods of empirical economics were a necessary adaptation to the unavailability of laboratory techniques, so some late-twentieth-century experimenters have been wrong to think that their use of such techniques renders attention to stochastic specification unnecessary? Even if laboratory techniques diminish or exclude some of the sources of stochastic disturbance in field data, it does not follow that they do so for all sources.

To motivate this issue in relation to theory testing, note that most economic theories are essentially deterministic. However, since the early development of econometrics,[22] applied economists have recognized that such models cannot be literal descriptions of the processes that generate the data typically studied because, relative to this standpoint, there is too much variability in the data. This is as true of experimental data as it is of field data. Indeed, arguably, it can be seen even more clearly in experiments than in the field, because the laboratory allows us to face the same subjects with essentially the same task on more than one occasion, with almost everything held constant except for the passage of time.

Part of the process of confronting a theory with data therefore involves stochastic specification of the model. This would be unproblematic if there were a clearly correct, all-purpose method of stochastic specification that could be applied to deterministic theories. But this is not so; and, worse, different methods may lead to different conclusions about a particular theory from a given set of experimental findings—another instance of the Duhem–Quine problem from chapter 3. Further, it may not be the case that employing routine econometric techniques when analyzing experimental data, without seriously considering the sources of variability in that data, will be helpful. We illustrate and discuss these problems in chapter 7, comparing and assessing alternative types of stochastic specification for economic theories of choice and strategic interaction. Our earlier discussion of the findings of tests of these theories is, to some extent, conditional on this later treatment. Chapter 7 also considers whether different branches of experimental economics

---

[22] See Morgan (1990) for a history of econometrics.

have something to learn from each other on the question of stochastic specification and extends the argument introduced in chapter 6 that experimenters should not be shy of new forms of experimental data.

Chapter 8 concludes by drawing the themes of the book together and, as a consequence, suggesting that a number of popular nostrums concerning experimental economics are misplaced.

1.5 Methods, Methodology, and Philosophy of Science

At the start of this chapter, we described this book as a *methodological* assessment of experimental economics. What does that mean? According to its dictionary definition, "methodology" is the systematic study of method, and, by extension, method considered in a systematic way. So, apart from sounding grander, is the methodology of experimental economics anything more than the body of methods that experimental economists use?

Professional methodologists sometimes distinguish between "methods" and "methodology," conceiving the former as part of the routine practice of a science and the latter as higher-order reflection. In a recent survey of economic methodology, Wade Hands (2001) defines "methods" as "the practical techniques employed by successful economists in the execution of their day-to-day professional activities." Methodology in the sense of "methods," he says,

> is essential to professional success, usually acquired tacitly, or by rote, in the context of actually working on specific economic research projects: initially under the guidance of one's research supervisor or thesis director, and then later through interactions with one's colleagues, department chair, and various journal editors. It is the source of answers to day-to-day questions like: Is an R^2 this low OK for this kind of model? Is it reasonable to assume the Jacobian matrix has this strange sign pattern? or, It's OK to drop all of the data from the first two quarters of 1929, right? As important as such questions might be, [method in this sense] is *not* what most economists mean when they use the term Economic Methodology. [This] is not generally what one will see published in journals like *Economics and Philosophy* or *The Journal of Economic Methodology*, which specialize in methodological research; and, whereas one might overhear such topics discussed by Nobel laureates, it is not what they write about when they write about "Methodology."
>
> Hands (2001, p. 3)

The suggestion seems to be that "method" is a set of relatively uncontroversial rules of good practice, internal to a scientific discipline, of which established scientists have a tacit understanding and into which novices are inducted. "Methodology" is a more elevated or abstract activity, pursued by professional methodologists (and, apparently, by Nobel laureates in their more reflective writings).

Clearly, there is a difference of some kind between the questions that Hands classifies as "method" and those that professional methodologists discuss. Still, we would have difficulty in classifying our subject matter either as "method" or "methodology," in Hands's terms. In relation to experimental economics, at least, we think this distinction is unhelpful.

Notice how Hands's examples of the processes by which "method" is learned involve scientists passing judgment on the scientific quality of other scientists' work. The research student's thesis is judged by the supervisor or examiner; the author's research paper is judged by the journal editor; the research record of the applicant for the academic post is judged by the department chair; the standing of the researcher in his field is judged by his colleagues. In all of these processes, judgments about what does and does not constitute good science are invoked. It is in these "day-to-day" processes that the battles which determine how the accepted methods of a science evolve are fought. If a new method is to establish its legitimacy, the scientists who favor it have to convince other scientists of its merits: research students have to convince skeptical supervisors or examiners, authors have to convince skeptical referees and editors, job applicants have to convince skeptical department chairs, colleagues have to convince skeptical colleagues. All of this has certainly been true of the introduction of experimental methods into economics: we, the authors, have taken part in these kinds of battles.

It is only after many day-to-day judgments have been made in favor of a new method that it is likely to come to the attention of professional methodologists or its pioneers to attain the status of Nobel laureates. These judgments involve more than the routine application of accepted rules of good practice, even though neither the judges nor the judged typically appeal explicitly to the higher-order principles of philosophy of science. Much of our book will be concerned with judgments of this kind. That is, we will be concerned with controversies *among practicing economists* about what the methods of their discipline should be. Or, since we are practicing economists addressing practicing economists, we can say: what the methods of *our* discipline should be.

A methodological assessment of a new development in a discipline must, we maintain, engage with issues of "method." But it must also be informed by "methodology" in its higher-order sense; methodology as practiced by professional methodologists. In the remainder of this section, we explain how our approach to our subject matter relates to methodology, so understood. We begin with a thumbnail sketch of what methodologists do.

Traditionally, methodological enquiry begins in philosophy of science or, more fundamentally, in *epistemology*—that branch of philosophy which studies the nature of knowledge and justified belief. Epistemology addresses questions such as, What are the defining conditions of knowledge? What are the substantive sources of knowledge? Does it have foundations, and if so, what are they? Are there limits to what can be known? The mainstream of work in philosophy of science has investigated the special characteristics of scientific knowledge, often implicitly presupposing that the received theories of natural science have especially strong claims to the status of knowledge.

For much of the twentieth century, philosophy of science was dominated by the search for a satisfactory *empiricist* account of knowledge: the aim was to identify general principles by which knowledge can be generated *from observation and experiment*. There was a presumption that these principles would be implicit in the best practices of the most "advanced" natural sciences, particularly physics. By identifying those principles, it would be possible to distinguish between science and nonscience; some disciplines that claimed to be sciences might then be revealed to be merely pseudosciences.

Perhaps because of the deeply rooted aspiration of economists to the status of practitioners of "hard" science, this program of philosophical investigation has had a particularly significant impact on economics. It has affected both the methods used in the discipline and economists' interpretations of them. That influence can still be seen in the language of practical economists. For example, the idea that there is a categorical distinction between "descriptive" (or "positive") propositions on one side and "normative" propositions (or "value judgments") on the other, and that economics as a science is concerned only with the former, entered economics from a particular strand of empiricist philosophy of science. So too did the idea that a theory has content only if it leads to hypotheses that can be tested against observations—an idea that has led generations of economists to append a list of testable hypotheses to every theoretical proposal. Economics has been particularly influenced by the empiricist philosophy of Karl Popper (1934), known as *falsificationism*, which we will discuss in relation to experimental economics in chapter 3. Popper's central idea is that scientific knowledge consists of a body of hypotheses that in principle are capable of being falsified by observation but in fact have withstood the best efforts of the scientific community to find disconfirming evidence. On this account, scientific virtue is identified with *bold conjectures*: that is, putting forward hypotheses which, a priori, appear improbable and which lay themselves open to many possibilities for falsification—and *severe tests*: that is, subjecting hypotheses to tests which, a priori, seem particularly likely to falsify them. Bold conjectures that survive severe tests are ones in which confidence can be placed.

Over the last two decades, issues of epistemology have become less central to philosophy of science. Perhaps this reflects a recognition of the problems posed for empiricism and positivism by the Duhem–Quine problem, but it might simply be a change in intellectual fashion. Whatever the reason, there has been a shift of emphasis in philosophy of science from issues of epistemology to issues of *ontology*—that branch of philosophy that studies the nature of existence. In particular, philosophers of science have proposed and discussed various theories of *realism*. In traditional empiricist accounts, knowledge is grounded on observation. Ultimately, knowledge is *about* observations; the problem for science is to find regularities in past observations that can be used to make reliable predictions about future observations. In realist accounts, in contrast, our observations can inform us about *forces* or *capacities* or *mechanisms*; those mechanisms, even if not straightforwardly observable, cause the regularities we observe.

The realist project can be pursued in different ways. Some realist philosophers—for example, Richard Boyd (1983)—start from (what they take to be) the fact that the natural sciences have been extraordinarily successful in predicting observable features of the world, and in showing us how to manipulate the world to produce chosen results. Those predictions and manipulations are based on theories that (it is claimed) postulate unobservable mechanisms. The most credible explanation of the success of science, it is then argued, is that the mechanisms it postulates, or mechanisms very like them, really exist. This brand of realism asks what properties the world would have to have in order for science as we know it to be successful, and then infers the existence of those properties from the success of science. A different approach, which does not presuppose the success of science, is to ask what properties have to be attributed to the world in order for scientists' *claims* to knowledge to make sense on their own terms. If we can make sense of those claims only on the supposition that scientists are postulating the existence of real mechanisms, then we can conclude that science *is committed to* realism. This argument is developed by Nancy Cartwright (1989) in relation to the practices of physics and economics.[23] A third approach, pursued

---

[23] Cartwright (1989, p. 158) argues that, in view of the success of physics, the capacities postulated by physics "are scarcely to be rejected." But she is explicitly agnostic about whether economics is a successful science, claiming only that economics is committed to realism.

by Tony Lawson (1997), turns Boyd's "argument from success" on its head. If a science is consistently *un*successful, perhaps the most credible explanation is that the mechanisms that it postulates do *not* exist. Thus, according to Lawson, one way to set about the reconstruction of an unsuccessful science is to start in ontology, by proposing new conceptions of the sorts of mechanisms that really operate beneath the surface of the phenomena that are to be explained. Lawson maintains that "orthodox" economics *has* failed, and recommends economists to start all over again with his preferred form of "critical realism."

As a first step in explaining how our book fits into the grand scheme of methodology, we declare that, in our roles as its authors, we do not set out to defend any particular philosophical position in either epistemology or ontology. We are not looking for foundational principles from which we can construct rules of good practice in experimental economics. Nor are we primarily concerned with uncovering ontological assumptions implied by current practice.

To illustrate our stance toward fundamental methodological issues, we return to the debate between empiricist and realist conceptions of scientific knowledge. Within this debate, interpretations of the concepts of "explanation" and "causation" are hotly contested. For realists, there is a categorical distinction between *observing* a regularity in the world and *explaining* it; an explanation appeals to a supposed causal mechanism, while an observation is just an observation. For empiricists, in contrast, science is simply about finding regularities in observations: the only sense in which some regularity can be "explained" is by showing it to be an instance of a more general regularity. Similarly, talk about "causation" is to be understood as just another way of referring to observed regularities.[24] But while methodologists argue about what scientists *really* mean, or *ought to* mean, by "explanation" and "causation," practicing scientists are generally able to use these concepts in a mutually intelligible way without getting ensnared in ontological debate. Our experience of economics suggests to us that this is not because scientists are all realists, or because they are all empiricists. It is because much of what they actually need to say about explanation and causation would be just the same whichever of these positions they maintained. In writing this book, our standpoint is that of practicing experimental economists. Our default position is that we too can write intelligibly about explanation and causation without committing ourselves to ontological assumptions.

---

[24] The classic empiricist account of causation is that of Hume (1739-40, see 1978 edition, pp. 155-72). Hume argues that causation is a property not of the external world, but of our mental perceptions. The perception of causation is a psychological response to the observation of certain kinds of regularity.

In the rest of this book, the distinction between empiricism and realism will appear if, but only if, it matters for the arguments we want to make.

More generally, our understanding of the relationship between methodology and methods can be expressed in the following way. Without claiming deep insight into the abstract reaches of philosophy of science, we declare our sympathies with the anti-foundational epistemology of Willard Van Orman Quine (1951). By this, we do not mean that we will be presenting arguments in support of Quine's philosophy, but only that our approach to our subject matter is broadly Quinean in spirit. For Quine, the idea of finding the *foundations* of scientific knowledge is misguided. No form of belief, not even in the reality of "raw" observations or in the supposedly "analytic" (that is, necessarily true) theorems of mathematics and logic, is totally secure, independent of support from other beliefs. In place of the metaphor of foundations, Quine offers that of the *web of belief*:

> The totality of our so-called knowledge or beliefs, from the most casual matters of geography and history to the profoundest laws of atomic physics or even of pure mathematics and logic, is a man-made fabric which impinges with experience only along the edges. Or, to change the figure, total science is like a field of force whose boundary conditions are experience. A conflict with experience at the periphery occasions readjustments in the interior of the field....the total field is so under-determined by its boundary conditions, experience, that there is much latitude of choice as to what statements to reevaluate in the light of any single contrary experience. No particular experiences are linked with any particular statements of the interior of the field, except indirectly through considerations of equilibrium affecting the field as a whole.
>
> Quine (1951, section 6)

Another vivid metaphor, with much the same meaning as Quine's, is the ship imagined by Otto Neurath (1937):

> We possess no fixed point which may be made the fulcrum for moving the earth; and in like manner we have no absolutely firm ground upon which to establish the sciences. Our actual situation is as if we were on board ship on an open sea and were required to change various parts of the ship during the voyage.
>
> Neurath (1937, p. 276)

The idea behind these metaphors is that the body of scientific knowledge has no foundations: every part of it relies on other parts for corroboration. If we think of the study of methodology in these terms, we have to recognize that what we can learn from the philosophy of science is neither more nor less "fundamental" than what we can learn from the practice of science: methodology is neither more nor less fundamental than methods. If abstract philosophical reasoning can generate particular conclusions about the nature of knowledge, and if those conclusions imply that particular scientific methods are more likely than others to generate reliable knowledge, then that provides some support for whatever knowledge claims are produced by the favored methods. But, conversely, if the application of particular scientific methods is found to produce successful predictions and to assist us in manipulating the world, then that provides some support for whatever lines of philosophical reasoning lead to the conclusion that those methods are reliable.

This general conception of the mutual dependence of methodology and method is compatible with much of the current practice of methodology. In particular, it is compatible with the reluctance of many modern methodologists to prescribe regulative principles of scientific method in the way that, for example, Popper saw it as his job to do, and with modern methodologists' interest in investigating how, in particular sciences, claims to knowledge are in fact established and contested.[25] This less regulative approach is sometimes presented as showing decent humility on the part of the methodologist. Is it not presumptuous for philosophers of science to claim to judge the validity of the methods used by practicing scientists? If we accept Quine's metaphor of the web of belief, it is natural to ask, In which part of the web do we have greater confidence—in the substantive claims of received scientific theories or in the philosophical claims of epistemologists? If the former, should we not respond to conflicts between the two by reevaluating our epistemology rather than by questioning the methods used by scientists?

A significant example of this argument can be found in the work of Thomas Kuhn. Kuhn has had a huge impact on methodology through his historical study of "scientific revolutions." According to Kuhn's account, a "paradigm"—an assemblage of cohering theories, questions, and practices—can continue to hold the allegiance of a scientific community in the face of what later comes to be recognized as a mass of disconfirming evidence. The overthrow of a paradigm is a social process as much as it is the systematic application of rules of scientific method (Kuhn 1962). In the eyes of some critics, Kuhn's uncritical acceptance of this alleged characteristic of science is irrational and relativist. Kuhn makes the following reply to these criticisms:

> To say that, in matters of theory-choice, the force of logic and observation cannot in principle be compelling is neither to discard logic and observation nor to suggest that there are not good reasons for favoring

---

[25] Cartwright's (1989) study of knowledge claims in econometrics is an example.

one theory over another. To say that trained scientists are, in such matters, the highest court of appeal is neither to defend mob rule nor to suggest that scientists could have decided to accept any theory at all.

Kuhn (1970, p. 234)

In other words, Kuhn is not denying that there are standards of good scientific method; but he *is* denying that philosophy of science is qualified to define or police those standards.

The development of experimental economics over the last few decades has some similarities with a revolution—or, at least, an attempted revolution—in Kuhn's sense. Previously accepted ideas about the proper methods of the discipline and the criteria that should be used to choose between rival theories are being fought over. The implication of Kuhn's argument is that philosophy of science should not be expected to provide metacriteria by which to adjudicate whether the cause of true science is represented by the revolutionaries or the ancien régime. Science has to regulate itself.

While this argument has force for someone who is thinking about science from outside, it cannot provide the structure for our work. In Kuhn's sense, we *are* trained scientists. With respect to issues of method and theory-choice in economics, we are *members of* Kuhn's "highest court of appeal." Our book is not a commentary on the judgments of this court; it is part of the judgment process itself. In saying this, we do not lay claim to any special authority. Rather, the metaphor of courts of appeal is not completely apt. Courts of justice are organized hierarchically; one appeals from lower to higher ones. In contrast, science has more of the nature of a spontaneous order. A knowledge claim in economics becomes accepted as the cumulative effect of many small acts of judgment. Notwithstanding the existence of major players, there is no supreme court, no committee of the great and the good of the discipline, which collectively certifies or overrules the outcomes of this process.

This naturally raises the questions, What status can we claim for our judgments? On what are they grounded? How can the reader test their validity?

Before answering these questions directly, we take a step back. Recall Hands's examples of the "day-to-day" contexts in which methods are learned, and which we redescribed as potential locations of contests about which methods should be preferred to which. These are situations in which judgments are made about knowledge claims. How are these judgments expressed? Think of a panel of examiners judging a dissertation, an editor and her referees judging a paper, an appointment committee judging a job applicant, a panel of distinguished scholars awarding a major prize. The reader may have noticed that, in each case, we have replaced the single judge from Hands's example with a *panel* of judges. This revision reflects the reality of scientific institutions: collective judgments are the norm. If the members of a panel disagree— if, for example, one referee thinks a paper should be published while another thinks it should be rejected—there is an expectation that each will provide *reasons* for his judgment, in a form which allows discussion about its merits. And even if a panel is in agreement, there is often an expectation (as in the case of rejection decisions by journals) that the agreed judgment is supported by reasons that can be communicated to the person whose work is being judged. According to the conventions of refereeing, it is not enough just to say: "I am a trained economist, with a feel for the tacit rules of economics. I have a sense, which I cannot articulate, that this paper is no good."

The point of these examples is that, as a matter of simple fact, scientific practice involves not only the making of judgments between alternative methods and between competing theories; it also involves the giving of reasons. And more than that: reasons can be judged to be good or bad, sound or unsound, strong or weak. For example, if two members of an editorial board disagree about the suitability of a particular paper for publication, each may challenge the validity or force of the reasons that the other has given for her judgment. And again, it is not enough for one just to say to the other: "I am a trained economist, with a feel for the tacit rules of argument within the discipline. I have a sense, which I cannot articulate, that your reasons are no good." Further reasons are expected.

At first sight, it might seem that this chain of reasons and metareasons must *either* lead back to the ultimate foundations of knowledge (if such things exist), *or* lead back to claims for which no reasons can be given, *or* lead to an infinite regress. But, when individuals are trying to resolve a disagreement, there is no need for them to go back further than propositions on which they agree. Since these propositions are not in dispute, reasons are not called for. In disputes between practicing scientists, the search for reasons will often stop well before the issues that concern professional methodologists are reached. For example, the two members of our editorial board might resolve their disagreement about the merits of the paper without ever becoming aware that one of them believes that scientific knowledge can only be about observation while the other believes that science can discover real but unobservable mechanisms. Sometimes, however, the parties to what appears to be a day-to-day disagreement may find that they are disagreeing about issues in philosophy of science. And then, contrary to the implication of Kuhn's metaphor of the highest court of appeal, issues of method may be resolved by appeal to principles of methodology. Our approach will allow both possibilities. We will neither start from professional methodology or philosophy of science, nor shy away from them if that is where the arguments lead us.

We can now answer the rhetorical question we asked a few paragraphs back, What status can we, the authors of this book, claim for our judgments? All we can claim is that we are contributing to ongoing debates within economics, following what we believe to be the implicit rules of engagement. Our aim is to support our judgments by appealing to premises that our readers will accept and by giving reasons that our readers will find convincing.

2

Theory Testing and the Domain of Economic Theory

2.1 Domain Restrictions: Economic Theory and the Laboratory

We begin with the classic function of experiments in science: namely, testing theories. As explained in chapter 1, theory testing must be seen in the context of a view of theory in which empirical claims result from it. Even though much of the work of economic theorists consists of formal deductive analysis, such claims arise from applications of the theory: for example, seeing it as informative about, or as predicting, some class of actual phenomena. In this chapter we consider *where* the theory may be applied to test it or, to put the question slightly differently, with *what types of evidence* it is legitimate to confront the theory. In discussing this we put other issues, such as the conjunctive nature of testing and stochastic variation, on hold as far as possible until later chapters. We also restrict ourselves, for the present, by confining attention to evidence of *behavior*, broadly interpreted, so ignoring forms of evidence such as neural images or reports of mental states. Colin Camerer et al. (2004b, 2005) argue that economic theory may one day be revolutionized by these types of data, but the view that they provide a test of economic theory has been vigorously resisted by others, such as Faruk Gul and Wolfgang Pesendorfer (2008).[1] We set this dispute to one side for now because the overwhelming majority of data generated by experimental economics is evidence of behavior.

What sorts of behavioral evidence provide legitimate tests is a question about the *domain* of economic theory. Different positions about it have, at different stages in the development of experimental economics, been at the heart of debates both about the role of experiments in the broader subject and, among experimenters, about competing designs.

---

[1] For responses to Gul and Pesendorfer (2008), see the papers in part II of Caplin and Schotter (2008). For other discussion of neuroeconomics, see Bernheim (2008), Camerer (2007), Rustichini (2005), Smith (2008, chapter 14), and the November 2008 special issue of *Economics and Philosophy*.

Economics was seen as nonexperimental for much of its history, on the grounds that feasible laboratory experiments would not contribute usefully to the evaluation of economic theory. This view restricts the domain of the theory by putting the laboratory outside the realm in which its performance should be assessed. Although the suggestion that economics only concerns the behavior of agents in the naturally occurring economy may seem prehistoric to many of today's experimental economists, it was conventional wisdom until recently and we suspect it to be a view that is still widely held by nonexperimenters. In fact, we concur with Smith's (2002) conjecture that a substantial majority of economists still regard economics as a nonexperimental science, if one counts among the conjectured majority those who, though aware of experimental economics and disinclined to criticize it directly, regard its findings more as entertaining vignettes than as serious matters that might affect their own professional activity.

Even among economists who conduct experiments, there are opposing and often strongly held views about whether certain design features are mandated by the subject matter of economics. For example, although the claim that experiments should offer response-related monetary rewards is endorsed by most experimental economists, there is less agreement about the required size or structure of those rewards, the need or otherwise for task repetition, and many other design features. Different positions on such matters reflect disagreements about the types of phenomena to which economic theory is supposed to apply. Thus, they too imply domain restrictions on the theory, albeit different ones from those implied by general denial of a role for the laboratory in testing economic theory. They draw a boundary for the domain of the theory *through*, rather than right *around*, the set of possible experiments.

Each of the controversies considered in the last two paragraphs concerns domain restrictions on economic theory that are endorsed by some but resisted by others. In this chapter, we suggest a framework for assessing such restrictions, insofar as they relate to experimental theory testing. For this purpose, we are neutral about the origins of the theory. In particular, as discussed in chapter 1, the theory might have been developed from abstract theorizing or to explain stylized facts; in the latter case, these stylized facts might or might not have included observations made in previous experiments. However, we assume that *one* of the purposes of the theory is to make predictions about the world beyond any stylized facts used in constructing it. This assumption is much milder than the instrumentalist view often attributed to Milton Friedman (1953) that prediction is the *only* function of a substantive economic theory, a view which is discussed further below. It is also neutral with respect to the claim, suggested by some passages of Friedman (1953) but attacked by Guala (2005a, chapter 5) and Mayo (1991, 1996), that evidence used in the construction of a hypothesis cannot be used as support for it. However, it does assume that economic theory can be taken to have empirical content in relation to some domain, thereby posing the question of what that domain is. For our purposes, the key aspects of this question are as follows: Does the domain of economic theory allow it to be tested legitimately in the laboratory? If so, does the domain of the theory govern the appropriate experimental designs? And, if so, how?[2]

These questions should really be posed about particular theories rather than about economic theory as a whole because, for example, it might be that the domain of consumer theory intersects with the laboratory whereas that of the theory of international trade does not. The purpose of this chapter is not to deny this possibility but rather to offer and apply a general framework with which our questions, when asked about a particular economic theory, can be addressed. In sections 2.2–2.5, we use the term "theory" to stand as a placeholder for any economic theory or model.[3] In sections 2.6 and 2.7, we discuss theories of individual choice and of equilibrium behavior respectively, as examples.

The case of individual choice is one where, prima facie, the results of testing in the laboratory have been unfavorable to conventional economic theory (Camerer 1995; Starmer 2000). Yet, notwithstanding the recent growth of behavioral economics, the standard theory of choice is still the foundation of most research in economics.[4] This suggests that many economists discount unfavorable evidence from choice experiments, either (i) because they discount experimental evidence in economics in general, or (ii) because they see the particular designs that have produced the most unfavorable evidence about standard choice theory as outside the proper domain of that theory, or at least as outside the domain relevant for their purposes. Charles Plott (1996), Ken Binmore

---

[2] These questions are posed and discussed in Cubitt (2005). The argument of sections 2.2–2.6 of this chapter draws on that paper, as well as Cubitt et al. (2001) and Starmer (1999a,b).

[3] For the present, it is not necessary to distinguish between a theory and a model; and we use the terms interchangeably. However, in chapter 5, we will distinguish between them.

[4] The process of applying nonstandard theories of choice and other elements of behavioral economics to economic phenomena "in the wild," to use the phrase coined by Camerer (2000), is gathering pace. For early steps, see part 5 of Kahneman and Tversky (2000). A complete selection would now include many more papers than that volume but we suspect that it would still run to no more than a few hundred papers, compared with thousands that routinely apply standard choice theory. For recent surveys of applied behavioral economics, see Diamond and Vartiainen (2007), but note that not all applications of behavioral economics invoke nonstandard theories of individual choice. (For example, an agent may have social preferences and still maximize expected utility.)

(1999), and Glenn Harrison (1994) take positions of type (ii). We suspect that they articulate views that are more widely, if sometimes only casually, held. Section 2.6 shows how the framework suggested in sections 2.4 and 2.5 can structure an assessment of such views. Section 2.7 uses the same framework to consider a different domain question, also raised by the arguments of Plott and Binmore, arising from the use of equilibrium concepts in economic theory.

Central to this chapter is the interplay between two requirements: that of generality on economic theory and that of external validity on experimental research. We begin by briefly discussing those requirements in isolation.

2.2 Generality and External Validity

2.2.1 Generality of Theory

Imagine a discussion between two macroeconomists on the first day of the current century. Their conversation turns to the future of the main Asian economies, in the light of their twentieth-century growth paths. Suppose one of the macroeconomists proposes an explanation of Japanese economic growth in the second half of the twentieth century (in which decades of rapid growth in real per capita GDP were followed by much slower growth), according to which the rapid growth is explained by Japan's capital–labor ratio rising toward its steady-state value and the slowdown by the ratio stabilizing at that value. She supports this account with evidence of growth in Japan's capital–labor ratio continuing up to, but not beyond, the end of the period of rapid GDP growth. Suppose, for the sake of example, that the second macroeconomist does not dispute this evidence but argues that, in China as the twenty-first century begins, there is little sign that its spectacular growth will soon be followed by prolonged stagnation.[5] The critic therefore attributes Japan's growth slowdown to inappropriate monetary policy in the late twentieth century. The first macroeconomist could respond that her claim is that Japan slowed down on reaching its steady-state capital–labor ratio, so rapid growth in China is not inconsistent with it unless China's capital–labor ratio has stabilized too. Even if the critic were (somehow) to convince her that China's capital–labor ratio had reached its steady state

---

[5] How sensible the second macroeconomist's view will look by the time the reader sees this may depend on events unfolding as we complete the final manuscript, to the accompaniment of the 2008 U.S. and European banking crises. But it was a common view in 2000, and still supportable in 2008 by the argument that even a recession in its major export markets is more likely to interrupt China's growth temporarily than to initiate prolonged stagnation.

by then, the first macroeconomist could still point to many economies besides Japan whose postwar experience was of rapid growth followed by slowdown and suggest factors that distinguish China from many of these economies, such as scope to grow by eliminating the inefficiencies of central planning. But she could *not* reasonably respond to her critic that her explanation applies only to Japan in the second half of the twentieth century and is therefore untouchable by evidence from other countries or time periods.

What this illustrates is that any reasonable explanation requires *some* component that purports to generality. If attributions of causation require "constant conjunction" between events (Hume 1739–40, 1748), causal explanations necessarily generalize across sufficiently similar episodes.[6] Thus, to the extent that economic theories purport to offer explanations, especially causal ones, they must have some degree of generality. However, the desirability of generality does not depend on the purpose of theories being to explain. Those who hold that the primary function of theories is to predict typically also favor theories with generality. Even Friedman (1953) favors theories with generality. For example, in his famous discussion of the distribution of leaves on a tree, he rates the theory that light stimulates organic growth over the theory that leaves consciously maximize their light exposure on the grounds that it has the potential to predict more phenomena (Friedman 1953, pp. 19–20).

Whatever the balance of explanation and prediction in the function of theory, the most useful theories perform well over a broad range of circumstances. It is a standard principle that, other things being equal, if one theory can account for everything that another theory can account for, and more besides, then the former theory is to be preferred. Thus, without knowledge of the evidence that may confront it, to interpret a theory as having broad generality is to interpret it *charitably*.[7] This grounds an entitlement, on the part of a scientist seeking to test some theory, to presume that the theory is intended as general unless or until there is some legitimate reason to qualify this. This is a mild claim. Specifically, it is not an unconditional requirement that theories

---

[6] Although the phrase "constant conjunction" is famously Hume's, our claim does not depend on a further assertion—more controversial, but also Hume's in the eyes of many commentators—that constant conjunction is all there is to causation. A realist view of science implies that causal explanations generalize because, on this view, the same constant conjunction would be observed whenever the same causal mechanisms are present.

[7] This, of course, does not imply that it is charitable to interpret a theory as making a prediction that one already knows will not be confirmed. Our point is simply that, other things being equal, generality is a virtue of a theory; and therefore that, other things being equal, attributing it to a theory is charitable.

be maximally general, as it freely admits the possibility of legitimate qualification. It merely asserts a potentially qualified entitlement to presume. Nor does it require that nature can be characterized by simple general laws, since a default presumption of generality would still be charitable if the virtue of generality arose from the cognitive function of theories, rather than from any simplicity of nature.

Further support for our claim can be found in the Popperian principle of exposing theories to severe tests (Popper 1934), explained in chapter 1 and considered further in chapter 3 (see box 3.2 (p. 108)). This principle contains two underlying ideas. One is that scientific theories should not lightly be insulated from testing; the other is that tests of theories should be of their most surprising predictions. The first component supports the entitlement to presume intended generality, since for Popper, shyness of empirical tests is a sign of unscientific activity.[8]

2.2.2 External Validity of Laboratory Experiments

Strictly, all that one observes in a particular laboratory experiment is what happens in it. The experimenter observes subjects' behavior, usually for a short time and always in a specific context. As this is actual behavior,[9] it is part of the subject matter of the science of human behavior (assuming subjects are human). But, *in itself*, this is not enough to make the behavior of laboratory subjects important for that science, because it is such a small part of its subject matter. As an analogy, consider Christian monastic communities. These are genuine societies, so what goes on in them is part of the subject matter of social science. But because there are now so few Christian monasteries and those that do remain are so small, study of them is not important for the study of modern society *unless* (as is actually very possible) we learn something from it about the social world outside the monastery. As for monasteries, so for laboratories. The importance of the behavior of laboratory subjects

---

[8] Although chapter 3 will discuss problems with simple forms of Popperianism, such problems do not undermine the charity of seeing a scientific theory as not seeking insulation from empirical evaluation.

[9] The claim that experimental economics creates real economic systems, for example, real markets in market experiments, has been influential in the development of experimental economics. Smith (1982a) and Wilde (1980) state well-known conditions for laboratory economic systems to count as real ones. We claim that all behavior that actually occurs, whether in the laboratory or otherwise, is real. But this leaves open that the Smith–Wilde precepts may govern whether laboratory behavior is significant for economics. We return to Smith's arguments in chapter 3.

for economics rests on it telling us something about the economy outside the laboratory, i.e., on external validity.

> **Box 2.1. Internal and external validity.**
>
> It is common for discussions of experimental methods in economics to distinguish between questions of internal validity and external validity. Each term can be, and has been, used in many different ways. However, one useful conception is to see each as a *joint* property of *inferences* and *experimental designs*. The joint property is possessed to the extent that a certain design licenses a certain inference.[10] The difference between internal and external validity is then a matter of the nature of the inference. Internal validity holds to the extent that an experimental design licenses conclusions about behavior in the experiment; whereas external validity holds to the extent that the design licenses conclusions about behavior outside the experiment.
>
> Internal validity might fail, for example, in an experiment in which measurements are unreliable or, more interestingly, in which control fails. Consider an experiment intended to investigate the effect of some factor x on some form of behavior. For there to be two treatments identical in all respects except for the presence or absence of x would militate for internal validity. But if the x-present and x-absent treatments also differ in other significant respects, then the ability of the design to inform about the effect of x is confounded.[11] Note that internal validity could fail even when the findings of the experiment are highly replicable: that is, when running essentially the same experiment in different conditions (e.g., with different subjects) would yield essentially the same results. Thus, on our definition, replicability and internal validity are distinct properties, even though nonreplicability would tend to indicate low internal validity.
>
> External validity fails if the design is such that the findings of the experiment, even when internally valid, are not informative about behavior outside the experiment. This might arise if, for example, the pool of experimental subjects responds to well-controlled experimental manipulations differently from how other agents would. A common view is that there is a trade-off between internal validity and external validity, in the

[10] One could also define analogous conditions of internal and external validity, where each of these properties is one which might be possessed jointly by a *class of designs* and certain inferences.

[11] For this reason, it is common when an experimenter wishes to investigate the effect on certain behavior of two factors, x and y, to employ a 2×2 design in which there are x-present and x-absent treatments for both y-present and y-absent conditions. This allows the effect of each factor to be considered, holding the other constant; and permits investigation of their interaction.

sense that design features that conduce to the former (typically through a high degree of control) may militate against the latter, perhaps because of increasing the artificiality of the laboratory environment. We discuss this view in the context of a broader assessment of external-validity concerns in chapter 5. Another notable discussion of internal and external validity is provided by Guala (2005a).

Critics of experiments in social science are typically skeptics about external validity. Even among experimenters, there is concern about whether some experimental findings—sharing in dictator games,[12] for example—would extend outside the laboratory. Such concerns are, at least up to a point, understandable. Many experimental sessions are so unlike most of "normal life" that it seems a considerable stretch to generalize from laboratory behavior to the behavior that economists are usually concerned with. The fact that many are swayed by this thought probably underlies the recent popularity of field experiments (Harrison and List 2004; List 2006; Levitt and List 2007). However, as noted in chapter 1, it is not clear that either field experiments or nonexperimental empirical methods have a fail-safe defense against problems analogous to that of external validity. For *any* empirical enquiry, there is a question of how far the findings generalize from the environment in which they were observed to other environments, which may vary in how like the first they are. While this puts external-validity concerns in a different light, it does not eliminate them.

2.2.3 Generality and External Validity Counterposed

Stated separately, the presumption of generality of theory and the concern with external validity of experimental findings seem almost banal. The interesting point about them is that they pull in opposite directions in the following way: the more general we presume our theories to be, the more legitimate it seems to test them anywhere, including in the laboratory if we choose to do so; on the other hand, the more doubtful we are about the external validity of experimental findings, the less importance it seems that we should attach to theory testing in the laboratory. In sections 2.4 and 2.5, we mediate between these two considerations.

---

[12] In a dictator game, one subject is given a sum of money to divide between himself and another subject, who has no decision to make. A typical finding is that the first subject allocates a substantial share to the other (Thaler 1988; Camerer and Thaler 1995). Critics have pointed out that giving much of one's wealth to a complete stranger is unusual, or questioned the external validity of the finding for other reasons. See, for example, Bardsley (2008), Levitt and List (2007), Samuelson (2005, pp. 87–88), Schram (2005, p. 233), and Smith (2008, pp. 220–27) for different views.

2.3   The Blame-the-Theory Argument

However, before proceeding to that mediation, we comment on an argument that may seem to defuse the tension that we have just set up between the presumption of generality in theory and the concern with external validity of theory tests conducted in the laboratory. It is sometimes known as the *blame-the-theory* argument.

Box 2.2. The blame-the-theory argument.

The blame-the-theory argument is a defense of certain kinds of experimental design used for testing economic theories, especially those which closely implement the assumptions of some theoretical model, against the charge that the laboratory environments they create are inappropriate testing grounds because they are too simple or unrealistic to represent the complexity of real economies. The argument is encapsulated in the following quotations:

> Microeconomic theory abstracts from a rich variety of human activities which are postulated not to be of relevance to human economic behavior. The experimental laboratory...consists of a far richer and more complex set of circumstances than is parameterized in our theories. Since the abstractions of the laboratory are orders of magnitude smaller than those of economic theory, there can be no question that the laboratory provides ample possibilities for falsifying any theory we might wish to test.
>
> Smith (1982a, p. 936)

> But what is most important to any particular experiment is that it be relevant to its purpose. If its purpose is to test a theory, then it is legitimate to ask whether the elements of alleged "unrealism" in the experiment are parameters in the theory. If they are not parameters of the theory, then the criticism of "unrealism" applies equally to the theory and the experiment.
>
> Smith (1982a, p. 937)

> Once models, as opposed to economies, became the focus of research the simplicity of an experiment...became an asset. The experiment should be judged by the lessons it teaches about theory and not by its similarity with what nature might happen to have created.
>
> Plott (1991, p. 906)

Four distinct claims are embedded in the argument, namely (i) that laboratory environments are typically richer than the theories that they are used to test; (ii) that when this is so, it immunizes an experimental test against the criticism that the laboratory environment is too simple;

(iii) that laboratory environments are immune from charges of being too unrealistic to provide legitimate tests of a theory, unless the charges relate to factors modeled in the theory; and (iv), especially in Plott's formulation, that the primary purpose of the experiment is to teach about the theory, not the world.

Of these, it is hard to disagree with (i). As an illustration, consider markets. In a typical theoretical model of a market, demand and supply curves are either postulated directly or derived from more basic ingredients (such as assumptions about preferences and endowments), and an equilibrium condition defines the predicted volume of trade and price; but, usually, no mechanism is specified through which trade takes place or equilibrium is reached.[13] In contrast, in a market experiment, trade is undertaken by subjects whose behavior could, in principle, be affected by factors other than the theoretical determinants of equilibrium; and a market institution or set of rules governing how trade occurs and prices are set is specified.

However, (ii)–(iv) are more controversial. They will be the foci of our discussion of the blame-the-theory argument in this chapter and when it recurs in chapters 3–5. For other discussions, see Guala (2005a, chapters 7 and 9), Schram (2005), and Starmer (1999a), as well as the sources of the quotations above.

The blame-the-theory argument recognizes that where an experimental design closely implements many of the assumptions of a theoretical model, this will tend to make the laboratory environment spare, compared with nonlaboratory environments in which the theory is applied. It asserts, plausibly, that the laboratory environment is still usually richer than the theoretical model. However, it also argues that when this holds it immunizes the experiment from a charge of being too simple relative to the outside world to be an appropriate testing ground; and that a similar immunity applies to charges of being too unrealistic, as long as the alleged unrealism is not captured within the theory. These *immunization claims*, at least if taken as postulating sufficient conditions for immunity, are inconsistent with the instrumentalist argument of Friedman (1953) to be discussed in section 2.4 and (perhaps surprisingly in the case of Plott) with the arguments of Plott (1996) and Binmore (1999) to be considered in section 2.6. For now, we simply point out that *if*

---

[13] An exception is when the "Walrasian auctioneer" is postulated who adjusts prices, through "tâtonnement," until equilibrium prices are reached and prevents trade from occurring before that. But even the Walrasian auctioneer is an idealized abstraction, compared with trading processes, such as open cry or computerized double auctions or posted-offer markets, often found in market experiments.

theories are only expected to hold within limited domains, and *if* those domains are "richer" than the theory, then it would *not* follow from the laboratory environment also being richer than the theory that it is sufficiently rich to be an appropriate testing ground. Nor would it follow that a laboratory environment that captures the factors represented by the theory captures all important features of the domain in which the theory is expected to hold. So the immunization claims of the blame-the-theory defense presuppose answers to questions about the domain of the theory, rather than removing the need for them.

The blame-the-theory argument also has a further component, expressed by the highlighted quotation from Plott (1991), that may also seem to defuse the tension between generality of theory and external-validity requirements. In particular, the second sentence of that quotation can be read as denying the legitimacy of *all* external-validity concerns about the findings of experimental tests of theories, on the grounds that their purpose is to inform about theory, not the world. We see such a denial as too strong. At least in the context of theory testing, what one seeks to learn about an economic theory is its ability to account for actual behavior. Thus, it would only be if behavior in the laboratory was intrinsically interesting, independently of what it shows about behavior in the outside world, that the purpose of experimentation being to investigate theories would make irrelevant the similarity between the experiment and "what nature might happen to have created."

To assert, as we have in this section, that the concerns of external-validity skeptics pose legitimate questions is not to say that they are insuperable objections to experimental theory testing. Our objective in this section has not been to debunk the blame-the-theory argument, but just to warn against premature acceptance of the view that it diffuses external-validity concerns completely. In the next section, we set out a framework for adjudicating between those who endorse laboratory tests of economic theories and critics of the tests motivated by such concerns. We return to other aspects of the blame-the-theory argument in later chapters.

2.4   The Concept of Domain

The concept of domain is central to this chapter. It is now time to unpack it. It may seem surprising that this should be necessary. One could be forgiven for thinking that the domain of an economic theory will be obvious. Is it not just what the theory is about? But actually, this is often not obvious. For example, the theory of international trade may at first seem to be about trade in physical objects between nations but, on closer inspection, there is no reason evident from the theory to exclude services or invisible goods from the "goods" of the theory. Nor, more fundamentally, is it clear that the theory gives any reason why the "countries" should be nations, rather than villages or even individuals. Seen like this, one might argue that the theory of international trade is really just a theory of trade. But if trade is viewed as requiring a market, then even that description is slippery because the notion of a market is also unclear. For example, one might argue that the theory provides a possible account of the production and distribution of resources within a household. Such vagueness about the possible application of the theory raises the question of whether it can only be tested by examining trade between nation states or whether it would be equally legitimate, for example, to test it (or, perhaps better, some of its components—a point to which we return in chapter 5) by examining intrahousehold behavior in the field or the trading behavior of laboratory participants.[14]

Although the boundaries of the domain of a theory may not be clear-cut, we need some way of discussing them. One approach is to start from the *formal objects* of the theory. These are internal to the theory and, in the case of economic theories, usually consist of mathematical concepts. Consequently, there is inevitably some judgment involved in specifying to what real-world phenomena they correspond. But this difficulty should not be overstated: just because judgment is required, it does not follow that it is always contentious. The formal objects of economic theories usually have *real*, if not always naturally occurring, *close correlates* that can be identified from the formal objects themselves and the natural language used to describe and introduce them.[15] For example, the theory of consumer choice has, among its primitives, vectors called consumption bundles. Formally, these are just vectors. But the natural language used to describe them indicates that we may take quantifiable collections of actual consumer goods as close correlates of theoretical consumption bundles. There may also be other model entities, such as agents, which while not formal objects nevertheless have naturally occurring close correlates, to which one is guided by the language that describes them.

The close correlates of the formal objects of a theory and other model entities indicate a *base domain* for it, i.e., the set of possible real phenomena to which application of the theory seems reasonably unambiguous, if

---

[14] See Noussair et al. (1995) for a laboratory experiment that purports to test theories of international trade.

[15] Mäki (2002) argues that, though represented differently in economic theory than in commonsense discourse, what economic theory talks about is the "commonsense furniture of the human world" (p. 95).

made. By "reasonably unambiguous," we refer here to how things would seem to a normal observer, acquainted with the theory but *not* yet with the results of any attempts to test it.[16] Typically, the base domain constitutes only a small subset of the set of phenomena to which the theory could conceivably be applied.

For example, expected utility theory attributes to agents preferences over *prospects*. These formal objects are probability distributions over some well-defined set of possible outcomes. The theory is actually applied to choices between many items, such as investment portfolios or careers, which are not identical to prospects because, for example, some outcomes or probabilities are unknown. However, monetary gambles implemented by randomly drawing balls from a bingo cage (where the number of balls and the prize associated with each ball are known) are close correlates of prospects. Again, the natural language used to describe the formal objects is significant. Formally, for a given ordered list of possible outcomes, a prospect is simply a correspondingly ordered list of nonnegative numbers, summing to unity. It is the fact that these numbers are called "probabilities" that, together with background knowledge about bingo cages, licenses the judgment that a draw from a bingo cage is a close correlate of a prospect, so that choices made among them can reasonably be taken as in the base domain of expected utility theory.

As another example, consider the theory of public goods. In this theory, a pure public good is both nonrival in consumption (i.e., consumption of the good by one person does not diminish the amount available to others) and nonexcludable (i.e., if some quantity of the good is provided for anyone, no one within some population can be denied access to that quantity). Although the theory is routinely applied to goods that only approximate this description, such as road space, experimenters have devised a technique that corresponds very closely to the theoretical concept. It is known as the *voluntary-contributions mechanism*.

Box 2.3. The voluntary-contributions mechanism.

In an experimental treatment using the voluntary-contributions mechanism, subjects are divided into groups of n members. Each group member has an endowment of T tokens, that they must divide between two mutually exclusive uses, often termed the private and public accounts, respectively—a usage we follow here. A subject's monetary reward is

---

[16] Once such attempts have been made, and especially if with unfavorable results, reinterpreting the correspondence between theoretical concepts and entities in the test environment is often a response to the findings. This is an instance of the Duhem–Quine problem to be discussed in chapter 3.

proportionate to the number of points that she earns, which in turn depends on the allocation of tokens made by all subjects in her group. Each token that a subject allocates to her own private account earns one point for her (and nothing for anyone else); in contrast, each token that any group member allocates to the public account is multiplied by m and then divided equally among all n group members. Thus, for every token allocated to the public account by *any* group member, *every* group member earns (m/n) points. This ratio is called the marginal per capita return. In the usual form of the voluntary-contributions mechanism (assumed below), $n > m > 1$, so that the marginal per capita return, though positive, is strictly less than unity.

A subject who allocates a token to her private account earns one point from it; whereas the same token allocated to the public account would earn her $m/n < 1$ points. Thus, for any given allocation by other group members, each subject maximizes her own points total by allocating all of her endowment to her private account. However, the outcome in which all group members do this is socially inefficient, as it yields T points for each member when, had all members contributed their whole endowment to the public account, each would have received mT points. As $m > 1$, the situation is analogous to an n-person Prisoners' Dilemma.

Ledyard (1995) surveys experiments that have used the voluntary-contributions mechanism. A typical finding is that, initially, the average subject contributes around 40% of their endowment to the public account, but if the game is repeated, this proportion decays. There are many variants on the basic design, some of which—including the punishment opportunities investigated by Fehr and Gächter (2000), described in chapter 1—are effective at stimulating contributions to the public account and/or at preventing their decay over repeat play. Nevertheless, the findings from the basic design pose a puzzle for game theory on the assumption that each subject's concern is to maximize their own monetary payoff. One type of explanation replaces this assumption with the alternative that some subjects have social preferences that lead them first to contribute and then to reduce contributions if other group members have not done the same; another sees contribution as indicating disequilibrium play that occurs in early rounds, but then disappears.

Experiments that use the voluntary-contributions mechanism have a strong claim to be in the base domain of the theory of public goods because monetary rewards arising from a subject allocating a token to the public account have, in relation to her group, precisely the nonrivalness and nonexcludability properties constitutive of a pure public good.

Note that the crucial property of the base domain of a theory is close correspondence to the properties of the relevant formal objects and theoretical entities, *not* natural occurrence in the world. Bingo draws would have crucial dimensions in common with prospects, even if bingo was not a leisure industry; and the fact that the voluntary-contributions mechanism, in the form described above, is rare in the field does not prevent it from being in the base domain of the theory of public goods because of the close fit between it and the theoretical concept.

There are at least two further senses of the "domain" of a theory, which we label as follows.

I-domain. Set of phenomena to which it is *intended* the theory will be applied for the purposes of *understanding or predicting those phenomena.*

T-domain. Set of phenomena to which the theory can legitimately be applied for the purpose of *testing the theory.*

As with the base domain, the exact boundaries of the I-domain and the T-domain may not always be clear, but the distinction between the three conceptions of the "domain" of a theory still allows us to state claims that are important below. We begin with two such claims, as a preliminary to a more extended analysis in the following section.

(1) Universality and the T-domain

A theory is *universal* if it holds wherever it can be applied.[17] Thus, any assertion that an environment in which it is accepted that a particular theory could be applied is outside the T-domain of the theory is inconsistent with reasonable claims to universality on behalf of the theory. For example, a suggestion that the theory of consumer behavior cannot legitimately be tested by examining the spending patterns of young children may or may not be reasonable.[18] Either way, it implies that the theory is not universal, since it would be just as easy (given data on their

---

[17] This conception of a universal theory comprises two requirements: (i) that of universal quantification over the elements of some set; and (ii) that this set is maximally extensive, given the possibilities for application of the theory. Some authors (e.g., Guala 2005a, chapter 7) reserve the adjective "universal" for the purely formal property (i). Introduction of (ii) raises the question of where a theory *can* be applied. One approach would be to rely on the natural language of the theory, so that, for example, the theory of the firm is universal if it holds for all firms, the theory of consumer behavior if it holds for all consumers, and so on. But, for the purposes of this chapter, a precise answer to this question is not needed.

[18] Some may see it as odd to test consumer theory on young children but others, such as Harbaugh et al. (2001a), and Harbaugh et al. (2001b), evidently do not. The theory has also been tested on various kinds of nonhumans, such as pigeons (Battalio et al. 1981) and rats (Kagel et al. 1981).

spending) to apply the theory to child consumers as to adult ones. Likewise, any claim that experiments or particular designs in which some economic theory could be applied are not legitimate testing grounds concedes that the theory is not universal. By doing so, it opens up the question of what the limits of the theory are.

We are not asserting that theories should purport to universality.[19] Such an assertion would be much stronger than the presumption of generality set out in section 2.2. Nor are we asserting that the boundaries in which a theory can be applied are always uncontroversial. We are simply saying that, if it is acknowledged that the theory could be applied in a particular environment E, then to deny that E provides a legitimate test is to deny that the theory is universal. Thus, rightly or wrongly, external-validity critics of experimental theory testing in economics typically abandon claims of economic theories to universality. They do not usually argue that the theory literally *cannot* be applied to laboratory environments, but only that it *should not* be tested there.

(2) The T-domain and the I-domain

It may surprise some readers that we identify, as separate concepts, an I-domain and a T-domain for the theory. However, this should not be a surprise. Economic theories are used for many purposes, such as informing policy interventions or private sector decision making, other than the "pure science" of assessing the theories themselves. Multiplicity of purposes immediately militates against *identification* of the T-domain with the I-domain. This leaves open the possibility that the T-domain should be constrained to be a subset of the I-domain, a possibility that may seem attractive to adherents of the brand of instrumentalism associated with Friedman (1953).

Box 2.4. Instrumentalism and Friedman's methodology of positive economics.

The contribution that most influentially introduced instrumentalist scientific principles to economists is, by some distance, Milton Friedman's classic paper on the methodology of positive economics (Friedman 1953). However, some commentators, such as Uskali Mäki (2003), have suggested that Friedman's paper is really a heady mix of instrumentalism with other doctrines; and, in any case, instrumentalism is itself a constellation of distinct, if closely related, doctrines.

---

[19] Guala (2005a, chapter 7; 2005b) argues against such a requirement.

At the most general level, the instrumentalist view of theories is that they are instruments that can only be evaluated *relative to a purpose.* However, the usual forms of instrumentalism are more specific. They adopt, as the purpose of theories, the making of *successful predictions*, sometimes additionally asserting that it is not appropriate to ask whether a theory is "true" or "false" but only whether its predictions succeed or fail. Friedman puts this view in characteristically robust style: "the only relevant test of the validity of a hypothesis is comparison of its predictions with experience" (Friedman 1953, pp. 8–9). In fact, Friedman's form of instrumentalism is more specific, as the following quotations indicate (our italics):

> Viewed as a body of substantive hypotheses, theory is to be judged by its predictive power *for the class of phenomena that it is intended to "explain."*
>
> (p. 8)

> Given that the hypothesis is consistent with the evidence at hand, its further testing involves deducing from it new facts capable of being observed, but not previously known, and checking these deduced facts against additional empirical evidence. For this test to be relevant, the deduced facts must be *about the class of phenomena the hypothesis is designed to explain*; and they must be well enough defined so observation can show them to be wrong.
>
> (pp. 12–13)

These quotations show how, for Friedman (though not for all instrumentalists), assessment of a theory turns on its predictive success or failure *only* within the limited domain in which it is intended to be applied. Putting this claim into our terminology, it asserts that the T-domain is a subset of the I-domain.

A further controversial aspect of Friedman's argument was his insistence, expressed for example as follows, that theories cannot legitimately be evaluated by the realism of their assumptions if that is taken as a separate criterion from the success of their predictions:

> The relevant question to ask about the "assumptions" of a theory is not whether they are descriptively "realistic," for they never are, but whether they are sufficiently good approximations for the purpose in hand. And this question can be answered only by seeing whether the theory works, which means whether it yields sufficiently accurate predictions. The two supposedly independent tests thus reduce to one test.
>
> (p. 15)

This view licenses the claim that if the theory predicts successfully in its intended domain, it is all right for its assumptions to be unrealistic. Put differently, the theorist does not claim that the assumptions hold but rather that, within the intended domain, matters are *as if* the assumptions held. This could be because of background conditions, not captured in the theory.

Instrumentalism is opposed by *realist* views of science. The claims that the aim of science is not just to predict, but also to explain; that it should do so by uncovering causal mechanisms that are actually at work; that entities postulated by a scientific theory should exist; and that those assumptions of the theory that describe what it takes to be important causal mechanisms should hold in the world are among those associated with different forms of realism. However, realist views of science do not provide the only viewpoint from which Friedman's brand of instrumentalism can be criticized. An important alternative attack is due to Daniel Hausman (1992, chapter 9), who denies that Friedman's "irrelevance of the realism of assumptions" claim is implied by the instrumentalist view that scientific theories should be evaluated by the success of their predictions. Caldwell (1984, chapter 8) summarizes some other aspects of the controversy surrounding Friedman's paper. For discussion of realism, instrumentalism, and other forms of antirealism in philosophy of science, see Bird (1998, chapter 4) and Chalmers (1999, chapter 15).

It is a superficially attractive thought that the domain in which a theory can legitimately be tested is restricted to that in which it is intended to apply the theory. After all, what does it matter how the theory performs anywhere else? To see what is wrong with this thought, consider an example that Hausman (1992, chapter 9) uses to criticize Friedman (1953). Friedman contends that the test of a substantive theory is the success of its predictions *in the class of the phenomena that it is designed to explain.* On some interpretations, he asserts that this is the *only* legitimate test. Hausman objects to the latter view, even granting the assumption (which Hausman contests elsewhere) that prediction is the only role of theory. He draws an analogy, which we now adapt, with buying a used car. Suppose that the only intended use for the car is to make short journeys through town to work. This does not mean that the only tests to which we would subject the car before purchase are test-drives along this particular route. We might do test-drives on other routes, including dissimilar ones (motorway driving, for example); we might, as Hausman suggests, have a mechanic "look under the hood." But why would we do either of those things if we are really *only* concerned with the performance of the car on the route to work? There are at least two answers. First, we might suspect that our intentions could change, making performance on other routes more important. Second, even if we were certain that this would not happen, having a mechanic check under the hood might help to gauge the future performance of the car on the route to work, mitigating the problem that we can only do a few actual test-drives along it.

The analogues of these points apply to theory testing. The I-domains of theories change; testing outside the current I-domain may help to guide that change, in the same way that examining the mechanical condition of the car might guide whether it would be wise to undertake a long journey in it. Even if this were not so, the results of tests conducted *outside* the I-domain may help to understand or to predict future performance of the theory *in* the I-domain. The latter view is in line with the Quinean metaphor of a web of belief. If the confrontation between scientific belief and observation is between the whole web of belief and all observations, and can in principle suggest adjustments to any part of the web, it would be inappropriate to restrict arbitrarily the types of observations used to assess a given part of the web.

In the next section, we outline a position that asserts that, despite these points, there still *is* a connection between the T-domain and the I-domain of a theory. So far our claim has merely been that there are no strong general reasons to identify the T-domain with the I-domain or to restrict the T-domain to lie within the I-domain.

2.5   The Laboratory and the Three Senses of Domain

There are few, if any, economic theories that are *primarily* intended for application in the prediction or understanding of the behavior of experimental subjects. For much of the history of economics, it probably would not have occurred to many theorists that explaining experimental findings should even be among their objectives but, as we discuss in chapter 4, it is now very common to develop theories to explain stylized facts from experiments. Even so, we take it that few proponents of these theories would claim that this is actually the main purpose of the theory.[20] The reason why this has not deterred experimenters from attempting to test economic theories in the laboratory is that the laboratory offers greater prospects for control than naturally occurring environments in the I-domain of a theory.

For many economic theories, laboratory environments with plausible claims to be in the base domain of particular theories can be created because of the possibility of close correspondence between laboratory

---

[20] Some, such as Schram (2005, pp. 234–35), have feared otherwise.

constructs and the formal concepts of the theory. For example, experiments to test expected utility theory can present subjects with real choices between close correlates of prospects. Similarly, experiments, such as those surveyed by Roth (1995b), that test theories about interpersonal bargaining can impose forms of interaction between subjects that correspond closely to the moves allowed in bargaining theory.[21] Smith's (1982a) suggestion that the laboratory can be closer to economic theory than are natural economic environments is probably the least contentious part of the blame-the-theory defense and has been an inspiration to a generation of subsequent experimenters, who have tried to instantiate theoretical models in the laboratory.[22] In a theory-testing context, this can be seen as an attempt to develop laboratory environments in the base domains of the relevant theories.

The possibility of creating environments in which the predictions of the theories are relatively unambiguous is a major advantage of the laboratory. Thus, although not all designs could plausibly be said to be in the base domains of the relevant theories, those for which this can be said provide an obvious starting point, since they will tend to provide relatively unambiguous tests. Consider the following assertion.

Naive experimental claim (NEC). *Any laboratory environment in the base domain of a theory is also in the T-domain of that theory.*

NEC asserts that experimental designs within the base domain of a particular theory provide legitimate tests of that theory. For theories that claim universality, this is immediate. If such a theory cannot be tested in its base domain, where its predictions are at their least ambiguous, it is hard to see how it could be tested anywhere. However, while the concept

---

[21] These are examples of close correspondence between laboratory constructs and concepts that, in the theory, are used to describe the choices or environment faced by *individual agents*. In such cases, there is also a close correspondence between the agent of the theory and a subject, at least to the extent that the latter is, and the former is referred to by terms suggestive of, an individual person. Whether the latter type of correspondence holds when the agent is described in the theory by terms (such as "firm" or "government") that seem to refer to entities of different natural kinds from experimental subjects is more problematic, a point to which we return in chapter 5.

[22] This is not to say that Smith would necessarily agree with matching experimental design as closely as possible to theoretical models. His market experiments have typically included features absent from such models (e.g., precise trading rules) or different from them (e.g., few traders). In his recent book, he writes:

... hence the importance of testing it [a theorem or theory] not only under the assumptions on the economic environment giving rise to the theorem, but under variations on those assumptions to test the breadth of its ecological rationality.

Smith (2008, p. 50)

of a universal theory may be an ideal type, it is not clear if many, if any, economic theories do purport to universality; and, for a theory that does not, NEC can easily be disputed. For example, a critic might assert that an experimental environment E, even if in the base domain of some theory, is not in its T-domain *unless* behavior in E can be shown to generalize to environments in the I-domain. This criticism need not equate the T-domain with the I-domain or assert that the former is a subset of the latter, and so could be consistent with our argument in the previous section about the relationship between those concepts. But, as just formulated, the criticism still demands too much because it may not be possible to establish whether behavior in E generalizes to environments in the I-domain. Conclusive examination of all such environments is unlikely to be feasible, because of resource constraints. More importantly, difficulty in interpreting behavior in the I-domain is often why experiments were conducted to test the theory in the first place. Further, the presumption of generality in theory entitles the experimenter presenting an experiment whose design is in the base domain of the theory to respond to the skeptic that the burden of explanation goes the other way. This response suggests a modification of NEC.

Modified experimental claim (MEC). *Any laboratory environment E in the base domain of a theory should be presumed to be in the T-domain unless there is some difference between E and the I-domain, that can reasonably be expected to make behavior in the I-domain markedly more consistent with the theory.*

Note that, like NEC, MEC does not make being in the base domain of the theory a *necessary* condition for a laboratory environment to be in the T-domain of that theory. Rather, MEC asserts a *qualified presumption of sufficiency*. In the remainder of this section, we discuss the "rules of the game" that it implies: that is, the obligations that it imposes on experimenters, economic theorists, and defenders of theories.

Suppose that a theory t is contradicted by evidence obtained in an experimental environment E, where E is in the base domain, but not the I-domain, of the theory. (For simplicity, continue to ignore Duhem–Quine problems with this supposition.) What lines are available to a defender of t?

MEC disallows a defense that just states that E is outside the T-domain of the theory because it is outside the I-domain. But it allows, as candidate defenses of t, assertions that behavior in the I-domain is likely to be more consistent with the theory than behavior in E. Although such assertions effectively abandon any claim that t is a universal theory, this may be a price that the defender of t is prepared to pay. But, even if it is, a defense of the suggested form would not be compelling unless accompanied by some explanation of *why* behavior in the I-domain should be expected to be more consistent with *t* than behavior in *E*. Thus, MEC implicitly imposes a *rationalization requirement* on the defender of *t*. To meet the rationalization requirement, it is not enough for the defender of *t* to point out differences between *E* and the I-domain. Some reason why they should be seen as relevant to conformity of behavior with *t* must be given too. This is a very mild requirement. It does not say that the defender of the theory must establish the success of the theory in the I-domain, so the burden that it imposes on the defender of *t* is one of explanation, rather than proof. Explanation is required for any useful debate to proceed.

In view of the rationalization requirement, the theory-defender's argument should typically be *suggestive* of further empirical hypotheses that could be tested, experimentally or otherwise. The idea that, in responding to unfavorable evidence, the defender of a theory should develop it in a way that generates novel empirical content is an important part of the "methodology of scientific research programmes" developed by Imre Lakatos (1970, 1978), to which we return in chapter 3.

In meeting the rationalization requirement, a defender of *t* might (implicitly or explicitly) limit the I-domain of the theory. Call this an *I-domain contraction defense*. (We discuss examples in sections 2.6 and 2.7 in the context of choice theory and equilibrium theory, respectively.) If the newly proposed boundaries of the I-domain are accompanied by plausible rationalizations, this is a legitimate defense strategy despite the obvious danger that the further the suggested I-domain for the theory contracts, the less useful the theory becomes.

I-domain contraction defenses may be more or less convincing. Critics are entitled to be skeptical if faced with repeated I-domain contractions accompanied by unrelated rationalizations; by rationalizations that do little more, in generating novel hypotheses, than suggest that the original theory will predict more accurately in the newly suggested I-domain than in the old; or if subsequent tests show the associated rationalizations to be unconvincing. These criteria have something in common with those that define the distinction between progressive and degenerating research programs (Lakatos 1970, 1978), to be discussed in chapter 3.

As an illustration, consider an example adapted from Friedman (1953). Suppose that a scientist tests Newtonian theories concerning the operation of gravity on bodies by dropping feathers and steel balls from a tall building. In normal atmospheric conditions, the results will almost certainly be unfavorable to the simple Newtonian prediction that all bodies accelerate at the same rate under gravity. A defender of the theory might rationalize such unfavorable evidence by pointing out the differing effects of air resistance on feathers and steel balls, thereby suggesting the new hypotheses (i) that the simple Newtonian prediction is more accurate in vacuums than in standard atmospheric conditions; and (ii) that it is also more accurate, in standard atmospheric conditions, for steel balls of different sizes than for objects as different as feathers and steel balls. Each of (i) and (ii) is an I-domain contraction defense. They become more convincing the more fleshed-out are the reasons for expecting air resistance to matter for acceleration under gravity and the more new hypotheses are suggested that go beyond (i) and (ii). For example, the rationalization might suggest the possibility of exploiting air resistance to make possible powered flight or to predict the relative effectiveness of different designs of airplane wing. The success of such predictions would give one more confidence that the I-domain contraction defense of the original theory is part of scientific progress.[23]

Note that although MEC allows a defender of a theory to offer suggestive rationalizations of apparently unfavorable evidence and/or to offer I-domain contraction defenses of the theory, either of these moves imposes further (if obvious) obligations on the defender. These are only to advocate use of the theory within its newly proposed I-domain and to accept the implications of subsequent tests of the rationalization for the success of the defense.

Now consider the case where an experiment whose design is in the base domain of some theory generates evidence that is consistent with that theory. Clearly this is a success for the theory. But the question remains of how far one can extrapolate that success outside the laboratory. Provided that they give reasons for doing so, in the form of relevant differences between the experimental design and the I-domain of the theory, critics can legitimately question the likely success of the theory in its I-domain. External-validity concerns about experimental findings are double-edged, in the sense that they can apply to successes of theory, as well as to failures. We return to the extrapolation of favorable results in chapters 4 and 5.

Finally, consider the position of experimenters seeking to design a test of some theory. There is nothing in our argument above that forces the

---

[23] In treating (i) and (ii) as I-domain contraction defenses of the theory, we have treated the theory as asserting that all bodies fall at the same rate under gravity. There is an alternative view that the theory merely asserts this as a tendency that would hold in the absence of countervailing factors. On this view, experiments conducted under atmospheric conditions merely indicate the presence of countervailing factors, not failures of the theory. However, one can see this form of the theory as itself I-domain contracted, relative to the unconditional version. We give further examples of I-domain contraction defenses in the next two sections.

experimenter to start with the base domain of the theory, since MEC is just a qualified presumption of sufficiency. But experimental designs in the base domain will often provide attractive, well-controlled tests. Suppose that the experimenter does take this route. Even if the theory does not purport to be universal, the "unless ..." clause in MEC can be sidestepped if the experimenter takes some account of the I-domain of the theory and of rationalizations suggesting that the base domain may differ from it in ways that can be expected to affect conformity of behavior with the theory. Two questions arise: What should the experimenter take the I-domain to be? Which rationalizations should they allow for?

One might expect that the I-domain could be identified from the *original statements of the theory* (and so that subsequent rationalizations are not relevant). Sometimes the original formulation of a theory is accompanied by comments about its domain of applicability. But often these are only fragmentary.[24] For example, it is quite common, when a theory is introduced, for a list of facts that the theory purports to explain to be given. Such a list may be indicative of an I-domain, but usually no more than vaguely so. In any case, some theories have no canonical original statement. Perhaps more importantly, the recent history of economics shows very clearly that theories initially intended for use in one area may spread to others: the development of public choice theory, through the application of economic theories of choice to politics, is an example. Not to recognize that evolution in the I-domains of theories is part of scientific progress would be absurd.

An alternative position is that *current practice among scientists who use the theory* for explanation, prediction, and policy recommendation provides the best guide to the I-domain. Relevant rationalizations are then those that indicate potentially important differences between areas of current use of the theory and its base domain.

However, the conventions of current usage may only adjust slowly in the face of theory testing. So a third position is that relevant rationalizations should be identified from the *specialist literature on tests of the theory*. By rationalizing previous ostensibly disconfirming evidence, this literature may implicitly or explicitly allow a residual

---

[24] Guala (2005a, chapter 7; 2005b) argues that economic theories cannot contain complete statements of their domain of applicability. His main arguments for this conclusion would not prevent scientists from appending to the theory supplementary statements of its intended domain, not formulated in the theory's own terms. But many original statements of economic theories are quite vague on such matters. It is interesting to note, in passing, that a Popperian view of scientific virtue requires scientists to specify the possible observations that would refute the theory. We discuss problems with this aspect of Popper's falsificationism in chapter 3.

I-domain to be delineated. This position would require experimenters to take account of rationalizations in the specialist literature even if they are not yet reflected in the practice of the wider scientific community.

The possibility that the practice of users and the specialist literature are out of line with each other is very real, as the case of choice theory discussed below will illustrate. If practitioners use the theory in domain D_1 and specialists advocate its use in domain D_2, where $D_2 \neq D_1$, it seems reasonable for experimenters to be concerned with both D_1 and D_2. In view of this, a fourth possible position is *pluralism* in the treatment of the I-domain. Only a mild form of pluralism would be required, in the case just considered, to allow investigation of the theory's performance in environments sufficiently like either D_1 or D_2.

An argument in support of a wider form of pluralism is as follows: the more tightly constrained is the set of environments in which a theory is tested, and the more that set is limited to situations in which there is prior expectation that the theory will not fail, the less chance there is that the theory will have surprising successes. As a nonexperimental analogy, consider the development of real business cycle theory in macroeconomics. The early proponents of the theory, such as Finn Kydland and Edward Prescott (1982), deliberately set out to investigate the ability of modeling approaches that had previously been used to explain very long term patterns in growth rates to account also for economic fluctuations at business cycle frequency. The result was a profound change in modern business cycle theory. For better or worse, this development could not have occurred if change in the domain of application of growth theory had been restricted only to come about through contraction in the face of unfavorable evidence. Such a restriction would also limit the implementation of the Popperian stricture in favor of bold conjectures and severe tests.[25]

On a pluralist view, the obligation on experimenters is not to ensure conformity of the design with a particular conception of the domain of the theory, but rather to ensure that only warranted conclusions are drawn from results (and, therefore, that the design makes as clear as possible which conclusions are warranted). Although the base domain was used above as the starting point from which MEC is built, a pluralist would allow others, especially if they satisfy an "unless..." condition analogous to that of MEC. For example, often the proponent of a new

---

[25] Hartley et al. (1997) commend Kydland and Prescott precisely for making a bold Popperian conjecture in developing the real business cycle model, even though, on balance, they regard the conjecture as refuted by the evidence.

theory advocates it partly on the grounds that it can explain some phenomenon, observed in some experimental environment E, that earlier theories could not account for. In doing so, the proponent accepts that differences between E and the I-domain are not such that the new theory is inapplicable in E, thereby grounding a presumption analogous to MEC that environments "sufficiently like" E are in the T-domain of the new theory, even if they are not in either its base domain or its I-domain. A second example is the case of designs that seek to "naturalize" the experimental experience in some way, perhaps through the use of field experiment techniques. Such naturalization may come at a cost of a weaker claim to being in the base domain of the theory but, as noted above, neither MEC nor NEC makes being in the base domain a necessary condition for being in the T-domain.

2.6 Application to Experimental Tests of Choice Theory

In this section we apply the framework discussed above to the standard economic theory of choice. By this, we mean the theory of utility maximization for conditions of certainty, and expected utility theory for those of uncertainty.

Sometimes it is asserted that the standard theory of choice is so flexible that it is not subject to experimental testing or any other empirical test. To dispose of this argument, it is enough for present purposes to distinguish the *general form* of the theory from *the theory as applied*.[26] When choice theory is applied in economic modeling, the first step is to postulate a universe of objects over which preferences are then defined. For example, in general equilibrium theory, preferences are defined over n-dimensional consumption bundles; in real business cycle models, preferences are defined over lifetime streams of consumption and leisure. Once it has been specified what preferences are defined over, standard choice theory *does* impose testable restrictions on choices over those things. If this were not so, the theory would have no falsifiable implications and no bite in applications. So, in needing to specify the objects of choice before proceeding, experimenters wanting to test standard choice theory are in precisely the same position as economists wishing to apply the theory in the field.

---

[26] This idea is similar to the Lakatosian distinction, to be considered in chapter 3, between the *hard core* and *protective belt* of a scientific research program (Lakatos 1970, 1978). Each consists of a set of assumptions; it is only by combining them that testable hypotheses are derived.

> **Box 2.5. Expected utility theory: Transitivity and Independence.**
>
> To formulate expected utility theory, we take as primitive a nonempty, finite set $X = \{x_1, \ldots, x_n\}$ of *consequences* and the concept of *probability*. A *prospect* is a probability distribution over X; for the purposes of this box, typical elements of the set of such prospects are denoted p, q, r. The probability of consequence x in prospect p is π_{px}. For any prospects p, q and for any $\lambda \in [0, 1]$, we use $\lambda p + (1 - \lambda)q$ as an alternative notation for the simple prospect r defined such that, for all $x \in X$, $\pi_{rx} = \lambda\pi_{px} + (1 - \lambda)\pi_{qx}$. The theory postulates a decision maker who has a (binary) weak preference relation $\succsim$ over prospects.[27] Different formulations of the theory vary in their details, but one thing is common to them all. It is the existence of a utility function $u(\cdot)$ that assigns a utility to each consequence, such that the decision maker weakly prefers p to q if, and only if, the probability-weighted sum of utilities of consequences implied by p is at least as great as that implied by q: that is $p \succsim q$ if, and only if, $\sum_{x \in X} \pi_{px} u(x) \geq \sum_{x \in X} \pi_{qx} u(x)$. This *expected utility representation* of preferences dates back to Bernoulli (1738), but the popularity of expected utility in economics is much more recent. It is largely due to formal results, known as expected utility representation theorems, that show that the expected utility representation of preferences holds if the decision maker's preference relation satisfies certain axioms.
>
> Various expected utility representation theorems have been proved, differentiated by different axioms and formal frameworks (see Hammond (1998) for some of the history.) But for our purposes, these differences are inessential. We focus on two principles, defined as follows.
>
> **Transitivity.** For all simple prospects p, q, r, if $p \succsim q$ and $q \succsim r$, then $p \succsim r$.
>
> **Independence.** For all simple prospects p, q, r, and for any $\lambda \in [0, 1]$, $p \succsim q$ if, and only if, $\lambda p + (1 - \lambda)r \succsim \lambda q + (1 - \lambda)r$.
>
> These conditions are fundamental to expected utility theory because, although different representation theorems use sets of axioms that sometimes do and sometimes do not contain precisely the conditions above, those conditions are *implications* of the expected utility representation. For Transitivity, this follows immediately from transitivity of weak inequality. For Independence, it follows from the fact that

---

[27] The decision maker is indifferent between p and q if he weakly prefers both p to q and q to p. He strictly prefers p to q if he weakly prefers p to q and is not indifferent between them.

for any prospects p, q, and r, and any $\lambda \in [0, 1]$, $\sum_{x \in X} \pi_{px} u(x) \geqslant \sum_{x \in X} \pi_{qx} u(x)$ implies (and is implied by)

$$\sum_{x \in X} \lambda \pi_{px} u(x) + \sum_{x \in X} (1 - \lambda) \pi_{rx} u(x)$$

$$\geqslant \sum_{x \in X} \lambda \pi_{qx} u(x) + \sum_{x \in X} (1 - \lambda) \pi_{rx} u(x).$$

Thus, when supplemented by the principle that the decision maker will choose p over q in a pairwise choice only if he weakly prefers p to q, Transitivity and Independence imply predictions about choice that are common to different formulations of expected utility theory with known probabilities.

A common application of expected utility theory is to situations where consequences are monetary, so that the elements of X may be ordered by their magnitude. For this case, we adopt the notational convention that $x_1 > \cdots > x_n$. Then, on the reasonable assumption that $u(\cdot)$ is strictly increasing in its monetary argument, the following is also an implication of the expected utility representation:

First-Order Stochastic Dominance. For all simple prospects p, q, if, for all $i \in \{1, \ldots, n\}$, $\pi_{px1} + \cdots + \pi_{pxi} \geqslant \pi_{qx1} + \cdots + \pi_{qxi}$, with strict inequality for at least one i, then p is strictly preferred to q.

First-Order Stochastic Dominance seems a minimal rational preference condition for agents concerned with maximizing their monetary rewards.

Box 2.5 outlines the formal structure of expected utility theory. Given a set of consequences and the *revealed preference principle* that, in any pairwise choice, the decision maker will choose an option only if he (at least weakly) prefers it to the alternative, the Transitivity, Independence, and (if consequences are monetary) First-Order Stochastic Dominance conditions of the theory imply restrictions on the choices that a decision maker can make. Unlike First-Order Stochastic Dominance, Transitivity and Independence do not restrict choices in any single decision problem, but only across certain sets of problems. These *cross-problem consistency conditions* have been studied extensively.[28] For example, Independence rules out particular patterns of choice in certain pairs of problems. Many studies have observed systematic violations of this prediction. One classic set of violations involves what is known as the *common ratio effect*, presented in box 2.6.

---

[28] First-Order Stochastic Dominance has also been studied (see Charness et al. (2007) for a recent example). We return to it in chapter 7, as part of a discussion of "errors" in choice.

Box 2.6. The common ratio effect.

Among the best-known violations of the Independence requirement of expected utility theory are the *Allais paradoxes* presented by Maurice Allais (1953), essentially as thought experiments. Subsequently, they have been the subject of much laboratory research. We focus on one branch of this research, concerned with the common ratio effect.

To introduce this effect, we present an example used in a famous experiment reported by Kahneman and Tversky (1979). Consider the following four gambles, each of which is denoted by a list of consequence-probability pairs, separated by semicolons, with consequences being amounts of Israeli currency:[29]

$$R_1 = (4{,}000, 0.8; 0, 0.2),$$

$$S_1 = (3{,}000, 1),$$

$$R_2 = (4{,}000, 0.2; 0, 0.8),$$

$$S_2 = (3{,}000, 0.25; 0, 0.75).$$

The gambles should be seen as comprising two binary decision problems, with subscripts identifying the decision problem and, in each problem, R denoting the riskier option and S the safer one. Kahneman and Tversky (1979) report that 80% of their subjects chose S_1 over R_1, whereas 65% chose R_2 over S_2. The modal pattern of choices, if made by an individual in accordance with strict preferences, would be inconsistent with expected utility theory and, more specifically, with its Independence axiom as formulated in box 2.5.

The inconsistency with expected utility theory is easily shown, on the assumptions that consequences are money prizes and that more is preferred to less. Expected utility theory allows the utility function to be "scaled" at will, by arbitrarily fixing the utility of two consequences, with the preferred of these two being assigned higher utility than the other. If more money is preferred to less, we may scale the utility function $u(\cdot)$ by specifying $u(4{,}000) = 1$ and $u(0) = 0$. Then, strict preference for S_1 over R_1 requires $u(3{,}000) > 0.8$; and the latter inequality in turn implies strict preference for S_2 over R_2. Thus, there is no value of $u(3{,}000)$ for which expected utility theory predicts strict preference both for S_1 over R_1 and for R_2 over S_2.

To show the inconsistency with the Independence axiom, we define, for each of the gambles R_1, S_1, R_2, S_2, a corresponding prospect, $r_1 = (0.8, 0, 0.2)$, $s_1 = (0, 1, 0)$, $r_2 = (0.2, 0, 0.8)$, $s_2 = (0, 0.25, 0.75)$, where

---

[29] Thus, for example, R_1 offers prizes of 4,000 with probability 0.8 and zero with probability 0.2; S_1 offers a prize of 3,000 with certainty; and so on.

each prospect is denoted by the vector of probabilities assigned to the consequences 4,000, 3,000, and 0, respectively. If $p = (0, 0, 1)$, then $s_2 = 0.25s_1 + 0.75p$ and $r_2 = 0.25r_1 + 0.75p$. Thus, Independence requires that s_1 is preferred to r_1 if, and only if, s_2 is preferred to r_2.

Intuitively, the gambles S_2 and R_2 can be obtained from S_1 and R_1 respectively by multiplying the probabilities of all nonzero prizes by the ratio 0.25. Thus, the phenomenon observed by Kahneman and Tversky (1979) is a strong form of what is now known as the *common ratio effect*: a tendency, contrary to expected utility theory, for such scaling down to increase the relative attractiveness of the riskier option. The intuition suggested by Allais was that, although scaling down all probabilities of nonzero prizes by a common ratio leaves ratios of such probabilities unchanged, the change in their absolute levels can be important if, for example, agents are particularly attracted to certainties such as S_1. There are several other possible explanations, some of which we discuss in chapter 4. Chapter 7 discusses the interpretation of the common ratio effect when there is some randomness in individual behavior, and considers whether stochastic variants of expected utility theory might account for the effect.

Kahneman and Tversky's experiment used hypothetical payoffs, but an example in which each subject faced just one problem knowing it was for real[30] is reported by Beattie and Loomes (1997). In their design, two groups (their groups 3 and 5) faced the following problems, in which the prizes are in pounds sterling. One group had the choice between $R_1 = (15, 0.8; 0, 0.2)$ and $S_1 = (10, 1)$, with 85% of subjects choosing the latter; and the other group had the choice between $R_2 = (15, 0.2; 0, 0.8)$ and $S_2 = (10, 0.25; 0, 0.75)$, with 54% of subjects choosing the former. It is easy to see that R_2 and S_2 are obtainable from R_1 and S_1 respectively, by multiplying all nonzero prizes by 0.25, with the result that the modal preference again violates expected utility theory. Many other studies of common ratio effects and other violations of Independence are surveyed by Camerer (1995) and Starmer (2000).

Transitivity rules out cyclical choices in trios of decision problems. Chapter 3 discusses tests of this prediction (see box 3.5 (p. 135)). Chapter 4 catalogs several other "anomalies" observed in choice experiments that standard choice theory cannot easily explain. More comprehensive surveys of the experimental economics literature on individual decision making are provided by Camerer (1995) and Starmer (2000).

---

[30] See Cubitt et al. (2001) for discussion of the merits of this kind of single task, individual choice, design.

Our aim in this section is simply to illustrate the framework we have presented for considering defenses of theories in the face of unfavorable evidence from within their base domains. For this purpose, details of the evidence pertaining to choice theory are not germane, so we will not discuss them further. What matters for now is simply that, although the standard theory of choice provides a central building block for most contemporary economics, there are many experiments that seem to disconfirm some of its central predictions. What to conclude from this is crucial: Does experimental evidence seriously undermine the foundations of economics?

This is a huge question, many aspects of which are outside the scope of this book. One issue, on which we refer the reader to Camerer (1995) and Starmer (2000), is the extent of the adverse evidence. A second issue, which we defer until chapter 7, is the interpretation of adverse evidence in the light of variability in the data. A third issue is how far it matters for economics to be founded on an accurate theory of *individual* choice at all. A fourth issue is how much difference it makes to applications of choice theory if conditions such as Independence and/or Transitivity are relaxed. In this section, we are not primarily concerned with any of those issues, but rather with whether it is legitimate to test the theory of choice in experiments of the kind that have produced the seemingly unfavorable evidence.

Debate on this point is starkly polarized, as shown by the fact noted in chapter 1 that, whereas a Nobel memorial prize was awarded in 2002 to one of the pioneers of choice experiments (Daniel Kahneman), the same person is implicitly accused by Binmore (1999) of an activity analogous to disproving chemistry with "dirty test tubes." To adjudicate, we apply the framework set out in the previous section, taking as our starting point that the laboratory environments used in many of the experiments that have produced unfavorable results are in the base domain of the theory because, at least when incentives are real, laboratory gambles are close correlates of prospects.

If results from these environments are unfavorable to standard choice theory, NEC implies that this counts unambiguously against the theory. However, MEC allows for lines of defense. We concentrate mainly on two candidate defenses, one suggested by the *discovered preference hypothesis* (Plott 1996) and the other by considerations about *markets*. It is notable that, although the domain in which choice theory is now applied is much wider than that of choices over consumption bundles or lotteries, narrowly conceived, each of these defenses implies a smaller I-domain for the theory even than traditional applications. They are prime examples of I-domain contraction defenses. A further argument, considered more briefly below and based on the *flat maximum critique* (Harrison 1992, 1994) can also be interpreted as an I-domain contraction defense.

To defend standard choice theory according to the rules of the game implied by MEC, given apparently disconfirming experimental evidence from the theory's base domain, one would need to rationalize that evidence (a) by identifying differences between a suggested I-domain for the theory and the experimental designs that produced the evidence; and (b) by formulating testable hypotheses about why these differences matter for conformity of behavior with the theory.

The discovered preference hypothesis (Plott 1996) can be seen as defending standard choice theory in this way. Its central feature is to allow that there may be a difference between revealed and underlying preferences.

Box 2.7. The discovered preference hypothesis.

The discovered preference hypothesis was formulated by Plott (1996), as part of a discussion of why economic theory performs better in some types of experiments than in others. According to Plott, individuals have *underlying preferences* that conform to the coherence properties, such as Transitivity and Independence, assumed by standard theory. However, on Plott's account, underlying preferences are not the basis from which all decisions are made; rather, before they become effective in governing choice, they have to be discovered through deliberation or learning.

Plott argues that choices can be considered in three stages. The first is when "experience is absent" and behavior "impulsive." At this stage, although behavior may display systematic patterns, it should not be expected to satisfy the assumptions of standard choice theory. The second stage is when there have been extended opportunities for deliberation, reflection on incentives, and, possibly, experience of play. At this stage, the individual's behavior can be expected to be coherent, in the sense of standard theory, but the beliefs of different agents about each other may not have converged to reality. At the third stage, these beliefs converge, at least to the extent that "choices begin to anticipate the rationality reflected in the choices of others."

Plott's metaphor of *discovery*, rather than of *construction*, is chosen deliberately. An important feature of the discovered preference hypothesis is that underlying preferences are independent of the processes by which they are learned (Plott 1996, pp. 227–28) in the same way that although European explorers had to discover America before they could know what it was like, what it was like did not depend on whether they discovered America by sailing east or west.

Further discussions of the discovered preference hypothesis are given by Cubitt et al. (2001) and Braga and Starmer (2005). On the rival preference construction hypothesis, see, for example Payne et al. (1993), Slovic (1995) and Payne et al. (1999).

If standard choice theory was intended for application only to choices determined by underlying preferences, as defined by the discovered preference hypothesis, this would contract the I-domain of the theory, relative to the domain of all choices, suggest rationalizations that insulate the theory from disconfirming evidence obtained using certain common experimental designs, and suggest further hypotheses open to testing. Thus, if one accepts that the I-domain of a theory is to be identified from rationalizations in the literature on tests of the theory, the discovered preference hypothesis has precisely the *form* required by MEC for a defense of standard choice theory against some of the apparently disconfirming experimental evidence. But just having this form is not enough to make the defense compelling. Assessment of it requires assessment of its specification of the theory's I-domain and of the rationalizations that it provides.

If the later stages of discovery described by the discovered preference hypothesis define the I-domain of standard choice theory, that domain is restricted to choices made by agents who have experience and understanding of the tasks they face, with strong enough incentives to deliberate over their responses. (For individual choice theory, Plott's "third stage" does not have to be reached.) Put briefly, the resulting domain is that of *important tasks for experienced agents* (ITEA). Plott's account of why behavior differs across his three stages would lead one to expect a difference between ITEA and non-ITEA environments in the extent to which they yield evidence unfavorable to standard choice theory. Given this argument, and providing that any claim that standard choice theory is universal is abandoned, MEC would allow the claim that experimental designs are not in the T-domain of the theory unless they create ITEA conditions.

Binmore (1999) specifies the conditions under which standard theory should be tested in the laboratory in a similar way, though without endorsing the discovered preference hypothesis. Specifically, Binmore (1999, p. F17) asserts that economic theory should only be expected to predict in the laboratory when tasks are reasonably simple, incentives adequate, and time for trial and error adjustment sufficient. Despite the similarities of the resulting domain for the standard theory of choice, this formulation differs from the discovered preference hypothesis by not making the preferences arrived at after deliberation independent of the learning process.

It is clear that ITEA conditions exclude many situations to which economists routinely apply standard choice theory. This is freely acknowledged by Plott (1996, p. 226) and Binmore (1999, p. F17). Many decisions that are very important for the individual are taken only infrequently by most people (e.g., choices between job offers or houses to buy); whereas, at least in their nonprofessional lives, most decisions that individuals face frequently involve low stakes on each occasion (e.g., choice of route for the journey to work). Although it is coherent to specify an I-domain for standard choice theory that consists of ITEA conditions, that specification is not much reflected in economics textbooks or applied research. Given the actual current practice of economists, experimenters can reasonably assert that the I-domain of choice theory is much broader than ITEA conditions and, therefore, that such conditions are not essential for legitimate tests of the theory. Either position on whether standard choice theory can legitimately be applied outside ITEA conditions seems, at least prima facie, defensible provided that it is taken consistently. But it would not be defensible to dismiss certain classes of experiment for not applying ITEA conditions while simultaneously advocating the application of the theory to understand the behavior of subjects facing novel or low-stakes tasks in the field.

Rather than trading slogans over the I-domain, a more constructive response to the discovered preference hypothesis is to pursue empirical testing of the new hypotheses that it suggests. These can be broadly summarized as (a) standard choice theory will predict better the stronger the incentives are and the more experience subjects have; (b) discovered preferences are independent of the process of discovery.

There is a substantial body of evidence relating to (a), some of which we discuss in chapter 6. For example, Camerer and Hogarth (1999) review many studies on the impact of experimental incentives, while Beattie and Loomes (1997) and Cubitt et al. (1998a) test for common ratio effects with controlled variation of incentives. Ariely et al. (2003), Bone et al. (1999), Braga et al. (2009), Charness et al. (2007), Cox and Grether (1996), Cubitt and Sugden (2001a), Hey (2001), Humphrey (2006), Loomes et al. (2002, 2003), Loomes and Sugden (1998), Myagkov and Plott (1997), Plott and Zeiler (2005), and van de Kuilen and Wakker (2006) all consider the effects of different kinds of *within-experiment experience* on particular violations of standard choice theory. List (2002, 2003, 2004) investigates the effect of *prior nonlaboratory experience* on (a form of) preference reversal[31] and on the endowment effect; the latter is also considered by Maffioletti and Santoni (2005). An interesting theme emerging from this literature is that there are many different kinds of experience, including task repetition or familiarity, feedback on, or experience of, outcomes or risks, engagement in group deliberation or social interaction, exposure to different types of market process, and so on. It seems that while experience sometimes leads to marked reduction in violations of expected utility theory, the exact form of the experience matters considerably for this, and violations are not always eliminated.

To date, there is less evidence impinging directly on (b); but there is some, including Braga et al. (2009), Knetsch et al. (2001), and Loomes et al. (2003). More research on this is needed.

It is probably still too early to provide a definitive judgment on (a) and (b) (except perhaps in relation to incentives, to which we return in chapter 6). In any case, our current purpose is not to do so, but just to make the methodological point that the appropriate response to the discovered preference hypothesis is to test the hypotheses it suggests and, by doing so, explore the boundaries of successful and unsuccessful performance of standard theory. It is not to dismiss as irrelevant unfavorable evidence previously found; nor to insist on narrow experimental protocols that would prevent researchers from exploring those boundaries.

An argument that shares with the discovered preference hypothesis a concern with incentives is also worth comment at this point. It is known as the *flat maximum critique* and is associated particularly with Glenn Harrison (Harrison, 1989, 1992, 1994). Harrison is concerned not so much with the overall *level* of incentives as with the *differences* in payoffs resulting from different actions or, when payoffs are a continuous, smooth function of a decision variable, with the *slope* of that function in the neighborhood of its maximum.[32] Harrison first presented his argument as a critique of experimental research on auctions, but later generalized it to other experiments including some of those that cast doubt on standard choice theory. In this context, his argument is that, in some tasks used in such experiments, subjects may be close to indifference between the options and therefore unwilling to apply the cognitive effort that would be required to identify their truly preferred option.

---

[31] Investigation of the effect of nonlaboratory experience on preference reversal has a long history, including the early replication of the phenomenon among gamblers in Las Vegas casinos reported by Lichtenstein and Slovic (1973).

[32] For simplicity, we assume here a single maximum. The slope of the payoff function is always zero at that maximum. Thus, the issue is the slope at values of the decision-variable close to, but not equal to, the optimum.

We consider this argument further in chapter 6. For now, we focus only on the point that if the flat maximum critique is interpreted as denying the validity of experimental tests of standard choice theory in which differences in the attractiveness of the options are relatively small on the grounds that the theory does not apply to such cases, then it is an I-domain contraction defense of the theory. Assessment of such a defense would turn on its specification of the I-domain of the theory and on the accompanying rationalization, limiting the theory to that domain. We consider these in turn.

It is not clear that, in fact, the general practice of economists applies standard choice theory only when the difference between values to the agent of the optimal action and of alternatives are substantial. Nor is it clear how such a restriction could be formulated, given the kinds of models that economists usually employ. In many economic models, the objective function is smooth and continuous in the decision variable. In such models, there is always *some* neighborhood of decisions around the optimal one that yield a value not far below that obtained at the optimum.[33] Thus, if agents' decision problems are in fact best seen as optimization of smooth, continuous functions, then there must be some suboptimal actions that are nearly as good as the optimal ones. So, if it is not to bite too hard, the intended restriction would have to be read as requiring that the neighborhood of decisions that yield near-optimal payoffs is, in some sense, not "too large."[34] Conceptually, this may not look more problematic than a requirement that the theory is only applied when incentives are not "too small." But it may be more difficult to implement. For example, it is clear that deciding which house to buy usually involves high stakes, in that the purchase price is a multiple of the buyer's annual income and (if she is to live in the house) a lot of her time will be spent there. But it is far less obvious whether the net benefit, all things considered, of the buyer's preferred choice greatly exceeds that of rival options.

---

[33] A further difficulty arises if the objective function is expected utility, since expected utility theory permits linear transformation of the utility function. Thus the difference in expected utility between two actions can always be made arbitrarily large or small by rescaling the utility function. To overcome this difficulty, any rescaling would also have to be applied to utility costs of effort.

[34] Instead of limiting the domain of the theory to cases where the range of near-optimal behavior is small, an alternative response to the flat maximum argument would be for economists to investigate the implications in their models of near-optimal choices being made. Examples are provided by Akerlof and Yellen (1985a,b). By definition, when objective functions are smooth and continuous, the costs to the individual of behavior that is nearly optimal are not great, *everything else held constant*. But Akerlof and Yellen show that the consequences of behavior that is near-optimal for each individual can be severe in aggregate.

While the idea that individuals will apply effort to a task only when it is expected to make a difference to the value of the outcome sufficient to justify the cost of the effort has an obvious initial appeal, it is difficult to formulate this rationalization more precisely, because the effect of deliberation is not known prior to its being undertaken.[35] Perhaps the most plausible variant of the idea is a supposition that agents can, using simple rules of thumb, form rough impressions of which tasks are likely to be worth expenditure of cognitive resources. However, notice that, on this view, it is tasks in which it is obvious that little hangs on the decision (as opposed to tasks in which, *after deliberation*, one can ascertain that no option is much the most attractive) that would tend to be denied cognitive resources.[36] Applied to choices between gambles, this would lead one to expect the agent not to apply much cognitive effort when the gambles are transparently similar on all important dimensions. But it would *not* necessarily lead one to expect low effort when gambles that differ in offsetting ways on different dimensions nevertheless yield similar levels of expected utility. A full evaluation of the rationalization for the I-domain restriction on standard choice theory suggested by the flat maximum critique would require, besides discussion of such issues, an empirical assessment of the determinants of effort supplied by subjects and of the impact of the latter on their decisions. We discuss evidence on these issues in chapter 6, in the context of a fuller discussion of incentives in experiments.

A further candidate defense of standard choice theory in the face of prima facie experimental evidence against it, the *market discipline hypothesis*, can be distilled from the joint claims that the experimental designs that produce apparently disconfirming evidence in relation to standard choice theory typically do not use markets and that economic theory performs better in market conditions. If the I-domain of standard choice theory is markets, and if markets induce conformity with the theory, then a defender of the theory could contend that nonmarket

---

[35] There is a notorious conceptual problem with the view that, for every decision problem P, in order to decide how much cognitive resource to apply to the task of solving P, the agent makes an optimizing decision based on the value of solving P and the cost of cognitive resources. The problem is that this lands the agent in an infinite regress.

[36] To return to the house purchase example, suppose a buyer is considering two properties, similar in most respects except that one is in West Bridgford and the other in Mapperley Park. These are prosperous suburbs of Nottingham (in the United Kingdom), of similar age, roughly equidistant from the city center, and each neighboring one of the city's more deprived neighborhoods. But there are respects in which they differ. (For example, the transport links, local shops, and schools are not identical.) For a particular buyer, it might on balance make little difference which area she locates in; but, equally, it might make a big difference. Prior to deliberation and research, it might not be clear which case holds.

experiments are outside the T-domain of the theory. Like the discovered preference hypothesis, this contention abandons the claim that choice theory is universal. Assessment of the contention according to the criteria set out in the previous section requires evaluation of its antecedents.

Before outlining how such an evaluation might proceed, it will help to introduce two distinctions. The first is between two possible roles of market experiments: namely, as testing grounds for standard choice theory and as vehicles for the investigation of market processes or institutions. In this section, we are concerned only with the former role. (We turn to the latter role, which is the one typically stressed by market experimenters, briefly in the next section and more fully in chapter 4.)

The second distinction is between two different claims: a claim that markets eliminate violations of choice theory at the level of the individual, either by inducing individuals not to violate the theory or by eliminating those who do, and a claim that markets suppress the implications of violations of standard choice theory because aggregate market outcomes, such as prices and trade volumes, are driven by individuals who do not display such violations. In this section, it is the claim about elimination of violations at the level of the *individual* with which we are concerned.[37]

If the general practice of economists determines it, the I-domain of choice theory is not restricted to markets. Many important insights of economics, for example concerning public goods, voting, crime, and the division of activity within firms and households, are about nonmarket activities. To the extent that economics is not exclusively concerned with markets, it is worth noting that market experiments actually have some drawbacks *as tests of choice theory*. One problem is the danger of contamination between responses of different subjects who condition their behavior on market outcomes (Loomes et al. 2003; Braga et al. 2009); another is the complexity of instructions needed to explain the trading mechanism to subjects, as well as the objects of trade. Given an I-domain defined by the general practice of economists, there is no obvious reason for any presumption in favor of market designs in experimental tests of standard choice theory.

However, if markets did induce conformity with standard choice theory at the level of the individual, this would rationalize some potentially disconfirming evidence and suggest a residual I-domain for the

---

[37] It is nevertheless interesting to note that Gode and Sunder (1993) have argued that aggregate market outcomes may conform to standard predictions even when traders have very limited rationality (though see Gjerstad and Shachat 2007); whereas Haltiwanger and Waldman (1984) and Fehr and Tyran (2005) show how the irrationalities of a few can have large effects on aggregate outcomes in the presence of strategic complementarity.

theory limited to markets. For example, it might be argued that markets drive out irrational behavior through arbitrage or "sobering effects" of experience. However, it is not clear that market disciplines can induce conformity with standard choice theory. As a matter of theory, Cubitt and Sugden's (2001b) analysis of "money pump" arguments shows that many forms of behavior that are governed by choice functions that violate standard theory can still survive arbitrage (see also Sugden 2004a; Mandler 2005). George Loewenstein (1999) argues that some types of irrational behavior are unlikely to lead to elimination from the market, or even to diminution of the irrational agent's role in it. Finally, experimental evidence does not suggest unambiguously that markets promote consistency with standard choice theory. Some of the literature to which we referred on the impact of experience relates to market experience; this literature suggests that the effects of experience are complicated and depend in part on the type of experience. Two other experimental literatures are sometimes seen as suggesting that markets induce conformity with standard theory.

One consists of papers, such as Berg et al. (1985), Chu and Chu (1990), and Cox and Grether (1996), that purport to show that the incidence of a particular anomaly—preference reversal in these cases—is reduced in certain market environments.[38] However, as discussed by Loomes et al. (2003) and Braga and Starmer (2005), such findings can also be interpreted less favorably to standard theory. It may be that although subjects learn to avoid a particular anomaly, they do so by adopting context-sensitive routines. If so, their behavior does not satisfy the context-free condition required by standard theory (and the discovered preference hypothesis). There are analogous investigations of other anomalies, some of which pose similar difficulties of interpretation. For example, Evans (1997) investigates violation of a generalization of the Independence axiom of expected utility theory, known as "Betweenness," and reports results of an experiment in which preferences were elicited in a market treatment, using pricing tasks, and in a nonmarket treatment. Although market equilibrium prices from the market treatment displayed lower rates of violation than individual bids in the nonmarket treatment, there was no significant difference between violation rates *in individual responses* between the two treatments. Further evidence concerning markets and the incidence of violations of standard theory is discussed by Braga and Starmer (2005).

---

[38] Although it is common to describe the Berg et al. (1985) and Chu and Chu (1990) environments as "market" ones, this is a stretch as they lack a crucial feature of most markets in the field: namely, the right not to trade.

Another literature that may initially seem to suggest that standard choice theory works better in market environments than in choice experiments is that concerning efficiency and convergence to equilibrium in particular types of experimental market. Davis and Holt (1993, chapters 3 and 4) survey double-auction and posted-offer market experiments, indicating that the former display stronger efficiency and convergence properties. However, the market experiments reported in this literature, which includes some of the classic contributions of Nobel memorial prizewinner Vernon Smith, usually concern different predictions of economic theory from choice experiments. Choice experiments investigate properties of the preferences that individuals have. Market experiments typically use incentive schemes that *induce* subjects to behave as if they had certain preferences.[39] They examine properties of markets and individual behavior in markets, *given that agents have the induced preferences.* They do not investigate the characteristics of the preferences that subjects actually have. Thus there is no inconsistency on the question of whether agents' actual preferences satisfy standard choice theory between the findings that in certain types of market experiment with induced preferences, theories of market equilibrium typically perform rather well, and that in certain types of choice experiment, standard choice theory predicts less well.

Like the discovered preference hypothesis, the market discipline hypothesis is an I-domain contraction defense of standard choice theory that defines the domain of the theory much more narrowly than current usage in economics. Nevertheless, and again like the discovered preference hypothesis, it defines a valuable research agenda, the fruits of which are only beginning to emerge. Whatever they turn out to be, this agenda should be seen as complementary to, rather than as overturning, the insights of earlier research.

2.7 Application to Experimental Tests of Equilibrium Predictions

While theories of individual behavior are crucial to conventional economic modeling, they can never be the end of the story because most

---

[39] Smith (1976) is the canonical statement of the induced-value technique (see box 3.1 (p. 99)), that we discuss in more detail in chapter 3. In experiments that use this method, subjects are induced to put particular values on (otherwise-worthless) tokens by the opportunity to sell those they hold at the end of the trading period to the experimenter, according to a preset schedule. This allows the induced marginal values to vary, both across individuals and across different tokens held by the same individual, thereby inducing demand and supply curves of different shapes, provided only that subjects wish to maximize their money winnings.

economic activity involves interactions between individuals. Further, some aspects of Plott's discovered preference hypothesis (in particular, the third stage of discovery) are only intelligible in an interactive context; and it is natural to suppose that one reason for Binmore's insistence on opportunities for trial and error learning in experimental designs is that they facilitate learning about the play of others.[40]

The overwhelming majority of economic models of interaction between agents use a notion of *equilibrium*, such as some form of competitive equilibrium in models of competitive markets or Nash equilibrium (or a refinement thereof) in game-theoretic models. Market models and games are the two types of model of interaction that we consider in this section. For convenience, we confine attention to models in which the equilibrium (of whatever type) is unique.[41]

Note that the equilibrium concepts mentioned in the previous paragraph are formal, theoretical concepts. However, if economic models of interaction are to be interpreted as having empirical content, their equilibrium concepts must be taken as somehow predictive. There are two quite different ways in which the predictions of equilibrium models can be interpreted. One, which we will call the *unconditional interpretation*, is to predict that observed behavior in some situation will correspond to the pattern of equilibrium behavior specified by the model; the other, which we will call the *conditional interpretation*, is to make such a prediction only conditional on achievement of equilibrium. On the latter interpretation, equilibrium is one of the conditions defining the I-domain of economic theories of interaction.

To make sense of the conditional interpretation, given that theories are to be interpreted as having empirical content, we require some empirical concept of "equilibrium" that is *independent* of the theoretical equilibrium concept, otherwise the equilibrium-conditional prediction would be true by definition. But there is no shortage of candidates to fill this role. Two types of candidate are notably different: one, defined in terms of *processes*, consists of the situation after some prespecified and potentially equilibrating process (e.g., twenty rounds of prior play) has run its course; the other, defined in terms of *outcomes*, consists of the situation after which behavior has stabilized in some specified sense. Where

---

[40] Binmore (2007, p. 1) repeats the trio of conditions from Binmore (1999), this time as an answer to the question of what kind of environment interactive game theory might reasonably be expected to predict well in, though he also (p. 2) indicates his view that, in fact, it sometimes performs well when not all the conditions are met and sometimes fails when they are.

[41] This avoids the question of what the prediction of such a model is when there are multiple equilibria. This question is well-known, important, but not germane to our current concerns.

necessary to avoid ambiguity below, we refer to (process- or outcome-defined) equilibria of these kinds as S-equilibria and to the formal equilibrium concepts of theoretical models as T-equilibria. Thus, the conditional interpretation of an equilibrium model has the form that, once an S-equilibrium of a given kind obtains in a certain situation, behavior will correspond to the pattern specified by the T-equilibrium of the model.

As an example, consider the Bertrand model of duopoly in which two profit-maximizing firms with identical, linear cost functions compete by setting prices, each unable to observe the price of the other, but knowing the market demand curve and that the entire market will be served by any firm that sets a strictly lower price than the other. As long as there is sufficient demand to support a market, the unique Nash equilibrium of this price-setting game is for each firm to price at marginal cost (Tirole 1988, chapter 5; Carlton and Perloff 2005, chapter 6). Now consider how this T-equilibrium can be translated into a prediction about a real duopolistic industry in which firms have the same costs. On the unconditional interpretation, the prediction is simply that the firms in the industry will price at marginal cost. On the conditional interpretation, it is that, once S-equilibrium obtains, they will price at marginal cost. Depending on the S-equilibrium concept, this might mean, for example, that once firms have had a certain number of opportunities to revise prices, they will be pricing at marginal cost; or that, once prices have settled at stable levels, they will equal marginal cost. Each of these conditional predictions is weaker than the unconditional one, but neither is true by definition.

Typically, equilibrium theories of economic behavior are unspecific about the equilibrating mechanism that is supposed to bring equilibrium about. This might be (timeless) pure reasoning, as in the classical interpretation of game theory, or some temporally extended evolutionary process, or some mechanism of price adjustment or arbitrage. The list of possibilities depends, among other things, on the theoretical model and T-equilibrium concept. But usually there are several. For some purposes, this lack of specificity does not matter. In particular, if the prediction of the theoretical model is *unconditional*, there is no need to specify an equilibrating process in making it. In contrast, if the predictions of an equilibrium model are interpreted as *conditional*, appropriate tests might depend on the conditions under which S-equilibrium will be said to obtain, and they might in turn depend on the equilibration mechanism envisaged. For example, when assessing the design of a test of a conditional prediction, it might matter whether the equilibration mechanism envisaged is a slow-acting evolutionary one or fast-acting arbitrage.

The unconditional and conditional interpretations of the predictions of equilibrium models correspond, respectively, to different views about the design of experiments to test theories of market and strategic interaction. The unconditional interpretation implies that the T-equilibrium behavior specified by the model generates the prediction that experiments should test, and that the theory makes this prediction unconditionally on S-equilibrium. In contrast, the conditional interpretation implies that S-equilibrium is something over which the experimenter should achieve control. How this should be done may depend on the candidate equilibration mechanism, but for example, one might expect design features such as repetition of tasks, perhaps supplemented by feedback on the choices and/or on the payoffs of other players.

If the purpose of task repetition is to bring about a situation in which the prediction of some *one-shot* equilibrium model of interaction can be expected to hold, care needs to be taken to ensure that repetition does not generate new T-equilibria, for example through the possibility of reputation-building in a repeated game. There are various solutions and palliatives to this problem, such as "strangers" and "perfect strangers" experimental designs.

Box 2.8. Partners and strangers designs.

Many experiments study subjects' play of games. Often in such experiments, subjects play the game not just once but repeatedly. Typically, within a given experimental session, subjects are put, at random and anonymously, into pairs or groups who start off playing each other. There are then two main types of protocol, if the game is to be played repeatedly over a series of rounds. In *partners* designs, the same group of subjects play the game together each round. In *strangers* designs, sometimes also called random rematching designs, the groups who play together are reselected, at random and anonymously, separately for each round. The main purpose of the latter protocol is to create a situation in which subjects can gain experience of the game, but without their play being influenced by the consideration that they are playing a repeated game with the same other players. Different forms of strangers protocol vary according to whether any restrictions are imposed on the random process that reselects groups in order to strengthen the divorce between a player's play in a given round and the consideration that it might affect the future play of her opponents. Some authors use the term *perfect strangers* design to indicate the imposition of a restriction that the probability of any two players playing each other twice is zero. However, in principle, this still leaves scope, for example, for player *i*'s choice in round t to be influenced by the consideration that it could affect player j's choice in round $t + 1$, that might in turn affect player k's choice in round $t + 2$, when i might be playing k. Arguably, the term perfect strangers should really be reserved for cases where, in each round, each subject i plays subjects who have not previously met i, or any of those whom i has met, or any of those whom they have met, and so on. This eliminates all scope for player i's play in round t to influence the play of those with whom i interacts in subsequent rounds, but is much more complex and costly to operate than unconstrained random rematching.

A famous comparison of partners and strangers protocols is Andreoni (1988), though some subsequent studies have found rather different results (see, for example, Keser and van Winden 2000). The findings of Fehr and Gächter (2000), discussed in chapter 1, illustrate the intuitively plausible idea that partners protocols might be more conducive to cooperative outcomes than strangers protocols.

As the base domain of a theory is defined by close correspondence to theoretical concepts, it is often straightforward to specify an experimental design in the base domain of a game-theoretic model, provided one assumes that monetary payoffs correspond to utilities. (The need for this assumption is an aspect of the Duhem–Quine problem, discussion of which is deferred until chapter 3.) It is harder to say exactly what the base domain of a market model is, when (as is often the case) that model does not specify any trading mechanism. One might think that the base domain of a competitive equilibrium model would require the existence of many traders, since that is a key assumption in such models. For these reasons, it may be better to see market experiments as exploring the successful applicability of the theory, rather than as attempts to test the theory in its base domain.[42] Nevertheless, the distinction between unconditional and conditional interpretations would still be relevant. When exploring whether some property of a theoretical competitive equilibrium describes actual trade in an experimental market with, say, six traders, one can ask this question either unconditionally or conditionally on S-equilibrium obtaining.

If the equilibrium predictions of economic models are taken as unconditional, there are cases where those predictions appear to fail (e.g., early trading periods of market experiments and early rounds of experiments

---

[42] We defer until chapter 4 discussion of market experiments that are best seen as investigating the properties of particular trading institutions, rather than the successes or failures of theory.

using the voluntary-contributions mechanism), as well as cases where they perform much better (e.g., later trading periods or rounds of similar experiments especially, in the case of market experiments, under double-auction conditions).[43] What should one make of this?

Plott (1996) and Binmore (1999)[44] can be interpreted as defending the relevant theories against evidence that is prima facie unfavorable, precisely by *reinterpreting the predictions of the theories as conditional predictions instead of unconditional ones.* Such a move is in line with the "rules of the game" implied by MEC and described in section 2.5. When made as part of a defense against unfavorable evidence, the move should be judged by the criteria for evaluating I-domain contraction defenses, since that is what it is. As noted before, such defenses carry obligations, including not using the theory outside the newly recommended I-domain (in this case, the domain in which some concept of S-equilibrium can be expected to obtain). Plott and Binmore accept this obligation but, in the absence of a specified equilibration process or conception of S-equilibrium, it is hard to say whether the general practice of economists satisfies it or not.

As before, our view is that the most constructive response to an I-domain contraction defense is a theoretical and empirical research program to investigate the limits of the theory. In this case, such a program might investigate the success in bringing about equilibrium of different candidate equilibration mechanisms, the amount of time and the feedback conditions required for such success under different mechanisms, and so on. Much existing experimental research on markets can be seen as contributing to precisely such a program. For example, many market experiments investigate properties of different trading institutions, such as the speed of convergence that they produce. To date, the results seem to indicate a bigger domain of success for competitive equilibrium models than might be expected in certain respects (e.g., convergence is often fast, even with only a few traders, under some trading systems), though smaller in other respects (e.g., trading rules matter for the speed of convergence and, under some rules, convergence is slow).

The position is less clear in the case of experimental games. It is very common for designs to include repeat play of a given game, but data analysis often focuses mainly on play in the final few rounds, or on average play over all rounds, or on play in those rounds after which a stable pattern of behavior has emerged. This analysis is most readily interpreted as investigation of an unconditional prediction, when it is average

---

[43] See Davis and Holt (1993, chapters 3 and 4) and Ledyard (1995) for relevant surveys.
[44] See also Binmore (1994, pp. 184–86) and Binmore (2007, pp. 5–10).

play over all rounds that is discussed, or as investigation of a prediction conditioned on S-equilibrium in the other two cases. It is less common to see the actual *process* whereby equilibrium is established—how much repetition is needed for it to emerge and which structures of repeat inter-action, which information and feedback conditions, or which games, pro-duce it most quickly—as *itself* the main focus of experimental analysis. However, there are notable exceptions such as investigation of contribu-tion decay in the voluntary-contributions mechanism (see, for example, Andreoni 1988, 1995), randomization in zero-sum games (Binmore et al. 2001), repetition and role-swapping in bargaining games (see, for exam-ple, Binmore et al. 1985), imitation and feedback conditions (Apesteguia et al. 2007), and subjects' information search in strategic environments (see, for example, Costa-Gomez et al. 2001; Crawford 2008).[45]

In the case of game-theoretic equilibrium, there is a further compli-cation. There are well-known theoretical grounds for *not* expecting play that corresponds to the one-shot equilibrium of the model, when play is repeated in certain ways, such as indefinitely by the same players. The "folk theorems" of game theory imply that repetition of a game can induce, as equilibrium outcomes, outcomes that do not correspond to equilibria of the constituent one-shot game.[46] Thus, *if* (i) game-theoretic predictions are conditional on achievement of S-equilibrium, and (ii) S-equilibrium is not expected unless play is repeated under appropri-ate conditions, the equilibrium predictions of *one-shot* game theory are caught on a Morton fork:[47] no repetition and the S-equilibrium requirement is not met; the wrong sort of repetition and the one-shot T-equilibrium is no longer the unique such equilibrium. This problem does not shrink the I-domain of the theory to zero; but, given premises (i) and (ii), it would restrict it to a domain of repeat interactions taking place under conditions sufficiently like perfect strangers designs. There are many games in the world that are played under such conditions, such

---

[45] There is also theoretical work on the question, as surveyed by Samuelson (1997, 2002), and an experimental literature on learning in strategic contexts (see, for example, Erev and Roth 1998; Camerer and Ho 1999; and, for a review, Camerer 2003, chapter 6). To date, the focus of the latter literature has been more on how to model subjects' learning in strategic contexts than on which conditions produce convergence to equilibrium, though clearly the two issues are connected.

[46] See Osborne and Rubinstein (1994, chapter 8) for a textbook treatment of folk theorems.

[47] Cardinal Morton was responsible for tax collection for the English Tudor king Henry VII. The two-pronged "fork" for which he is famous is a forerunner of Catch 22, consisting of a pair of arguments, conditioned on the observed hospitality of nobles toward the king, which he is said to have used: those who entertained the king lavishly should be taxed heavily as they clearly had money to burn; whereas those whose entertainment was modest should be taxed heavily as they clearly had savings in hand.

as road junction games; but there are also many, such as intrafirm bargaining, that are not. Thus, the conditional interpretation of theoretical equilibrium predictions has a cost in terms of the size of the potential I-domain of single-period game-theoretic models. The bolder unconditional interpretation does not carry this price tag because it does not condition the equilibrium prediction on the presence of a mechanism that requires repetition.

To sum up the methodological conclusion of this section: whether the equilibrium predictions of economic models of interaction are interpreted unconditionally or conditionally has crucial implications for the I-domain of the theory and consequently, via MEC, for experimental design. *If predictions are unconditional*, there is no need for experimenters wanting to test them actively to bring S-equilibrium about or to verify that they have done so. But *if predictions are conditional*, then S-equilibrium is something over which experimenters must establish control; designs that fail to achieve such control are then outside the T-domain of the theory because they fail to implement what, according to the conditional interpretation, is a key feature of the I-domain of the theory: equilibrium itself. The difference between the conditional and unconditional interpretations of the predictions of the theory probably explains the contrast between the practices of experimental gamers who routinely insist on task-repetition and those who more often run one-shot games. As with the case of choice theory, this provides an example of how different design principles flow from different interpretations of the domain of the theory.

2.8   Conclusions

In this chapter we have discussed an issue that marks important divisions between those who do and do not see experiments as useful for testing economic theories, as well as between the advocates of different types of experimental design. The issue is about the proper domain of economic theories. More specifically, we have presented a framework for adjudicating between those who stress the requirement that theories have generality, and, consequently, are disinclined to draw tight boundaries within which they may be tested and those who see theories as having narrowly specified domains of application, beyond which their performance is irrelevant.

We have argued that even those who see an economic theory as having a narrow domain of application should accept that testing outside that domain may be legitimate. We have delineated "rules of the game" for design and discussion of experimental theory testing which balance concerns about external validity of laboratory findings with the requirement that theories are not unreasonably protected from the implications of unfavorable findings. These rules derive their authority from an initial, but overridable, presumption in favor of legitimacy of laboratory testing using designs that closely correlate with theoretical concepts. The initial presumption is grounded in the control that such designs afford, combined with the charitability of interpreting a theory as intended to be general. But, because of the override clause, this position does not divorce the question of whether some experimental test is legitimate from that of the intended domain of application of the theory. It strikes a middle path between the view that experimenters need only concern themselves with implementing the assumptions of a theoretical model on the one hand, and extreme forms of external-validity skepticism on the other.

This middle path raises the question of how to identify the intended domain for application of the theory. The example of choice theory shows that the normal practice of users of a theory may reveal a very different domain of application from rationalizations of apparently disconfirming evidence in the specialist literature. Although it can be argued that standard choice theory should only be applied to important tasks undertaken by experienced subjects, or only to behavior in markets, the general practice of economists still applies it to nonmarket situations and to tasks that are relatively unimportant or infrequent. Equilibrium theory provides a further example in which distinct interpretations of the domain of applicability of the theory can be entertained. Although it can be argued that predictions derived from competitive or game-theoretic equilibrium models should only be expected to hold after an adjustment phase, and that earlier periods of disequilibrium in which the predictions do not hold should not be taken as evidence against the theory, the usual practice of economists is not normally to qualify their conclusions in this way. Rather, it is just to apply equilibrium models.

In such cases, those who advocate narrow domains for the testing of a theory are constrained also to do so for its application; whereas those who advocate broad domains of application must accept results from a correspondingly broad set of tests. When the domain of successful performance of some theory is in doubt, further research can clarify whether the theory works better in some areas than in others and, if so, what their boundaries are. Because of the control that they allow, experiments are likely to be well-suited to this research. For them to contribute to it requires a pluralist predisposition to countenance a range of experimental designs, not narrow insistence on any single design blueprint.

The idea that when a theory is confronted by unfavorable experimental evidence, what follows is likely to be, and often most constructively can be, not immediate consignment of the theory to the dustbin of history, but rather a process that gradually probes the effects of design features that seem untypical of domains to which the theory might be taken to apply, is an early hint of the dynamic perspective on theory appraisal that we develop in chapter 3. Relatedly, the idea that a program of controlled experiments can help to map the boundaries of a theory's successful and unsuccessful performance is an early hint of a relationship between theory testing and empirical regularity-refinement to be explored in chapter 4. The framework presented in this chapter asserts an initial presumption of legitimacy of tests that use experimental designs in what we called the base domain of the theory. To this limited extent, it is reminiscent of the blame-the-theory defense. But, unlike that defense, it allows challenges to the effect that a laboratory environment differs from the theory's intended domain of application in important respects; our criteria for assessing such challenges are the plausibility, suggestiveness, and empirical success of the accompanying argument, not whether the challenges can be formulated within the original theory. A further issue is whether all designs for which the blame-the-theory defense is routinely invoked actually are in the base domains of the relevant theories. We take up this issue in chapter 5, in the context of broader discussion of external validity. Finally, we return to the issue of incentives in chapter 6 and to the interpretation of findings from choice experiments in chapter 7.

3

Experimental Testing in Practice

3.1 Preliminaries

This chapter continues the discussion of experiments in their theory-testing role. While chapter 2 addressed questions about where economic theory can legitimately be tested, this chapter is about what testing (in a given domain) involves and what it delivers. An important theme of the chapter will be that experimental tests (in economics and elsewhere) are always relatively complex affairs that, by virtue of their complexity, never provide acid tests of individual hypotheses. Consequently, judgments about whether a particular hypothesis has withstood or failed some experimental test will always involve some element of interpretation.

If the evidence cannot entirely "speak for itself," that may make it less surprising to know that there are disputes about the status of particular claims arising from experimental tests in economics. On the one hand, these may be part and parcel of the normal process of scientific discovery and reflect legitimate, but competing, interpretations of the evidence. On the other hand, the identification of a seemingly judgmental element in the process raises questions about whether some interpretations are better than others and whether disputes can always be resolved satisfactorily through the application of more tests. This chapter explores these and related issues and arrives at a perspective on them that shares some of the spirit of the "methodology of scientific research programmes" proposed by Imre Lakatos (1970, 1978). We argue that while isolated experiments never provide completely decisive tests of individual hypotheses, extended programs of experimental economics research can and do deliver significant advances in knowledge.

3.2 Experimental Testing and the Duhem–Quine Thesis

As an opening move, consider the following question. What do theory-testing experiments test? The answer might seem trivially obvious:

surely, if they are set up properly, such experiments test the relevant theory? Yet some care is needed here. As explained in chapter 1, in thinking of what is involved in (experimental or nonexperimental) theory testing, it is important to distinguish between formal theorems of economic models and empirical hypotheses associated with them. Experimental tests must be tests of the latter and the step from formal model to empirical hypothesis requires an application of the model—a matter we explore in more detail in chapter 5. As discussed in the last chapter, deciding whether the predictive success of a model, in a particular application, provides a good test involves judgments about whether the domain in which it has been applied is an appropriate one for testing it. In this chapter, we identify and consider the implications of another dimension of judgment that arises in any attempt to test a theory. There is a well-known and widely accepted argument due to Pierre Duhem (1906) and Willard Van Orman Quine (1951, 1953) that—we believe rightly— contends that there are no definitive tests of *single* hypotheses. This is because all hypothesis tests involve (possibly complex) bundles of hypotheses and, consequently, interpretation is always needed to decide whether a particular hypothesis, within the set brought to test, has survived or failed. We will refer to this claim as the Duhem–Quine thesis (or DQT for short). While some readers may be very familiar with this argument, since the DQT will play an important role in this chapter we take a little time here to set it out in the context of experimental economics.

In order to illustrate the logic of the DQT, imagine what would be involved in constructing a convincing test of some aspect of economic theory. Consider, for the sake of argument, a simple experiment aimed at testing the hypothesis that human subjects choose among lotteries as if maximizing their expected utility. Let us call this the *target hypothesis* of this particular investigation. Suppose that in seeking to test this target, our experimenter proceeds, as many have done, by offering experimental subjects a series of pairwise choices between lotteries with payoffs and probabilities structured so that, on natural interpretations, expected utility theory permits particular patterns of choice while ruling out others. To fix the example a little more, suppose that included among the tasks are choices between pairs of gambles that we denote g^+ and g^-, where the former (first-order stochastically) dominates the latter. Since preferences in expected utility theory satisfy First-Order Stochastic Dominance (see box 2.5 (p. 72)), one way to test our target hypothesis is to observe whether subjects in the experiment (typically) select the g^+ options in these choices as the theory would lead us to expect. On the face of it, this design provides an especially simple way of testing the conformity of human behavior with a basic property of expected utility theory (and, indeed, the many other theories of risk preference that embody the same property).

Now suppose that, contrary to the target hypothesis, the data from this experiment show that subjects choose g^- options just as frequently as g^+ options: that is, they fail to reveal any systematic preference for dominating options. Is this convincing evidence against the target? Before reaching that conclusion, it seems reasonable to think that we might want to know more about the way in which the experiment was conducted: more: that is, about the *conditions* under which these data were collected. For instance, for this to count as persuasive evidence of subjects failing to respect First-Order Stochastic Dominance, one might at least want to be assured that subjects were actually informed about the probabilities and payoffs associated with the various (g^+, g^-) choices. Imagine, for instance, that subjects were presented with options described simply by the labels (g^+, g^-) and told to "pick one." If this had been the design and subjects had not been given any basic information about the probabilities and payoffs, or opportunities to learn them, then rather than concluding that the target had failed, one might be more inclined to read it simply as evidence that subjects cannot guess the relevant probabilities or payoffs. In this case, one might reasonably conclude that this was not a good test of the target.

The proposition that "subjects knew the relevant payoffs and probabilities" may be interpreted as an *auxiliary hypothesis* that forms part of a bundle that is tested when we attempt to test the target hypothesis. In principle, the evidence of subjects choosing dominated options (g^-) might be explained either as a failure of the target hypothesis or, alternatively, as a failure of this auxiliary hypothesis (or both). In this case, it might be relatively straightforward to get more information bearing on whether the particular auxiliary (call it a^1) was satisfied—a good report of the experiment, for instance, would make this clear. However, we may rapidly, and perhaps indefinitely, expand the list of auxiliary assumptions that must hold in order for us to be able to *unambiguously* interpret the data from the experiment as evidence bearing on the target. For example, we may require not only that subjects were told probability information but also that it was explained and presented in a way that would be comprehensible to them (call this a^2). We might require that subjects were given an incentive to attend to the experimental tasks and consider their decisions carefully (a^3). We might require that they were given sufficient time to think about their decisions (a^4).

And so on.[1] Notice that while the validity of some auxiliaries (e.g., a^1) may be relatively easy to verify, in other cases it may be a matter of judgment whether the relevant auxiliary holds. For instance, there may be some ambiguity with respect to what would count as "sufficient time," or "sufficient incentive," for thinking about a decision.

So, were it to be observed, using the design described, that subjects choose dominated just as frequently as nondominated alternatives, this would permit multiple interpretations. This is because the experiment is a joint test of a set of hypotheses $(T, a^1, a^2, a^3, a^4, \ldots, a^n)$, including the target ($T$) plus a (possibly large) number of auxiliary hypotheses. The observation of frequent g^- choosing is inconsistent with the presumption that the entire set of hypotheses simultaneously hold. However, choosing g^- could logically be accommodated in a variety of ways: it might be explained by rejecting T; or by rejecting one or more of the auxiliary hypotheses; or by doing both. The same general point holds for evidence appearing to confirm T: for this to be interpreted as definitive evidence in favor of T we must (at least implicitly) invoke a set of auxiliaries to rule out a variety of possibilities (such as offsetting failures of different assumptions) that could have generated apparent consistency with a false T. The DQT points to generic issues that arise in any form of hypothesis testing: we always test sets of hypotheses; consequently, the outcomes of hypothesis tests always require interpretation. Parallel issues exist, for instance, in relation to econometric testing. Consider attempting to test the target hypothesis that purchasing power parity holds for a particular data set. While a researcher may report a single test statistic examining the value of a specific coefficient in a regression analysis, the validity of such a test will turn on a plethora of auxiliary hypotheses about the validity of the underlying model, the choice of functional forms, the stochastic specification, and so on (see, for example, Taylor 2003). Our primary interest, however, is in exploring the implications of the DQT in the context of experimental economics. This is an important enterprise relative to the ambitions of this book not least because, as we now explain, some key methods of experimental research are apparently erected on foundations that require particular auxiliary hypotheses to hold. To illustrate the point, consider the so-called *induced-value methodology* (IVM), which has become a standard

---

[1] What counts as an auxiliary hypothesis may itself be a matter of interpretation, and may be connected to issues of domain. For instance, consider two theorists who hold to different opinions regarding the domain in which a theory (T) can be applied. Suppose that one theorist assumes that T only applies in domains where the stakes are high enough to promote careful decisions while a second interprets T as applying to decisions regardless of stakes. For the first theorist, the assumption that "the stakes were high enough" is an auxiliary tested alongside T, but for the second it is not.

technique for attempting to implement particular sets of preferences in market experiments. To introduce the topic, we take a step back to an early article by Smith (1962) that helped lay the foundations for the approach.

Box 3.1. A classic market experiment "inducing" supply and demand in a double auction.

Vernon Smith's paper "An experimental study of competitive market behavior" (1962), reports a series of experiments that refine and extend Chamberlin's (1948) first market experiments (see box 4.1 (p. 152)). The research is explicitly motivated—at least in part—by an attempt to test hypotheses derived from competitive equilibrium price theory. Smith takes it to be a prediction of (Marshallian) competitive price theory that, in a stable environment with downward-sloping demand and upward-sloping supply, observed prices and quantities should converge to those at which the demand and supply schedules intersect. His underlying strategy is to create an experimental market setting with demand and supply conditions that are known to the experimenter, and that are stable over a sequence of market periods. Smith sees the stability of demand and supply as something atypical of real markets but intentionally builds it into his laboratory environment for the purpose of testing a particular economic hypothesis: that behavior will converge to equilibrium in a stable environment. He then observes whether behavior consistent with competitive equilibrium in fact emerges when real people trade via a particular exchange institution.

With a view to implementing specific supply and demand conditions in his experimental markets, participants were randomly divided into buyers and sellers who then had the opportunity to transact in a simple market; values were "induced" by giving each buyer a card that specified the maximum they were permitted to pay for one unit of an experimental good; these values were private information that varied across the buyers; similarly, each seller was given a (private) minimum price at which they could sell a unit of the experimental good.

The experiments involved sequences of market periods during which buyers and sellers had the chance to make bilateral contracts via an oral *double-auction institution*: in any market period, the supply and demand schedules were implemented by distribution of the private values, then buyers could tender for a contract by announcing a price they were willing to pay for a unit (constrained by their private maximum); similarly, sellers could tender for a contract by announcing a price at which they were willing to sell a unit (constrained by their private minimum). Any

buyer (or seller) was at liberty to accept an announced ask (bid) subject
to the constraints already described. Such acceptances resulted in binding contracts and the pair then dropped out for the rest of that market
period. The market period continued (usually for between five and ten
minutes) until bids and offers were no longer leading to contracts. In
each period, anyone who formed a contract received a payoff equal to
the absolute difference between their private value and the contracted
price and participants were instructed to try to maximize their own total
payoff. The process was repeated with the same individuals participating
in multiple market periods under identical conditions.

Taken together, the individual maxima that constrained particular
buyers determined the maximum possible demand in the market at every
conceivable price. Likewise, the minimum selling prices imposed on individual sellers jointly determined the maximum possible supply of goods
to the market at any conceivable price. Hence, we may think of the sets of
(private) constraints on buyers and sellers as "inducing" specific demand
and supply conditions in the market.

Smith points out that while competitive equilibrium theory presumes
some device for eliminating any excess demand or supply (e.g., a Walrasian auctioneer), real people interacting via the double-auction institution may or may not produce close convergence on the competitive
equilibrium prediction. So, while the implemented demand and supply
schedules constrain what can happen in the market, the exact pattern
of trade is underdetermined by those constraints. So it was an entirely
open question as to what would happen in this market, and, in particular, whether behavior consistent with competitive equilibrium would
emerge. For instance, it is conceivable that, contrary to equilibrium predictions, different units could sell at different prices, with no tendency
for prices to settle down; the volume of trade could be less than the
equilibrium volume and, in this case, all units could sell at disequilibrium
prices. Consequently, we could think of Smith's experiment as testing the
equilibrating properties of a particular experimental trading institution
(the double auction).

Smith observed a remarkable degree of convergence of prices, across
periods, on the equilibrium prediction. The paper also investigates how
the equilibrating tendencies of the institution respond to variations and
shocks in supply and demand conditions.

Our primary interest lies not in Smith's specific findings—pathbreaking though they were—but in the more general testing strategy that his
experiment exemplifies. That strategy reveals one of the key attractions

of laboratory testing: the possibility to control the environment. Tests of whether equilibrium pertains in any naturally occurring market are complicated both by the fact that supply and demand conditions must be inferred from behavior in the market and by the fact that supply and demand may not be stable. In contrast, Smith's experimental approach illustrates the possibility of implementing specific demand and supply conditions, and holding these constant over a number of market periods. The theoretical equilibrium given by the intersection of supply and demand can then be read off from conditions imposed in the laboratory, so permitting the testing of competitive price theory.

Notice, however, that in Smith's experiment the assumption that the intended supply and demand schedules have been induced must presuppose something about what the participants in the experiment are trying to do. Specifically, it implicitly assumes that buyers really do want to buy units at values at or below their maximum and prefer deals that increase their surplus; similarly, it assumes that sellers really do want to sell units at values at or above their minimum and that they prefer deals that increase their surplus. In other words, the experimenter really wants the participants to have preferences consistent with the intended supply and demand conditions, or at least to be acting as if they had them. The question of how to achieve this is what has motivated discussions of IVM.

In the experiments reported by Smith (1962), the participants made hypothetical decisions and consequently, by today's standards, this would not be regarded as a design that properly "induced" preferences. However, the conventional wisdom on what is required to do so flows largely from subsequent papers in which Smith (1976, 1982a) proposed a set of conditions (he called them "precepts") that, if satisfied, would be sufficient to guarantee that the experimenter has induced the intended sets of preferences. The discussion presupposes that participation in an experiment should lead to a concrete reward (that in practice is usually money). All of the precepts then relate to the reward structure of the experiment and we discuss them following Smith (1982a).

The two most basic precepts are *nonsatiation* and *saliency*. Nonsatiation is the requirement that subjects prefer more to less of the reward medium and do not become satiated by it in the range of rewards possible in the experimental setting. Saliency is the requirement that rewards are tied to decisions in the experiment in an appropriate fashion. Specifically, rewards should be monotonically increasing in the objective the experimenter is trying to induce. In the context of Smith's 1962 experiment, paying each subject according to the amount of private surplus generated by their individual trades would have promoted saliency because subjects would then have been given an incentive to do what the experimenter wanted them to try to do: that is, to maximize their surplus. By contrast, paying subjects a fixed fee for participating would not satisfy saliency. Two further, but subsidiary, precepts are intended to rule out other significant motivational factors interfering with the reward structure. *Dominance*[2] requires that other costs (or benefits), such as transaction costs, do not override the motivation provided by the experimenter's intended reward medium. *Privacy* requires that a subject knows only their own reward, which is intended to rule out motivations arising from interpersonal considerations such as altruism or envy. Smith argues that in an experimental setting where all four precepts hold, we are entitled to interpret participants' behavior as being driven by a desire to maximize extraction of reward from the experiment. Since the experimenter knows the structure of the environment (e.g., endowments of goods, etc.), having created it, *if* she also knows the agents' objective functions, we have the basis for deriving equilibrium predictions from competitive price theory. She knows the latter (to be maximum extraction of the reward medium from the experiment) *if* the precepts hold.

As such, Smith's arguments can be read as leading to a set of conditions, defined on the experimental reward structure, that are sufficient for inducing known preferences. But since knowledge of preferences is necessary for deriving equilibrium predictions for the laboratory market setting, the precepts are, indirectly, conditions for testing theories of market behavior in the lab. Smith's analysis has been hugely influential and has been widely endorsed as a canonical statement of experimental economics methodology. For example, Glenn Harrison (1994, p. 223), speaks of the precepts as "widely accepted sufficient conditions for a valid controlled experiment."[3]

The relevance of the DQT is easy to spot here. In any particular study using IVM we can think of Smith's precepts as auxiliary hypotheses that are tested alongside the target that motivates the investigation. If the

---

[2] The term "dominance" as used by Smith in the context of induced-value methodology refers to a completely different concept from that of the First-Order Stochastic Dominance that has figured in our discussion of expected utility theory.

[3] This statement by Harrison, while providing a good illustration of the importance that is often attached to Smithian precepts, also reflects what we suspect may be a fairly common methodological misunderstanding. While it has become common to speak of Smith's precepts as general principles for valid experimental design, the degree of control implied when the precepts hold would not always be desirable across all uses of experimental method. For example, some experiments are designed with the explicit intention of investigating the impact of motives (e.g., envy or altruism) that successful implementation of the Smithian precepts would control out. When the purpose of the experiment is to investigate what motivations subjects actually have, there is unlikely to be a strong general argument for imposing all of the IVM assumptions, so doing so might be neither necessary nor sufficient for a well-designed experiment.

predictions of the theory appear to be falsified, there are always a number of possible interpretations: one possibility is that the target is false; another is that the theory is true but some auxiliary assumption, perhaps including one or more of Smith's precepts, has been violated. To decide which inference to draw, one must judge how likely it is that the auxiliary assumptions have held. But such judgments may not be straightforward to reach. For instance, to determine whether dominance has held, one needs to ask whether the rewards in the experiment were sufficiently large to outweigh other possible influences. Since economic theories typically tell us little or nothing about how big incentives need to be to provide appropriate motivation, experimenters must make assumptions about what kinds of rewards are necessary.

Smith is clearly aware of this and argues for using "payoff levels that are judged to be high for the subject population" (Smith 1982a, p. 934). Such judgments, however, clearly leave room for disagreement and, as we will see later, questions about the levels of incentives needed to motivate subjects in particular experimental tasks are complex and vexed (this issue is taken up in detail in chapter 6). Similarly, for saliency and nonsatiation to hold: it is important that subjects properly understand the experiment, in particular, how the reward medium is related to their actions. But can we ever be *sure* that subjects understand an experimental design "sufficiently" well? Even if they did understand what was described to them, there may be questions about whether subjects trusted the experimenter: that is, did they believe what they were told, even if they understood it?

Scope for residual doubt in relation to such questions can never be completely eliminated and that provides a potential foothold for critics to question the interpretation of results from major branches of experimental enquiry. Take, for instance, this skeptical commentary on the interpretation of evidence from market experiments offered by John Cross (1980, p. 405) who argues that "it seems to be extraordinarily optimistic to assume that behavior in an artificially constructed 'market' game would provide direct insight into actual market behavior." Included among his criticisms is the following:

> Experimental situations often project a gamelike atmosphere in which a "subject" may see himself as "matching wits" against the experimenter-designer of the game. Even with relatively large payoffs, a subject may derive personal satisfaction from perceived "victories" that are not necessarily correlated with the performance indices used by the experimenter.
>
> Cross (1980, p. 404)

Cross is casting doubt on whether Smith's precepts can be expected to apply in the setting of an experimental market; he is suggesting some possible motivations of subjects, additional to those intended by the experimenter, the presence of which would mean that the subjects' preferences are not those assumed by the experimenter. The presence of such motives would confound interpretation of the data and frustrate attempts to test theoretical predictions that are contingent on assumptions about the subjects' preferences.

While we do not endorse the thoroughly skeptical interpretation of market experiments advocated by Cross, one can point to cases where, with the benefit of hindsight, it is apparent that uncontrolled motivations have confounded their interpretation. Take for instance work by Vivian Lei et al. (2001) that extends the literature around illustration 7 in chapter 1 by exploring the causes of "bubbles" in the types of asset market used in Smith et al. (1988).

The underlying experimental strategy of Smith et al. had two key elements. First, they aimed to create markets where the motives for trade usually built into market experiments were turned off. Previous markets experiments had used the induced-value technique to create motives for trade by making experimental "goods" have different values for different agents, thus providing potential for mutually beneficial trades that transferred goods from low- to high-value holders. Smith et al. aimed to eliminate these motives for trade by running markets for goods with the same induced value for all traders.[4] The second key feature of their design was to allow each trader to act as both a buyer and a seller, hence "turning on" the possibility of speculative trading (e.g., an agent buying assets at one price in the hope of selling them on at a higher price). Recall that Smith et al. (1988) repeatedly observed bubbles (sustained episodes of trading at prices above fundamentals) followed by crashes and they diagnosed it as a consequence of rational agents pursuing speculative gains in an environment where the behavior of other agents is uncertain (Smith et al. 1988, p. 1,148).

The experiments conducted by Lei et al. (2001), however, suggest a very different interpretation. Their research replicates bubbling in an environment similar to Smith et al. (1988) but then explores the effects of two changes in the design. The first turns off the possibility of speculation by constraining traders to be either buyers or sellers. In this environment neither the induced-reward structure nor speculation provide any motive for trade. While this creates some reduction in bubbling, it does not eliminate it. Consequently, Lei et al. (2001) conclude that trading and

---

[4] Though this did rest on the assumption that subjects were risk neutral.

bubbling must be, to some extent, supported by motives that are independent of both the intrinsic values of the goods and any speculative
motives. They propose the *active participation hypothesis*:

> The hypothesis that a fraction of the volume in the markets is related to
> the fact that participation in the asset market is the only activity avail-
> able for subjects, and to the fact that the protocol of the experiment
> encourages them to participate in some manner.
>
> Lei et al. (2001, p. 847)

To test this hypothesis they run further asset markets like their previous ones except that subjects have the option of engaging in another
activity besides participating in the asset market. They stress to subjects that it is entirely up to them to decide to what extent they wish to
engage in the two activities. In line with the active participation hypothesis, they find that bubbling is attenuated by these changes, suggesting
that some of the bubbling reported by Smith et al. (1988) and others may
be attributable to a design feature that has been typical of, but peculiar
to, *experimental* asset markets: that is, while participating in these experiments, trading in a single asset market has been the sole activity that
the participant could engage in (aside from, say, daydreaming).

The extra asset trading that arises from constraining individuals to
a single activity might stem from boredom (subjects want to do something to occupy their time in the experiment) or from subjects thinking
that they ought to participate in the activity the experimenter has set
them, in which case we might think of it as a form of "demand effect"
(see chapter 5). But on either interpretation this is an instance of a failure to satisfy Smith's dominance precept: that is, for the participants
in these experiments, if the active participation hypothesis is correct in
its account, the experimental rewards apparently did not dominate the
psychological rewards from doing something.

The significance of this example, however, runs beyond it simply being
an instance of a Smithian precept failing. Notice that in this case, the failure relates to a feature of the decision context that previously, we suppose, most researchers would have taken to be irrelevant (i.e., whether or
not there is another activity for subjects to engage in). In relation to IVM,
this case illustrates that Smith's precepts are *not* well-defined auxiliaries
that researchers can readily know how to implement and check. Instead,
they have the character of open-ended principles requiring guesswork
to judge what might be required to implement them. For instance, in
thinking about whether dominance is satisfied, we must try to guess
what other motivations, beyond maximizing money returns, the subjects
might have. More generally, the example illustrates a further dimension

to the DQT issue: deciding which auxiliaries are relevant to a particular test involves imagination and guesswork and particular interpretations of experimental tests may rest on auxiliaries that the experimenters (or those consuming their results) have not even entertained.

3.3   On the Significance of the DQT for Testing

The DQT suggests that tests always involve sets of hypotheses and that, consequently, drawing conclusions about what they have "shown" requires judgments about which auxiliaries may be relevant to the test and whether those auxiliaries have held or failed. While this provides a more refined picture of what experimental testing involves, we have not identified special reasons for thinking that problems of interpretation raised by the DQT are worse in relation to testing in experimental economics than they are for testing elsewhere in economics or beyond. Indeed, some argue that these matters of interpretation are *more* readily addressed in experimental research than they are in other forms of empirical investigation in economics (see, for example, Smith 1994). There is some merit in this idea. The notion of a controlled experiment in which one variable is manipulated while holding everything else constant suggests an ideal vehicle for checking the sensitivity of particular laboratory findings to specific auxiliary hypotheses. Moreover, compared with field studies where auxiliary checking may be constrained by the data set that was collected or can be accessed, experimenters can *create* new data in the lab via designs intended to probe the reliability of findings to variations in any number of auxiliaries that may not have been previously explored. Viewed in this way, we might think of experiments as tools for investigating competing interpretations of particular data and for grappling with the problems set by the DQT. The relevant question is then how effectively experiments do that.

There is a logical question about the extent to which a series of experiments could settle questions of interpretation set by the DQT. Suppose we run an experiment that appears to refute the conjunction $(T, a^1, a^2, a^3, a^4, \ldots, a^n)$. We then have to decide which subset of these hypotheses should take the blame for the refutation. But can we resolve this by running more experiments? It is not obvious that the answer is yes, because any new experiment must also be a joint test of a bundle of hypotheses with multiple possible interpretations of whatever outcome is observed. So how can more experiments help to pin down the right interpretation for some initial experiment? The issue has been formally analyzed by, among others, Elie Zahar (1983) and Morten Søberg

(2005). Their arguments work roughly as follows. Suppose that some specific experiment leads to observation O being inconsistent with the conjunction of some target hypothesis T with some single auxiliary a^1. Now imagine running another experiment where the conjunction (T, a^2) implies not-O, and another where (T, a^3) implies not-O, and so on for a long series of alternative a^i. Zahar and Søberg each argue that if the recalcitrant O is consistently observed, then T should be considered "refuted" in the sense of being implausible.

While the Zahar–Søberg argument seems appealing from a logical point of view, it does presuppose a highly stylized series of experimental tests and there are reasons to doubt whether routine experimental practice will conform closely to this ideal. One such reason relates to whether experimenters can in practice create anything remotely like the corresponding series of environments in which a prediction rests on the conjunction of a target plus just one auxiliary that is then repeatedly substituted by others while maintaining the same predictive content. Even if we could create the right series of experiments, some might doubt whether there would be good incentives to carry them out. For example, Rubinstein (2001) has raised doubts about whether the incentives of the discipline are really geared toward supporting experiments aimed at checking, challenging, and probing experimental findings over sustained periods of time.

Others, however, are more optimistic. For example, Smith (2008, pp. 304–6) argues that the business of checking auxiliaries comes very naturally to experimental economists and that there are cases where the incentives for checking are strong, such as when experimental results are perceived to pose a significant theoretical challenge.[5] Moreover, one can readily point to cases in experimental economics where extensive literatures have emerged around the testing of particular auxiliaries. Indeed, several examples are discussed later in this chapter and in subsequent chapters. The issue is then whether disputes about auxiliaries tend to progress in satisfactory ways or gravitate toward reasonable conclusions. Notice that this question presupposes the existence of some prescriptive viewpoint from which to judge whether progress is "satisfactory" or conclusions "reasonable." We suggest that it is in consideration of this question that we find the real bite of the DQT because it tells firmly against the most celebrated attempt to set out prescriptive criteria for theory selection: that due to Karl Popper.

---

[5] For example, Smith (p. 306) argues that "Whenever negative experimental results threaten perceived important new theory, the resulting controversies galvanize experimentalists everywhere into a search for different or better tests—tests that examine the robustness of the original results."

Box 3.2. Popper and the methodology of falsificationism.

Much of Popper's work was directly concerned with attempting to identify prescriptive principles for scientific practice with a view to weeding out poor science (or indeed "pseudo science" merely masquerading as science). Popper takes a clear and firm prescriptive line on a set of key questions related to theory testing including what counts as a legitimate theory, what counts as a convincing test of a theory, and on how scientists should respond when theories fail tests.

Central to Popper's approach is his distinction (or "demarcation") between science and nonscience based on the notion of *falsifiability*. According to Popper, for a hypothesis to be considered as part of science it must generate statements that are falsifiable: that is, it must identify conceivable states of the world that, if observed, would show the hypothesis to be false. The motivation for this demarcation stemmed partly from Popper's belief that intellectual resources are wasted in developing theoretical frameworks with little or no predictive content (see Popper 1963). He argued that by constructing vague or loosely articulated hypotheses it is relatively easy to create "theories" that, superficially, seem to fit events. But if the fit derives from them being cast so loosely that they can in fact be molded to fit any course of events in the domain of interest, they are empty of scientific content and devoid of explanatory power. Thus for a "theory" to be considered part of scientific discourse at all, it must pass a first benchmark test: it must be potentially falsifiable.

Popper advocates *falsificationism* as a strategy for promoting the advance of scientific knowledge. The essential idea is that any proposed hypothesis is a legitimate scientific conjecture so long as it is falsifiable and, as yet, unfalsified. However, the onus should be upon the proponents of scientific hypotheses to state, in advance, the conditions under which they would consider their hypotheses rejected. Members of the scientific community should then focus on conducting tests aimed at falsifying the proposed hypotheses.

For Popper, the orientation toward falsification (as opposed to the earlier, logical positivist, concern with *verification*) is required by a *logical* asymmetry in the relative discriminatory power of confirming versus disconfirming evidence. Specifically, while no amount of confirming evidence can prove a hypothesis true (a reflection of Hume's famous problem of induction), a single negative result can, in principle, show a hypothesis to be false. As Popper puts it:

> Real support can be obtained only from observations undertaken as tests (by "attempted refutations"); and for this purpose criteria of

> refutation have to be laid down beforehand: it must be agreed which
> observable situations, if actually observed, mean that the theory is
> refuted.
>
> Popper (1963, p. 38)

Hence, on Popper's view, falsificationism provides a recipe for the growth
of knowledge because, while the problem of induction implies that there
is no method for arriving at theories that are demonstrably true, we can,
by adopting the method of falsificationism, aim at the rejection of false
ones.

On the Popperian view, scientific advance is best fostered by proposing
bold theories (i.e., theories that lay themselves open to refutation by
specifying a wide range of potentially observable falsifiers and/or make
surprising predictions) and by subjecting theories to *harsh tests* (e.g., by
running tests we might expect them to fail rather than those we expect
them to pass).

Popper also proposes rules governing the development of new hypotheses in the face of evidence that rejects an existing theory. These include
the requirement that a new theory should be *encompassing* in the sense
that it should explain the previous successes of a theory it replaces.
A further, crucial, requirement is *novel content*: that is, a new theory
proposed in order to explain data inconsistent with a previous theory
should generate *novel* predictions. These requirements are intended to
foster theories with expanding, rather than contracting, content and a
nice intuition for why they are necessary is provided by this example
due to Lakatos:

> To give a very simple-minded example: suppose you put forward that
> all swans are white, and then produce a black swan. You have to reject
> "All swans are white." Let us call the black swan "Peter." According to
> Popper, you are not allowed to put forward the new theory "All swans
> are white except for Peter," because this is an ad hoc maneuver, and
> this kind of exception-barring is not allowed.
>
> Lakatos (1973)

Classic works in which Popper sets out the falsificationist agenda
include Popper (1934) and Popper (1963). Critics of falsificationism, at
least in its undiluted form, include Lakatos (1970), Feyerabend (1975),
and McCloskey (1983). General discussions of falsificationism and its
critics can be found in Blaug (1992), Hausman (1992) and Hands (2001).

Over the last half century, many economists have explicitly endorsed
aspects of Popper's methodology in monographs and textbooks (see,
for example, Friedman 1953; Lipsey 1979; Blaug 1992) and a distinctly

Popperian tone often pervades methodological writing in economics even when there is no explicit reference to Popper. A recent example, laden with Popperian overtones, is Larry Samuelson's (2005) article examining the relation between theory and experiment in economics. The spirit of Popper is manifest in several passages including this one in which Samuelson (2005, p. 100) urges theorists to identify potential falsifiers: "It would be useful for theory to identify behavior for which the theory cannot account, in the sense that observations would force the theorist to reconsider." Shortly after, he points to the desirability of novel content in discriminating between theories.

That said, the Popperian approach has been heavily criticized by philosophers of science and economic methodologists who have pointed to a range of difficulties. Perhaps the most fundamental problem confronting falsificationism—or at least unrefined versions of it—is the DQT. As we noted, an important part of what recommends falsificationism is a view that there is a *logical* asymmetry between confirming and falsifying evidence because theories can be falsified but not confirmed. But the DQT implies that it is never possible to isolate a single (target) hypothesis and definitively falsify it. There are *always* additional assumptions that must be taken to hold in order for evidence to be interpreted as telling for, or against, a particular target. Consequently, there can be no "acid tests" of theories because in the face of any evidence, positive or negative, it is always logically possible to adjust some auxiliary hypotheses in ways that allow any target hypothesis to stand or fall (see Hesse (1970) for further discussion).

Many view the DQT as a serious problem for falsificationism, or at least naive formulations of it, and some interpret this as reflecting deeper, ultimately insurmountable, problems inherent in *any* attempt to construct a prescriptive or rules-based methodology for science (see, for example, Feyerabend 1975; McCloskey 1983). Others, however, have sought to build on Popperian foundations in attempts to salvage the hunt for principles of rational theory appraisal. The most prominent of these is the "methodology of scientific research programmes" (MSRP) due to Lakatos (1970).[6] We argue that *aspects* of MSRP provide a useful perspective on the problems set by the DQT and, with that in mind, we now sketch some of the salient features of it.

While MSRP is often referred to as a form of "sophisticated falsificationism" (Lakatos 1970) it also has some rather non-Popperian roots in the work of Thomas Kuhn. One key element of the Kuhnian perspective

---

[6]We acknowledge that contemporary economists, such as Samuelson (2005), who appear to express sympathy with various Popperian ideas could have the MSRP in mind.

reflected in MSRP is a rejection of any simplistic version of empiricism in which "bare facts" play a decisive role in the development and selection of theories. Kuhn (1962) argued for a sociological perspective on science highlighting the role that "paradigms" play in the evolution of knowledge. The notion of a paradigm refers to a complex fabric of common practices and background beliefs that shape the evolution of knowledge in any research community. Kuhn argues that paradigms play a crucial role in the evolution of scientific knowledge by influencing, among other things, the questions that a given research community will consider relevant and the conceptual and theoretical tools they will use to address them.

On some readings of Kuhn, the day-to-day practice of science (or what Kuhn calls "normal science") aims to bring observations of phenomena that challenge current beliefs into conformity with the existing paradigm. For the Popperian this may sound like a process involving dogmatic resistance to evidence but, in contrast, Kuhn sees the existence of a paradigm, and the shaping role it performs, as a *prerequisite* for any properly functioning science. The defense of something akin to a paradigm as a necessary backdrop to healthy scientific endeavor is also apparent in MSRP. There are, however, major differences between the approaches of Kuhn and Lakatos: perhaps the most important of them is that while Kuhn is primarily concerned with descriptive analysis, MSRP is also intended as a framework for prescriptive evaluation. In order to explain this, however, it is first necessary to set out some key features of the descriptive framework.

In its descriptive function, MSRP is intended as a conceptual framework for aiding understanding, or reconstruction, of historic episodes in particular research fields. The unit of analysis is the *research program:* a complex entity consisting of a body of evolving theory (assumptions, methods, predictions, etc.) and rules or conventions governing scientific activity. At a given point in time, any active research program will be characterized by a partial fit between the implications of the current body of theory and observations of phenomena in the world. Relevant empirical phenomena that are not adequately organized by the program ("anomalies") then provide impetus for its future development. One key rule governing activity within any program is its "negative heuristic": that is, a convention according specific statements or assumptions a privileged, or "hard core," status. Hard core statements are, in consequence of the choices and actions of the researchers, effectively insulated from the possibility of refutation: that is, researchers look to resolve mismatches between the implications of the program and empirical evidence by adjustments elsewhere in the program (adjustment to what

Lakatos calls the "protective belt" of assumptions). Other conventions (Lakatos refers to them collectively as the "positive heuristic") shape activity within the program by, for example, delineating the problems for the program to address, the appropriate methods for tackling them, and so on. Applying MSRP descriptively involves fitting the history of events, in the relevant field, to the conceptual framework of MSRP: that is, one tries to identify or distil the hard core, the positive heuristic, and so on.

In relation to its prescriptive dimension, a key move relative to Popper is to shift the focus from assessing the success or failure of particular hypotheses to evaluation of the performance of research programs *over time.* For Lakatos, long-run adherence to a particular hard core is defensible, from a scientific point of view, only if it delivers "progress." Lakatos identifies two dimensions of progress. A program is said to be *theoretically progressive* if refinements lead to new versions of it that (i) encompass the unrefuted content of prior versions; (ii) absorb anomalies relative to previous versions by extending the predictive content to include previously unexplained phenomena; and (iii) lead to the prediction of *novel* phenomena.[7] A research program demonstrates *empirical progress* when there is confirmation of at least some of its novel predictive content. For the Lakatosian, a well-functioning research program should deliver progress on both fronts.

For those who endorse it, MSRP could provide prescriptive guidance at two levels. On the one hand, it might inform decisions (of, say, individual researchers, university departments, or funding agencies) about which research programs are most worth investing in. On the other, at the level of day-to-day research within a program, we take it that the prescriptive message of MSRP is to urge researchers to develop and test new theories with a view to delivering theoretical and empirical progress. At this level the Lakatosian framework has considerable resonance with the Popperian approach. It urges individual scientists to put forward and test new hypotheses with the intention of expanding explanatory power—the key test of success being the delivery of successful novel predictions.

While we think Lakatos may go too far in distilling the notion of scientific progress down to just these two dimensions, we think there is considerable appeal to his presumption that empirical scientists—including

---

[7] Lakatos (1970, p. 118) defines novelty as predictions of phenomena that would have seemed "improbable or even impossible in the light of previous knowledge." In subsequent literature, Lakatos acknowledges other, less-demanding, standards of novelty. One is the ability of a theory to accommodate known facts that were hitherto unexplained in the program to which the theory belongs. Such predictions may be regarded as novel if they arise as unintended consequences of attempts to explain other phenomena.

economists—should aim for expanding empirical content of their theories[8] and to the idea that success in novel predictions is one meaningful indicator of success. So, while we do not view MSRP as providing a definitive statement of what progress in science really is, it does provide some broadly appealing prescriptive orientation. More importantly in the context of this chapter, we think that MSRP provides the outlines of a descriptive and prescriptive view of science, and the role that testing plays within it, that is more credible than earlier vintage Popperianism. In MSRP, the problem posed by the DQT is partly defused by allowing some assumptions to be treated as hard core (thereby reducing the number of auxiliaries implicated in a given test) and, more significantly, by shifting the focus of theory evaluation from the single test to the time profile of a program. The DQT bites hard in Popper's scheme because it undercuts the power of the very thing that is supposed to drive scientific discovery (the possibility of definitive falsifications). Lakatos maintains that, to paraphrase, all theories will be born into and die in a sea of anomalies. The job of science, therefore, cannot be to weed out theories with apparent falsifiers. Instead, scientists should aim, over time, to improve the imperfect theories at their disposal. In this scheme, it is the long-run accumulation of evidence that counts. So, while it remains the case that all individual tests must be fallible (by virtue of the DQT), since the single test no longer plays the crucial role that it has in the Popperian scheme, the blow delivered by the DQT in the context of MSRP is correspondingly reduced.

Of course we recognize that MSRP has its own limitations. Some critics point to problems at its philosophical foundations (see Hands (2001) for discussion), while others identify difficulties in applying it to research programs in economics (see, for example, De Marchi and Blaug 1991). But at least some of the criticisms leveled at MSRP seem entirely misplaced in the context of experimental economics research. For example, De Marchi (1991, p. 5) notes that some economists (he cites, for example, Hutchison, Leijonhufvud, and Hicks) have doubted the applicability of MSRP to economics because of "the difficulty of experimentation in economics and the nonrepeating character of economic data and circumstances." In similar vein, De Marchi (1991, p. 9) argues that some economists dispute the relevance of MSRP because it is a framework in which testing plays a crucial role, whereas when one considers empirical economics he claims that "rarely does it have to do with testing." These criticisms simply dissolve in the context of debates about *theory*

---

[8] This is not to say that any expansion of content is desirable ex post because there may naturally be trade-offs between complexity and fit.

testing in *experimental economics*: if the critics thought MSRP inapplicable because economics is nonexperimental and does not involve testing, then, with the benefit of hindsight, and with respect to experimental economics research, we can now see that they were *wrong*. The development of experimental economics has transformed the scope for theory testing as well as showing that (some) economics can be experimental.

It is not our aim, however, to defend the entire machinery of MSRP. Instead we wish merely to argue that certain elements of MSRP can be helpful in understanding what testing in experimental economics involves. There are three main aspects of the Lakatosian framework that we seek to borrow and apply. The first is the essentially Kuhnian claim that in order to understand research activity it is necessary to appreciate background assumptions that operate around any program of research. We think this claim applies clearly in the context of experimental testing and that one can only make proper sense of what experimenters are trying to achieve via particular programs of testing by taking account of the operation of, sometimes tacit, background assumptions. Second, we will argue that in surveying programs of experimental research it is possible to identify the operation of quasi-Lakatosian hard cores: that is, assumptions that researchers involved in those programs appear to accord a privileged status relative to the data. We will suggest that hard-core commitments are evident in various spheres of experimental research and play an important role in shaping the development of such research. Third, we will argue that while hard-core attachments can be a defensible aspect of proper scientific activity, long-run adherence to them should be justified through the delivery of some form of empirical progress. We think that applying these concepts sheds light on what it is that experimental economists are trying to do when "testing" theories and we illustrate this claim with examples from game theory and choice theory.

3.4   On Testing Game Theory

A considerable amount of experimental economics research observes behavior in strategic settings where the reward to a participant's decision depends partly on what other participants do (see, for example, illustrations 4–6 in chapter 1). In the reports of such exercises it is common for researchers to use the tools of game theory to derive "predictions" and to report behavior in the experiment as tests of them. The purpose of this section is to explore in more detail what such exercises actually involve and, more specifically, whether they can be sensibly interpreted as tests of game theory. As we will see, the question quickly connects with the DQT because of the role that so-called bridge principles necessarily play in such activities.

To approach this issue, it is helpful to consider an aspect of how game theory works by noting the distinction between the *statement* and *analysis* of a formal game. The statement of a formal game involves a specification of the structural features of the game (e.g., how many players there are; what strategy choices are available to them; whether the game is one-shot or repeated; and so on) together with a specification of the players' preferences over possible "outcomes" of the game. For the purpose of this illustration we will focus on games represented in extensive form (i.e., as trees). In this case, specifying preferences amounts to assigning a utility number, for each player, to each possible route through the tree such that, for every player, the ranking of routes according to their own utility numbers reflects their own preference ordering over outcomes, all things considered. The game so stated is a formal or mathematical construct that we will call an *abstract game.* The standard analysis of an abstract game involves the application of a *solution concept* (such as Nash equilibrium or some refinement of it) that picks out some outcomes as equilibrium ones.

Now consider what is involved in conducting an experimental test of a prediction derived from game theory. A typical approach is to construct a laboratory analogue of some abstract game. In this laboratory game—which we will call the *implemented game*—concrete entities in the lab substitute for abstract concepts in the theory: real people serve as substitutes for theoretical agents, material payoffs (e.g., money) substitute for utilities, and so on. Assuming that the implemented game contains the necessary correlates, one may derive predictions for it by applying some solution concept of interest, using the relevant concrete features of the implemented game as inputs. The degree of correspondence between these predictions and observed behavior in the implemented game then forms the basis of the experimental test. But what exactly would be tested via such an exercise? Such tests are clearly joint tests of the solution concept together with any assumptions involved in connecting together the concepts in the abstract and implemented games. The latter include what philosophers of science sometimes call *bridge principles* (see, for example, Guala 2006).[9] For present purposes, we may

---

[9] There are, of course, additional auxiliary assumptions implicated in any such test, such as "the subjects understood the instructions," "the data were properly recorded," and so on. In this section, we take that as read but abstract from these other auxiliaries to focus on questions relating to bridge principles.

think of bridge principles as assumptions about what count as satisfactory laboratory analogues of game theory concepts. While such bridging assumptions are, more often than not, implicit rather than explicit, some assumptions of this sort are necessarily involved in connecting the theory to the lab (for more discussion of this point, see Hausman (2005), and Grüne-Yanoff and Schweinzer (2008)).

The adequacy (or otherwise) of bridging assumptions can be a crucial issue when it comes to the interpretation of test results. We illustrate this point with a discussion of game payoffs. In game theory, it is conventional to interpret the utilities written into abstract games as representing everything that is relevant to the players' rankings of alternative routes through a tree. On the other hand, experimenters motivate subjects with concrete payoffs (usually money):[10] and they usually read off game-theoretic predictions by taking the money payoffs as proxies for utilities. In other words, treating money payoffs as counterparts of utilities has been a widely used bridging principle in tests of game theory. We will call it the *standard payoff bridging principle* or just the "standard bridge" for short. The standard bridge is questionable from an empirical point of view given the evidence pointing to "other-regarding" motives as a factor in human decisions. This literature has early roots in the analysis of field data (Sugden 1982, 1984) but there is now a very large and growing experimental literature, and related to that an expanding theoretical literature. While we mention some particularly relevant work below, a broader overview of this literature is provided in Camerer (2003, chapter 2).

The possibility of other-regarding motives generates a Duhem–Quine problem in the interpretation of experimental tests of game theory. Any observed discrepancy between game-theoretic predictions in an implemented game played for money payoffs immediately permits at least two interpretations: one is as a "rejection" of some component (such as the solution concept) of the game theory leading to the prediction; the other is that—because of the presence of some other-regarding motive—the experimenter has failed to implement the intended game. As a more specific illustration of this general point, consider the *ultimatum game*.

Box 3.3. The ultimatum game.

The ultimatum game was introduced by Werner Güth et al. (1982). In the standard version of it, two players ("proposer" and "responder") move in

---

[10] We discuss other ways of motivating subjects in chapter 6, including the binary lottery mechanism in which the proximate rewards are measured in chances of winning a fixed lottery prize.

sequence and "bargain" over the division of some fixed money amount (say 10 pounds, euros, or dollars). Bargaining is structured so that the proposer moves first by offering some split of the pie (e.g., proposer gets 8, responder gets 2). The responder then has a choice between two actions: they either "accept," in which case the proposed division is implemented; or they "reject," in which case both players get nothing. If each player is motivated only by maximization of their own money payoff, any division can be supported as a Nash equilibrium of the game, but there is a unique subgame-perfect equilibrium in which the proposer offers a split that gives the responder the smallest allowable positive payoff (e.g., one penny or cent) and the responder accepts.

The subgame-perfect equilibrium is derived through the application of *backward induction* (an algorithm for identifying optimal play in sequential games). In the context of the ultimatum game, this involves first identifying the responder's optimal decisions (conditional on any offer), then working back to identify the optimal proposal. Assuming that the responder cares only about their own money payoff, it follows they would accept any offer that gives them a positive payoff. If the proposer aims to maximize their own money payoff (and believes this to be the motive of the responder) it follows that they should offer the smallest possible amount in the expectation that this offer will be accepted.

An extensive literature shows that behavior deviates from the subgame-perfect equilibrium in predictable ways: responders frequently reject "low" offers and proposals of close-to-even splits are common (often modal). Surveys of the evidence are available in Thaler (1988), Güth and Tietz (1990), Davis and Holt (1993), and Camerer (2003).

One possible interpretation of behavior in the ultimatum game is that it reflects the failure of individuals to apply backward induction reasoning. Some evidence for this interpretation is provided in experiments reported by Binmore et al. (2002). But the possibility of "other-regarding" motives suggests a range of other potential explanations. In recent years, various new game-theoretic models incorporating other-regarding motives have been developed, partly as a response to observed behavior in these and other experimental games. In some of these models, agents have preferences over the distribution of final payoffs. Theories in this spirit include the models of inequity aversion due to Fehr and Schmidt (1999) and Bolton and Ockenfels (2000). Other theories capture other-regarding motives via propensities for positive or negative reciprocity (that is, tendencies to reward kind acts or punish unkind acts). Models in this spirit include those due to Rabin (1993) and Dufwenberg and Kirchsteiger (2004). In principle, either type of model could provide an account of the basic facts described above. We further explore how experiments have been used to probe causes of behavior in the ultimatum game in chapter 4.

The possibility of other-regarding motives seeds uncertainty about the standard payoff bridging principle. As the ultimatum-game example illustrates, this complicates the interpretation of experiments that attempt to test aspects of game theory. If behavior deviates from theoretical predictions, do we regard it as a failure of the theory, or should we question whether the right game has been implemented?

But having granted that there is a problem in principle here, one might reasonably wonder how serious it is in practice. If the extent of uncertainty about which game subjects are playing is limited, that might mediate the problem of interpreting experimental tests. For instance, if money payoffs were reasonably close proxies to utilities and/or discrepancies were rare or at least confined to known cases, the presence of such uncertainty would not be a *general* obstacle to testing. At least some commentators, however, do judge the uncertainty to be profound and the issue to be—at least currently—a serious general obstacle to testing principles of game theory. Take for instance Hausman (2005), who argues:

> There are, however, very serious difficulties in the way of determining the payoffs or preferences of experimental subjects. These payoffs must be determined in order for game theory to make any substantial predictions concerning laboratory behavior. Until the preferences are specified, the experimenter only knows "the game form," not the game. Determining the player's preferences might not seem all that difficult. If experimenters insure that subjects are completely anonymous—thereby eliminating all sorts of extraneous motives—it might seem a reasonable first approximation to regard the preferences of an experimental subject over the outcomes as tracking the monetary payoffs he or she would receive. But as I read the literature, this turns out to be unsatisfactory, even as a first approximation. It is in fact very difficult to know what motivates subjects in a laboratory for experimentation in economics.
>
> Hausman (2005, p. 216)

While the literature on social preferences does suggest a wide range of motives influencing behavior that run beyond a narrow desire to maximize one's own money payoff, one might wonder whether that same literature allows one to make some reasonably reliable inferences about how money payoffs translate into utility, at least for some basic games. Given the present state of the literature, however, the prospects for this are not very promising. While there are theoretical models that explicitly propose such mappings (see, for example, Rabin 1993; Fehr and Schmidt 1999), this literature is itself developing and there are currently competing models with predictions that are only partially supported in a relatively limited range of applications. Difficulties here are compounded by the evidence of heterogeneity in subject motives. Some studies point to the existence of different subject types in experimental games (Brandts and Schram 2001; Park 2000; van Dijk et al. 2002; Bardsley and Moffatt 2007). For instance, in studies of voluntary contributions (see box 2.3 (p. 58)) it seems that some individuals can be classified as conditional cooperators, whereas others are persistent free-riders (Fischbacher and Gächter 2006, forthcoming). This suggests that we could not successfully map from concrete payoffs to utilities without filtering in some individual level characteristics. To deepen the problem further, the extent to which other-regarding motives come into play might sometimes depend on contextual dimensions of decision environments (see, for example, Hoffman et al. 1994, 2000; Cookson 2000; Levitt and List 2007). Yet other studies point to a significant cultural element in other-regarding behaviors (see Henrich et al. 2001). We suggest that, taken together, these considerations make it implausible to suppose that researchers could— given the current state of knowledge—reliably construct good proxies for utilities from concrete payoffs even in rather basic experimental games. So if there is significant uncertainty about how material payoffs should be mapped into utilities, what does that imply for the scope, conduct, and interpretation of experiments aimed at testing game theory? In what follows, we consider three possible lines of response.

One possible reaction would be to argue that, given uncertainty about mapping from concrete experimental payoffs to utilities, there is no point in trying to test (purported) predictions of game theory. If the experimentalist does not know what the game is, in most cases,[11] they cannot claim to know what a particular solution concept (such as subgame perfection) predicts about play in the game. If they do not know what the theory predicts in the lab, they cannot test it there. Moreover, since game theory has flexibility regarding what could count as a bridging principle (e.g., as the theories of inequity aversion illustrate, standard solution concepts can be applied in contexts where the utilities of individual players depend on the distributions of concrete payoffs across players), it is possible that any behaviors that seem deviant, given the standard payoff bridging principle, could be absorbed by a suitably modified one. Hence, absent a commitment to a particular payoff bridging

---

[11] In some cases, that might be too strong. Suppose all strategy profiles yield zero (in money) for every player, except for one profile that yields £10 for all players. Modest payoff restrictions then imply a unique strict Nash equilibrium.

principle, it is completely unclear what would count as evidence against game theory.

While this position seems a coherent one, we think that adopting it amounts to an unnecessarily restrictive interpretation of game theory. Notice that the problem of finding a workable payoff bridging principle is not specific to experimental applications of game theory. The issue necessarily arises in the course of *any* attempt to apply game theory to predict empirical phenomena such as the behavior of real firms in oligopolistic markets, or the behavior of governments negotiating trade agreements, or any other strategic setting that you might think of. This brings us back to a now-familiar argument: in order for game theory to say anything about the world at all, game-theoretic models must be applied, and that necessarily involves making assumptions about how to map from theoretical constructs to real strategic settings. For instance, we must identify players, the strategies available to them, and, crucially, we must make assumptions about how different strategy combinations translate into utility for them. Only then can we apply some chosen solution concept. And while we may do these things relatively quickly and implicitly in our own everyday thinking as economists, we must be making some such moves whenever we attempt to apply game-theoretic logic to the behavior of real agents, be they in the lab or anywhere else. So unless there is some reason to suppose that making good payoff bridging assumptions is more difficult in experimental applications than it is in other nonexperimental applications—and we do not think it is (indeed, quite possibly, the reverse might be true)—then taking the line that this problem prevents derivation of game-theoretic predictions, if applied consistently, entails that game theory makes no substantive predictions about behavior in the world. In other words, it leads to an interpretation of game theory as an entirely nonempirical enterprise.

There is, of course, intellectually interesting and important work in pure game theory that could sit easily within this nonempirical interpretation: for instance, conceptual analysis exploring intellectual questions about ideally rational play (e.g., the theory of equilibrium selection developed by Harsanyi and Selten (1988)) or mathematical properties of games (such as existence theorems). Researchers pursuing such questions might interpret their analyses as having no intended empirical content and thus as entailing no predictions about anything outside their models. Researchers who confine themselves to such self-contained theoretical worlds could, in principle, completely avoid the difficult problems of how to map from abstract game-theoretic models to the world of real agents in live strategic settings. But anyone wanting to use game theory to say anything about behavior in the world outside their models must, at least implicitly, confront issues of how to apply them, including the question of what bridging assumptions should be used to map from concrete payoffs to utility. So, since our interest lies in understanding how game theory can be applied as an empirical tool, we reject this first line of response.

A second possible response would be to accept that ambiguities about the relationship between material and utility payoffs confound experimental tests of game theory, but to propose that the problem might be solved by developing experimental procedures designed to check whether the intended game has been properly implemented (i.e., whether the subjects' rankings of material payoffs in the implemented game correspond with those of the intended abstract game). An experimenter pursuing this strategy, and wishing to clarify the interpretation of behavior in a particular implemented game, would need to establish each subject's ranking of the possible outcomes in that game. We will say that an experimenter who has found this out has successfully *identified* the game.

At first blush, one might wonder whether game identification could be achieved through some relatively straightforward procedure, comparable perhaps to methods used for attaching individual utilities to consequences in the context of risk and uncertainty (see Farquhar 1984). If so, questions about which game the subjects are really playing might be tackled via application of some standard test procedure. On closer inspection, it seems doubtful that the problem can be successfully addressed in this way.

To appreciate why, consider the difficulties involved in eliciting preferences in the relatively simple "mini" ultimatum game of figure 3.1. This describes a simplified version of a standard ultimatum game. The first mover has a binary choice between proposing an even split of the pie (in which case the game ends with that division) or keeping 90% of it (in which case the second player has the option of accepting or rejecting the proposal). We will call any distinct path through the tree, starting at A and terminating at one of the end nodes ($w_1, \ldots, w_3$), a *play* of this game. So, in this game, there are exactly three plays. The size of the pie fixes the material payoffs at each node and completes the description of what we call the *game form*.

Thus far, we have said nothing about players' preferences over plays in this game form. Indeed, what we are aiming at is a technique for identifying each player's ranking of plays. That is, for each player, we wish to know for each possible pair of plays (w_i, w_j) whether they would prefer that w_i happens or that w_j happens. How might we establish that?

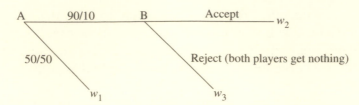

Figure 3.1. Game form for simplified ultimatum game.

We cannot distil a player's rankings of plays directly from their behavior in the game because reading off preferences from actions in this game would require additional assumptions about the rationality of the players and/or their beliefs. For instance, the play of 50/50 by A, permits multiple interpretations: it could be the rational move of an agent with a preference for fairness (that is, they prefer w_1 to w_2 and w_3); or the rational move of an own-payoff-maximizing A who prefers w_2 to w_1 but chooses the play of w_1 because they fear rejection from a possibly irrational or vengeful B, and so on. But if behavior in the game does not identify it, how else might we do it?

One possibility would be to ask each subject to verbally state their ranking over plays. So, for instance, players might be asked to respond (privately) to questions, for each (w_i, w_j) pair, of roughly the form, Which would you prefer to happen out of w_i or w_j?[12] One might discount this approach purely on the grounds that it relies on subjects reporting hypothetical introspections about their preference orderings over plays.[13] But even setting this aside, we suspect that verbal elicitation procedures create further issues of interpretation analogous to those we are seeking to resolve. To illustrate the point, consider how a reasonable person, comparing two plays, would interpret the request, Tell us what you would prefer to happen. There seem to be several possibilities. One is that the subject simply reports the play that gives them the best material payoff. This may be so, even if they would be moved by other considerations—such as fairness—in actual plays of the game. For one thing, identifying the play giving "you" the best material payoff may be

---

[12] We borrowed the idea for such a procedure from a discussion paper by Jorgen Weibull. A later version of that paper is published as Weibull (2004), though the discussion of this type of procedure does not figure so prominently in the published version. Discussions of such mechanisms, however, have older roots in the literature of game and decision theory (see Guala 2006).

[13] While we would not want to make a general case against the usefulness of hypothetical responses (and we discuss this further in chapter 6), there may be particular reasons for doubt about hypothetical responses in this case. For instance, if the subjects are ultimately to play the game, there may be incentives for them to misrepresent their preference orderings.

cognitively less demanding than including and balancing other considerations in the frame. Perhaps more significantly, the request "tell us what you would prefer to happen" does not make it clear that considerations such as fairness *should* be built into a response to this task, even if they would be relevant to the responder's *action* in a corresponding decision. Notice that the request is ambiguous with respect to how the responder should conceive of plays coming about: should they think of themselves as a passive recipient of the various material payoffs consequent on particular plays, or should they imagine themselves an active player implicated in bringing them about, in which case issues of fair play may become more salient? (For instance, I may prefer it if I could be richer than my neighbor, but I may not be prepared to bring it about by stealing from them, even if I was sure I could get away with it.)

If verbal elicitation will not work, would it be possible to identify the game of figure 3.1 by observing the players' choices in simpler but related games? So, for instance, could we establish A's ranking of w_1 and w_2 by observing their behavior in a dictator game where they face a binary choice between sharing the pie 50/50 with B or taking 90% (leaving 10% for B)? Notice that since there is no strategic element in this decision, A's choice has an apparently straightforward interpretation as revealing their preference ranking over sharing versus taking 90%. Since these are also the material outcomes associated with, respectively, plays w_1 and w_2 of figure 3.1, can we take it that A's choice in this dictator game reveals their ranking of the corresponding plays in the mini-ultimatum game? If so, could we proceed in similar fashion to establish each player's ranking for all pairs of plays in figure 3.1 via suitably constructed dictator games?

The approach would be valid if preferences over pairs of plays depended only on the distribution of consequences associated with the terminal nodes of those plays. There is, however, considerable evidence, much of it associated with the literature on reciprocity, that preferences over plays with identical distributions of consequences can depend on other features of trees in which they are embedded (see, for example, Charness and Rabin 2002; Falk et al. 2003; Cox 2004). As an illustration, consider the following example provided by Gary Charness and Matthew Rabin (2002). They compare behavior in the game of figure 3.2(a) with behavior in a situation where that game is embedded in the slightly more complex tree of figure 3.2(b). In both games there are two players (A and B) and the numbers in brackets represent the payoffs (in US$) associated with each play (with A's payoff on the left).

In the game of figure 3.2(a), player B is a dictator who decides between two allocations: one is an equal split; the other is a Pareto-superior

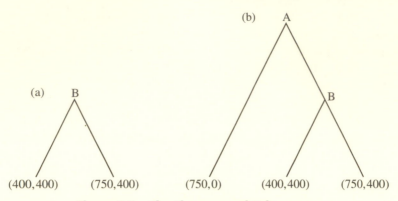

Figure 3.2. The Charness and Rabin games.

allocation giving A the higher payoff. In this game, Charness and Rabin found that while the majority of dictators chose the Pareto-superior distribution, almost a third (31%) selected the equal payoff option. In the game of figure 3.2(b), if player A chooses the right-hand branch, the remaining subgame for player B is identical to the game in figure 3.2(a). In this case, however, almost all B-players (94%) selected the Pareto-superior division. One interpretation of the different plays observed in these games is that behavior in the game in figure 3.2(a) shows some B players to be averse toward taking a smaller share, but that motive is not decisive in the game in figure 3.2(b). Indeed, its operation would seem perverse following a trusting act by A that increases B's payoff but cannot increase their own. But whatever the right interpretation, the example provides a clear illustration of an important general conclusion supported by a range of experimental literature: that preferences over plays in particular subgames may depend on the structure of any larger game in which they are embedded (see Samuelson 2005; Guala 2006). This stylized fact is often interpreted as evidence of "reciprocity" and it tells against the general possibility of identifying games through any process that involves observing choices in different games from those one seeks to identify.

Some interpret the reciprocity evidence as presenting a serious challenge to game theory because it raises questions about the coherence of assuming that game "outcomes" can be ranked in the way that game theory has traditionally presupposed. Or, to put things differently, it raises a conceptual question about whether utilities of the form presupposed in game theory can really be assumed to exist (see Sugden 1991; Guala 2006). To motivate that radical thought, consider this example adapted from Weibull (2004).

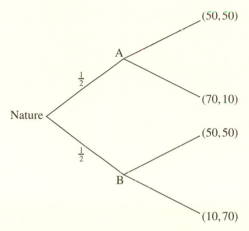

Figure 3.3. The Weibull game.

In this game, nature moves first and selects either A or B to decide upon the allocation to implement in a dictator-like game with two alternatives. The payoffs at the end of the tree are to be interpreted as *material* pay-offs (with A's written first as usual). Whoever nature selects as dictator then gets to choose between "UP" (giving each player 50 material payoff units) or "DOWN" (giving the dictator 70 while the other gets 10). Weibull argues that it is coherent to imagine that players of this game could have *interdependent* preferences such that A prefers UP at their choice node *if* B prefers UP at theirs, but A prefers DOWN at their choice node *if* B prefers DOWN at theirs. The conjecture seems a plausible one. But note that if it were true, there would be more than one set of preference rankings associated with the single game form described in figure 3.3.

This example suggests that the problem of game identification may run deeper than we have so far entertained in this chapter, and it pro-vides a new type of reason for being circumspect about the "check the game" response to the issue of uncertainty about the relationship between abstract and implemented games. That response presupposes that the problem of knowing what game is being played, in an experi-ment, is essentially a problem of measurement. It presumes that unique preferences over terminal consequences exist, and that the issue is one of how to elicit or measure them. But another interesting possibility, suggested by the last example, is that some implementable game forms may not have associated with them preferences of the sort that game theory assumes or requires. That is, there may be well-defined imple-mentable game forms that have no unique abstract game associated with them. Were that to be the case, it may be more appropriate to judge that the issue of knowing which game is being played is, at least in part, a conceptual problem in game theory and not simply an issue of measurement. Hence, we have both practical and conceptual reasons for thinking the "check the game" response unsatisfactory.

On the basis of the discussion so far, we think it reasonable to conclude that it will not be possible to eliminate uncertainty about "what game the subjects are playing" in some strategic settings of interest to experimentalists. There is, we suggest, some irreducible Duhem–Quine issue here that, in general, we cannot expect to resolve through more testing and checking. That being the case, what should we make of experiments that purport to test game theory? We suggest that a quasi-Lakatosian perspective throws some helpful light on this. To the extent that one conceives of the act of theory testing as primarily aimed at grappling with underlying theoretical concepts, auxiliary hypotheses (e.g., payoff bridge principles) do seem, frustratingly, to get in the way. However, the framework of MSRP provides a different, and potentially useful, way of construing the nature of theory testing. This is our third, and preferred, line of response. On this view, testing within a given program is not really about attempting to dig down with the aim of exposing core principles to test. Instead, it conceives of research developing as part of a program. Researchers associated with a program should have the objective of expanding its ability to explain phenomena in the world, and testing plays a key role in establishing whether the program is succeeding—the ultimate test for Lakatos being whether it generates novel predictions that turn out to be supported. Within this scheme it is taken for granted that individual propositions—core or otherwise—never face the "tribunal of experience" alone. Instead, predictions arise from relatively complex theoretical frameworks and they form part of a Quineian style web of belief (see chapter 1) that, ultimately, we cannot expect to unpick piece by piece.

This perspective helps to make sense of, and potentially rationalize, various practices evident in contemporary experimental research on games. To begin with it leads us to expect that empirical research with games will involve working with composite hypotheses (e.g., solution concepts plus bridge principles, and so on). It then leads us to structure our interpretation of the literature in new ways. In attempting to impose the interpretive machinery of MSRP on the record of research, we will be directed to look for distinct research programs, defined partly according to which parts of their composite they take as hard core (i.e., as given for the purpose of the program) and which parts of their composite are potential targets for modification and change.

Approaching the literature in this way, we think it is possible to distinguish some quite distinct avenues of experimental games research.

For instance, one stream of research (we will call it the *preference refinement program*) takes certain positions about which solution concepts are predictive as its hard core and treats hypotheses about payoffs as open to adjustment. We interpret much of the literature on social preferences as falling within this preference refinement program, including illustration 5 from chapter 1 (Fehr and Gächter 2000). In contrast, another stream of literature (we will call it the *applied game theory program*) takes hypotheses about payoffs as part of its hard core and treats claims about the predictive success of particular solution concepts as open to investigation and adjustment. We would regard illustrations 4 and 6 from chapter 1 (due to Goeree and Holt 2001 and Morgan et al. 2006) as exemplars of this genre.

In this second program, it has been standard to derive equilibrium predictions for behavior in experimental games by treating the money payoffs subjects may receive as if they were valid counterparts of their utilities. In other words, this program has the standard bridge as part of its hard core. A (naive) critic might complain that this research is based on what appears, from viewing the literature on other-regarding preferences, a suspect assumption. Would they then have grounds for denying the significance of any particular research findings involving the standard bridge? One possible way to defend this literature would be to argue that it generally focuses on classes of games where money payoffs are a reasonably good proxy for utilities. While this could be true for at least a subset of the relevant research, including Morgan et al. (2006), given the practical obstacles to identifying games that we have discussed, we think it would be hard to construct a convincing general defense for the standard bridge across the wide range of applications where it figures. On the other hand, we suggest that borrowed concepts from MSRP provide a way of rationalizing research using it.

The crucial aspect of MSRP needed here is the presumption that in evaluating predictive performance it is programs—not individual propositions within them—that constitute the appropriate level for assessment. To appreciate the significance of this change in emphasis, suppose that the results of some experiment, conducted within the applied game theory program, show that behavior is not well organized by some equilibrium concept currently in standard use within the program. While we cannot argue that this constitutes a direct rejection of that concept, from the point of view of MSRP, such evidence should count toward marking out the limits of the program's current explanatory power. But such predictive "failure" could also provide the impetus for future program refinements that might lead to the development of some more successful solution concept. Were such refinements to occur, if they ultimately led to surprising predictions that turned out to be supported, that should count as evidence of empirical success, and hence progressiveness, of the program. So, while we cannot expect to unambiguously trace the success or failure of particular predictions to particular components within the program, we can ask meaningful questions about whether research conducted within the program is leading, over time, to progress as measured by expanding empirical content. Hence, while it is correct to judge that the results of particular tests cannot unequivocally be pinned on specific components of theories involved in generating predictions that are tested, there is a coherent sense in which programs can use experimental testing strategies to explore the ability of a particular theoretical framework to explain the world.

The arguments of this section also suggest a particular perspective on the question, Is game theory testable? Our view is that game theory cannot be tested in isolation from assumptions that, while extraneous to its central logic, are fundamental to its application as an applied theory in the lab or elsewhere. And, while assumptions standardly used to operationalize game theory (e.g., assuming money payoffs equate to utilities) are at best approximations, economists must face up to the fact that without some such operationalizing assumptions game theory does not really provide them with a theory of behavior in the world at all. Applied game theory necessarily involves a conjunction of conceptual tools and assumptions connecting those to the world. Consequently, to the extent that we seek an empirical game theory with improving capacity to explain behavior in the world, it cannot be a satisfactory defense of predictive failures in the lab to argue that the underlying theory has not been tested. Instead such failures should be seen as setting a challenge for us to refine our empirical theory.

3.5   Hard Cores, Progress, and Experiments

In experimental economics, it is relatively easy ex post to spot analogues of Lakatosian hard cores, operating in the background of various streams of research. We will argue that hard core commitments play an important organizing role in experimental economics research and exert significant influence over the ways in which theories face the tribunal of evidence. As such, we will argue that hard cores have an important mediating function in the process of theory evaluation and that understanding this role constitutes a significant step in appreciating what programs of testing, using experiments, really involve. We illustrate these points via a discussion of developments in the theory of risk preference.

While expected utility theory has been the standard model of risk preference since the 1950s, numerous alternative theories have been proposed in attempts to explain descriptive failures of it, including the famous counterexamples identified by Allais (1953): one of these—the "common ratio effect"—is set out in box 2.6 (p. 74). For present purposes, the details of these anomalies are less important than how economists have responded to them. In a review of this literature, Starmer (2000) argues that a particular style of explanation has dominated attempts to explain anomaly evidence and he refers to theories in this mold as "conventional" theories. Theories following this approach relax the Independence axiom of expected utility theory with a view to accommodating known violations such as the Allais examples, but they retain common structural elements of the standard model. Specifically, they assume that preferences can be represented by *some* function that attaches a unique value to any prospect and that this function is also "well-behaved." This assumption implies that preferences satisfy standard conditions, such as Completeness, Transitivity, and First-Order Stochastic Dominance. Example theories in this mold include generalized expected utility theory (Machina 1982), disappointment theory (Loomes and Sugden 1986), rank-dependent expected utility theory (Quiggin 1982), and cumulative prospect theory (Tversky and Kahneman 1992). While Starmer (2000) does not use this language, we think it is natural to interpret these conventional theories as being part of a research program with a hard-core commitment to building models of well-behaved preference.[14]

This hard core is evident in several features of the literature. One is the set of anomalies that this research has focused upon. While considerable attention has been devoted to explaining some phenomena such as the Allais examples, economists have shown much less interest in explaining other, equally well-documented, deviations from expected utility theory. For instance, there is substantial evidence that minor changes in the presentation or "framing" of choice alternatives can have dramatic impacts upon decisions and illustration 1 from chapter 1 due to Tversky and Kahneman (1981) provides one classic example (for additional evidence see Camerer 1995 and Starmer 2000). On the face of it, such framing effects look like significant empirical phenomena relevant for the assessment of conventional theories since they challenge a principle implicit in them: specifically, the principle of *description invariance* that holds

---

[14] There are, of course, some well-known alternatives to expected utility theory that do not follow this conventional approach, including prospect theory (Kahneman and Tversky 1979) and regret theory (Loomes and Sugden 1982); so, on this interpretation of the literature, these theories must be interpreted as falling outside of the conventional research program.

that choices should not be systematically influenced by mere redescriptions of choice alternatives that do not affect the logical structure of the decision problem. Yet, compared with the effort devoted to explaining phenomena such as the Allais examples, very little attention has been directed, by economists, toward explaining framing effects.

A similar point can be made regarding the principle of First-Order Stochastic Dominance (defined in box 2.5 (p. 72)). While there is considerable evidence showing violation of it (see Tversky and Kahneman 1986; Loomes et al. 1992; Birnbaum and Thompson 1996; Bateman et al. 2007), economists have not been busy trying to explain it.[15] In fact, the situation is quite the reverse because theories that allow such violations have been subject to some strong criticism. One example of this relates to theories that extend expected utility theory by attaching simple decision weights to probabilities, as in the first version of prospect theory (Kahneman and Tversky 1979). They show that the Allais examples can be explained by nonlinear decision weights, but this strategy for accommodating them has the side effect that preferences must violate First-Order Stochastic Dominance. This has generally been regarded as a fatal flaw sufficient to damn theories of this type. Arguments to this effect have been made by Fishburn (1978), Machina (1982), and Quiggin (1982), each of them heavyweights in the arena of choice theory. No doubt conscious of these potential criticisms, as an adjunct to the central features of their theory, Kahneman and Tversky (1979) assume that individuals adopt a choice heuristic (or mental shortcut) that eliminates dominated options, so long as they are detected. But this strategy for inducing First-Order Stochastic Dominance in choices has attracted further criticism from some economists. Quiggin (1982), for example, has criticized the approach on two counts. First, he argues that by appropriate specification of the preference function this heuristic element of the theory could be rendered redundant. Second, he criticizes their heuristic strategy for imposing First-Order Stochastic Dominance because it has the further spin-off effect that the theory then admits violations of Transitivity. Quiggin (1982, p. 327) describes this as an "undesirable result."

What is the basis of this claim? It is not sensibly interpreted as a straightforward appeal to empirical evidence. There is at least some support for the editing "fix" for imposing First-Order Stochastic Dominance adopted in prospect theory (Kahneman and Tversky 1979): specifically, evidence showing that the likelihood of an individual choosing a dominated option from a choice set depends on how easy it is to spot the relation of dominance. Such dependence is an implication of prospect

---

[15] There is further discussion of violations of stochastic dominance in chapter 7.

theory's (nonconventional) heuristic approach and it cuts against the conventional presumption of universally dominance-respecting preferences. Secondly, there is well-established evidence that cyclical choice is a robust and reasonably general phenomenon: Tversky (1969) produced some of the early evidence and we present a more contemporary example shortly in box 3.4. It is true to say that the type of cyclical choice predicted by prospect theory is of an unusual kind and distinct from forms of intransitivity known when prospect theory was proposed. That, however, presents a useful opportunity for testing a novel implication of prospect theory and a test of that prediction appears to find strong support for it (Starmer 1999c).

Notwithstanding this evidence, the economics literature continues to be dominated by models that assume description invariance, First-Order Stochastic Dominance, and Transitivity. We suggest this can be sensibly interpreted as evidence of a *hard-core commitment* of those working in this literature to preference theories based upon utility maximization and hence to particular principles of rational choice that most researchers have taken to be fundamental to the structure of maximizing theories. That commitment has, in turn, delimited certain problems as interesting (i.e., those that appeared at least potentially soluble in terms of the precommitted assumptions) and others as, at least presently, uninteresting (i.e., those that researchers have presumed could not be so handled). Consequently, the effect of adopting this hard core has been to insulate theories associated with it from specific forms of disconfirming evidence by treating that evidence as falling outside the conventional program of risk research.

But in addition to this insulating function, hard-core commitments also steer researchers in their interpretation of particular test results. That is, in the face of competing interpretations of data, researchers associated with a particular program are more likely to pursue interpretations of evidence that are more favorable to their hard-core presumptions. Hence in practice, hard-core presumptions to some extent mediate problems associated with the DQT. As an illustration of this, consider the literature related to the preference reversal phenomenon.

Box 3.4. The preference reversal phenomenon.

Preference reversal is a behavioral tendency for the revealed preference ordering of a pair of alternatives to depend, in a predictable way, on the process used to elicit it. Much of the empirical literature has examined decisions relating to pairs of simple gambles where one of them (the

"*P*-bet") offers a relatively good chance of winning a modest prize (otherwise nothing or a small loss) while the other (the "$-bet") offers a relatively small chance of winning a larger prize. In classic preference reversal experiments, subjects are required to make straight choices between the pairs of bets and to provide separate (usually monetary) valuations for them.

Conventional economic theory implies that the chosen gamble should be valued at least as highly as the rejected bet. But while many individuals are so consistent, a significant proportion typically are not. The existence of some such inconsistency, by itself, is not especially surprising. People might, for instance, make a mistake in one or more task, leading to some level of inconsistency in comparisons of rankings. Interest in preference reversal stems largely from the fact that observed inconsistencies tend to be patterned in a systematic way: the usual finding is that subjects will frequently choose the *P*-bet and value the $-bet more highly (let us call this the *standard reversal*), while very few commit the opposite reversal ($-bet chosen and *P*-bet valued more highly). It is this asymmetric pattern of inconsistencies between the revealed rankings based on choice and valuation that constitutes the intriguing preference reversal phenomenon.

Preference reversal was first observed by psychologists Lichtenstein and Slovic (1971) and Lindman (1971). It was later brought to the attention of economists by Grether and Plott (1979), who described its potential significance for economics in the following passage:

> Taken at face value the data are simply inconsistent with preference theory and have broad implications for research priorities within economics....It suggests that no optimization principles of any sort lie behind even the simplest of human choices.
>
> Grether and Plott (1979, p. 623)

To clearly explain the challenge that preference reversal sets for conventional preference theory, let P and $ represent the two bets; let $M^\$$ and M^P represent their elicited money valuations. An individual who commits the standard reversal reveals $P \succ \$$ in the choice task and records $M^\$ > M^P$ in the valuation tasks. Assuming this individual prefers more money to less, we may write $M^\$ \succ M^P$; and, if the valuation tasks correctly elicit certainty equivalent values, we can write $M^\$ \sim \$$ and $M^P \sim P$. Putting this all together, the observation of preference reversal entails the following set of *intransitive* preferences: $P \succ \$ \sim M^\$ \succ M^P \sim P$.

So, assuming that agents have a unique set of preferences that govern their behavior in choice and valuation tasks and that those preferences are correctly elicited, the occurrence of preference reversal is evidence of nontransitive preferences. While there is some support for this interpretation (see Loomes et al. 1989, 1991), there are other possibilities. One is that different preferences govern decisions in choice and valuation tasks: on this interpretation, preference reversal is a failure of *procedure invariance* (that is, the principle that preferences should be independent of the method of eliciting them). Tversky et al. (1990) present evidence for this interpretation. Yet another is that behavior is not governed by preferences at all (see, for example, Lichtenstein and Slovic (2006), who interpret preference reversal as evidence that preferences are "constructed" through, rather than revealed in, human decisions). While each of these interpretations conflicts with some basic aspect of conventional preference theory (by denying either Transitivity, uniqueness, or existence of preferences) there are other interpretations that would be much less, if at all, challenging to economic theory. For instance, one might challenge whether the experiments that report preference reversal have accurately elicited preferences. Indeed, as we discuss below, a large literature has grown around investigations of whether preference reversal might be explained in terms of biased elicitation procedures and, in particular, biases in the elicitation of valuations.

There is now an extensive theoretical and empirical literature on preference reversal exploring these and other accounts of it. We discuss some further dimensions of this in chapters 4, 6, and 7, and broader reviews are available in Hausman (1992, chapter 13), Seidl (2002), and Cubitt et al. (2004a).

From the early days of this literature, psychologists working on preference reversal tended to treat it as evidence against conventional preference theory and, instead, took it to be a stylized fact to be explained via a genre of theory referring to capacities and limitations of human decision-making processes (see, for example, Tversky et al. 1988). In contrast, most of the research by economists working on preference reversal has looked for ways of explaining it while retaining conventional preference assumptions. A substantial part of this economics literature has consisted in proposing auxiliary hypotheses the failure of which might explain preference reversal without the need to give up the conventional hard core. Research in this spirit has examined whether preference reversal might be explained as a product of biases caused by limitations of the experimental procedures used to elicit preferences. For example, early research of this genre—including Grether and Plott (1979), Reilly (1982), and Pommerehne et al. (1982)—investigated issues such as whether preference reversal might be a consequence of subjects failing to understand the tasks confronting them, or of having insufficient motivation to take those tasks seriously.

We examine aspects of this literature more closely later in the book (see chapters 4, 6, and 7). For present purposes, however, the significance of the example lies in the clues it gives to the existence and function of a hard core operating behind the scenes of the economic theory of risky choice. Why should it be that economists, as compared with psychologists, thought it necessary and worthwhile to invest so much more effort in probing and checking whether apparent failures of conventional preference theory might be explained in some other way? While one possible reading is that economists apply more rigorous scientific standards than psychologists, another—and we think more plausible—reading is to suppose that the effort in such checking was motivated, at least in part, by a precommitment to assumptions challenged by preference reversal data. To the extent that this latter interpretation is correct, we do not think this in itself reveals the presence of an undesirable bias on the part of economists. Rather, we suggest that it provides an illustration of the role that hard-core assumptions play in mediating the DQT issues by steering the interpretation and evolution of testing activity in everyday scientific life.

But if economists do cling to some assumptions demonstrably more tenaciously than others, this begs the prescriptive question of whether such tenacity is justified. We share the Lakatosian instinct that although particular assumptions may be privileged (i.e., treated as hard core) for good scientific reason in the conduct of particular streams of research, long-run attachment to a particular hard-core demands some kind of empirical "progress" in return. While we do not wish to slavishly apply the Lakatosian test for progress, we think that programs of experimental research in economics do display track records of concrete success that compare very favorably with other spheres of economics research. Moreover, as we now argue, the application of experimental methods has been a key factor in stimulating and fostering some demonstrable forms of progress.

One fundamental role of experimental research has been as a generator of anomaly evidence that has provided the initial impetus for extensive and long-running programs. The demonstration of anomalies is often just a first step in a new literature prompting the development of alternative theories to account for them. This is certainly the case in the risk literature, where the 1970s and 1980s witnessed a wave of theoretical activity aimed at accounting for anomaly evidence. Moreover, it is significant that this research program did not come to a halt with the development of new theories but instead moved into a second phase of testing aimed at evaluating the performance of new theories. One can often characterize alternatives to expected utility theory as assuming specific "mechanisms" to explain anomalies (e.g., nonlinear decision weights in prospect theory). Theories then absorb anomalies by "tuning" these mechanisms to predict specific deviations that prompted their development (e.g., specifying a particular nonlinear weighting function in prospect theory consistent with the Allais examples). But the consequence of such tuning is that those mechanisms then imply many deviations from conventional theory in other cases. In other words, these theories explain specific anomalies by postulating more general patterns of deviation from the standard theory. Those predicted patterns then provided the basis for testing essentially novel implications of competing theories.

A considerable literature has grown around testing alternatives to expected utility theory (see Starmer 2000) and it reveals mixed predictive success for the new generation of theories. On the one hand, this literature does not produce convincing support for the general patterns of violation predicted by any of the alternatives to expected utility theory and there has yet to emerge a theory that can unambiguously outperform expected utility theory (Starmer 1992, 2000; Hey and Orme 1994). On the other hand, there is evidence that some alternatives to expected utility theory outperform it in specific domains of application allowing for sensible trade-offs between parsimony and fit (see Harless and Camerer 1994). Consequently, many economists now accept the usefulness of a subset of these new theories for modeling a range of economic phenomena where the mechanisms they embody may be particularly relevant. For instance, the concepts of loss aversion and probability weighting that feature in different variants of prospect theory are slowly becoming part of the everyday landscape of contemporary research, with considerable work now focused on their broader economic implications.[16]

Another striking output of experimental economics research has been the discovery of new empirical phenomena that were unexpected prior to the development of particular theories. An example of this in the context of choice theory relates to the discovery of *choice cycles* predicted by regret theory.

Box 3.5. Regret theory and the novel prediction of choice cycles.

Regret theory was proposed simultaneously by David Bell (1982), Peter Fishburn (1982), and Graham Loomes and Robert Sugden (1982). In the

---

[16] For some examples of this literature see part 2 of Camerer et al. (2004c).

version due to Loomes and Sugden, preferences are defined over pairs of acts, where an act maps from states of the world to (monetary) consequences. Let A_i and A_j be two potential acts that result in outcomes x_{is} and x_{js}, respectively, in state of the world s. The utility associated with having chosen act A_i when state s occurs is given by a function $M(x_{is}, x_{js})$ that is increasing in its first argument and allows the basic utility from having x_{is} to be reduced by "regret" when $x_{is} < x_{js}$ or enhanced by "rejoicing" when $x_{is} > x_{js}$. Regret theory then assumes that individuals behave as if maximizing the expectation of *modified* utility $\sum p_s M(x_{is}, x_{js})$, where p_s is the probability of state s. This is a nonconventional model (because it does not imply a value function defined over individual prospects) though it reduces to expected utility theory in the special case where $M(x_{is}, x_{js}) = u(x_{is})$ and $u(\cdot)$ is a von Neumann–Morgenstern utility function.

Loomes and Sugden (1982, 1987) show that, if preferences in this theory satisfy particular restrictions, regret theory provides a possible explanation of several well-known violations of expected utility theory including some cases of the Allais examples and the preference reversal phenomenon. The most important of these restrictions is a property called "regret aversion" (Loomes and Sugden 1987). This can be stated as a restriction on a further function $\Psi(x_{is}, x_{js}) = M(x_{is}, x_{js}) - M(x_{js}, x_{is})$ such that, for any three consequences $x > y > z$, $\Psi(x, z) > \Psi(x, y) + \Psi(y, z)$. This property gives the model empirical content consistent with previously observed behavior; and as a rough-and-ready intuition, one interpretation of it is that "net regret" grows disproportionately with the distance between the consequence an agent gets and what they might have got, had they chosen differently.

Regret theory (with regret aversion) generates several distinctive properties, including a prediction of nontransitive cycles of pairwise choice. We focus on this implication of regret theory as an example of novel theoretical content. To see how this prediction arises, consider the three acts (A_1, A_2, A_3) described by the matrix below. They are defined over three states of the world (s_1, s_2, s_3), and the numbers in the matrix are monetary consequences.

	s_1	s_2	s_3
A_1	5	0	0
A_2	3	3	0
A_3	2	2	2

Regret theory allows choices over acts with this structure to be nontransitive. If preferences are regret averse, any cycle will be in a specific direction: with A_2 chosen over A_1, A_3 over A_2, and A_1 over A_3. This property of regret theory is explained in more detail in Loomes et al. (1991) but, to gain an intuition for why being motivated by regret may have this consequence, assume an extreme form of regret aversion that results in pairwise preferences being driven by the state of the world with the biggest payoff difference for any given pair of acts. For the comparison of A_1 and A_2, this occurs in s_2 (where the payoff difference is 3) and favors A_2; for the comparison of A_2 and A_3, this occurs in state s_3 (where the payoff difference is 2) and favors A_3; and in the comparison between A_1 and A_3, it occurs in state s_1 (where the payoff difference is 3) and favors A_1. This illustrates, in a much simplified form, why regret theory predicts intransitivity: not in general, but in specific cases and directions.

This prediction has been extensively tested and several experiments, including Loomes et al. (1991) and Steven Humphrey (2001), report observing specific patterns of nontransitive choice predicted by regret theory. To provide a feel for the magnitude of cyclical behavior, in Humphrey's study, the pattern for a typical triple is that between 10% and 20% of subjects displayed preference cycles, the large majority in the direction predicted by regret theory.

While the accumulated evidence provides strong evidence for the existence of a replicable cycling phenomenon, the interpretation of its origins and theoretical implications remains a matter of ongoing debate.

Examples like this last one illustrate the possibility of something akin to empirical progress in the Lakatosian sense being associated with economic research programs involving experiments. That said, there is an interesting sequel to the story of regret cycles. Some tests indicate that the motive of avoiding regret (at least as currently formulated in regret theory) cannot be the primary cause of these cycles (Starmer and Sugden 1998). So, while this cycling is a new and interesting phenomenon, it is probably not ultimately explained by the theory that led to its discovery. So the upshot of this stream of research has been to produce a new puzzle for which there is, as yet, no satisfactory explanation. Examples like this prompt interesting questions about whether economic theory is developing at a satisfactory rate relative to the growing stock of anomalies created by experimental evidence. So, for instance, are the successes we have pointed to in the development of new tools in the risky choice literature essentially swamped by the flow of challenging data from experiments?

We think these are interesting open questions. But whatever one concludes about the success of economics in absorbing anomalies, the case of risk research provides a good illustration of a demonstrably positive role that experiments can and do play in research programs. First, it illustrates how experiments can fuel streams of literature by identifying "anomalies" to be explained. Second, it illustrates the role that experiments play in probing evidence and sifting competing interpretations. Third, it illustrates how experiments can be marshaled to provide direct comparative tests of competing theoretical hypotheses, a process that has aided the selection of new applied tools. Finally, it illustrates how experimental research can sometimes lead to the discovery of genuinely surprising new facts about the world.

3.6 Conclusion

In this chapter we have focused on what the enterprise of testing economic theories, via experimental methods, involves in practice. We began by arguing that, like all forms of testing, it is complicated by the fact that tests necessarily bear down on sets of, as opposed to individual, hypotheses. Consequently, test outcomes are always open to interpretation, leaving scope for quarrels about what the data show. This fact about scientific research provides one obvious motive for engaging with prescriptive methodology because it leads us to ask whether some interpretations are better than others.

On the other hand, the very problem that prompts this case for prescriptive criteria also undermines one of the most celebrated attempts to lay prescriptive foundations for science: that is, Popperian falsificationism. We have argued that while the DQT is a fundamental problem for what is sometimes called "naive" Popperianism, it is considerably less problematic in the context of the reformulated or "sophisticated" version of Popperianism advocated by Lakatos. In this chapter we have drawn on aspects of Lakatos' framework and, in doing so, we think we have sketched out a more accurate and helpful account of what experimental testing is and how research involving it should be appraised.

An overarching theme is that for the descriptive purpose of understanding what testing involves, it is helpful to conceive of it as going on, over time, within communities of researchers who hold to (perhaps implicit) conventions and background assumptions. Our discussion of testing game theory illustrates that experimental research involves (among other things) attachments to an underlying conceptual machinery (e.g., standard solution concepts) plus various assumptions required to connect that machinery to the world (e.g., the assumption that money payoffs be read as utilities). We have argued that without some such connecting assumptions, game theory is untestable and devoid of empirical content. Thus, while assumptions about, for example, how concrete payoffs map into individual utility are extraneous to the abstract conceptual machinery, they are nonoptional if the theory is to be used empirically in the lab or beyond. Perhaps, then, we should get more used to thinking of these connecting assumptions as fundamental components of our applied theories that play crucial roles in determining what our theories predict about the world. Viewed in this way, they are an integral part of the applied theory.

A second key feature of MSRP that we have borrowed is the presumption that researchers working in particular fields will privilege various assumptions and methods. It is as if researchers, working within given programs, are setting sail in their selected sea of anomalies, taking with them a bag containing only their own peculiar tools and thus having a precommitment to explain what they find on their travels using, largely, what they packed before they left home. In our discussion of the risk program, we suggested that one can readily find evidence of various precommitments at work, shaping the evolution of research activity. From the point of view of MSRP, some such precommitments are a necessary part of properly functioning science. On the other hand, some critical appraisal of what is achieved via their specific commitments is fundamental if scientific communities are to avoid slipping slowly from science to prejudice. The key test proposed by Lakatos is that research programs should generate "progress" by way of a stream of theoretical developments with expanding content and leading to the discovery of novel empirical phenomena. While we are inclined to interpret the notion of progress more broadly than Lakatos, the demand that continued attachment to research programs be conditional upon *some* measure of demonstrable progress with an empirical component seems a sensible goal that we thoroughly endorse. In relation to research on risky choice, we have argued that experimentation has played a key role in fueling theoretical developments. And while we have signaled some reservations about the extent to which the relevant *theory* has so far progressed, our assessment is that the application of the experimental method has played an effective and positive role in challenging existing theory, and in enriching the evidential base against which theories can be judged. We take this to be a common and very positive characteristic of all the major programs of experimental research in economics.

Finally, the discussion of this chapter leads to a modified picture of what testing is, against which the DQT seems much less problematic. While we endorse the force of the DQT in telling us that there can be no decisive tests, its significance is diluted by dispensing with a view of testing that sees it as a hammer delivering knock-down blows. To the extent that testing provides robust answers to questions of interest, it probably does so only in the long run through sustained programs of research. Perhaps, then, it is better to think of testing as being about asking many questions of roughly the form, What do we see if we look at such and such? While the questions may be motivated by particular theoretical frameworks, the individual answers are rarely, if ever, decisive facts determining the fate of those frameworks. But, hopefully, as a result of observing the answers to many such questions, we slowly revise our picture of how the world looks. Putting things in this way hints at a more inductive account of the role that testing plays in the growth of knowledge. At this stage, that is no more than a hint, but it sets the rudder toward the theme of the next chapter.

4

Experiments and Inductive Generalization

4.1 Preliminaries

The two previous chapters have looked at the use of experiments to test theories. When experimental economics was taking off in the 1980s, most practitioners interpreted their work as theory testing. But as experimental methods have become established in economics, there has been a gradual change in practice. Increasingly, experiments are used not only to test preexisting theories but also as part of the process by which theories are created, and even as alternatives to theory as ways of understanding the world. The present chapter considers these other uses of experiments.[1]

The idea that the role of experiments is to test theories coheres with a general view of economics in which theory takes center stage, and in which theorizing is seen as a deductive exercise. More precisely, the view we have in mind rests on two tacit presumptions. The first is that knowledge in economics is primarily encoded as a collection of theories, and as the record of how successfully those theories have withstood empirical tests. The second is that the way to construct a useful economic theory is to start with assumptions that are as credible as possible—either because they are taken from a standard set of uncontroversial theoretical assumptions, or because they correspond with common experience or with common-sense intuitions—and then to deduce some significant and perhaps counterintuitive conclusion that can be applied to some area of real economic life. Conversely, the newer uses of experiments that we discuss in this chapter go together with a less theory-centered view of economics, in which knowledge can be encoded as untheorized regularities or "stylized facts," and with an approach to theory building that gives more emphasis to organizing previously discovered regularities. In this respect, we shall argue, developments in

---

[1] This chapter draws on ideas first presented in Sugden (2005, 2008).

experimental methods are part of a significant shift in the methodology of the discipline. We try to explain this shift, and to characterize and codify its implications for the practice of experimental economics.

4.2 Deduction versus Induction

At least until the 1980s, the prevailing approach to explanation in economics was deductive. The *deductive method* begins with general propositions—"axioms," "laws," "assumptions," or "hypotheses"—that are accepted as true or assumed to be true. These are combined with more specific assumptions about the environment for which predictions or explanations are required. Conclusions are then arrived at by a process of logical deduction. In its most traditional a priori form, the deductive method starts from general "laws" whose truth is claimed to be beyond reasonable doubt. Over the years, this approach has been defended by many methodologists of economics, beginning with John Stuart Mill (1843, book 6, chapters 1–4). It was endorsed by Lionel Robbins in one of the most influential works of economic methodology of the twentieth century:

> The propositions of economic theory, like all scientific theory, are obviously deductions from a series of postulates. And the chief of these postulates are all assumptions involving in some way simple and indisputable facts of experience relating to the way in which the scarcity of goods that is the subject matter of our science actually shows itself in the world of reality....These are not postulates the existence of whose counterpart in reality admits of extensive dispute once their nature is fully realized. We do not need controlled experiments to establish their validity: they are so much the stuff of our everyday experience that they have only to be stated to be recognized as obvious.
>
> Robbins (1935, pp. 78–79)

In the decades after Robbins wrote this, economists became less willing to claim the status of known truth for the "lawlike" propositions from which their deductions were made. Instead, those propositions were interpreted as provisional hypotheses. This variant of the deductive approach is known to methodologists as the *hypothetico-deductive method*. A crucial feature of this method is that theoretical propositions need not be directly grounded in observations of the world: it is the *conclusions* of the theoretical reasoning, not the premises, that are required to be confirmed by real-world evidence. If some conclusion of a theory is not confirmed, one or more of the premises from which it has been derived must be revised. Thus, the hypothetico-deductive method can

be thought of as the pursuit of theoretical hypotheses whose implications are consistent with the evidence of observation; the resulting
theories are interpreted as *explanations* of the evidence. In practice,
however, economists have been strongly committed to a core set of
assumptions about rationality, usually expressed as particular restrictions on individuals' preferences and beliefs. Until relatively recently,
the idea that those assumptions might need to be revised in the light
of regularities found from below was not seriously entertained. Thus,
economic theory retained many of the characteristics of earlier a priori
analysis.

This does not mean that model building was carried out without reference to evidence. Even though the core rationality assumptions had a
privileged status, it was still possible to move from observed regularity
to theory, as well as from theory to empirical test. This was possible
because of the room for maneuver in constructing a model of any concrete situation. For example, in the 1970s, a major research program in
economics was concerned with the application of rational-choice theory
to public choice. One of the most intractable problems in this program
was (and remains) that of explaining why people vote in elections.[2]

Although most of the theories that were put forward to explain voting were constructed within a rational-choice framework, many different specifications of voters' preferences were proposed, with different
implications for voting behavior. In choosing between alternative specifications, theorists responded to evidence about how, in real elections,
participation rates varied with voters' education, voters' income, the
expected closeness of the result, voters' self-reported sense of obligation, the cost of voting, and so on. Rational-choice theories could then
be configured to fit the evidence. For example, an observed positive correlation between participation and education could be interpreted as
suggesting that voting behavior is influenced by the costs of gaining
information about relevant outcomes (which might be less for people
with more education). Alternatively, it could be interpreted as suggesting that voting behavior is influenced by voters' sense of civic duty (which
might be greater for people with more education).

But even though the hypothetico-deductive method allows theoretical
premises to be revised in response to evidence, its advocates have had
little to say, either descriptively or normatively, about the methods by

---

[2] The problem is that, for an individual voter, the act of voting seems to involve significant costs, while in a large electorate, with the rates of participation typically observed
in national elections, the probability that any individual vote will affect the outcome is
vanishingly small. For a review of public choice theorists' attempts to explain voting
behavior, see Mueller (2003, chapter 14).

which scientists construct hypotheses in the light of observation. The emphasis has been on how hypotheses, once formulated, are tested, and on the inferences to be drawn from those tests.

In the language of philosophy of science, the process of inferring general theoretical propositions directly from observations of the world is "induction." Traditionally, the deductive method is contrasted with the *inductive method.* The inductive method proceeds by observing regularities in the world; further observation allows more refined descriptions of these regularities to be made; theories are then distilled from the observations to explain (or, an empiricist might say, to organize) what has been found. One of the big questions of philosophy of science is whether there are rational principles of "inductive inference," in some way analogous with the logic of deduction, that can be applied in the context of scientific discovery.[3] The philosophers who have thought that such principles exist (and have tried to formulate them) include Mill (1843), who, despite characterizing economics as a deductive science, saw nothing problematic in the idea of inductive science. However, a pervasive view in twentieth-century empiricist philosophy, and one that has been particularly influential in economics, holds that induction is not subject to rules of rationality or logic, while deductive theoretical reasoning and hypothesis-testing are. If one accepts this view of induction and if one sees the purpose of methodology as being to formulate a "logic" of scientific method or of scientific knowledge (as the title of Karl Popper's great work implies), the inductive side of science is something of an embarrassment. One has to conclude, as Popper (1934) does, that the creation of hypotheses takes place outside this logic.

The idea that induction is outside the scope of methodology is expressed with characteristic force by Milton Friedman in his famous essay on economic methodology:

> On [the construction of new hypotheses] there is little to say on a formal level. The construction of hypotheses is a creative act of inspiration, intuition, invention; its essence is a vision of something new in familiar material. The process must be discussed in psychological, not logical, categories; studied in autobiographies and biographies, not treatises on scientific method; and promoted by maxim and example, not syllogism or theorem.
>
> Friedman (1953, pp. 42–43)

---

[3] The "inductive method," as we interpret it, is not adequately represented by the principles of Bayesian probability, even though there is a sense in which those principles support a logic of induction. In the Bayesian logic, prior subjective probabilities about the truth of general propositions are revised in the light of specific evidence, but there is no way by which observation can lead to the discovery of genuinely new propositions about the world.

A similar reluctance to engage with induction can be found in an influential account of the methodology of economics written almost forty years later by Daniel Hausman (1992). Hausman argues that economics uses a version of the hypothetico-deductive method (that he calls "the economists' deductive method"). Although Hausman does not endorse Friedman's position, and suggests in passing that the hypotheses that serve as premises for the deductive method might be generated by some inductive "logic of discovery" (Hausman p. 302), he does not pursue the question of what this logic might be. His book has almost nothing to say about inductive methods in economics. One of the main aims of the present chapter is to show that a method of systematic inductive enquiry is now evolving in experimental economics.

4.3   How Inductive Investigation Works

We begin with an example of a research program whose methods have been predominantly inductive.[4] We have deliberately chosen a non-experimental research program from outside economics, so that we can highlight some fundamental features of inductive enquiry before raising issues specific to experimental economics. We do not claim expertise in the relevant research area, epidemiology; we rely for our information on a popular work by one of its leading investigators, Michael Marmot (2004). Our interest is not in the validity of the inferences that Marmot draws from the evidence he reviews, but in the methodological strategy that he is following.

Starting in 1967, Marmot and his associates have carried out two large-scale longitudinal studies of the health of British civil servants, the results of which began to be reported in 1978. The initial focus was on heart disease in men; the reasons for studying civil servants were simply the need for a large number of participants and the convenience of using employees in a single organization. One of the most surprising findings has been that mortality rates show a steep "social gradient": they decline progressively as one moves up the civil service hierarchy. For men aged between forty and sixty-four, the mortality rate for the lowest of the four civil service grades (office support) is four times that for the highest (administrative). This difference persists after retirement age; even for men aged between seventy and eighty-nine, the mortality rate is twice as high for the lowest grade as for the highest. This finding is surprising, since there seem to be no obvious health-related

---

[4] The idea of using this example was borrowed by Sugden from a lecture given by Nancy Cartwright, but what follows is our analysis of the example, not Cartwright's.

differences in working conditions between the grades (they are all office-based jobs); although incomes increase with occupational status, even the lowest-grade workers have job security and do not live in poverty.

Taken at face value, this result suggests that low occupational status may be a cause of ill-health. However, other explanations might seem more plausible. For example, it is well-known that smoking and unhealthy diets are more common in lower social classes. So perhaps what are being picked up are the effects of a social gradient in lifestyle, rather than the effects of status itself. Since children tend to inherit the social class of their parents, people in the higher civil service grades will, on average, have had more affluent childhoods. So perhaps what is being picked up is the effect of childhood environment on health in later life. Higher-grade workers are better paid, and so may be buying better-quality medical care. So perhaps low status does not cause illness, but only affects how people's illnesses are treated. Marmot investigates these possible explanations by using statistical controls. For example, in studying mortality from heart disease, he controls for the main recognized risk factors: smoking, high blood pressure, high cholesterol level, high blood sugar level, low height. These risk factors have their own social gradients (this is true even of height, which is positively correlated with social status); but, after controlling for all of them, a large part of the social gradient in mortality remains. The incidence of disease shows the same social gradient as mortality, so the latter cannot be the effect of better health care. It seems that the original finding is not just a spurious correlation.

Another way of trying to understand this finding is to investigate whether the correlation between occupational status and health appears in other populations. Looking within his civil service population, Marmot investigates whether the social gradient in mortality is found for some diseases but not others, and finds it to be a feature of most causes of death. He points to evidence of similar social gradients in health in other populations. Analogous gradients have even been found for non-human primates. For example, a study of a population of laboratory monkeys has found that higher-ranking monkeys are less susceptible to heart disease, even though there is no difference in their diets. In a controlled experiment, social ranking has been manipulated by moving monkeys between groups. When the ranking of a monkey is changed in this way, its health status changes accordingly. This suggests that, for these monkeys, there is a direct causal relationship between status and health. Since there is a presumption that similar effects have similar causes, these findings make more credible the hypothesis that, for human beings, there is a direct causal relationship between status and health, and that the causal mechanism is common to monkeys and human beings.

What could this causal mechanism be? Marmot points to various findings that suggest that the mechanism may be related to stress. For example, studies of wild baboons have found both a status gradient in health and a negative correlation between status and biological stress markers. Among humans, stress is known to be negatively associated with the perception of being in control of one's life, and high-grade jobs allow greater control. Biologically, stress is a response to threat, involving physiological mechanisms (for example, increases in heart rate, increases in blood pressure, the secretion of particular hormones, the diversion of blood from the intestines) that are known to be associated with heart disease and diabetes. A hypothesis that at first sounded far-fetched—that occupational status in the civil service has a causal effect on health—is beginning to look credible.

Notice how Marmot's investigation starts from the discovery of a surprising empirical regularity that needs to be explained, not from a surprising theoretical hypothesis that needs to be tested. That is not to say that the regularity is a collection of "raw" or "untheorized" observations, but only that the conceptual framework within which it is described does not provide an explanation for it. For example, the regularity that initiated Marmot's project is formulated in terms of a hierarchy of civil service grades. That conceptual structure would have been salient to anyone who worked with British civil servants in the 1960s, but civil service grades are not simple facts of observation. Similarly, the concept of a mortality rate can be understood only within a framework of statistical theory. To understand Marmot's discovery, we need to see the world in a very particular frame. But we are still left with a surprising and unexplained regularity.

The main strategy of investigation is to try to arrive at more precise, more useful, or more suggestive specifications of that regularity. In this respecification, some factors that initially had seemed to be candidate explanations are eliminated, making the regularity simpler and sharper. In parallel, possible generalizations of the regularity are explored. Progressively, we move from an apparently arbitrary and isolated observation (among male civil servants in Britain, mortality is lower at higher grades) to propositions that are more promising candidates for theoretical explanation (after controlling for the effects of lifestyle and upbringing, there is a negative correlation between mortality and occupational status; among several primate species, there is a negative correlation between mortality and social rank). In order to achieve this kind of respecification, researchers draw on their knowledge of already-established theories and empirical regularities. (The fact that smoking has a social gradient and is a major cause of death suggests the usefulness of controlling for smoking behavior when investigating the relationship between status and mortality; the fact that primate species have many physiological and behavioral characteristics in common suggests the usefulness of investigating whether social gradients in human health have analogues in other primate species.) As the specification of the regularity is refined, the range of possible explanations is narrowed down, and so the likelihood increases of discovering underlying causal mechanisms. But it is possible to progress a long way in specifying a regularity without having any definite hypothesis about its explanation.

As the investigation proceeds, ideas about possible causal mechanisms may suggest themselves, and these may guide subsequent work. Marmot's account hints that, from a relatively early stage in his research, he had the hunch that there might be *some* direct causal link between status and health, even though he did not have a clear idea about the nature of the link. Later, the idea that the link might be through stress began to seem credible but, even when the book was published in 2004, this was still only a promising speculation. It had some support from a range of research findings, and it suggested new lines of enquiry, but it was not a formal theory whose implications could be worked out precisely and subjected to testing.

In this respect, Marmot's hypothesis about stress is not at all like the heroic hypotheses that provide classic examples for discussions of the hypothetico-deductive method. Take Albert Einstein's theory of gravitation, with its prediction that, as seen by an observer on the earth, light passing the sun's surface is deflected by 1.7 seconds of arc. This astonishing prediction is a precise implication of a well-defined theory; it provides a means of testing that theory. The test was in fact carried out under the leadership of Arthur Eddington in 1919, when the sun was eclipsed while in line with bright stars, and Einstein's prediction was confirmed.[5] Popper's account of bold conjectures and severe tests (see box 3.2 (p. 108)) fits this episode perfectly. It is hard to imagine a bolder conjecture than Einstein's theory, which challenged what had long been thought to be the immutable laws of Newtonian physics. Since this

---

[5] Mayo (1996, pp. 278–93) gives a methodological account of this experiment. She shows that many of the issues involved in interpreting the experimental data concerned statistical inference from noisy data: given the margins of error in observation and possible confounding effects, what should be inferred about the actual deflection of light at the time of the eclipse? These issues are analogous with those we discuss in chapter 7.

theory, and no other known at the time, predicted a deflection of 1.7 seconds, Eddington's experiment was an extremely severe test. In contrast, untheorized hunches about causal mechanisms, such as Marmot's hunch about stress, cannot be tested like this.

This is not to say that formal hypothesis tests have no role in inductive research: quite the contrary. The difference is that, in an inductive research program, the hypotheses being tested are not typically reached by deduction from well-specified theories. Instead, they are propositions about empirical regularities. For example, consider Marmot's most basic empirical claim: that mortality rates are higher at lower grades in the British civil service. If that claim is to be interesting, it must be a claim about the whole population of British civil servants and not merely about the sample that happened to be picked for the study. Whenever inferences are made from samples, there is the possibility of sampling error: the observed properties of the sample may not hold for the whole population. A standard way of dealing with this problem is to specify null and alternative hypotheses. In the present case, the obvious null hypothesis is that, in the whole population, mortality rates are the same for all grades. A simple alternative hypothesis is that mortality in the two highest grades is different from that in the two lowest. Then we can ask the following statistical question, What is the probability that, were the null hypothesis true, a random sample (of the same size as the actual sample) would show a difference in mortality between high and low grades at least as great as the difference actually observed? If this probability is very small, we are entitled to infer that the alternative hypothesis is (very probably) true.[6]

Hypothesis tests of this kind are fundamental to any empirical research program, whether the aim is to test theoretically derived hypotheses or to discover previously unknown regularities. Our point is that while null and alternative hypotheses must have precise specifications, neither needs to be supported by any theory. There need be no bold conjecture to put to a severe test. Inductive enquiry can use formal statistical methods while investigating the flimsiest of hunches, expressed in the vaguest of terms.

Many philosophers of science have thought that an inductive methodology requires formal principles for deriving general propositions from evidence. Some have doubted whether any such principles can be justified: this is the skepticism about the existence of a logic of induction that we mentioned in section 4.2. For example, Popper presented his

---

[6] This is clearly the case in Marmot's study, which uses a massive sample of 18,000 individuals.

account of scientific theories as a way of escaping this problem. In Popper's account, no theory is ever proved to be true; the most that can ever be said of a theory is that it has so far withstood all attempts to disconfirm it. Others have thought that the propositions of inductive science need to be understood as statements of subjective belief. This leads to the idea that inductive methodology should be based on the principles of Bayesian statistics, in which subjective degrees of belief are expressed as probabilities, and these probabilities are revised as new evidence becomes available. We suggest that inductive enquiry does not need to be structured in terms of principles for deriving general propositions from particular evidence. Consider how, in Marmot's research program, evidence is collected, collated, and used. Certainly, when Marmot *interprets* the body of evidence generated by this program, he expresses subjective judgments of the kind that are represented in Bayesian statistics—for example, that it seems *likely* that there is a direct causal link between status and health, working through some stress-related mechanism. But the evidence itself is structured in terms of formal statistical tests that make no use of subjective probabilities. (Take the proposition discussed in the preceding paragraph, that there is less mortality in the higher civil service grades than in the lower ones. From the evidence of Marmot's sample, we can infer that this proposition is very probably true. The "very probably" here is not a degree of belief, derived by updating prior probabilities; it is a statement about the frequency with which data of the kind observed would be generated by a particular null hypothesis.) The basic building blocks of inductive enquiry are not subjective judgments: they are regularities in observations of the world.[7]

4.4   Experiments as Tests

If one thinks about the subject matter of economics from outside the discipline, it might seem obvious that inductive research methods could be productive, and that controlled experiments might play a useful part in such research. But when, in the 1980s, experiments first began to be widely accepted in economics, their main role was seen as theory testing. Why was this? We will argue that the explanation is to be found in the methodological practices of economics at that time. Conversely, the inductive use of experiments has become possible only because of a change in methodological conventions.

---

[7] Mayo (1996) gives an account of scientific method that is compatible with this suggestion.

As we pointed out in section 4.2, the prevailing methodology of economics before the recent growth of experimental research was hypothetico-deductive. The emphasis was on building, testing, and estimating models of economic behavior, constructed within the framework of a set of core assumptions about rationality. Theorizing could be responsive to observed regularities in the world (recall the example from public choice theory); but there was no tradition of using *experimental* evidence to guide the formation of hypotheses. In order to think that experimentally observed regularities are relevant for economics, one must have some confidence in the *external validity* of experiments (see box 2.1 (p. 52)). It seems that economists did not have that confidence.

The relevance of experiments was much less contestable when they could be presented as tests of theories that, if taken at face value, applied to laboratory behavior as much as to behavior in the field. Twentieth-century economics prided itself on its generality. Up to the 1980s, the main trends in economics were toward expansion of the domain of rational-choice modeling. The theory of rational choice, first developed to explain consumer choice under certainty, had been extended to choice under uncertainty, public goods, collective choice, and the family. Rationality-based theories, such as rational expectations theory and search theory, were being used to create "microfoundations" for macroeconomic theories that previously had been grounded on assumptions about psychological propensities. Game theory was seen as a way of analyzing the interactions of agents who had common knowledge of their rationality, and there were hopes that the "refinement program" would resolve outstanding problems of equilibrium selection within a framework of perfect rationality. In this climate of optimism—not to say hubris—about the potential of rational-choice theory, there was a prior expectation that the core components of that theory would apply wherever people made choices. If the theory could be expected to explain the behavior of voters in elections, gamblers in casinos, donors to charities, unemployed workers looking for jobs, even men and women choosing marriage partners, why not also that of university students in controlled experiments with real money payoffs? The idea, discussed in chapter 2, that rational choice is an emergent property of particular environments became prominent only much later, after the development of behavioral and evolutionary approaches to economics.[8]

---

[8] When rational-choice theory was first introduced into economics, displacing a previous tradition of psychologically grounded theorizing, there was some recognition that its domain might be limited. In particular, Pareto, one of the founding fathers of rational-choice theory, proposed a version of the discovered preference hypothesis: see Bruni and Sugden (2007).

Thus there was a niche in economics for experiments that tested core components of economic theory. Many early experiments were presented as tests of this kind, in which experimental controls were used in place of the more familiar statistical controls of regression analysis. The experimental strategy can be described as follows: take some preexisting theory from the core of economics; configure the laboratory environment so that in most respects it reproduces the abstractions of the theory, but allows subjects some of the freedom of action that agents have in the field; then investigate whether the theory's predictions are confirmed. As we now show, this strategy was common to two of the first sustained research programs of experimental economics.

Our first example is the experimental investigation of *the determination of market prices*. This program began as an investigation of one of the most fundamental theoretical hypotheses in economics: that in markets with many buyers and sellers, prices are determined by the equilibrium of supply and demand. Its first experiment now has classic status: Edward Chamberlin's experimental market (see box 4.1). Chamberlin's design creates a laboratory (or classroom) market in which participants are induced to act according to supply and demand functions constructed by the experimenter. The experiment tests whether bilateral trades between these participants take place at the prices, and in the quantities, predicted by the theory. Chamberlin's design provided the template for a later program of market experiments, initiated by Vernon Smith (1962)—who, as a student, had participated in Chamberlin's experiment. Smith's first experiments added minor variations to Chamberlin's design and investigated what happened when the same market was repeated several times: his most famous experiment of this kind is described in box 3.1 (p. 99). Subsequently, this line of research diversified to study many different market institutions. The investigation of bubbles and crashes in asset markets, described in illustration 7 in chapter 1, is an example.

Box 4.1. Chamberlin's experimental market.

According to economic theory, in markets with many buyers and sellers, trade takes place at the prices and quantities of competitive equilibrium. This theory is used throughout neoclassical economics, even though there is no generally accepted explanation of how equilibrium is reached. The classic theoretical analyses of equilibrium rely on clearly unrealistic as-if mechanisms, the most famous of which is the "Walrasian auctioneer." (The Walrasian auctioneer announces provisional prices, to which traders respond as if those prices were fixed and final. The auctioneer then revises the prices in response to excess demands and supplies, as signaled by the traders' bids. This mechanism is iterated until all markets clear. No trade is permitted until market-clearing prices have been found.) Implicit in microeconomic theory is the claim that in a real decentralized market, the interaction of profit-seeking or utility-maximizing traders leads to the same outcome as would occur in a Walrasian auction.

Chamberlin (1948) realized that this hypothesis could be tested experimentally. His strategy was to create experimental markets in which subjects played the roles of buyers and sellers. Each seller was endowed with one unit of a commodity (the same commodity for all sellers); he was instructed to try to sell the commodity for the highest possible amount of money, provided this was not less than some given reservation price. Each buyer was instructed to try to buy the commodity for the smallest possible amount of money, not greater than some given reservation price. Different subjects had different reservation prices; each subject knew only his or her own reservation price. The arrays of sellers' and buyers' reservation prices allow the experimenter to construct supply and demand functions, and thus to identify the competitive equilibrium. But instead of implementing a Walrasian auction, Chamberlin brought his subjects together in a room and allowed them to circulate and engage in bilateral bargaining. When a contract was made, the price was written on a blackboard, visible to the other subjects. This setup can be interpreted as a simple model (in flesh and blood, rather than in mathematics) of a decentralized market in the field, such as private trading in second-hand cars.

Walrasian theory makes clear predictions about the price and quantities at which trade will take place, but the subjects in Chamberlin's experiment are free to trade at any mutually agreed prices. Thus, a genuine test of the theory is possible. In fact, Chamberlin found a systematic deviation from Walrasian predictions; on average, his subjects traded larger quantities than were predicted, at lower prices.

Our second example is the investigation of *individual decision-making behavior*. Here, the received theory is that economic agents act on preferences that satisfy standard conditions of rational consistency. In the theory of consumer choice, preferences are defined over bundles of goods and are assumed to satisfy conditions such as Completeness, Transitivity, Nonsatiation, and Convexity; built into the conceptual framework is an assumption of reference-independence (that preferences do not vary according to the individual's current endowment or expectations). In the theory of choice under uncertainty, preferences are defined over prospects (arrays of consequences and associated probabilities) or acts (assignments of consequences to uncertain events); they are assumed to satisfy the axioms of expected utility theory (see box 2.5 (p. 72)). These theories are used throughout economics, but there is no generally accepted explanation of why they work—if indeed they do. Economists have been reluctant to claim that human beings "really" are hyperrational, and have usually treated rationality as an as-if hypothesis. For example, in his essay on the methodology of economics, Friedman (1953) denies the relevance of asking whether the assumptions of a theory are realistic (see box 2.4 (p. 61)). All that matters is whether the theory's predictions are reliable.

A number of early experiments set out to test these rationality-based theories of individual choice. Two classic, if informal, experiments were reported by Maurice Allais (1953) and Daniel Ellsberg (1961); the effects that were discovered are described in box 2.6 (p. 74), and in box 4.2. This research program took off in economics with the publication of the work of Daniel Kahneman and Amos Tversky (1979). Experiments in this program confronted subjects with simple, well-defined decision problems. For example, in tests of expected utility theory, subjects typically faced choices between pairs of lotteries, with consequences described in money and risk described either by explicit numerical probabilities or by fully specified random mechanisms, such as rolling dice or drawing balls from urns. Decision problems were constructed to test hypotheses derived from the theory.

Box 4.2. The Ellsberg paradox.

This effect was discovered by Ellsberg (1961). Here is a typical example. An experimental subject is to draw a ball from an urn that contains ninety balls. Thirty of these balls are known to be red. The other sixty are some mix of black and yellow balls, but the numbers of the two colors are not revealed. The subject is asked whether he would prefer to have, say, $50 conditional on drawing a red ball (gamble I), or $50 conditional on black (gamble II). Then he is asked whether he would prefer $50 conditional on "red or yellow" (gamble III), or $50 conditional on "black or yellow" (gamble IV). According to expected utility theory, the subject assigns subjective probabilities to the events "draw a red ball," "draw a black ball," and "draw a yellow ball." These probabilities (that must sum to 1) can be denoted $p(R)$, $p(B)$, and $p(Y)$. The theory implies that the subject will prefer I to II if and only if $p(R) > p(B)$, and will prefer III to IV if and only if $p(R) + p(Y) > p(B) + p(Y)$. Since these two inequalities are equivalent to one another, a preference for II over I implies a preference for IV over III. In fact, people typically choose I and IV.

In each of these research programs, much of the apparent simplicity of the experimental environment is achieved by reproducing the abstractions of the theory being tested. In the market experiments, there is a single homogenous commodity for which each trader has a given reservation price. These are properties of standard theoretical *models* of markets, but it is not clear that they are properties of the real markets that are being modeled. In a real market for second-hand cars, for example, every car has distinct properties, and it is not self-evident that traders have the well-defined preferences from which reservation prices can be inferred. In the decision experiments, the binary nature of the choices reflects the binary structure of the preference relation that is fundamental to theories of rational choice; the lotteries between which subjects choose are constructed to resemble the prospects or acts of expected utility theory. Prospects and acts are properties of theoretical *models* of choice under uncertainty, not of the reality that is being modeled. For example, think of an investor choosing which shares to buy. In conventional theories of the capital market, shares are modeled as prospects, over which agents have expected-utility preferences; but, to the investor, a share does not come with an array of alternative money consequences and associated numerical probabilities. These experimental designs are sacrificing "realism"—that is, similarity to economic problems in the field—to allow sharp tests of received theories.

However, the designer of such an experiment has a ready-made defense against the criticism that the laboratory environment is unrealistic, and that laboratory experiments lack external validity. This is the "blame-the-theory" argument: however unrealistic the experiment may be, its unrealistic features are also properties of the theory that it is testing (see box 2.2 (p. 54)). This argument was commonly used in the early years of experimental economics. It had more force then than it does now because, as we have already pointed out, economists of that period often made very ambitious claims about the domain of application of their theories. By presenting their approach as a theory-testing method, experimenters were able to avoid having to respond to the external-validity challenge while securing a bridgehead in economics. It was only later that an inductive approach to experimentation began to be widely accepted by economists.

4.5 Exhibits

Experimental economics began to expand beyond theory testing as it accumulated a stock of what, following Sugden (2005), we will call "exhibits." An *exhibit* is a replicable experimental design that reliably produces some interesting result.

One way of thinking about exhibits is to imagine preparing a presentation on experimental economics to be given to a large and skeptical audience. Suppose that, as part of your presentation, you have the opportunity to use the audience as participants in just one experiment. The results of this experiment will be analyzed immediately by an assistant, so you will be able to include them in your presentation. You want an experiment that you can rely on to produce a result that will surprise and impress the audience. Unless you are very good at thinking on your feet, you will want to be fairly sure in advance what that result will be. What experiment would you choose? What you are looking for is an effective exhibit.

If you were addressing an audience of economists, you might want to choose an experiment that would produce an *anomaly*: that is, behavior contrary to some well-established theory. We now list seven reliable exhibits of this kind, that will be used as examples in the remainder of the chapter.

One of these is the *Ellsberg paradox*, described in box 4.2 above. Three others have been described in previous chapters; the most salient features of these are recapitulated below.

The common ratio effect. This experiment involves four lotteries. S_1 gives some amount of money (say, 3,000 units of some currency) with certainty. R_1 gives a relatively high probability (say, 0.8) of winning a larger amount of money (say, 4,000). The parameters of these two lotteries are set so that neither is obviously more attractive than the other. R_2 and S_2 are derived from R_1 and S_1 respectively by "scaling down" the probabilities of winning in the same proportion (say, by a factor of $\frac{1}{4}$, so that S_2 gives a 0.25 probability of winning 3,000 while R_2 gives a 0.2 probability of winning 4,000). Subjects choose between R_1 and S_1, and between R_2 and S_2. Expected utility theory implies that a person who prefers R_1 to S_1 will also prefer R_2 to S_2, and a person who prefers S_1 to R_1 will also prefer S_2 to R_2. In fact, there is a tendency for people to switch from choosing S_1 in the scaled-up problem to choosing R_2 in the scaled-down one. For more details, see box 2.6 (p. 74).

Preference reversal. This experiment involves two lotteries, the "P bet" and the "$ bet," that are approximately equal in expected value. The P bet offers a large probability of winning a small prize, while the $ bet offers a small probability of winning a larger prize. In one part of the experiment, subjects are asked to say which of the two lotteries they would choose. In the other part, they are asked to state, for each lottery separately, the smallest amount of money for which, if they owned the lottery, they would be willing to sell it. According to conventional economic theory, choice and valuation provide different ways of eliciting a subject's preference between the two lotteries: someone who prefers, say, the $ bet to the *P* bet should *both* choose the $ bet in the choice task *and* give a higher value to the $ bet than to the *P* bet in the valuation tasks. In fact, there is a tendency for people to choose the *P* bet in preference to the $ bet, but to report a higher money valuation for the $ bet. For more details, see box 3.4 (p. 131).

The ultimatum game. Two subjects are given the opportunity to divide a sum of money, say $10, between themselves. One subject, the "proposer," proposes a division of the money. The other subject, the "responder," then chooses whether to accept this division, in which case each subject gets the amount of money proposed, or to reject it, in which case neither gets anything. On the assumption that individuals are self-interested, conventional game theory predicts that the proposer will propose taking $9.99 for himself, and the responder will accept this. In fact, proposers tend to offer substantial shares to responders, and proposals that offer small shares to responders tend to be rejected. For more details, see box 3.3 (p. 116).

The remaining three exhibits—the *endowment effect*, the *trust game*, and *focal points*—are in boxes 4.3, 4.4, and 4.5.

Box 4.3. The endowment effect and the willingness-to-accept/willingness-to-pay disparity.

The experimental design we describe here is based on one first used by Jack Knetsch (1989). Subjects are divided at random into two groups. Each subject is given a small gift, but the gift is different for the two groups—say, one group gets coffee mugs, the other gets chocolates. A short time later, the experimenter offers each subject the option of exchanging the object she has been given for the other one. If preferences are independent of endowments, the proportion of individuals revealing a preference for the mug over the chocolate should be the same in both groups (apart from sampling variation). In fact, the proportion tends to be higher in the group that has been endowed with mugs. A closely related effect can be generated by the following design (used, for example, by Bateman et al. (1997)). In one group of subjects, each individual is endowed with some good, say a coffee mug, and is asked to state his *willingness-to-accept* (WTA) valuation for the mug: that is, the money price at which he would be indifferent between selling it and keeping it. In another group of subjects, each individual is given no initial endowment of goods (in some variants, a small endowment of money is given). Each is then asked to state her *willingness-to-pay* (WTP) valuation for a mug of the same type that the first group was given: that is, the money price at which she would be indifferent between buying the mug and not buying it. If preferences are independent of endowments, the distribution of valuations in the two groups should be virtually the same, apart from sampling variation.[9] In fact, WTA valuations are usually much higher than WTP valuations: this is the *WTA/WTP disparity*.

Box 4.4. The trust game.

The design we describe was first used by Joyce Berg, John Dickhaut, and Kevin McCabe (1995). It is a game with two players, the "sender" and the "responder." The sender is given a sum of money, say $50. He chooses how much of this to keep for himself. The remainder is tripled and transferred to the responder. The responder then chooses how much of this sum to keep for herself. The remainder of this sum (without further multiplication) is returned to the sender. On the assumption that players are self-interested, conventional game theory predicts that the responder will keep everything she is given and that, predicting this, the sender will keep the whole $50 for himself: that is, there will be no trusting behavior. In fact, senders typically transfer about half of their endowment to the responder. There is a lot of variation in the amounts returned by responders, but the average is typically around one-third of the amount received, so senders get back about as much as they sent, while responders make substantial gains.

Box 4.5. Focal points.

The concept of a focal point is due to Thomas Schelling (1960). Schelling reports informal experiments in which each member of a group of subjects is paired with one other member, but does not know who his partner is. Each is given the same question, with the instruction that he

---

[9] If money endowments are not given to the group that reports WTP valuations, conventional economic theory predicts that WTA will be slightly greater than WTP because of income effects. But this predicted effect is far too small to account for observed WTA/WTP disparities (see Sugden 1999; Horowitz and McConnell 2003).

should try to give the same answer as his partner: for example, "Write down any positive number." In conventional game theory, this is a "coordination game" with many Nash equilibria, all of which are indistinguishable from one another in terms of concepts recognized by the theory. In fact, Schelling's respondents were highly successful in coordinating in this kind of task (the most common answer to the number question is "1"). Schelling argues that people are able to solve such coordination problems by their common recognition that one equilibrium is particularly "prominent" (later theorists have used the term "salient") in some respect that traditional game-theoretic models strip out as irrelevant for rational players; an equilibrium that has this form of prominence is a "focal point." Schelling's experiments have since been replicated, with very similar results, using the kinds of incentive mechanisms and controls that are now standard in experimental economics (Mehta et al. 1994).

The exhibits we have described so far generate surprise—at least for an audience of old-fashioned economists—by revealing behavior that conventional economic theories cannot explain. But what if your audience is not made up of economists? Then you might prefer to surprise them by using an experiment that shows economic theory being successful. Here is an obvious choice (already described in a previous chapter).

Smith's double auction. This experiment is a variant of Chamberlin's market experiment, described in box 4.1. Subjects participate in an experimental market. Demand and supply functions are induced by the experimenter. The market is organized as a double auction in which all traders' offers to buy or sell are announced openly to everyone. The same market, with the same subjects and the same reservation prices, is repeated several times. When this design is used, competitive equilibrium does not appear immediately (just as it was not reached in Chamberlin's nonrepeated experiment). But with repetition, prices and quantities tend to converge to their equilibrium values. As we explain later, this result can be produced in markets with surprisingly few buyers and sellers. For more details, see box 3.3 (p. 116).

Finally, we list an exhibit that lies somewhere between the obvious anomalies and the success stories.

Voluntary contributions to public goods. A small number of subjects is formed into a group. Each subject is given an endowment and is instructed to allocate this between a "private account" and a "public account." All money put in the public account is multiplied by some factor greater than one but less than the size of the group, and then divided equally between the group members. Each person keeps whatever he put in his own private account. On the assumption that subjects are self-interested, conventional game theory predicts zero contributions. In fact, many subjects put significant amounts of their endowment in the public account. However, if the experiment is repeated with the same group of subjects, contributions to the public account fall. For more details, see box 2.3 (p. 58).

With these examples to fix ideas, we consider the role of exhibits in the research programs of economics.

4.6   Why Be Interested in Exhibits?

At the beginning of section 4.5 we defined an exhibit as "a replicable experimental design that reliably produces some interesting result." But what makes a result interesting? An exhibit can be thought of as a mechanism that induces some specific *regularity* (or "effect," or "phenomenon") in human behavior. In a phrase used by Kahneman in informal exposition, the exhibit is a "bottled phenomenon": the regularity is *captured* by the design. Our question can be rephrased as, What makes a regularity interesting?

Often, an exhibit is of interest because the regularity it captures contravenes—or at least, is not adequately explained by—some received economic theory. As we have explained, this is true of the common ratio effect, the Ellsberg paradox, preference reversal, the endowment effect, focal points, the rejection of positive offers in ultimatum games, reciprocating behavior in trust games, and positive contributions to public goods in the voluntary-contributions experiment. Any program of experimental testing of received theories will necessarily create exhibits whenever a theory can genuinely be said to have failed a test. There is a genuine failure only if the test can be replicated with the same negative result; and, if this is the case, there is a replicable experimental design that induces a regularity that contravenes the theory: that is, an exhibit. Thus, the early theory-testing experiments provided a rich source of exhibits.

What about exhibits that confirm received theories? At first sight, it might seem that these do not have any particular value in their own right, since a more general regularity is implicit in the theory itself. For example, if we are convinced that the predictions of the Walrasian theory of markets are *generally* true, there seems to be no extra information content in the proposition that it makes correct predictions about double-auction markets with homogeneous goods. As an analogy, consider Eddington's eclipse experiment that confirmed Einstein's theory of gravitation (section 4.3). That experiment played a major role in convincing physicists of the truth of Einstein's theory, but now that the theory is accepted, it is of only historic interest. However, there are at least two reasons why theory-confirming exhibits are interesting, independently of the support they give to received theories.

First, if a theory passes some tests but fails others, it is important to keep track of both. For example, we now know that Walrasian equilibrium theory works well in the later stages of repeated double-auction markets, but poorly in the initial stages. There is nothing in the theory itself that predicts this combination of observations. Thus, the experimental evidence reveals an empirical regularity—the tendency for market experience to induce *convergence* to equilibrium—for which the received theory provides no explanation.

Second, the received theory may do *better* than was previously expected. As Smith (1962, 1982b) points out, most economists have interpreted the Walrasian theory as a theory of perfect competition, applicable to markets in which the number of traders is so large that none of them has a perceptible influence on the price. For reasons of practicality, experimenters began by studying markets with relatively small numbers of traders. In his first experiments, Smith used numbers of traders (typically, between twenty and forty traders in each market) which, he claimed, were "a replica of real markets," in contrast to the indefinitely large number assumed in theories of perfect competition (1962, p. 115). These numbers proved sufficient to induce convergence to equilibrium. In fact, the same result is found with much smaller numbers. In some of the experiments reported in the later paper, Smith finds convergence in markets with only four buyers and four sellers. With justification, he says: "a priori these experimental results have not been considered intuitively plausible" (1982b, p. 177). This is just as surprising a regularity as the anomalies captured by the theory-disconfirming exhibits.

It seems that *all* of the exhibits we have described are surprising from the viewpoint of received theory. That is, each captures a regularity within what one would take to be the base domain of the received theory, but that would not have been predicted by someone who knew only that theory.

In some cases, the regularity captured by an exhibit is not surprising when it is considered intuitively, rather than viewed through the lens of an existing theory. Indeed, many of the earliest exhibits began as thought experiments. The exhibit was presented to a scientific readership, not as a report of a controlled experiment that had in fact been carried out, but as an experimental design. Each reader was asked to imagine taking part in this experiment; the designer of the experiment reported his prediction about what the reader would do, confident that this prediction would be confirmed. When actual evidence was presented, this was done informally, often with explicit disclaimers concerning its scientific respectability.[10] The common ratio effect, the Ellsberg paradox, and focal points were all introduced in this way. Since such thought experiments draw attention to the reader's own intuitions, their results cannot be completely surprising. Exhibits of this kind are perhaps what Ariel Rubinstein (2001) has in mind when he suggests that robust phenomena can be recognized as such by intuition alone and that, in consequence, pure theorists may be able to substitute their gut feelings for controlled experiments (see chapter 1).

If one thinks of science in terms of bold conjectures and severe tests, the scientific value of an "obvious" exhibit may seem to be low. From a Popperian perspective, it is crucial whether such an exhibit is interpreted as a disconfirmation of a received theory or as positive evidence that a particular regularity or mechanism can be found in the world. Take the case of the Ellsberg paradox. If we interpret Ellsberg's experiment as a test of expected utility theory, it clearly meets the Popperian demand for severity—precisely because there is such a strong intuitive expectation that the theory will fail when subjected to this test. But if this interpretation is used, the conclusion to be drawn from the Ellsberg paradox is simply that a prediction of expected utility theory is disconfirmed: the paradox is not an exhibit of anything positive. In this chapter, our concern is not with tests of received theories, but with the use of exhibits to demonstrate particular regularities in the world. The Ellsberg paradox is usually interpreted as evidence that individuals are averse to "ambiguity" (that is, *uncertainty about* probabilities, as contrasted with "risk," which is defined in terms of *given* probabilities). In this context, a Popperian might reasonably say that there is no boldness in conjecturing what is intuitively obvious. Against this, it could be claimed that the general hypothesis of ambiguity aversion has surprising implications for *some* aspects of decision-making behavior, even if the Ellsberg paradox itself is obvious; but then the Popperian can reply that evidence of the confirmation of one of those surprising implications would have made a more convincing exhibit.

---

[10] For example, Schelling (1960, p. 55) reports some of the results of trying his problems "on an unscientific sample of respondents"; Ellsberg (1961, p. 651) gives a very brief qualitative summary of "a large number of responses [collected] under absolutely nonexperimental conditions."

Still, we want to claim, boldness and surprise are not essential to the value of an exhibit. Even if the regularity captured by an exhibit seems obvious, that exhibit can serve an important function. This function is expressed in Kahneman's metaphor of *bottling* a phenomenon. The exhibit records the existence of the phenomenon in a form that other scientists can verify or challenge, and that they can use as a fixed point in subsequent work. Exhibits impose a structure on regularities that cannot be provided merely by shared intuitions.

In contrast, there are exhibits whose regularities are genuinely surprising implications of controversial theories. One such exhibit was described in box 3.5 (p. 135). One of the most surprising implications of regret theory is that, over certain kinds of sets of three lotteries, there is a tendency for individuals' preferences to cycle in a particular direction. When that theory was first proposed by David Bell (1982), Peter Fishburn (1982), and Loomes and Sugden (1982), there was no evidence of such cycles; the theory was proposed as an explanation of previously established exhibits, particularly the common ratio and related effects. However, subsequent tests of regret theory led to the development of an experimental design that reliably generates such cycles (Loomes et al. 1991; Humphrey 2001). In cases like this, the process by which an exhibit is discovered can be thought of as a Popperian test of a bold conjecture.

There are also exhibits whose regularities were entirely unexpected, even by the researchers who first discovered them. For example, Sarah Lichtenstein and Paul Slovic (1971) discovered preference reversal as a by-product of an investigation of how different modes of assessment of lotteries are affected by lottery characteristics. They found that monetary valuations were best explained by properties of the payoffs, while judgments of attractiveness were best explained by properties of the probabilities.[11] It was only after this discovery that they conjectured that choices between lotteries might be governed by the same mental processes as judgments of attractiveness. Notice that exhibits of this kind are discovered by what Rubinstein (2001) regards as the dubious practice of "sifting results ex post" (see chapter 1). Does this detract from their value as exhibits?

Rubinstein presents this objection in the context of a criticism of what he sees as the lax scientific standards of experimental economists. He argues that experimenters should maintain *protocols*, that is, systematic records of the course of each experiment—that can be accessed by other researchers. His objection is:

---

[11] This earlier investigation is reported in Slovic and Lichtenstein (1968).

> Obviously, if some pattern of behavior, from among an endless number
> of possibilities, is discovered in the data *ex post*, the results are much
> less informative [than if a prior hypothesis has been confirmed]. In the
> absence of rules of maintaining a research protocol one cannot check
> whether the results were conjectured before or after the results were
> obtained.
>
> Rubinstein (2001, p. 626)

We agree that, *in interpreting the results of a single experiment*, there
is an important distinction between hypotheses proposed prior to the
experiment and hypotheses constructed in the light of the results. If an
experiment is carried out to test a single prior hypothesis, and if there
is a regularity in the results that is predicted by that hypothesis but
that would be very unlikely to occur if the relevant null hypothesis were
true, then the proposer of that hypothesis is entitled to claim that it has
passed a severe test. But, as Rubinstein says, there may be many *potential* regularities; the prior probability that one such regularity (*which* one
not being specified in advance) will be found in the results may be quite
high. There is always a temptation for experimenters to overinterpret
their results by giving unanticipated regularities more importance than
they deserve. However, this argument cannot be used to discount the significance of exhibits that were first discovered by ex post sifting of data.

An exhibit, by definition, is a *replicable* experimental design that *reliably* produces particular results. Rubinstein's argument warns us that
most of the apparent regularities that are found by ex post sifting will not
be replicable. It provides reasons for doubting the efficiency of unstructured sifting as a method of discovering exhibits. Nevertheless, if this
method leads us to discover an interesting regularity that *does* turn out
to be replicable, we have an exhibit. Its status as an exhibit is independent
of how we found it.

Even if the regularity captured by an exhibit was initially unexpected,
that exhibit typically attracts attention by virtue of its allegedly illustrating the effects of some specific causal mechanism that the received
theory does not take into account. Often, however, the alleged explanatory factor is described only in broad-brush terms. A common rhetorical
strategy is to focus on the limitations of the received theory, showing its
inability to take account of a certain causal mechanism, and then to rely
on more informal and intuitive arguments to make plausible the claim
that that factor might be the cause of the exhibited regularity.

For example, Ellsberg (1961) presents his paradox alongside the argument that the theory of subjective expected utility cannot distinguish
between risk and ambiguity. The paradox is used to show that "reasonable people" are averse to ambiguity in a way that the received theory

cannot accommodate. Ellsberg's paper ends with a very simple formal model of decision making under ambiguity, but this is presented only as an illustration of the theoretical possibilities, not as a hypothesis to which he is firmly committed. Comprehensive theories of choice under uncertainty, capable of differentiating between risk and ambiguity, were developed only later, by other theorists.[12]

Similarly, Berg et al. (1995) introduce their trust game experiment with the claim: "A fundamental assumption in economics is that individuals act in their own self interest." They contrast this assumption with the hypothesis that "trust is an economic primitive": that is, that economic agents have some direct motivation to trust others and to repay other people's trust in them (pp. 122–23). They refer to a number of different theoretical explanations of trust that have been developed by economists, such as that provided by Matthew Rabin's (1993) theory of "fairness," but they do not apply these theories to the trust game itself, and they do not interpret their results as confirming any specific theoretical prediction. Summarizing their findings, they point to a well-defined negative conclusion—the rejection of the self-interest hypothesis. They are much less specific about the nature of the regularity they *have* found, describing their experiment as "provid[ing] evidence that people are...willing to reward appropriate behavior" and "provid[ing] strong support to...efforts to integrate reciprocity into standard game theory."

Although the researcher who first presents an exhibit normally offers some explanation of the regularity it captures, the exhibit can outlive its association with that explanation. For some of the most important exhibits of behavioral economics, many alternative explanations have been proposed. For example, Allais (1979) explained the common ratio effect and the closely related common consequence effect[13] as the result of complementarities between consequences that occur in mutually exclusive states of the world. (Roughly: if consequences in different states of the world combine to form certainties, those consequences are complementary with one another.) This has remained one of the

---

[12] These theories are reviewed in Sugden (2004b).

[13] The following is an example of the common consequence effect. Lottery R_1 gives a 0.1 probability of $200, a 0.85 probability of $50, and a 0.05 probability of winning nothing. S_1 gives $50 with certainty. R_2 gives a 0.1 probability of $200 and a 0.9 probability of nothing. S_2 gives a 0.15 probability of $50 and a 0.85 probability of nothing. Subjects choose between R_1 and S_1, and between R_2 and S_2. Notice that R_2 and S_2 differ from R_1 and S_1 respectively by the substitution of a 0.85 probability of nothing for a 0.85 probability of $50. Expected utility theory implies that a person who prefers R_1 to S_1 will also prefer R_2 to S_2, and that a person who prefers S_1 to R_1 will also prefer S_2 to R_2. In fact, there is a tendency for people to switch from choosing S_1 in the first problem to choosing R_2 in the second.

main strands of nonexpected utility theory, further developed in Mark Machina's (1982) generalized expected utility theory. However, Kahneman and Tversky (1979) have explained the same effects in terms of properties of the subjective transformation of probabilities into "decision weights"—an explanation embodied in their prospect theory and in rank-dependent theory. And regret theory explains these effects as the result of individuals' disproportionate aversion to large regrets.

Preference reversal provides another example. In presenting this exhibit, Lichtenstein and Slovic (1971) explained it as the effect of differences between the cognitive processes used in choice and valuation tasks. Loomes and Sugden (1983) have explained it as an instance of the cycles of pairwise choice predicted by regret theory. More recently, Sugden (2003) has shown that preference reversal can be induced by loss aversion, while Butler and Loomes (2007) have shown that it can be induced by imprecision in people's preferences.

The point we wish to emphasize is that an exhibit has a scientific status that is independent of any particular theory that may be proposed—whether by the exhibit's creator or by anyone else—to explain the regularity that it captures. Some exhibits are the subject of several rival (or perhaps complementary) explanations; for others, only one explanation has been offered; for yet others, no explanation has been offered at all. Putative explanations may be fully specified theories or mere hunches. Typically, these theories or hunches present the specific regularity captured by the exhibit as illustrating some causal mechanism (or, as some empiricists might prefer to say, some more general regularity) that is claimed to exist. However, in thinking about an exhibit, it is important not to conflate the specific regularity and the causal mechanism. The former has been demonstrated; the latter is only a hypothesis. However it is to be explained, the specific regularity exists. The experimental design that reliably induces it is the proof of this fact.

4.7   Do Exhibits Need to Be Explained?

As a result of experimental research, much of which was initially directed toward theory testing, economics has accumulated a stock of exhibits and associated regularities. These regularities are surprising in that they contravene, or are not explained by, received theory. It seems natural to go on to say that they call for explanation, and that they point to flaws in existing theory that it would be good to remedy. Indeed, it is hard to see how anyone could consistently accept experiments as legitimate tests of a received theory while denying that experimental disconfirmations of the theory call for explanation.

Even so, a momentous methodological step is taken when a discipline starts to treat experimental observations as part of the material that it is to explain. We have suggested that economists' long-standing resistance to experimental methods was based on a reluctance to take exactly this step (section 4.3). So let us pause and consider whether exhibits *should* be seen as necessarily in need of explanation. Of course, that means that we must also reconsider whether the corresponding experiments are legitimate tests of received theory.

A possible argument to the contrary, encapsulated in the slogan "all theories are false," has been put forward by John Hey (2005a). The idea is that no theory in economics can credibly claim to take account of *every* factor that influences the behavior of agents in the relevant environment; thus, no theory can be expected to pass every test to which it is subjected. One way of expressing this thought is to interpret theories in economics as attempts to describe particular *tendencies* or *mechanisms* that operate alongside other mechanisms that are not taken into account.[14] This idea has traditionally been expressed as the formula that a theory's predictions hold "other things being equal," with no precise specification of what those other things might be, or what it would mean for them to be equal or unequal. The operation of these other mechanisms can cause systematic deviations from the theory's predictions in certain circumstances. (Thus, a theory of rational choice might be understood as an attempt to describe those aspects of decision-making behavior that result from sound instrumental reasoning about the consequences of actions. It might be allowed that actual decisions are also influenced by various psychological mechanisms that induce errors of reasoning. The discovered preference hypothesis (see box 2.7 (p. 77)) is an example of just such an argument.) If one thinks of theory testing in terms of a literal-minded Popperianism (with the implication that, contrary to the Duhem–Quine thesis, a theory can be destroyed by a single knockdown blow from the evidence), and if one neglects the "other things being equal" qualification, the theory is liable to fail if it is tested in the presence of the other mechanisms. The greater the statistical power of the tests, the weaker those other mechanisms can be while disconfirming the theory. Since this is a feature of *all* economic theories, it would be nihilistic to claim that any theory that (in the statistical sense) fails a test has thereby been shown to be a failure as a theory.

---

[14] This idea is developed in different ways by Cartwright (1989), Hausman (1992), and Mäki (1992).

Hey draws the conclusion that economists should be concerned with *estimation* rather than *testing*. We should look for theories that offer good combinations of parsimony and predictive power, "good" being interpreted relative to the uses to which the theories are to be put. By expressing rival theories in parametric form and estimating the relevant parameter values, we can find out how well each theory fits the kind of data we are interested in explaining, and then, depending on the relative importance we attach to predictive power and simplicity, we can choose a "best buy." On this view, systematic deviations between prediction and observation are not a cause for concern unless they are large enough and frequent enough to impact on a theory's usefulness in practice. Experimental exhibits merely demonstrate the existence of deviations: they cannot tell us whether those deviations are of practical significance.

We agree that questions about the usefulness of a theory cannot be settled by looking at exhibits. The idea of looking for a theory that works well across a broad range of applications makes a lot of sense, even if it is difficult to give a precise formulation of the concept of a "best buy." (One problem is the need to define a set of cases, supposedly representative of the intended applications of the theory, against which the performance of rival candidates can be assessed. Another problem, that we will discuss in chapter 7, is that, in order to estimate the parameters of a theory, one has to specify an "error mechanism"; the question of which theory is best is difficult to disentangle from the question of which error mechanism should be preferred.) Nevertheless, we maintain that systematic violations of a received economic theory call for explanation. By "call for explanation" we do not mean that any particular economist has an obligation to try to explain any particular anomalies. We mean that an unexplained violation of a received economic theory is a problem *in economics*: it belongs on the discipline's agenda of research questions. It is a signal that some mechanism, not yet understood, is operating in the domain of the theory. It is not possible to know in advance whether a search for that mechanism will yield valuable new knowledge; but it might.

It is a mistake to assume that, just because an anomaly is "small," the mechanism that induces it is not important. Consider an example from the history of astronomy. Early astronomers assumed that planets had circular orbits. Later, it was discovered that their orbits were in fact ellipses, but the error involved in treating them as circular was very small, and a circle is a simpler function than an ellipse. In this sense, the noncircularity of planetary orbits is a minor anomaly. Still, the recognition of this anomaly led to Newtonian physics. Significantly, it revealed that comets were not mysterious exceptions to the normal laws of astronomy: they, too, were satellites of the sun, following elliptical orbits. The point of this particular example is that the domain of the received theory is not necessarily the same as the domain of the as-yet-unknown theory that will supersede it. It is quite possible that the domain of the received theory has come to be defined by that theory's predictive power, excluding cases (in the example, the movements of comets) that, seen from another viewpoint, are glaring anomalies.

To take an example from economics, think of the status of gambling in relation to the theory of choice under uncertainty. Before experimental economists began to investigate the common ratio effect and related exhibits, it was well-known that gambling behavior could not be adequately explained by expected utility theory. (The theory can explain the behavior of people who are risk-loving with respect to *all* decision problems, but it cannot credibly explain why people who are risk averse in many aspects of their lives buy lottery tickets and other gambling products.) That is certainly not a minor anomaly: gambling is a major industry. However, by conceptualizing gambling as a form of entertainment rather than as choice under uncertainty, economists were able to exclude it from the domain of expected utility theory, and so avoid seeing it as an anomaly at all. But the search for explanations of experimental anomalies led to the development of theories that can also explain some forms of gambling. For example, prospect theory postulates the "overweighting" of small probabilities. This is important in explaining some deviations from expected utility theory that are observed outside the gambling world, but it also implies a tendency for small-stake, large-prize gambles to be preferred to actuarially equivalent certainties (Kahneman and Tversky 1979). In regret theory, the same tendency is induced by the assumption that individuals show disproportionate aversion to large regrets (Loomes and Sugden 1982).

4.8 Multiple Causation

We have pointed out that some of the best-known exhibits of behavioral economics have inspired rival explanations (section 4.6). That this is so is partly a reflection of what we mean by "well-known": a well-known exhibit is, as a matter of definition, a center of attention, and having rival explanations is a form of attention. It is partly a product of the incentive structure of the scientific community: the better known an exhibit is, the more prestige there is to be earned by finding a new explanation for it. But, we maintain, deeper causal factors are at work too: the criteria by which exhibits are selected as worthy of exhibition favor phenomena that are capable of being explained in more than one way.

Consider the characteristics of a "good" exhibit—good in the senses of memorable, interesting, and influential. Given that the regularity captured by an exhibit is a violation of received theory, the exhibit is more likely to attract attention the stronger it is (that is, the larger the deviation from the received theory) and the more robust it is (that is, the less sensitive it is to small variations in the experimental design or in the subject pool). Other things being equal, the stronger a regularity, the higher the probability that it will be found as a statistically significant effect in an experiment with a given number of subjects. The more robust a regularity, the more likely it is to be replicated by other investigators.

Suppose that, ranging over the whole domain of possible experiments, there are many independent causal mechanisms, each of which is liable to induce systematic deviations from some received theory. In any specific decision context, some of these mechanisms may work in one direction and some in another. In some cases, they tend to counteract one another; in others they are mutually reinforcing. Some people may be more susceptible to the factors that contribute to one mechanism, others to those that contribute to another. Some experimental designs make one factor more salient, others favor others. Clearly, the strongest and most robust deviations from standard theory will be found in those decision contexts in which these independent causal mechanisms happen to coincide, each inducing deviations in the same direction. Thus, if exhibits are selected for strength and robustness, the regularities that are captured by the "best" exhibits will tend to have multiple causes.

Preference reversal provides a good example. We have already pointed out that preference reversal has attracted several different explanations. Our conjecture about multiple causation suggests that preference reversal may lie at the intersection of more than one causal mechanism. If this is so, apparently rival explanations of preference reversal may in truth be complementary: each may be describing a mechanism that contributes to the phenomenon we observe. In fact, there is good evidence that preference reversal *is* the product of several causal mechanisms. Since the mental-processing mechanisms proposed by Lichtenstein and Slovic (1971) have been found in experimental designs that do not involve lotteries and in which neither loss aversion nor nontransitive preferences would have any effect (see, for example, Tversky et al. 1990), there is strong reason to believe that a major cause of preference reversal works through mental processing. It now seems probable that more than one mental-processing mechanism contributes to preference reversal (Slovic et al. 1990; Cubitt et al. 2004a). At the same time, Sugden's (2003) explanation of preference reversal as a form of loss aversion is based on a close relative of prospect theory; and prospect theory is supported by a very large amount of evidence, quite independent of preference reversal. Cycles of pairwise choice, analogous with preference reversal, have been found in designs in which Lichtenstein and Slovic's mechanism is screened out (Loomes et al. 1991; Humphrey 2001). And this certainly does not exhaust the list of credible explanations of preference reversal for which there is empirical support.

If there is a systematic tendency for "good" exhibits to have multiple explanations, that reinforces a precept we have already proposed: that researchers should be cautious about accepting the initial account of what an exhibit is an exhibit *of*. In presenting exhibits, researchers often claim that what they have found is not just a replicable experimental design but some more general phenomenon or underlying causal mechanism; the regularity revealed in the design is (it is said) just a particularly sharp illustration of that phenomenon or mechanism. As readers of these presentations, we should distinguish between evidence and hypothesis.

It may be tempting to think that the experimenter who first presents an exhibit is somehow at fault if he presents it as evidence of just one mechanism when in reality it reveals the combined effects of two or more. Certainly, one might expect the experimenter to consider causal mechanisms other than that of his preferred account, and to alert the reader to credible alternative explanations of the regularity he is displaying. But he cannot be expected to scan the universe of all possible mechanisms, including those that no one has yet proposed. And it is only natural that a researcher who has a special interest in a particular mechanism will be predisposed to see that mechanism at work in the world. Rather than demanding that the presenter of an exhibit can defend his preferred explanation against all alternatives, it is more constructive to recognize the exhibit for what it is: a regularity that has been shown to exist independently of the truth or falsity of any alleged explanation.

A further implication of the "multiple causation" hypothesis is that the accumulated evidence of anomalous exhibits is likely to overstate the true limitations of received theory. The best-known and most-studied exhibits have been selected for their ability to induce strong and robust deviations from received theory, and so are likely to be located at those points in the space of possible experiments at which several different mechanisms induce the same deviation. This thought provides further support for Hey's argument against using exhibits as tests of the usefulness of received theories. Nevertheless, we stand by what we said in section 4.7: systematic violations of a received theory do not show that that theory is not useful, but they do call for explanation.

4.9   Explaining Exhibits Inductively

We now consider some of the strategies that can be used in trying to explain surprising exhibits. Some of these strategies are hypothetico-deductive in spirit, others are more inductive.

If some implications of an existing theory are disconfirmed, the obvious hypothetico-deductive response is to try to find a way of revising the assumptions of that theory so that the defective predictions are no longer implied, while significant predictions are still made; the revised theory can then be tested. There have been many such responses to the experimental evidence of anomalies. In most cases, new theories have been constructed by making a relatively small number of revisions to a received theory, usually encompassing the received theory as a limiting case. For example, Kahneman and Tversky's (1979) prospect theory, Machina's (1982) generalized expected utility theory, Loomes and Sugden's (1982) regret theory, and Quiggin's (1982) rank-dependent theory make different revisions to expected utility theory so as to explain anomalies observed in choice under uncertainty. Tversky and Kahneman's (1991) theory of reference-dependent preferences revises neoclassical consumer theory so as to explain anomalies associated with the endowment effect. Rabin's (1993) theory of fairness and Fehr and Schmidt's (1999) theory of inequity aversion revise the self-interest assumption of conventional game theory in different ways so as to explain observed behavior in ultimatum, trust, and public-good games. Bacharach's (1993) variable frame theory revises game theory so as to explain coordination on focal points.

In this chapter, however, we are primarily concerned with inductive approaches to the explanation of anomalies. Recall our epidemiological example, in which a program of investigation was initiated by the discovery of a surprising empirical regularity—a relationship between mortality and occupational status in a sample of civil servants. We showed that much of the subsequent investigation was structured around attempts to find ways of respecifying the original regularity in forms that were more susceptible to theoretical explanation. The same general approach can be seen in many experimental investigations of exhibits. In the following subsections, we consider various strategies for respecifying the regularities captured by exhibits. In discussing examples of the use of these

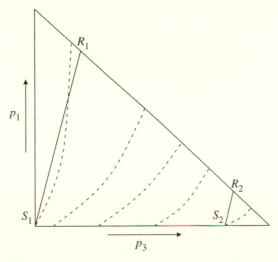

Figure 4.1. The Marschak–Machina triangle and the common ratio effect.

strategies, we focus on methodological issues rather than substantive findings.

4.9.1 Unification

We begin with an inductive strategy that has often been used to guide the development of new theories. This is to take two or more exhibits, previously regarded as distinct, and to *unify* them by describing them as instances of a single phenomenon. Usually, this requires that the regularities that are to be unified are characterized in more abstract terms than have previously been used. For this reason, unification tends to be more reliant on theory than some of the other inductive strategies we will describe.

A classic example of unification provided the starting point for Machina's (1982) development of generalized expected utility theory.[15] Surveying the currently available evidence of systematic violations of the Independence axiom of expected utility theory, Machina realized that many of these anomalies could be described by using a diagram invented by Jacob Marschak, now usually called the *Marschak–Machina triangle*. This is essentially a system of coordinates for representing the set of all probability distributions over three distinct money consequences. Taking the example used in box 2.6 (p. 74), consider the consequences 4,000, 3,000, and 0 (expressed as money values in some currency). Any probability distribution over these consequences can be described by

---

[15] The theoretical and empirical developments sketched in the following paragraphs are explained more fully in Starmer (2000) and Sugden (2004b).

two parameters: the probability of the best consequence (i.e., 4,000), denoted by p_1, and the probability of the worst consequence (i.e., zero), denoted by p_3. Obviously, $0 \leqslant p_1 + p_3 \leqslant 1$, and the probability of the middle consequence is $1 - p_1 - p_3$. In the triangle diagram, p_3 is measured on the horizontal axis and p_1 on the vertical. Figure 4.1 shows the four lotteries of the common ratio effect in a Marschak–Machina triangle. Notice that the line joining S_1 and R_1 is parallel to that joining S_2 and R_2. Expected utility theory implies that an individual's preferences over lotteries can be represented by a family of upward-sloping indifference curves that are linear and parallel. (The upward slope is an implication of the assumption that higher probabilities of better outcomes are preferred to lower probabilities; linearity and parallelism are implications of the Independence axiom.) Machina noticed that several different anomalies (including the common ratio and common consequence effects) could be explained by postulating upward-sloping indifference curves that, contrary to the Independence axiom, "fan out": that is, are more gently sloped toward the bottom right of the triangle and more steeply sloped toward the top left (represented by the dashed curves in figure 4.1). He then found a theoretically elegant way of generalizing the fanning-out hypothesis to all lotteries, by weakening the Independence axiom of expected utility theory while retaining its other axioms.

Subsequent experimental investigations have shown that Machina's fanning-out hypothesis is too simple; but the idea of representing patterns of choice under uncertainty in terms of indifference curves in Marschak–Machina triangles has proved very fruitful. It has provided a structure for experimental and theoretical work, with the common aim of finding general characterizations of preferences over lotteries, consistent with experimental evidence. This has allowed hypothetico-deductive approaches (working downward from allegedly credible axioms about preferences) and inductive approaches (working upward from observed regularities in behavior) to develop in partnership.

4.9.2 Checking for Confounds

In experimental terminology, there is a *confound* when two or more putative mechanisms are capable of explaining the same experimental result: the attempt to isolate one mechanism is confounded by the possibility that another mechanism is operating. When an experimental result is presented as evidence for the existence of one mechanism, critics who suspect that the result has been caused by a different mechanism sometimes say that the result is an *artifact*, with the connotation that it is artificial rather than real. However, the distinction between artificial and real can be unhelpful: one man's artifact is another man's phenomenon. What matters is whether the result is caused by the mechanism that has been proposed as its explanation. When this is uncertain, further experiments can be used to try to resolve the issue. If these attempts are successful, the result is a sharper specification of the regularity captured by the original exhibit.

For example, preference reversal was presented by Lichtenstein and Slovic (1971) as evidence of differences between the mental processes used for choice tasks and for valuation tasks. Charles Holt (1986) responded with a theoretical argument that showed that, in certain experimental designs and under certain assumptions, preference reversals can be the result of subjects acting on preferences that violate the Independence axiom of expected utility theory in a manner consistent with Machina's fanning-out hypothesis. According to this argument, choices and valuations are governed by the same preferences. The argument applies to experiments that use the random-lottery incentive system, by which subjects face more than one task but are paid only for one of these, selected at random at the end of the experiment. (See chapter 6 for further discussion.) Holt's analysis depends on the assumption that subjects treat the whole experiment as a single choice problem, rather than treating each task in isolation. Many of the preference reversal experiments carried out before Holt's critique had used the random-lottery incentive system. One way of testing the conjecture that preference reversals are caused by Holt's mechanism is to rerun the preference reversal experiment with a different incentive system. (Or with no incentives at all. In fact, when Holt's paper was written, it was already known that preference reversals occur when subjects respond to hypothetical choice and valuation tasks, and this is sufficient to cast doubt on Holt's conjecture.) Tversky et al. (1990) carried out such a test, finding preference reversals in an experiment with a completely different incentive system. A complementary strategy for testing Holt's conjecture is to carry out controlled tests of the random-lottery incentive system itself, to see if subjects respond differently to a given task depending on whether it is embedded in a random-lottery incentive system or whether it is the only task for which they are being paid. Tests of this kind have found no systematic differences between responses in the two cases (Starmer and Sugden 1991; Cubitt et al. 1998a).

A second example concerns the ultimatum game. Observed behavior in this game—proposers offering significant shares to responders, responders rejecting small shares—has usually been presented as evidence that subjects have some kind of taste for fairness. Elizabeth Hoffman et al. (1994) suggest an alternative explanation: that subjects are responding to what they perceive as the experimenters' expectations of them. In experiments previous to that of Hoffman et al., anonymity had been maintained *between the players*, but the behavior of each individual player was known to the experimenter. Hoffman et al. rerun the ultimatum-game experiment with a *double-blind design* in which there is anonymity between subject and experimenter as well as between subject and subject. Their results suggest that behavior is closer to the predictions of conventional game theory when the double-blind design is used. However, subsequent experiments, with additional controls, have cast doubt on this conclusion (Bolton and Zwick 1995).

Our final example concerns the observation that, in experimental investigations of voluntary contributions to public goods, contributions tend to decline as the experiment is repeated. This has usually been interpreted as evidence that subjects are learning that the dominant strategy is to make a zero contribution: positive contributions in early rounds are the result of errors that subjects gradually learn to avoid. An alternative explanation is that the perception, common to all players, that a game is the first in a series tends to induce positive contributions. For example, suppose some players are motivated by reciprocity; they are willing to contribute in a "first" game to signal their willingness to cooperate but, after that, will contribute only if enough others have done so in previous rounds. In a group that contains both reciprocators and free-riders, interaction between the players may produce a pattern of declining contributions. One way of discriminating between these two explanations is to run a public-good experiment in which there are periodic "restarts"— breaks in the sequence of repeated games that are framed so as to suggest to the players that they are starting a new series of games, rather than continuing the previous one. James Andreoni (1988) found that contributions tend to increase after restarts, a result that suggests that the perception of a "first" game has a direct effect on contributions.[16]

4.9.3 Decomposition

The regularity captured by an exhibit can sometimes be usefully respecified by being broken down into finer-grained component regularities. For example, consider the ultimatum game. As far as the behavior of proposers is concerned, the surprising observation is that of the stock of money available for division, most proposers offer relatively large

---

[16] By means of a microeconometric analysis of the behavior of individual subjects in a repeated public-good game, Bardsley and Moffatt (2007) find more direct evidence of a mixture of free-riders and reciprocators in the subject pool. See also Burlando and Guala (2005) and Fischbacher and Gächter (2006, forthcoming).

shares to their coplayers. One possible explanation is that proposers have a "taste for fairness": they *want* their coplayers to receive relatively large shares. An alternative explanation is that proposers act out of self-interest, in the belief that responders will reject small offers. (Of course, this requires that proposers believe that responders are not motivated solely by self-interest.) One way of trying to distinguish between these explanations is to investigate what happens if the rules of the game are changed so that responders are not able to reject proposers' offers. The resulting game is the *dictator game.*

The idea behind this game, first studied by Kahneman et al. (1986), is that proposers who act on self-interest have no reason to offer anything, while a taste for fairness still provides a motivation for positive offers. Thus, by comparing behavior in ultimatum and dictator games, we can break down the positive offers of the ultimatum game into two components: a component that persists in the dictator game, and the residual. The former seems to be most naturally interpreted as resulting from some form of nonselfish motivation, the latter as the effect of self-interest.[17] Kahneman et al.'s experiment allowed proposers to choose between only two alternative divisions, giving either 10% or 50% to the coplayer; a large majority chose the equal division, suggesting that a taste for fairness might be the main factor at work in ultimatum games. However, subsequent dictator-game experiments in which proposers' choices have been unconstrained have found that the modal offer to coplayers is around 20%, roughly half the value observed in ultimatum games (e.g., Forsythe et al. 1994).

As another example of decomposition, consider the phenomenon of focal points. Schelling's explanation is that the players of his games identify focal points by some mode of reasoning. For example, he argues that in the "write down any positive number" game, the players look for an obvious and unambiguous "rule of selection" that, if followed by both of them, would have a high probability of success; the rule "choose the smallest number" meets these criteria (Schelling 1960, p. 94). An alternative hypothesis—the hypothesis of *primary salience*—is that each player simply writes down the first number that comes to mind, and

---

[17] Each of these interpretations can be questioned. Some commentators have argued that positive offers in ultimatum games are the effect of proposers' attempts to meet what they perceive as the experimenters' expectations of them (see section 4.9.2). Such an effect might occur in a dictator game too: by allowing the proposer to *give* to the responder but not to *take* from her, the standard dictator-game design may suggest to subjects that giving is expected of them (Bardsley 2008). Because responders play a more active role in the ultimatum game than in the dictator game, the idea that responders are entitled to a fair share might be more salient in the ultimatum game.

that the players' success in coordinating is explained by positive correlation between what comes to mind for different individuals. It is possible to separate these two mechanisms by investigating what people do when they are simply asked to write down any positive number, without any suggestion that they are trying to coordinate with someone else. By comparing behavior in this "picking" task with that in a corresponding coordination game, we can discover how much of the coordination in Schelling's games can be explained by primary salience. This design is used by Mehta et al. (1994), who find that primary salience accounts for a relatively small part of total coordination. (In the "write down any positive number" task, the frequency with which two of Mehta et al.'s paired subjects chose the same number was 0.21 when they were trying to coordinate, but only 0.05 when they were just picking.)

A regularity can be decomposed in an informative way even if, for some or all of the mechanisms that are being separated out, there is no well-developed theoretical explanation. Take the case of the first dictator-game experiment. The rhetoric of the opening paragraphs of Kahneman et al.'s (1986) paper strongly suggests that their prior expectation was that ultimatum-game behavior is explained by a taste for fairness. (Conventional economists are teased about their "true belief in nonfairness" and their "embarrassment" in the face of supposedly transparent evidence to the contrary.) Yet Kahneman et al. do not propose any particular theory or definition of fairness; they simply use the findings of ultimatum-game experiments as prima facie evidence that people are motivated by "preferences . . . for treating others fairly." Nor do they present or cite any theory that would predict positive offers in ultimatum games and zero offers in dictator games, presumably because (as far as they knew, and as far as we know) no one had ever proposed such a theory. This is not surprising, since a theory of this kind would require proposers to be self-interested while believing responders to have a taste for fairness—not a particularly credible combination of assumptions. So the dictator-game experiment is neither a test of a theory of fairness nor a test of a theory of self-interest. Kahneman et al. present the experiment as a way of answering the question, How prevalent is "fair" behavior in the absence of enforcement? The implication is that "enforcement" (working through the power of respondents to reject unfair offers) might be expected to *reduce the frequency of* fair offers; the experiment is a way of finding out *by how much* that frequency is reduced.

The methodological approach being used here is similar to that of checking for confounds. Indeed, if the ultimatum game is presented as evidence of a taste for fairness, the self-interested motivation of proposers—to avoid making offers that will be rejected—can be interpreted as a confounding mechanism. The distinction between "decomposition" and "checking for confounds" is a matter of presentation rather than substance. To speak of "confounds" is to treat one putative causal mechanism as the received or privileged explanation of an exhibit, and other mechanisms as rival explanations. To speak of "decomposition" is to take a more neutral stance with respect to the various mechanisms. Whichever word one uses, the aim is to find more refined specifications of previously observed regularities.

The focal point experiment illustrates the same methodological principles. Prior to Mehta et al.'s experiment, the primary salience hypothesis had not been explicitly proposed as an explanation of Schelling's findings. Mehta et al. did not propose this hypothesis as the sole, or even principal, explanation of coordination in Schelling's games. Rather, they recognized that it might *contribute to* Schelling's results, and their experiment was designed to investigate *how much* it contributed. Or, to use the language of confounds, they used an experimental design that allowed the effects of primary salience to be filtered out, revealing the regularity identified by Schelling in a more refined form.

4.9.4 Robustness

To say that a regularity observed in one experimental design is *robust* is to say that similar regularities are found in similar designs: minor differences in parameter values, instructions, incentives, subject pools, and so on do not make major differences to the results. After an exhibit has been discovered, its robustness is typically tested by running variants of the original design.

In many cases, these variants are not motivated by any specific hypotheses about how the results will be affected. Small variations on previously used designs are often introduced without any intention to test anything in particular. For example, it is sometimes said that no experimenter accepts a surprising result until it has been replicated in his or her own lab. If this it true, that is at least partly because different research groups have their own preferred experimental practices. Thus, when one group tries to replicate a result reported by another, it does not usually replicate every detail of the original design. Instead, it adapts that design to its own "house style"—its own methods of subject recruitment, forms of instruction, display formats, currency units, average subject earnings, methods of payment, and so on. By a succession of undirected variations, the class of experiments that is understood as constituting a particular exhibit can expand. The gradual discovery that repeated experimental markets can generate competitive equilibria with very small numbers of traders (see section 4.4) may be an example of this kind of process.

In contrast, other robustness tests are done deliberately, prompted by skepticism about the external validity of particular exhibits. As we pointed out in chapter 2, many economists have doubted whether the behavior of student subjects, facing "artificial" tasks without prior experience and with only small (and sometimes no) financial incentives, is representative of the behavior of "real" economic agents. This skepticism has been expressed in more specific questions about the robustness of exhibits to such design variations as increases in incentives, changes in incentive mechanisms, changes in instructions, repetition of tasks, and the use of different subject pools. Questions of this kind are routinely investigated through further experiments.

Some commentators seem to suggest that unless an exhibit is robust to *all* minor variations in the original experimental design, its claim to capture a regularity in the field is compromised. For example, Charles Plott and Kathryn Zeiler (2005) report an investigation of the WTA/WTP disparity. Their investigation is motivated by the conjecture that this disparity is not (as is often claimed) evidence of loss aversion; rather, it results from subjects' misperceptions of the experimental environments in which valuations are elicited. Following what they call the *revealed theory methodology*, Plott and Zeiler use a design that is intended to include "every procedure used in previous experiments to control for misconceptions." They claim that if, in such an experiment, no "gap" between WTP and WTA valuations were observed:

> The results would support the conjecture that the [experimental] procedures themselves produce gaps and that gaps are unrelated to the nature of preferences, loss aversion and prospect theory. If the gap can be turned off and on using different sets of procedures, then it likely does not reflect an asymmetry between gains and losses as posited by loss aversion.
>
> Plott and Zeiler (2005, pp. 531–32)

Having claimed that this is what their results *do* show,[18] Plott and Zeiler consider the judgment, expressed by Russell Korobkin, that "it is

---

[18] Plott and Zeiler find no significant difference between WTA and WTP valuations of plastic mugs in three experiments with a total of thirty-six WTP observations and thirty-eight WTA valuations. Significant WTA/WTP differences *are* found for a series of tasks involving lotteries, carried out in the same experiment but not reported in the final paper. Plott and Zeiler argue that, because of potential contamination, the latter data are not appropriate for testing the endowment effect. However, the same WTA/WTP differences have since been found in a replication of Plott and Zeiler's experiment in which the possibility of contamination was removed (Isoni et al. 2009).

extremely unlikely that [the WTA/WTP disparity] is merely an artifact of the experimental methods that demonstrate it." Plott and Zeiler reject this judgment as "clearly misleading" (2005, p. 544).

On a first reading of the passage quoted above, Plott and Zeiler might seem to be saying that if an effect occurs in some designs but not in others, when the differences between the relevant designs are merely matters of experimental "procedure," then that effect must be considered an experimental artifact, not informative about behavior outside the laboratory. But that cannot be right. To say that an anomaly can be turned off and on by experimental procedures is also to say that the received theory—the theory that is disconfirmed when the anomaly occurs—can be turned on and off by those same procedures. Thus, if the failures of the received theory must be regarded as artifacts, so too must the successes.

Presumably, Plott and Zeiler's remark about the "turning on" and "turning off" of effects by experimental procedures is intended to apply only to procedures that control for misperceptions of the experimental environment. Their idea seems to be that if an anomaly is not found when all known controls for misperception are in place, we should infer that the anomaly is an artifact, caused by some misperception. We do not agree.

A crucial problem for the revealed theory methodology (an instance of the Duhem–Quine problem discussed in chapter 3) concerns the definition of a maximal set of experimental controls. This methodology implicitly assumes that it is possible, by decomposing an experimental design, to identify a set of discrete controls, each of which contributes positively to the total level of control in the design as a whole. Then, if the set of controls implemented by one design is a proper subset of that implemented by another, the latter design is said to be unambiguously more controlled. But this approach takes no account of the trade-offs and judgment calls that are intrinsic to the practice of experimental design, or of the ways in which different features of a design interact with one another. A design feature that reduces the likelihood of one form of misperception may increase that of another. Since human subjects have only limited powers of attention and memory, it is unavoidable that they will tend to focus on those aspects of an experiment that are made most salient to them. And salience is comparative: it is not possible to give maximal salience to *every* feature of a design.

For example, in many experimental investigations of WTA/WTP disparities, subjects who report WTA valuations do so while actually possessing the relevant good; those who report WTP valuations can *see* the good, but do not *possess* it. In Plott and Zeiler's design, this difference between the framing of the tasks is removed; subjects are merely *told* whether or not they own the good. Plott and Zeiler argue that their procedures are more controlled, because the framing of the two tasks has been made more similar. But one might argue instead that, by making the difference between ownership and nonownership more salient to subjects, the traditional design reduces the chance that subjects will misunderstand the experimental procedures. Thus, if the WTA/WTP disparity is found in the traditional design but not in Plott and Zeiler's, it is not clear whether the presence or the absence of the disparity should be attributed to misperception.

Indeed, the concept of "misperception" may be unhelpful when thinking about the interplay of experimental procedures and psychological mechanisms. In conventional rational-choice theories, a given decision task has an uncontroversially "correct" specification; to think of it in any other way is to make a mistake—to misperceive reality. But many psychological theories are *about* perceptions. In particular, loss aversion is defined relative to reference points, and reference points are matters of subjective perception. Thus, from the observation that reference points can be manipulated by experimental procedures, we cannot infer that loss aversion is a laboratory artifact, without real-world correlates.

More generally, we need to keep in mind the truism that all theories are false. If a theory is understood as a description of a particular mechanism that in reality works alongside other mechanisms, then we should not expect its predictions to hold in *every* experimental design. By identifying the cases in which a theory works and the cases in which it does not, we can learn more about the interplay of causal mechanisms. This, as opposed to the possibility of relegating exhibits to the status of artifacts, is the principal value of robustness tests.

There have been many investigations of the effects of rerunning classic experiments with larger incentives and unusual subject pools. Preference reversal provides an early example. Lichtenstein and Slovic's (1971) first experiments used student subjects and payoffs that were either hypothetical (in two cases) or small (in the third). Having found a strong effect, they replicated their design with larger payoffs and participants recruited at a Las Vegas casino (Lichtenstein and Slovic 1973). A strategy that has become popular is to rerun experiments in low-income countries, where payoffs can be made very large relative to wage rates without putting too much strain on research budgets (e.g., Kachelmeier and Shehata 1992). On the whole, experimental anomalies have proved to be fairly robust to increases in payoffs and changes in subject pools.

Another standard robustness test is to investigate whether the regularities found in an exhibit persist if subjects face the same task repeatedly.

We have already described Smith's repeated-task variant of Chamberlin's market experiment, and the repetition of public-good games. A different approach to testing the robustness of exhibits to experience is to investigate whether the behavior of subjects varies according to the extent of their experience, outside the experiment, of relevant tasks. For example, John List (2003) investigates the strength of the endowment effect (as expressed in differences between willingness-to-pay and willingness-to-accept valuations of goods) among participants in sports card conventions; he finds that the strength of the effect is inversely correlated with participants' trading experience. Other experimental investigations of the effect of experience on anomalies were discussed in chapter 2, in relation to the discovered preference hypothesis. This is not the place for a general review of the rather mixed evidence about the effects of experience, but it seems clear that at least some anomalies are made less prevalent by at least some kinds of experience.

It is significant that most of the robustness tests we have described were not prompted by preexisting theories that predicted the effects of incentives or experience on the prevalence of anomalies. Rather, they started from curiosity or skepticism about the robustness of exhibits, supported by a background belief that received theories worked reasonably well in the domains in which they were usually applied. The hypotheses that people might be less likely to violate received theory if their decisions had more substantial consequences, or if they had more experience of relevantly similar problems, were not predictions of formal theories. They had more of the nature of conjectures or hunches.

There is a suggestive parallel here between experiments and theoretical models. Conjectures and hunches often provide the starting points for exercises in modeling. When a theoretically inclined economist has a hunch that some mechanism is at work in the real world, causing some observed phenomenon, his characteristic response is to build a model. The aim is to create a simple model world in which the postulated mechanism can be seen to work and to have the conjectured effects. Success in constructing such a model is a first test of the coherence and credibility of the economist's hunch.

Some experimental tests for robustness and for confounds are mediated by models of this kind. That is, a commentator has the hunch that some experimentally observed regularity is not robust, or is the result of some confounding effect. He then expresses this hunch as a theoretical model that might subsequently be tested experimentally. Holt's hypothesis about the distorting effects of the random-lottery incentive system (section 4.9.2) is a good example. Holt expressed his skepticism about Lichtenstein and Slovic's explanation of preference reversal by creating a theoretical model in which preference reversals were generated by a different mechanism. It was only after this model had been published that other experimentalists tested Holt's hypothesis. But, as several of our examples have illustrated, tests for robustness and confounds are not always mediated by theoretical models: it is possible to move directly from hunch to experiment.

For example, we do not need any very specific theory about how incentives impact on behavior in order to recognize the credibility of the idea that anomalies might be less frequent if payoffs were larger, and to understand the value of investigating this issue experimentally. If, up to now, all the evidence of some anomaly has been collected in experiments with small payoffs, it is not unreasonable to be skeptical about whether the same anomaly would be found in situations in the field where much more was at stake. (We do not mean that all economically relevant situations in the field involve higher stakes than typical laboratory experiments: many do not. Consider impulse purchases of soft drinks and confectionery.) If the relevant experimental result can be shown to be robust to increases in payoffs, we have stronger grounds for confidence in the external validity of the original findings. Conversely, if the anomaly disappears when payoffs are increased, we have less reason for such confidence. Either of these conclusions can be reached, depending on the evidence, without anyone proposing a theory of the mechanism by which incentives affect behavior.

In cases such as these, we might say that experiments are *substituting for* theoretical models as means of firming up hunches and appraising their credibility. To firm up a hunch, a theorist builds it into a well-specified formal model; an experimentalist builds it into an experimental design. The theorist's hunch gains credibility if his conjectured mechanism works in his model; the experimentalist's hunch gains credibility if her conjectured mechanism is exhibited in her experiment. We will say more about the substitutability of experiments and models in the next section.

4.10   Investigating Exhibits without Trying to Explain Them

So far we have been concerned with inductive methodological strategies that aim to explain exhibits. We now consider some other inductive strategies that, while investigating the regularities captured by exhibits, are not primarily directed at explanation. The essential idea behind these strategies is to investigate how the strength or prevalence of a regularity is affected by factors that are not interpreted as potential causal mechanisms, but are of interest in the field.

One version of this approach, now quite common in experimental economics, is to investigate whether the prevalence of a regularity varies according to the demographic characteristics of the subject pool. For example, one might ask whether, after controlling for other factors, the probability of observing a particular anomaly varies according to subjects' age, gender, educational attainment, social class, or ethnicity. Among experimental economists, there seems to have been a gradual shift in opinion about the usefulness of investigating such issues.

Three of the current authors were experimentalists from the mid 1980s. Initially, our main focus of interest was individual choice under uncertainty; we were seeking to explain anomalies such as preference reversal and the common ratio and common consequence effects. In the early years, most economists viewed experiments with a mixture of skepticism and amused curiosity; whenever we presented our results to audiences of economists, we had to justify our methods. We were often asked whether it was valid to draw general conclusions from experiments carried out using demographically unrepresentative subject pools. (Most of our experiments recruited subjects from populations of British university students. These were clearly unrepresentative of the general British population with respect to age, educational attainment, and social class.) Less frequently, and probably more in a spirit of idle curiosity, our audiences would ask whether we had found any differences between the behavior of different categories of students, particularly males and females, and economists and noneconomists. Our short answer to the first question was that the inferences we were drawing *were* valid, even though our subject pools were unrepresentative. Our short answer to the second was that we had not investigated gender or subject-of-study differences in any systematic way; these issues were orthogonal to the topics we were concerned with. At the time, most experimental economists would have responded in much the same way as we did. Why has experimental practice changed since then?

We suggest that this change in attitudes to demographic variables is another symptom of the shift of emphasis from theory-testing to inductive generalization. When an experiment is being used to test a general theory of decision-making behavior, such as expected utility theory or one of its more recent rivals, it *is* legitimate to ignore demographic variables. (Of course, between-subject tests should compare the behavior of groups that have been randomly selected from *the same* subject pool; but it does not matter whether that pool is representative of a wider population.) Take the case of expected utility theory. That theory assumes that every individual has preferences over lotteries that satisfy certain general principles, such as the Independence axiom; in other respects, such as the degree of risk aversion, preferences are allowed to differ between individuals. The theory has nothing to say about how such differences in preferences relate to demographic variables. However, by virtue of the general assumptions made about preferences, it implies that *every* individual's behavior has certain general properties in common, such as the absence of the common ratio effect. Thus, the theory can be tested by taking *any* group of individuals and investigating the frequency of the common ratio effect in their behavior. A similar analysis applies to rival theories of choice under uncertainty. For example, prospect theory allows the degree of loss aversion to differ between individuals, and has nothing to say about how loss aversion relates to demographic variables. However, it has certain implications that apply to the behavior of all individuals, and these can be tested experimentally using any group of subjects.

This is not to say that when economists *use* expected utility theory, they have no reason to be interested in demographic effects on preferences. For example, economists often want to explain gender-related phenomena. It is sometimes credible to suppose that gender-based differences in preferences or in attitudes to risk might provide part of the explanation of observed gender differences in economic outcomes. (Why are men overrepresented at the very top of most professions, even when the majority of entrants are women? Why are men also overrepresented in the population of convicted criminals? One possible explanation is that women are more risk averse than men.) In applying expected utility theory to real economic problems, we may need to investigate whether attitudes to risk vary with gender. But it is still true that in testing the general properties of expected utility theory, there is no need to take account of the gender of subjects.

The idea that it is useful to investigate how demographic variables impact on exhibits depends on seeing exhibits as something other than tests of received theories. We have to think of them not in relation to theories, but in relation to behavior in the field. If the regularity captured by an exhibit is interpreted as a representation of some feature of field behavior, we may try to learn about the latter by manipulating the exhibit so as to represent different field conditions, or by using subject pools that represent different field populations.

This strategy is illustrated by the ways in which the trust game has been used since it was first exhibited by Berg et al. (1995). As we have explained (in section 4.4), Berg et al. present this exhibit as a test of the hypothesis of self-interest, and as evidence that people are motivated by positive reciprocity (glossed as being "willing to reward appropriate behavior"). While they do not claim to have tested any specific theory of reciprocity, Berg et al. argue that their results give general support to the enterprise of building such theories. Eight years later, however, in an authoritative review of experimental investigations of games, Colin Camerer (2003, p. 85, italics added) describes the trust game as "a beautiful simple game *to measure* trust." By this, he means that summary statistics of behavior in a trust game experiment can be used as measures of participants' propensities to trust others and to repay others' trust. (The first is measured by the proportion of senders' endowments that is transferred to responders; the second is measured either by the proportion of responders' receipts that is returned to senders or by the ratio of what senders get back to what they transfer to responders.) While Camerer's interpretation of the trust game does not accord with that of its progenitors, it captures the spirit of many subsequent experiments.

These experiments have taken two basic forms. The first is to investigate, for a given subject pool, the effects of different experimental conditions on the extent of trust. The second is to investigate, for a given experimental design, the extent of trust in different subject pools. An experiment reported by Nancy Buchan et al. (2002) provides an example of both approaches. In this experiment, student subjects in four countries (China, Japan, Korea, and the United States) play either the original trust game or one of two variants. In the original trust game (the *direct* condition), each sender (say A_1) is paired with one responder (say B_1): A_1 sends to B_1, who then responds by sending money back to A_1. In the *group* condition, two senders and two responders form a group; A_1 sends to B_1 and A_2 sends to B_2, but B_1 returns money to A_2 while B_2 returns to A_1. In the *strangers* condition, each sender sends to a randomly assigned responder (who could be any subject in a large group of subjects); each responder returns to a randomly assigned (but not his own) sender.

The comparison between the three conditions is presented as a way of discriminating between different forms of reciprocity; the main finding is that in the group and strangers conditions, the proportion of receipts returned is about half that in the direct condition. This part of the experiment can be thought of as an attempt to refine a regularity by decomposition (see section 4.9.3).

For our present purposes, the cross-country comparison is more significant. Buchan et al. do not set out to test any specific hypotheses about cross-country differences in trust; they merely measure the extent of trust in each of the four subject groups. However, this investigation is presented as an attempt to learn about differences in trust *in the field.* While Buchan et al.'s measures of trust are *descriptions* of the behavior of student subjects in particular experimental designs, they are interpreted as *indicators* of factors that are both much more general and much less precise—trust and reciprocation in a country as a whole, understood as factors that might have implications for "national prosperity, economic growth, or stability" (Buchan et al. 2002, p. 201). "Trust" and "reciprocation," as measured in the trust game, are being treated as what in psychology are called *constructs.* A construct is a concept that is defined operationally, in terms of a method of measurement, that is intended to represent something that might otherwise be only vaguely defined, but is conceived of as real. For example, in psychology, the concept of a person's "subjective well-being" is defined in terms of her responses to specific survey questions about how she feels about her life; but this construct is intended to represent something of the person's inner experience of happiness.

In fact, it is difficult to draw general conclusions from Buchan et al.'s international comparisons. The proportion of endowments transferred by senders was highest in the United States (60%), followed by China (52%), Korea, and Japan (44% in each). The proportion of receipts returned by responders was highest in Korea (74%), followed by China (65%), Japan (34%), and the United States (32%). Some of the differences between these measures are statistically significant, but there are no obvious patterns in the data. In any case, extreme caution is required when using experimental evidence to make inferences about cross-country differences in behavior in the field. When, as in Buchan et al.'s experiment, subjects are recruited by "convenience sampling" (i.e., subjects are not statistically representative of relevant field populations), and when subject groups are defined by characteristics external to the experiment (e.g., nationality or gender), a difference in behavior between two groups could be the product of *any* difference between those particular samples.[19] Thus, a difference in behavior between a convenience sample of Korean students and a convenience sample of American students, however statistically significant, is only weak evidence of a difference between *Koreans* and *Americans* (or even between Korean students and American students) in the field. For related reasons, when

---

[19] Notice the difference between this type of design and one in which a given convenience sample is divided at random into two groups and different experimental treatments are used for those groups. In the latter case, if there is a significant difference between the behavior of the two groups, we are entitled to infer that this is very probably the result of the treatment variable. This inference is legitimate because, if the experiment has been properly controlled, the treatment variable is the only source of nonrandom differences between the groups.

parameter values for theoretical models are estimated from the behavior of convenience samples, these values cannot be treated as reliable indicators of properties of the corresponding field population.

We suggest that experiments of this kind are best interpreted as first steps in a search for new exhibits. Isolated instances of differences between the behavior of different subject pools are not, in themselves, of great interest. (See our discussion of "ex post sifting" in section 4.5.) But suppose we find a design that, when applied to different subject pools, reliably induces the *same* cross-country effect. (For example, suppose that in many different experiments using matched convenience samples of Americans and Koreans—some of American and Korean students, some of American and Korean office workers, and so on—we consistently find greater reciprocation among Koreans.) To find such a design is to find an exhibit. The exhibit would be interesting by virtue of its suggesting that there is some real difference between behavior in the relevant countries. Notice that, in this kind of case, the exhibit can be interesting, independently of any prior theory. It is not a striking disconfirmation of a received theory; it is just a striking empirical regularity, analogous with Marmot's findings about the health of civil servants (section 4.3). Such an exhibit could serve as the starting point for further investigations, using methodological strategies of the kinds we described in section 4.9.

4.11 Experiments as Models

The investigations discussed in section 4.10 are examples of a more general methodological strategy in which experiments are used *as models*. Take Buchan et al.'s cross-national comparison of propensities for trust and reciprocation. In this investigation, the experimental trust game is being used as a model of trust in the field. Economists are more accustomed to theoretical models, constructed in terms of mathematical propositions, but the essential idea of modeling is more general than this. It is to represent some real-world mechanism (in methodological discussions, this is sometimes called the *target system*) by a simpler mechanism (the model or *substitute system*) constructed by the modeler. The intention is that, because of similarities between the two mechanisms, an investigation of the substitute system will be informative about the target system. Just as a theoretical model represents some feature of the real world by a well-specified abstract mathematical system, so an experiment can represent some feature of behavior in the field by a well-specified set of experimental procedures. The idea that experiments and theoretical models can play similar roles in scientific enquiry has recently been argued by a number of philosophers of science, including three specialists in the methodology of economics: Francesco Guala (1998), Uskali Mäki (2005), and Mary Morgan (2005). Unlike Mäki, we do not want to make the generic assertion that "models are experiments, experiments are models"; our claim is only that experiments can sometimes be used as models.

Experimental models may be more useful than theoretical ones when the modeler has an intuitive understanding of the target system but is not sure how the mechanisms at work in that system are best described. This seems to be true of trust. It seems clear enough that a sender in the trust game who transfers money to a responder is "showing trust," and that a responder who transfers money back to the sender is "returning trust," using these expressions in their everyday senses. Thus, it seems uncontroversial to interpret the trust game as a model of a class of interactions in the field in which trust can be (but need not be) shown and returned. However, we may be quite unsure about what motivates trust and reciprocity—both in the game and in the field. For example, we might be unsure whether people who show trust are motivated by self-interest (in the expectation that trustees will reciprocate), by altruism toward trustees, by a Kantian sense of duty, by reciprocity (that is, a desire to benefit people whom they expect to be willing to benefit them), or by team reasoning (that is, identifying with a group and then playing their part in joint actions by group members that promote their common interests). If we, as modelers, have this kind of uncertainty about the motivation of trust and reciprocity, it will be difficult for us to construct *mathematical* models of trust that we can be confident will respond to our manipulations in ways that correspond with behavior in the field. One way of getting round this problem is to use *experimental* models, in which the actors are real human beings. The intention is that the experimental environment will activate in the subjects the same motivations as determine their behavior in trust problems in the field— whatever those motivations may be. A person's propensity for trust and reciprocity can then be represented by constructs that are defined in terms of an experimental design rather than a theory.

Once one understands how experiments can be used as models, one begins to see that this methodological strategy has been a part of experimental economics all along. An early example of the substitution of experimental models for theoretical ones can be found in Schelling's study of focal points, and its reception by game theorists. Schelling (1960) presents the idea of focal points through a discussion of a wide range of coordination games ("write down any positive number" being

one). These games are clearly intended as simple models of coordination and bargaining problems that are faced in the field (in particular, by
military strategists: in the 1950s, Schelling was particularly concerned
with the problem of managing conflict between the United States and
the Soviet Union so as to avoid nuclear war). However, these models are
not theoretical models in the usual sense. They are not self-contained,
formally described worlds in which abstract agents act according to prespecified principles. Rather, they are well-specified games to be played by
real individuals. In other words, they are *experimental designs*. Following
the practice of the time at which he was writing, Schelling reports only
the results of "unscientific" experiments; often he merely offers conjectures about how these games would be played in reality. Nevertheless,
his methodological approach is clearly inductive: he is inferring general
principles for identifying focal points from (conjectured) experimental
regularities.[20]

Following Schelling's work, the concept of a focal point has become
part of the standard toolkit of game theory, used to resolve otherwise-
intractable problems of equilibrium selection. However, there is still
nothing approaching a received *theory* of focal points. Game theorists
work with an intuitive rather than formal understanding of focal points,
grounded in experimental rather than theoretical models. Because received game theory is (or at least has been until very recently) constructed by deduction from a priori principles of rationality, focal points
have had an ambiguous—one might say, awkward or embarrassing—
status. Game theorists recognize that Schelling has identified a real phenomenon, and that this is exhibited in his coordination games; they
understand that phenomenon intuitively; but they have been unable to
incorporate it into their theoretical framework satisfactorily.

As an even earlier example of an experimental model, consider Chamberlin's market experiment. As we noted in box 4.1, this classroom market is a flesh-and-blood model of decentralized markets in the field.
In this design, the range of possible actions available to each individual is vastly richer than anything that can be represented in a tractable
mathematical model. (Recall that subjects move around a room at will,
approaching other subjects and bargaining with them as they see fit.
There is no predetermined process to decide who meets whom in what
order, no predetermined set of possible messages that subjects can send
to one another, and no anonymity controls to screen out their knowledge
of the visible characteristics of the people with whom they bargain.) But

---

[20] The methodology of Schelling's analysis of focal points is reconstructed by Sugden
and Zamarrón (2006). For Schelling's use of the word "unscientific," see footnote 10 on
page 162.

this does not mean that the *experimental design* is complicated. As a model of real-world markets, it is beautifully simple. The rules of Chamberlin's market are well-defined and easy to understand; they are just difficult to express in the mathematical language of economic theory.

Chamberlin's experiment might be interpreted as a test of the theory of competitive equilibrium. As we noted in section 4.5, this design was the prototype for Smith's early market experiments; the main result of these experiments—that repeated double auction markets converge to competitive equilibrium—constitutes an exhibit that supports some features of received theory while raising questions about others. But subsequent work in this research program has been at least as much concerned with investigating a wide range of experimental models of markets as with testing preexisting theories or with finding theoretical explanations for surprising results.

Reviewing the findings of this program, Smith (2008) points to the failure of "standard theory" to account for observed convergence to equilibrium in markets with few traders and imperfect information, or to explain "the emergence of the institutions that we have copied from the world of practice into the laboratory" (Smith 2008, pp. 29–30). Characterizing conventional theorizing as based on a "constructivist" or "Cartesian" conception of rationality, he offers an alternative understanding of economic institutions as "ecologically rational": that is, as the unintended results of processes of cultural and biological evolution, "adapted to the structure of [their] environment" (p. 36). Smith's vision, inspired by the writings of Friedrich Hayek (e.g., Hayek 1945), is of markets as ordered systems of unwritten rules and practices, whose workings may be imperfectly understood by even the best economic theorists. Experimental research allows us to learn some of the general properties of different market institutions even if we cannot explain those properties theoretically. In this account, the organizing framework for our understanding of the world is provided by experiments rather than by theoretical models.

One line of development of the research program pioneered by Chamberlin and Smith has been to use experiments to guide the design of new market institutions. A particularly important class of applications of this method concerns the design of auctions for selling complex packages of assets, such as emission permits for pollutants or spectrum licenses for telecommunication networks. In the design of such auctions, many problems are confronted simultaneously. Some of these problems, such as the possibility of collusion among bidders and the fact that a public bid by one agent can convey information to other agents, are common to all auctions, but appear in more complex forms. Other problems are created by the heterogeneity of the assets to be sold: a potential buyer may see some assets as substitutes for one another and others as complements. (To get a feel for the difficulties this creates, suppose that three buyers i, j, and k are bidding for two indivisible assets x and y. Suppose that i wants to buy only x, j wants to buy only y, while k wants to buy the two assets as a package but not either on its own. An efficient auction mechanism has to compare k's willingness to pay for the package with the sum of i's and j's willingness to pay for the separate components. In effect, i and j together are bidding against k, but each wants his own share of any winning bid to be as small as possible. This is liable to create incentives for the misrepresentation of willingness to pay.)

One way of approaching this design problem, and the one that would most immediately occur to an economic theorist, is to build theoretical models of the relevant market, and to investigate the effect of different auction rules *within the models*. An alternative approach is to create experimental designs that mimic the various auction rules as applied to the real market, and to investigate the effects of these rules *within the experiments*. Or, to put this another way, experiments are used as models of the real-world system about which knowledge is sought.

It has become standard practice, when designing major auction institutions, to use both methods in combination.[21] It seems that, in at least some respects, experimental models are more informative than theoretical ones. Smith (2008) offers some possible explanations for this.

One reason for using experimental models to inform institutional design is that theoretical modeling is always constrained by the modeler's imagination. A theoretical model can contain only those causal factors that the modeler has thought of, while an experiment typically leaves space for other, unforeseen factors to come into play. As Smith puts it, experiments can "provide a window on forms of human competence that are not part of our traditional constructivist modeling" (Smith 2008, p. 41). (Although he does not say this, they may also reveal previously unsuspected forms of human *in*competence.) By using experiments as "test beds" for trials of proposed institutions, errors and omissions in the designers' reasoning can be picked up and corrected at an early stage.

A more general argument is implicit in Smith's claim, discussed above, that experimental research has discovered regularities in the workings of markets for which theorists have yet to find adequate explanations.

---

[21] Smith (2008, pp. 115–48) describes the role of experimental research in the design of spectrum auctions to be used by the United States Federal Communications Commission. Binmore and Klemperer (2002) describe a parallel process in the United Kingdom.

The suggestion is that we have inductive reason to believe that certain kinds of experimental market mimic their real-world counterparts, even though we cannot explain this "parallelism" by deductive analysis. In the absence of such an analysis, we do not know how to translate experimental models into theoretical ones.

Analogies can be found in the history of civil engineering, in which physical models have often preceded mathematical ones. For example, if one wants to know whether a specific masonry structure will support itself, one can learn a lot by building a scale model in some other homogeneous material, such as plaster. The theoretical explanation for this parallelism is that some crucial features of the "real" structure, such as the relative position of its center of mass, are replicated in the scale model despite the different material used. When modern engineers use physical models, the materials of the models are typically chosen to induce the relevant parallelisms. For example, to investigate how a chimney stack would behave in wind, a scale model might be used. The roughness of the surface of the structure that represents the chimney must be calibrated with the viscosity of the fluid that represents the air. If (as is normal) air is modeled by air, surface roughness must be adapted to the scale according to a theoretical formula. For many purposes, engineers no longer need to use physical models because the relevant theoretical principles are sufficiently well understood that they can be represented more conveniently in mathematical models. Historically, however, the reliability of certain kinds of scale models may have been learned by experience by craftsmen who had only an intuitive understanding of the theory. On Smith's account, economists who advise on the design of market mechanisms may be more like medieval stonemasons than modern structural engineers.

4.12   Conclusion

With hindsight, Chamberlin's market experiment and Schelling's investigation of focal points can be seen as early incursions by inductive research methods into a science whose traditional methodological practices were hypothetico-deductive. Now, half a century later, we are beginning to see the emergence of an alternative—or perhaps complementary—methodology for economics, in which inductive generalization plays a central part. In this chapter, we have tried to characterize this emerging system of methodological conventions. We have argued that the expansion of experimental methods in economics has been associated with a profound shift in prevailing understandings of the role of theory.

Traditionally, economists have prided themselves on what they have seen as the rigor and unity of their theory, grounded in a common core of formal principles of rational choice. They have been predisposed to see the world through the lens of this theory. Empirical hypotheses have been arrived at by deduction from theoretical assumptions, and empirical investigations have been interpreted as the testing of such hypotheses. In this perspective, the principal role of experiments is to test theories.

This traditional methodology has given economics a body of theory characterized by mathematical sophistication, generality, and internal coherence. But in doing so, it has set up a hierarchical relationship between theory and empirical investigation. Empirical investigation may expose inadequacies in existing theory, but the job of repairing or reconstructing the theory is seen as the preserve of theorists. If theorists are committed to the values of generality, parsimony, and elegance, they will be reluctant to compromise the core principles of existing theory in order to accommodate what appear to be isolated anomalies. However, the perception that anomalies are isolated may be generated by the conceptual framework within which they are being viewed: to see that there are underlying regularities in the anomalous evidence, one may need first to organize that evidence in terms of a different framework. This loop tends to insulate established theories from fundamental empirical challenges and from ideas originating in other disciplines.

This kind of insulation is less likely if there are accredited methods for discovering and organizing knowledge that do not depend on prior theoretical structures. The methodological shift we have described in this chapter consists in the use and acceptance of such inductive methods. At the heart of this shift is the idea that experiments need not be understood only in relation to preexisting theories; they can also be understood in direct relation to behavior in the field, unmediated by theory.

This is not to say that inductive research methods can or should *replace* hypothetico-deductive ones. The two approaches are better seen as complementary. But in order to understand the directions in which economics is developing, it is important to recognize that there can be useful experimental investigations of regularities prior to the development of explanatory theories. It is sometimes possible to organize our knowledge of the world in terms of experimentally observed regularities, rather than in terms of overarching theoretical systems.

5

External Validity

5.1 Introduction

Conditions in experiments usually differ markedly from those in naturally occurring situations. This may give rise to uncertainty and sometimes even skepticism about how, or indeed whether, the results will generalize. This concern and the particular character it assumes in experimental economics are the focus of this chapter. At least within experimental social sciences, laboratory economics seems to be distinguished by the close resemblance that designs often bear to formal models. Notwithstanding the argument of chapter 4, many, perhaps most, designs seek to recreate at least some features of such a model. This might appear especially contrived to an outsider. For many experimentalists, however, the correspondence between models and designs actually provides a robust defense against external-validity skepticism, a line that has been developed in their methodological writings as the "blame-the-theory" defense of box 2.2 (p. 54).

In our view, this defense does not diffuse all external-validity concerns because, as discussed in chapter 4, testing theory is not the only goal experimentalists pursue. Also, even for those experiments that are conceived purely as theory-testing exercises, the framework set out in chapter 2 offered only qualified support, encapsulated in the modified experimental claim (MEC) principle, to the blame-the-theory defense. According to MEC, it is reasonable to test a theory outside its intended domain of application (I-domain) in some other environment E such as the lab if E is in the base domain of the theory and absent differences between E and the I-domain that make E substantially less favorable to the theory than the field. In this chapter, we consider an argument to the effect that implementing the assumptions of a theoretical model is not, as is often supposed, sufficient to locate the design in the base domain of the theory.

The argument is especially pertinent for what we will call applied economics (AE) designs. By AE, we mean the use of general economic modeling tools such as expected utility theory (EUT) and game theory to analyze particular real-world economic institutions, actors, and circumstances; by AE designs we mean experiments based on such theories. We also argue, in relation to some AE designs, that a close fit between an experimental design and a theoretical model does not prevent important differences from arising between the laboratory and the I-domain of the theory. For these reasons, and because conclusions about theories are not the only ones drawn from experiments, external-validity concerns should be taken seriously; the purpose of this chapter is to explore them more fully.

Doubts about external validity are typically expressed as respects in which laboratory experiments are "artificial." The chapter considers the different senses of artificiality at issue and associated lines of debate. The existing economic methodology literature concentrates mainly on ways in which the laboratory might omit or introduce various influences on the behavior being studied, but we also consider a contrasting line of argument focusing on the alleged context dependence of human actions. We start by considering the relationship between experiments and models.

5.2 Are Economics Experiments Models?

The proximity of many economics experiments to models has not gone unnoticed by methodologists. Uskali Mäki (2005) appears to assert that laboratory economics experiments literally are models:

> An isolated system is a simple and controlled mini-world in contrast to the complex and uncontrolled maxi-world. The isolation of such controlled mini-worlds is accomplished in order to utilise and enhance the capacity of such experimental systems to serve as epistemically successful substitute systems, as resembling representatives. The equation models = experiments is supposed to hold precisely for such manipulable and manipulated systems.
>
> Mäki (2005, p. 306)

The sense of "model" in this quotation includes, but is not restricted to, formal models: that is, the mathematical propositions from which economists draw their conclusions in theoretical work. It also encompasses physical structures, for example, used in a representative capacity, such as engineers' scale models of bridges used for load testing. While experiments certainly can be used as substitute systems, as we saw in chapter 4, a general equivalence between models and experiments is contentious. Morgan (2005) argues that mathematical models, in particular, are in important ways conceptually distinct from experiments. Her argument is that different properties of experiments and formal models follow from their different ontology: that is, materials.

When we consider models in the broader sense of resembling represen-tatives, though, models may or may not use the same materials as their targets. For example, when a structural engineer uses a scale model to test the behavior of a chimney in wind (discussed in section 4.11), the model structure might be made of a different material from the planned structure, while the air in which it was tested might be ordinary air. In this case it seems that a scale model made entirely of the same materi-als might be inferior, but it would still be a model. We nonetheless think there is another reason to distinguish between a central class of exper-iments and models. We suspect that the relevant general feature of a model is that it substitutes for its object of investigation, as in Mäki's account. It seems jointly sufficient for something to count as a model that it substitutes in this way and that it is used in a representative capacity. Let x denote some phenomenon of research interest. Whereas models use (formal or physical) substitutes for x, the class of experiments we have in mind uses, in contrast, instances of x. For example, experiments on natural selection use organisms, such as fruit flies, rather than com-puterized representations of organisms. Galileo's experiments on the pendulum used pendula; Newton's demonstration of the refraction of light through a prism used light; and so on.

Consequently, experiments have different potentials to contribute to knowledge, or to provide epistemic success in Mäki's terms. Because experiments may use that which they investigate, they may, in ideal cir-cumstances, *demonstrate* properties of x.[1] It is always possible, in con-trast, that a substitute introduces some failure of analogy: a potential source of error absent from an experiment on the target. This is not to say that models are somehow generally inferior. Clearly, models can also demonstrate facts about x, as when load testing on a scale model, or computer modeling, demonstrates that a bridge design is structurally unsound. However, this kind of example seems to depend on prior know-ledge of relevant properties of x that does not always seem necessary in the case of experiments that actually use the target.

One simple way that experiments can demonstrate is evident in the following schema. The environment E implements the same conditions $c_1,...,c_N$ in each of two treatments of a design that records outcomes

---

[1] We do not intend here to belittle the complexity of the relationship between evi-dence and knowledge. Very significant caveats to read into this statement include, for example, that single pieces of evidence are not decisive, that an experiment's results are generally open to alternative interpretations, and that observation is theory-dependent. Nonetheless, demonstration seems to be a significant element of the language of experimentation.

on x. In addition, a single factor is varied across treatments. A statistically significant difference in outcomes is evidence that the manipulated variable had an effect, given that the various auxiliary assumptions of the experiment hold, including that there were no major differences in the samples of x between treatments.[2] If z is the variable that is being manipulated, the conclusion reporting this is one of an effect of z on x. Since x is the object of research interest, the design is (relatively) directly informative about the target of research. If, alternatively, the experiment uses a substitute, inferences to the target are less certain because of the possibility of failure of analogy.[3]

Although experiments are not generally reducible to models, many economics experiments do construct environments that in significant respects resemble the formal models of economic theories. (In what follows we shall restrict the sense of "model" to "formal model" unless we specify explicitly the more general sense of a resembling representative.) In Selten et al. (1999, illustration 3 of chapter 1), for example, lotteries were used that closely resemble the formal objects, prospects, defined in EUT. Morgan et al. (2006, illustration 6 of chapter 1) and Smith et al. (1988, illustration 7 of chapter 1) offer examples where a market environment is constructed to resemble that depicted in a model. This is done by attempting to satisfy the bulk of the model's assumptions (though by no means all of them): that is, "implementing" them.

To many, a high degree of such model–experiment correspondence represents part of the official canon of experimental economics. Vernon Smith's (1982a) methodological piece seems indicative of such a point of view, with its "precepts" of nonsatiation, saliency, dominance, and privacy we encountered in chapter 3. A fifth condition, "parallelism," is also proposed but, confusingly, this appears to be a stipulation of when external validity has been achieved, unlike the other precepts that advise experimenters on how to set up their designs.

The four precepts have had considerable influence. While they were presented primarily as providing sufficient conditions for "real" microeconomic systems, and in turn sufficient conditions for legitimate experiments, some experimentalists, notably Harrison (1989, 1992, 1994), have apparently insisted on them. The precepts effectively impose individual preferences that closely mirror their representation in theory. For

---

[2] If x's properties are equalized across treatments by random sampling, this yields the randomized control trial (RCT) common in medicine. We do not intend that either the text schema or RCTs are generally representative of experiments. For a critique of the claim that RCTs are representative see Pawson and Tilley (1997, chapter 3).

[3] For completeness we note, however, that insofar as its results are also supposed to generalize to *other* kinds of instances of the target phenomena than those observed, an experiment that uses an instance of its target also models those other kinds of instances.

example, and as Smith (1982a) discusses, "altruism" might be allowed, but only via interdependence in the reward medium, mirroring its theoretical depiction as interdependence in utility. It is intended that the experimenter should be in full command of any preferences subjects can act upon, in order that there be a high degree of similarity between model and experiment. It is important to consider the basis for this resemblance.

One good reason for an experiment to resemble a model would be that the theory in question leaves something unspecified and the "gap" can be filled empirically. There are numerous designs that might be interpreted as gap-filling exercises. For example, a convergence path to equilibrium, some parameter of preferences, or an equilibrium selection criterion may be left open. One may then investigate this issue experimentally. This could be seen as licensing various types of investigations, including studies of equilibrium convergence in market designs, of the extent of risk aversion in individual choice and of equilibrium selection in games. The claim would be that the designs are to fill gaps in a theory. For gap-filling exercises, a close fit with a model, meaning recreating its assumptions as far as possible, seems a sensible objective, even if this cannot be done perfectly. For the findings will not genuinely "fill the gap" if there is too much mismatch between theory and experiment. It should be apparent, though, that in any such cases the experiment is not intended to (and does not) tell us whether the assumptions themselves are appropriate for the domain of the theory in question. Whether the experiment teaches us about the world will depend on the quality of the specified model.

Many AE experiments, however, do not address questions left open by theories but rather aim either to test theories or to conduct exploratory or inductive investigations. Further examples of AE designs are set out in boxes 5.1–5.3 below. The class of AE experiments is broader, however, than our examples suggest, and it continues to broaden. Subfields have even emerged of experimental macroeconomics and international economics, as in Noussair et al. (1995, 1997), using essentially the same approach.

Box 5.1. Holt (1985), "An experimental test of the consistent conjectures hypothesis." *American Economic Review*.

The design is motivated by a model, based on that of Bresnahan (1981), that depicts the relationship between price and total output in a market with two firms, assuming homogeneous products, zero variable costs, and linear industry demand. In this model, equilibrium predictions are derived using a solution concept, consistent conjectures equilibrium, that is an alternative to Nash equilibrium.[4] The analysis is conducted for Cournot competition: that is, with firms who compete by setting quantities. Prices are assumed to adjust to a market-clearing level set by a postulated industry demand curve.

The experiment examined the relative performance of consistent conjectures equilibrium and Nash equilibrium predictions for an environment that implements the model apart from substituting student subjects for the model's firms. Numerical values are assigned to parameters in the equations to generate profit functions. These give the profits a firm would receive conditional on each possible combination of outputs. Subjects had to choose an integer between 4 and 22, representing output units, resulting in a symmetric payoff matrix with nineteen rows and columns. Consistent conjectures equilibrium outcomes entailed higher joint outputs than Nash equilibrium behavior, which in turn yielded higher outputs than collusion. Subjects were given the payoff matrix and effectively had to choose a column from it. As in the model, subjects made simultaneous choices, which determined earnings in a period.

The game was repeated, with payment given between periods. In the first experiment, subjects were paired for a whole repeated game. The number of periods was set by initial die throws, but not revealed, to yield an indefinite repetition protocol with probability $\frac{1}{6}$ that the current round was final. A subset of the subjects was rematched and played a second iteration of the repeated game; there were thirteen rounds in the first game and nine in the second. A second experiment, with ten rounds, was run introducing rematching in each period to remove repeated game effects.

The results are analyzed for last-period contributions, in line with a conditional interpretation of equilibrium predictions, as discussed in chapter 2. In the first experiment, outcomes clearly favored Nash equilibrium over consistent conjectures equilibrium, in both iterations, since only one observation of output pairs was close to consistent conjectures equilibrium. Overall around $\frac{3}{4}$ of paired outputs were at or around Nash equilibrium, with the remainder consistent with collusive behavior. In the second experiment, outcomes were close to Nash equilibrium, with far less apparent collusion, with data suggesting that some subjects were motivated by relative earnings considerations. Collusion disappeared after five out of ten periods. Consistent conjectures equilibrium outcomes were again not observed.

---

[4] A consistent conjectures equilibrium can be defined as a set of best replies on the assumption of correct beliefs about others' reaction functions (Bresnahan 1981, p 936).

Box 5.2. Alm et al. (1992), "Why do people pay taxes?" *Journal of Public Economics.*

Subjects were given a randomly determined endowment ranging from $0.25 to $2 in each period of a forty-five-round game. In each round, subjects had to report how much they had been given. Their balance then became 60% of the amount reported plus 100% of any amount unreported. A chip was then drawn from a bag containing 100 red and white chips; if and only if the chip was red, an audit of all subjects was conducted. In that event, underreporting subjects were fined fifteen times any money they stood to gain by the discrepancy in question. A second stage occurred within each period, in which the 40% of reported income in the first stage gave rise to a second payment to each subject. These revenues were multiplied by a factor m and divided equally between the eight subjects in a group, thus implementing public-good payoffs.

Experimental variables were the audit probability, p ($p = 0$, $p = 0.02$, $p = 0.1$), the multiplication factor for the public good, m ($m = 0$, $m = 2$, $m = 6$), and the language used to describe tasks to the subjects: that is, "neutral" versus "loaded" framing. There were nine sessions. Three varied p in counterbalanced, fifteen-round blocks, with $m = 2$. Three were the same with loaded framing. And three varied m in counterbalanced, fifteen-round blocks, with $p = 0.02$.

The rationale for this exercise is that the monetary incentives used resemble those involved in the decision to evade or pay taxes when filling in a tax declaration; the loaded framing consisted in describing the tasks in terms of taxation. The authors are interested in why honesty in tax declarations is substantial, which for many commentators is difficult to justify by self-interested calculation alone, since the risk of detection is typically rather low. The audit probabilities were chosen to determine whether overweighting of probabilities is a cause of tax compliance. By varying the task framing between neutral and tax-specific terminology they aimed to determine whether moral attitudes to taxes cause compliance.

The results were that the proportion of income reported increases with both the audit probability and the productivity of the public good. The increases in p from 0 to 0.02 and 0.1 each increased reported income from around 20% to around 50% and 67% respectively. The authors conclude that overweighting of small probabilities is a cause of tax compliance, since the results cannot be accounted for by risk aversion. The productivity of the public good increased compliance, but the manipulation of framing had no discernible effect. The authors conclude that people pay taxes because they value the public goods that are financed, but not because they believe tax evasion is morally wrong.

Box 5.3. Forsythe et al. (1993), "An experiment on coordination in multi-candidate elections: the importance of polls and election histories." *Social Choice and Welfare.*

Elections were implemented by paying subjects conditional on one of three events obtaining, framed as which "candidates" win an "election." Subjects then voted to determine which candidate won. The study assigned subjects to one of three types, O, G, and B, according to whether they received their highest payoff under events Orange, Green, and Blue respectively. Payoffs and subject numbers in a group were as shown in the table below.

	Election Winner			Total number of
Voter type	Orange	Green	Blue	each type
1 (O)	$1.20	$0.90	$0.20	4
2 (G)	$0.90	$1.20	$0.20	4
3 (B)	$0.40	$0.40	$1.40	6

There was an incentive for types O and G to combine on either orange or green to defeat type B subjects, who would win if each subject voted for their preferred outcome but lose either two-candidate race. That is, candidate B was a Condorcet loser.

In each round subjects could vote or abstain and payoffs were determined according to whichever candidate received most votes, with random resolution of ties. Each subject played twenty-four elections, with random recomposition of groups within twenty-eight-subject sessions. In one treatment, groups reformed after each election, and in a second treatment, groups reformed after blocks of eight. The experimenters also manipulated whether subjects received feedback between elections to determine whether subjects use past results to coordinate. Further, in half of the sessions, subjects' intentions were surveyed before each election, to investigate the effects of "opinion polls" on candidate choices.

The results showed support for "Duverger's law," that majority voting leads to a two-party system, in that last-placed candidates only received substantial votes when there were neither polls nor shared election histories to draw upon. The Condorcet loser won at least $\frac{2}{3}$ of votes in these cases but no more than $\frac{1}{2}$ in the other cases. Without prior information, types O and G were equally likely to win; with polls but no history, those that listed first won twice as frequently, a form of ballot order effect. Over $\frac{1}{3}$ of voting was strategic, with subjects choosing their second-best outcome. When groups stayed together for a sequence of elections, history was also an effective coordination device. Because they reduced the likelihood that the Condorcet loser won, the authors conclude that opinion polls may exert a benign influence on elections.

5.3   Tests of Applied Economics Theories

The usual reason for using a model-like environment is that this is an appropriate testing ground for a theory. In chapter 2 we considered this rationale primarily in relation to tests of general theories of choice and strategic interaction. We now examine cases in which an experimenter seeks to locate a design in the base domain of an AE theory by implementing enough of its assumptions. An important source of such designs is experimental industrial organization (IO); Plott's (1982) classic statement of the theory-testing defense of experiments occurs in the context of a review of IO designs. For a later review see Holt (1995). In this section we consider in depth a problem arising for the defense in an AE context, beginning by setting this out in general terms. In the remainder of this chapter we find it useful to adhere to a terminology that recognizes the distinction between a formal model and a theory, alluded to in chapter 1, which we now explore further and formulate more precisely. The natural idiom of economics, which we adopt elsewhere, does not emphasize the distinction, perhaps because theorizing and modeling activities tend to go hand in hand.

Key to the discussion is the relationship between economic theory and the world. Though this is a matter of ongoing debate among methodologists, a basic observation is that a theory cannot consist only of assumptions and deductions, or a postulated world, if the activity of testing it empirically is to make sense. The relevant sense of "assumption" here is a proposition that is supposed for the sake of argument; it has a different logical "mood" from an assertion. Assumptions and the deductions made from them, the constituent propositions of formal models in economics, therefore do not make claims about the world that invite empirical investigation. Conclusions derived are of the form: $\Box((P_1 \& P_2 \& \cdots \& P_n) \rightarrow (Q_1 \& Q_2 \& \cdots \& Q_k))$, where $P_1, \ldots, P_n$ are the (often formal) propositions of the model, $Q_1, \ldots, Q_n$ are implications of

$P_1, \ldots, P_n$, and □ is the operator, for necessity, which distinguishes the conclusions from empirical claims. So, if by a formal model we mean assumptions in abstraction from an application, it makes no sense to speak of testing a *model*.

In contrast, a *theory* makes assertions about various phenomena or entities. While a theory will typically concern many features of the world, we stipulate for simplicity a singular target, retaining our earlier notation, x. A theory will also, typically, make many assertions about the world, which we will represent as the compound assertion Tx. For example, EUT makes assertions about decisions, the theory of public goods makes assertions about behavior in the presence of nonrival and nonexcludable goods, the theory of contestable markets makes assertions about firms' pricing in markets with low entry and exit barriers, and so on. However, the theorizing typically *involves* models and their associated deductions. Therefore, in these cases, formal models are being used in such a way as to make these assertions. We can represent Tx in slightly more detail to make this explicit as $\{P_1, \ldots, P_n\}Cx$, where C is a predicate relating the model to x. For example, in illustration 6 of chapter 1, $P_1, \ldots, P_n$ comprise various assumptions about the demand and supply conditions of the market, price competition, and risk-neutral, symmetric, mixed strategy Nash equilibrium; x corresponds to some class of market with firms and consumers; and C might be "as if" truth. Tx would then be the assertion that it is as if $P_1, \ldots, P_n$ are true of certain markets.

This use of a model to make assertions about the world, in a rather oblique way, seems to be one of the "language games" characteristic of modern economics.[5] Indeed, much of the key disputed territory in economic methodology can be seen as the analysis of this practice. Of particular interest has been the question of how to understand the predicate C, for example as realist or instrumentalist, on which see chapter 2, or as representing an as-if truth claim or a type of parable. See, inter alia, Friedman (1953), Gibbard and Varian (1978), Hausman (1992), Blaug (1994), Morgan and Morrison (1999), Sugden (2000), and Cartwright (2007).

We assume for the time being that for AE theories Tx says that the formal model represents the economically essential features of some context. AE experimental designs typically implement an environment E that closely mimics the model (M) of interest, where $M = \{P_1, \ldots, P_n\}$.

---

[5] We are using "language games" in the sense of Wittgenstein (1953): that is, to paraphrase roughly, as the various rituals and activities involving language, which, according to Wittgensteinians, give rise to and determine its meanings.

In this context the blame-the-theory defense can be represented as the following argument:

(1) M represents both E and x;

(2) M represents E especially well, since E is constructed to resemble M; and therefore

(3) testing M's predictions in E gives the theory every chance of success.

On our analysis, however, (3) does not follow from (1) and (2) because of the distinction between theory and model. For E to test Tx requires the right kind of relationship between E and x, whatever the relationship between E and M. One requirement is that E provides some observations of x, specifically, ones in the domain of Tx. For in order to qualify as a test some possible experimental outcomes must be consistent, and some inconsistent, with the theory. But (1) and (2) only establish that E and x have a common representative, M, an implication that says nothing about the relationship between E and x. So these premises might hold in cases where E provides no observations of x and so cannot contradict Tx.

Such cases can arise, we argue, because the model's propositions imply nothing testable, independently of a theory which uses the model to make claims about the world. An AE theory uses a model to make those assertions about a specific domain, not more generally. For example, Tx may involve assertions that *firms* are rational, or behave as if they are, that *the government's* objectives can be represented by a certain function, that *migration* is a rational response to differentials in labor market prospects, and so on. Therefore, observations in E would neither confirm nor contradict the relevant theoretical prediction unless E provides observations of firms, the government, or migration, respectively, even if the formal model provides an excellent representation of the lab setup. These examples suggest that proposition (3) above may be false for many AE designs. As chapter 2 noted, the natural language of a theory is relevant to the determination of its base domain. And one must have extraordinarily elastic concepts of "government," "migration," and so on if one wishes to claim that they are observed in experimental economics laboratories.

It therefore seems that model-implementing tests of AE theories may be both faithful to the formal language of the model and unfaithful to the theory's natural language that directs the model at the world. In contrast, decision theory and game theory are general theories of decision making. Using stylized laboratory tasks may therefore be faithful to both the formal and natural language of the theory, with the latter relating the model to the world through the use of terms such as "probability," "outcome," and "choice." In other words, in these cases E provides instances of x. While theorists may have other decisions in mind than the kinds studied in the lab, specifically naturally occurring choices, the relevant terms in the theory still pick out suitably constructed laboratory tasks.

What then do we learn from model-implementing tests of AE theories? Any such design leaves unimplemented at least some of M's behavioral components. This is because the full implementation of a determinate model is both pointless, preempting the outcome, and impossible with human subjects, since an experimenter cannot decide how participants behave. In deriving predictions for E, these unimplemented behavioral components are applied to the kinds of subjects used in the experiment. On our analysis of theories, this application of a subset of the model propositions amounts to a distinct theoretical claim, say $T'y$, where y represents the entities studied in the lab: namely, individuals and their decisions. For example, if Tx is a game-theoretic analysis of multinational enterprises, the behavioral elements of which are profit maximization and Nash equilibrium, $T'y$ would then be selfish game theory applied to student subjects. If the predictions fail, this is inconsistent with $T'y$ but consistent with Tx, given that Tx does not imply $T'y$. Although selfish game theory involves a subset of the model propositions from our theory of multinationals, the latter concerns a very specific set of agents, and therefore, it seems, makes no prediction for the lab.

These conclusions, which locate E outside the AE theory's base domain, depend on judgments about the meaning of the natural language of the theory. In this example, it seems reasonably clear that randomly selected student subjects would not normally qualify as "multinationals." We note, however, that experiments are perfectly possible in which this would not be so clear-cut. For example, if subjects had to produce and trade something internationally, during the experiment, in conjunction with partners in many other countries, they might qualify as "multinationals" for the purpose at hand. Such cases are unlikely to involve maximal model implementation, though, for reasons considered later in this section.

To summarize, there are two key differences that predictably arise between the theories that AE designs target and those the designs actually test: namely, which propositions the theories comprise (the full set versus its behavioral elements) and their references (the applied domain versus individual people). It therefore seems reasonably clear that a model-implementing AE design will typically support decision-theoretic conclusions, rather than AE ones, *unless* the design has claims to external validity. The theory-testing defense of experiments, which eschews such claims, therefore seems out of place. In pressing this conclusion, we do not deny that an AE design may have external validity; rather, we deny that the question of its external validity can be sidestepped by blaming the theory. To make matters concrete, we now consider Holt's (1985) AE design described in box 5.1.

Since this experiment consists of student subjects choosing columns from a payoff matrix, it would be straightforward to report the experiment as a game-theoretic exercise. The AE context here, namely IO, is principally a matter of the labeling of actions and outcomes, both in the experiment and the research report. The paper is explicit about testing a behavioral proposition, since it is titled as a test of consistent conjectures equilibrium, but describes this as an IO theory and reports subjects' decisions as choices of "output" by "firms" and "industry" behavior. Because of this vocabulary, it might be predictably accused of artificiality. "Why should students' choices of columns from a monetary payoff matrix count as evidence about firms' strategic decision making?" a critic might ask.

The blame-the-theory response would be to argue that in the IO theory, a firm is represented in the same way that economic theory treats an individual, so that testing it on individuals gives the theory its best chance. On this view, Holt's experiment is only as unrealistic as the theory, since the model portrays no difference between firms and agents in general. However, the theory's natural language applies the model to firms. The defense requires that this natural language factor be regarded as less important than the formal model propositions in determining its base domain. The distinction between model and theory introduced in this chapter, however, implies that the natural language content cannot be suppressed in this manner without changing the theory under consideration.

An analogy may be useful here to illustrate this. Consider the theory (Tx) that traffic (x) behaves according to equations describing a flow (M), originating in studies of liquids. The example is not far-fetched, since engineers' models of traffic flow have actually drawn on fluid dynamics (see Bellomo et al. 2002). One can use a model originating in fluid mechanics, then, or a corresponding physical system, to derive predictions or putative explanations of traffic phenomena. One cannot test a theory of traffic, though, by experimenting on water in a pipe, even if M is supposed to represent both! This is a consequence of the natural language of Tx identifying x as traffic; any experimental outcome on water is consistent with the flow equation's working for traffic.[6] A water-based experiment, rather, tests the equations as descriptions of water in a pipe, and by extension the generality of the theory of flows on which Tx draws. For all that the model depicts a flow, the theory is a theory of traffic. Likewise, for all that the IO model depicts agents, the theory concerns firms' behavior. Conditional on the truth of the claim that traffic and water flows are analogous, the pipe experiment would be indicative of the likely behavior of traffic. However, neither the theory of traffic nor the condition are tested by it.

Holt himself cites Plott's (1982) version of the blame-the-theory defense, but also provides a bespoke methodological comment along ostensibly similar lines:

> Can laboratory experiments with individual decision makers be used to evaluate theories of the behavior of business firms? Many economists will give a negative answer, but I see nothing in the computation of a consistent-conjectures equilibrium that suggests that the arguments apply to business organizations but not to individuals.
>
> Holt (1985, p. 324)

If interpreted as the standard defense, our analysis implies that this argument is deductively invalid. It then reads as claiming that, since consistent conjectures equilibrium *can* be applied to either individuals or firms, one can test its application to firms with data on individuals. Since a theory's empirical claims depend on how a model is *actually* applied though, this does not follow. Consistent conjectures equilibrium's applications to firms and to individuals constitute distinct theories if those individuals do not count as firms. To judge whether the IO theory is being tested we therefore need to consider the meaning of the term "firm," not just the formal definition of consistent conjectures equilibrium. We interpret Holt's use of "evaluate" rather than "test" here, however, as a sign that he is aware of this. Holt appears to be arguing that if consistent conjectures equilibrium fails as a general decision-theoretic concept, the likelihood that it is suitable for application to IO problems is diminished. If so, his justification is actually subtly different from the generic blame-the-theory argument.

We note, however, that *every* potential application of a general solution concept may be said to be evaluated when it is tested in a laboratory

---

[6] Alternatively, to revisit an example from chapter 2, suppose that one "tested international trade theory" on within-household data. The exercise might be adequately described as an exploration of whether household activities obey the principle of comparative advantage. The findings could be a useful input to an evaluation of trade theory, or perhaps more likely have independent value, but it seems to stretch a point too far to say that they constitute a test of international trade theory.

experiment that implements the other components of a model. It seems reasonable to expect some of these applications to work better than others. The experiment's specific relevance to the IO domain, rather than to any other context suggesting a similar payoff matrix, therefore depends upon the degree of relevant similarity between laboratory subjects and firms. We conclude that consistent conjectures equilibrium's failure in the lab is, by itself, only a prima facie cause for concern for IO applications.

Returning to our analogy, for evaluative conclusions specifically about a theory of traffic to follow from the water-based design requires that the physical system in the experiment is a *good* model, in the resembling representative sense, of traffic. In our IO example, we similarly require students' decisions to be a good model of those of firms. These are external-validity considerations. Holt (1985, p. 324) does in fact recognize external validity as an issue, by going on to discuss whether business experience might make a difference. Other aspects to consider might include, for example, the need to justify decisions and to engage in joint deliberation in firms. The relevant considerations are factors that provide grounds for thinking that firms and laboratory subjects are potentially dissimilar types of decision makers.

The reader should not mistake the thrust of this section. To reiterate: our contention is not that AE theory-testing designs are necessarily externally invalid. It is that their ability to inform assessment of AE theories depends on their external validity; thus external-validity considerations cannot be ignored just because the design implements nonbehavioral components of a model. Model-implementing experiments test general hypotheses and theories about decision making. Unless there is reason to believe that the results generalize to the applied domain in question, this would appear to be their contribution to knowledge. Readers of experimental literature should therefore be aware that an ostensibly AE design may sometimes be better described as a test of decision-theoretic principles. Further, if the hypotheses tested are really behavioral, it seems logical that E should be optimized for testing them. A preoccupation with implementing M may detract from that. In the experiment of box 5.1, for instance, it is arguable that a smaller strategy space might have been used if the only aim were to decide between different general solution concepts based on evidence from interpersonal interaction. It seems that the payoff matrix in Holt (1985) could have been simplified by removing every second row and column, for example, while retaining the required analytical features.

A possible counterargument is that although a given design may not actually test an AE theory, it may be of interest to observe whether ordinary people can perform the types of actions that theory says are performed by governments, firms, investors, and so on. For example, it may be of interest not only to test behavioral hypotheses as general propositions, but to test them in the kinds of environment that the theories specify. It is often worth knowing whether ordinary people can perform the kinds of actions depicted in the theory, since the actions economists are interested in depend ultimately on individual human agency.

This reply is an assertion of a degree of external validity on the dimensions of both agents and tasks. So it would concede the main argument of this section.[7] The strength of such claims will have to be considered on a case-by-case basis. In our duopoly example, setting aside the issue of the relevance of student subjects, the framing of the experiment comes from a reduced form of the model, so it seems implausible to claim similarity for the tasks. Choosing rows or columns from a payoff matrix is not the kind of task the theory attributes to managers; rather it depicts them determining production quantities of a good. The payoff matrix is a useful device to illustrate the analyst's theoretical understanding of that task, but many different types of decision problems, in different contexts, might be represented in the same way.

Consider in contrast the design by Reinhard Selten et al. (2007). This experiment reports lab experiments on a "route choice" game, in which eighteen subjects have to choose either a major or minor "road" to reach a common destination. The lab environment represents a road network, with people choosing "routes" via PCs, instead of actually driving anywhere. One could implement this problem by having subjects choose actions from an abstract choice set, giving them a payoff table under the seventeen possible combinations of others' choices. In contrast, in the experiment subjects were not told any payoff contingencies, only that "journey time" increases with the number of others choosing the same route. Thus the design stopped short of implementing the assumptions of the analyst's model of route choice, in order to incorporate informational features of the target situation imported from the world. In addition, a graphic was used that, arguably, helps subjects to visualize the congestion problem in a concrete manner, strengthening the claim that subjects are performing actions of a similar kind to those the AE model specifies.

Selten et al.'s (2007) design therefore has a plausible claim to be studying behavioral components of the theory *in a relevant context*:

---

[7] By arguing from similarity in context between the lab and the target, the reply argues against the usual abstract experimental environments for applied designs. For related evolutionary arguments concerning abstract framing see Hagen and Hammerstein (2006).

one involving many ordinary human subjects, repetition, congestion-like payoffs, and limited feedback, as one would have in a road choice that people face on a habitual route. By checking the equilibrium prediction against the data, the behavioral performance of the model can be assessed, for what is to some extent a targetlike environment. It is of course possible that the lab excludes significant factors that real route choice typically involves: traffic accidents being an obvious example. This is consistent with the behavioral components' being tested at a strong point, though.

A second crucial feature is that the road traffic context is one in which ordinary people make the decisions, as opposed to a social institution. The lab agents used are therefore clearly relevant. It would be contentious to assert that the design was in the applied theory's base domain, however. For subjects may not be drivers, and there is no driving going on. Driving behavior might differ, for example because of habituation to regular routes. What we can learn from the exercise, uncontroversially, is whether the theoretical approach works for a particular context motivated by the route choice problem rather than a formal model.

A moral here is that if one implements assumptions maximally, one tends to arrive at an abstract context, because model assumptions simplify the situation to the point where it can be analyzed by applying general economic principles. One arrives at a certain monetary payoff matrix, or a certain set of monetary gambles, for example. There is a plausible argument, then, that claiming external validity on contextual grounds requires the implementation of *fewer* assumptions than is possible. The point also extends beyond theory testing to induction. If model implementation results in the study of a certain game, for example, behavioral patterns observed may transfer to other instances of that game, but not necessarily to the target, for the formal modeling may still be deficient for that particular target.

The considerations above indicate that it is neither necessary nor sufficient to implement a theory's assumptions to test it. The relevant criterion appears rather to be that the theory predicts what will happen in the experiment, which in turn implies that the laboratory observes the right kind of phenomena.[8] That will often favor some degree of match between the theory in question and the experimental environment, for example

---

[8] The view criticized here, that a theory applies where its model assumptions are satisfied rather than wherever its targets occur, is sometimes echoed outside experimental economics. For example, Noussair et al. (1995) aim to test international trade theory by implementing a simplified version of a trade model. Harrigan (2003) objects that the experiment is an oversimplified version of an economy, but nevertheless regards the Japanese economy prior to 1854 as an excellent case for empirical investigation on the grounds that it seems to satisfy the theory's assumptions.

the use of close correlates of the objects of a theory as we argued in chapter 2. However, this will typically fall short of maximal implementation of its model assumptions. This is because a theory typically consists of many components. If enough of these components are implemented, the exercise becomes a test of the decision-theoretic principles it comprises, if, as is almost always the case, these decision-theoretic principles are not implemented. The point therefore extends beyond the class of AE designs. For example, suppose one were somehow to implement the reflexivity, completeness, transitivity, and continuity axioms on preferences of the theory of choice under certainty, to test it in a choice experiment. Since this guarantees the existence of a preference ordering, the exercise would only test whether people choose their most preferred alternative. This proposition is an ingredient of the theory but is also ubiquitous in economics.

The discussion thus far deals with the question of what a laboratory experiment teaches us about a theory in cases where the aim is not to complete the theory but to evaluate it. We have concentrated on the case of realism, where the relationship the theory posits between the model and phenomena is one of approximate truth. This is not the only or even the "standard" account of the supposed relationship between economic models and the world. One might therefore consider other possible candidates for C in the representation of Tx as $\{P_1, \ldots, P_n\} Cx$. Each candidate for C, however, states a relationship between the model propositions and the world. So $\{P_1, \ldots, P_n\}$ might predict behavior in x, or they say that it is "as if" they are true of x, or they might illustrate a mechanism that may operate in the domain of x, and so on. In each case, therefore, the appropriate empirical exercise to assess the theory is to inform ourselves about x. If the experiment does not use its target, its relevance for evaluating the theory is therefore a function of its external validity.

The content of the theoretical claim C, however, may make a difference to which dimensions of "relevant similarity" are likely to be key. Suppose, for example, that Tx asserts that events in the field unfold "as if" the assumptions obtained. The justification for this claim may be that there is some enforcing mechanism in the field that makes behavior conform to the model's assumptions. However, that mechanism might not be written into the model. In that case, to consider only whether the entities in the model are sufficiently close to those in the lab would be to omit any consideration of the enforcing mechanism.

For example, the theory of the firm can be interpreted as saying that real firms behave as if they maximize profits. The justification might be a background supposition that, in the field, managers who deliver sub-optimal profits will be ousted by takeover. The theory, though, does not always specify shareholders or even managers, only firms. To concentrate only on the entities represented in the theory, even if we somehow had firms under observation in the lab, doing the kinds of tasks targeted in the theory, would be to leave out the capital market. This would, however, destroy the conditions under which the theorist believes the behavioral propositions hold. That theory did not predict well in the lab would therefore not challenge this theorist's position. So under this reading of the theory, judging likely external validity goes beyond considerations of the kinds of agent and tasks involved to include forces operating on the agent that are not represented in the formal model.

5.4   Types of Artificiality Criticism

That the "blame-the-theory" defense is not equally applicable across the board provides one reason for taking external validity seriously. However, there are other considerations backing this up. We saw in chapters 1 and 4 that theory testing is too narrow an objective to cover all experiments. Experimental inquiries also include inductive exercises such as regularity-finding and causal investigation, and such investigations are designed to support substantive claims about economic phenomena. Also, even if a theory survives initial testing in the lab, there is no guarantee that it will perform well in its intended domain of application. Whether or not a design is in the base domain of a theory, inductive inferences from an experiment depend upon its external validity and are sensitive to relevant differences between the environment and targeted domains.

For all these reasons it is important to evaluate arguments that purport to show that the results of economics experiments are unlikely to hold outside the lab. There are at least three senses in which a critic might claim that laboratory experiments are too artificial to tell us about the world. These are usefully distinguished by John Greenwood (1982), albeit in the context of social psychology designs. Artificiality may refer to the isolating function of the lab, its potential contaminating effects, or its alteration of objects of investigation. We alter this schema slightly since the contamination concern has a parallel in the claim that some key factor has been omitted.

As a preliminary it is useful to recall the distinction between internal and external validity, introduced in box 2.1 (p. 52). The latter may be conveniently defined as the lab's ability to identify facts and causal relationships that hold outside the lab, while internal validity refers to the lab's ability to identify facts and causes operating *in* the lab (Guala 2002, p. 262). Internal validity therefore depends on getting the technical details right, such as random allocations to treatments, holding nontreatment conditions constant, ensuring accurate measurement, and so on. It is common for authors to refer to an inverse relationship between these two dimensions of validity for the social science laboratory. Loewenstein's (1999) and Schram's (2005) methodological discussions, for example, take the alleged trade-off for experimental economics as a given, and Francesco Guala (2005a) also endorses it. A straightforward, axis-to-axis trade-off seems to lead to a contradiction however, if, as seems very plausible, there are no findings whose external validity is at issue unless a design has a reasonable degree of internal validity. This indicates that the relationship between internal and external validity is in need of clarification. The following discussion also aims to explore this and to identify what doubts there may be about external validity that might give rise to the trade-off view. We also aim to outline strategies to critically assess such misgivings.

5.4.1 The Artificiality of Isolation

In the naturally occurring world, a riot of constantly changing factors typically exerts simultaneous influences on almost anything one might wish to study empirically.[9] Labs implement a controlled environment, in which various factors can be manipulated while holding others constant (ceteris paribus) or excluding them entirely (ceteris absentibus). For example, economics experiments often attempt to hold constant subject characteristics by random allocation to treatment and to exclude communication between subjects entirely. A critic might therefore argue that the lab environment is too simple to tell us about the more complicated and multifaceted world outside.

However, if this criticism were generally valid it would also jeopardize the highly successful experimental traditions of natural science. Isolation seems to be the great strength of the lab, though, since without it the interplay of causes in the outside world cannot be disentangled. Consider what follows if an experiment following the schema in section 5.2 discovered a treatment effect. The weakest experimental conclusion that follows bears the ceteris *paribus* and *absentibus* qualifications: holding factors $c_1, \ldots, c_N$ constant across treatments, and excluding other factors, manipulation of the treatment variable affects the outcome in the

---

[9] The arguments of this subsection and subsection 5.4.3 draw on Greenwood (1982).

direction observed. Typically an experimenter would make a less explicitly qualified claim, for example, simply that the treatment variable has an effect in that direction on the outcome, or quantify the effect too. If a different pattern of outcomes is observed in the field, it may merely indicate that relevant controlling conditions, whether stated or not, were not met.

Indeed, when one considers a natural scientific example of this simple control trial schema, it seems hard to make sense of the notion that one might uncover a relationship that only ever holds in the laboratory. For the natural science laboratory setting is essentially a set of physical, chemical, and/or biological circumstances that just happens to be set up by an experimenter. If "the same" circumstances were to arise by some other contingency and did not give rise to the same results as the experiment, the qualified, weak conclusion from the experiment would be contradicted. We can think of that conclusion as a "local" external-validity claim, that wherever the same conditions obtain, the effect observed will follow. This seems to be roughly coincident with internal validity, the more so the more respects in which the conditions obtaining in the world are the same as those in the lab.

It should also be noted that local external validity may have considerable practical significance. Guala (2005a, chapter 7) describes "same conditions, same effects" as a metaphysical principle of the uniformity of nature. This may mean that, as just noted, perfect replication of conditions without replication of results defies comprehension. However, in practice many claims made on the basis of "same conditions" seem to be based on looser criteria of identity. Consider, for example, Greenwood's (1982) example of a result from social psychology experiments: that private use of marijuana may provoke psychosis in uninitiated smokers. Suppose this is internally valid. Whether the result also has practical importance is likely to depend on the frequency of private use in society, rather than on, say, whether the color of the walls in users' homes is the same as it is in the lab. Conditions will never be "the same" absolutely because there are an indefinite number of ways in which conditions in the lab and the world might differ.

Criteria of identity seem in practice to be relative to specific frames of reference that weight the importance of various dimensions of similarity. Overlooking this gives rise to paradoxes, discussed notably by Nozick (1981, chapter 1). We note that replication of experiments in different laboratory environments will tend to screen out many contextual specifics of particular laboratory trials—the color of the walls, the trial's timing in terms of the lunar cycle, and so on. In the marijuana smoking example, sameness would appear to be relative to the theoretical background of the experiment, broadly understood but certainly including its social-psychological features. "Same conditions, same effect," in practice, therefore, seems rather to depend on an ontological assumption that the world exhibits uniformity within the experiment's frame of reference. Such assumptions seem weak but may fail. For example, folk mycologies to determine the edibility of fungi on the basis of their physical appearance have been overturned. Any rule based on the appearance of fungi generated from controlled experiments on a sample would fail to generalize. For edible and poisonous or distasteful lookalikes are very common and sometimes discernible only by microscope (Garnweidner 1994). In this case we would expect replication to return "inconsistent" results across different samples.

What might be called "broader" external validity, in contrast, involves the lab's being able to inform us about circumstances different in relevant respects to those observed. Newton's laws of motion would appear to have a high degree of such broader external validity, for example, since they have proven to be very good approximations at the dimensions and velocities most relevant to daily life. The relevant assumption for broader external validity seems to be one of an additional uniformity to the world, an idea that is explored in the next section. In naturally occurring circumstances where a larger range of causal factors is at play than in the lab, for example, the presumption is that relationships observed in the lab remain an input into what happens, and this is a key desideratum of many kinds of results. It is often held, for example, that fundamental physical laws retain their form when multiple causes apply, so that they are considered globally valid.

However, there are problems in justifying claims to broader external validity. In the philosophy of physics this has been a matter of considerable debate following the work of Cartwright (1983); see, for example, Chalmers (1993) and Clarke (1995). Cartwright's influential, though controversial, thesis is that high-level physical laws only state truths for appropriately circumscribed circumstances; if they are not so qualified they *lie*. This is argued on the basis that the laws state the form of singular forces, whereas objects in nature are subject to combinations of these forces and the laws do not combine to form a unified system.

Greenwood's (1982) drug-use example raises an analogous multiple determination problem in a social science context. For he cites evidence that when smoking in the normalizing company of supportive users, the unfamiliar state of consciousness marijuana induces tends to be interpreted as pleasurable, confounding the tendency to paranoia. Characterizing the relationship between this drug and psychiatric problems remains a subject of ongoing debate, but the facts of the matter are of less interest here than the possibilities raised. Greenwood's description suggests that the tendency to psychosis is absent when use occurs in what is arguably the predominant social setting. If so, his description of the drug's paranoia-inducing capacity as a "tendency law" is misleading.[10] For it would *not* then remain an input into what happens when a very relevant condition is varied. The relevant experiments' external validity could therefore justifiably be regarded as lower than one might hope.

The awkward question arising from these considerations is, How reasonable is it in a given case to assume that in the wild, where a broader set of influences may operate, the effect in question *does* remain operative? It seems difficult to proceed other than by considering the kinds of reasons a result might not generalize and what can be done to check. The problem is not isolation per se, as that seems the only sensible way to conduct experiments, but the possibility that relevant features of the world may not be uniform. By omitting certain key features of the contexts we are interested in, we may be misled when we generalize to those contexts. We discuss this further in the next section under the heading of "omission."

5.4.2   Artificialities of Omission and Contamination

Guala (2005a, chapter 7) argues strongly that the principle of "same conditions, same effects" leaves many important questions about external validity unanswered.[11] The conditions in the social science lab are often nothing like "the same" as those in situations of interest even with specific, relevant criteria of identity. For example, with the exception of the context of the casino, actions rarely have both the well-defined probabilities and consequences characteristic of most choices studied in decision-theoretic exercises. Real-life choices typically involve messier, fuzzier, and more multifaceted problems, embedded in an ongoing context of other unclear judgment calls. One reason a critic might assert that laboratory results are unlikely to generalize to such contexts is that the causal relationships they involve may be complex. The criticism may be read as the suggestion of an "interaction effect," meaning that the presence (absence, or different value) in the world of a factor absent (present)

---

[10] This problem is hidden in Greenwood's formalism (1982, p. 230). A causal explanatory proposition is represented there by $(x)(Fx \rightarrow (Gx \veebar (c_1 \vee c_2 \vee \cdots \vee c_n)))$ where F is a causal mechanism and G is its effect, $\veebar$ is exclusive and $\vee$ inclusive disjunction, and $c_1, \ldots, c_n$ represent *all* confounding mechanisms. This represents in the same way both operative tendencies that are swamped by other factors, and factors that are rendered inoperative by confounds.

[11] The arguments of this subsection draw on Guala (2002, 2005a).

in the lab might negate or reverse a treatment effect. As just indicated, the critique that the lab does not contain the right set of causal influences may be a charge of omission, that is, that there are more factors present in the field, or contamination, that the lab introduces extraneous factors.

Experimentalists often argue, as Schram (2005) does, that critics are obliged to give specifics of circumstances where a result might not hold, and reasons why the alleged missing or contaminating factor might be a problem there. This seems to be a reasonable requirement, for a general doubt to the effect that there is some circumstance that makes a relevant difference somewhere cannot be critically assessed. When such specifics have been supplied, an appropriate response, wherever possible, is to rectify the alleged problem in the lab, to check empirically whether it makes a difference to the results. This is in principle a generally available strategy in the face of omission or contamination concerns to establish external validity, discussed by Starmer (1999a), which Guala (2002) terms "checking by exhaustion." For each factor cited by a critic as missing (or extraneous), it is often possible to come up with a design that incorporates (or excludes) it. The more factors that are added or excluded in this way, the less reasonable it will be for a critic to refuse to accept the result in question if it fails to disappear. For the list of factors that the social science community considers plausible ways of explaining the result away will typically be finite.

The history of the preference reversal effect arguably illustrates checking by exhaustion. Lichtenstein and Slovic's (1971) experiment seemed to provide evidence against optimization in individual decision making. The initial response by economists was to suggest many factors omitted from the original design, such as significant real payoffs and incentive-compatible valuation procedures. Gradually these and other omissions were introduced in designs such as those of Grether and Plott (1979) and Berg et al. (1985) in a largely unsuccessful research program to make the phenomenon disappear. For a review of the preference reversal literature, see Seidl (2002). Eventually, Chu and Chu (1990) had more success, but they had to use a combination of repetition and "money-pumping." Under money-pumping, subjects are forced to conduct a set of trades according to any inconsistent stated preferences and valuations they gave, which ultimately leaves them with the same set of assets as before trading but less cash. An insistence that factors such as repetition and money-pumping obtain for decision theory to apply would significantly curtail its scope, according to the argument of chapter 2. Overall, preference reversals would now appear to be generally accepted as robust results, even if they have not led to the abandonment of EUT—see chapters 3 and 4, in particular box 3.4 (p. 131).

A problematic case to check would appear to be contamination by subjects motivated either to help or to frustrate the experimenter. For designing this problem out of experiments apparently requires going beyond the lab: that is, using a design in which subjects are not aware of being in an experiment. While this is a solution in principle, in practice many designs rely heavily on subject–experimenter interaction. This is perhaps unavoidable for there are reasons in many cases for using highly stylized tasks to test particular hypotheses. Since these tasks often bear more resemblance to decisions as depicted in theory than naturally occurring ones, one would not expect to find them in a naturally occurring context. It is therefore unclear how one could conduct certain types of experiments as field experiments. Examples include many decision-theoretic exercises. For example, it is rarely clear what game theory predicts of a given real situation. In the lab one may implement a particular game, including its knowledge structure, using money to proxy utilities to test rival solution concepts. In most naturally occurring situations, in contrast, one will not know, inter alia, participants' views of which outcomes result from which action combinations, their preference orderings over these outcomes, nor their beliefs about others' payoffs, so one will typically not be able to calculate equilibrium strategies with a reasonable degree of certainty.

As long as the potential problem of subjects' compliance or subversion is that the particular personal encounter between experimenter and subjects influences the results, however, there seems to be no general cause for concern. We shall call such cases "experimenter effects," whereby the experimenter influences the results by being present in person. This is the usage of Rosenthal (1966). For example, a particular experimenter or assistant *might* unwittingly convey through his body language or facial expressions an obvious and different message about what subjects are desired to do in each treatment of a design. And subjects *might* respond to that message. Since these problems may or may not occur, though, and one might expect the risk to be minimized with competent implementation, it would seem arbitrary for a critic to dismiss experimental evidence on these grounds without specific reasons justifying the allegation. There is another type of compliance issue that may be harder to deal with, though, and this is considered in subsection 5.5.2.

One example of a specific contamination concern that *can* be investigated in the lab is that subjects identify an intended treatment effect and *deliberately* produce it. By using between-subject tests of the common ratio effect, preference reversals, and so on, we can eliminate the possibility that subjects are deliberately trying to make their preferences consistent (or inconsistent) to please experimenters. Regarding other conventional experimenter effects, some experimentalists have claimed that the experimenter, who knows what results he or she desires, should not be in the lab when the experiment is carried out. The assistants could be professionals, as are the people who administer opinion polls, who have no idea what is wanted. If critics of experimental economics really thought that these contamination effects were serious, experimenters could use this anonymous methodology. In like fashion, experimental economists have adopted the real-incentives methodology because their audience is skeptical of results without incentives.

Another important omission criticism is that the constituents of society or the economy are too interconnected for labs to provide useful findings. Guala (2002) attributes this position to critical realists, pointing out that it can be interpreted as an assertion of holism, which might be seen as a systemic version of the interaction effect concept. A system may be said to be holistic if relationships between some of its components depend on the state of other components. Checking by exhaustion might then be practically infeasible because what is excluded may be a whole chain of interconnected factors.

To grasp what such a systemic holism critique involves, consider Mae-Wan Ho's (1998) critique of genetic modification biotechnology (GMB). Ho claims that GMB takes a reductionist stance toward its subject matter. She means in part that genetic engineering interventions to create transgenic organisms typically presuppose that the function of a gene does not vary with the complex biological and environmental nexus of its occurrence. Ho documents a large body of evidence to the contrary. Supposing that this criticism is correct, however, it does not provide an argument against laboratory experimentation.[12] For the evidence cited of the holistic character of gene functions is itself furnished by controlled experiment, including failed gene transfer exercises themselves. Rather it would frustrate the project of using gene functions identified in context A in contexts B, C, and D of research and development interest. Assuming for the sake of argument that this is correct, it would follow that while the results of the gene-function-in-A investigations are externally valid in our local sense—that is, wherever the same conditions obtain the same results will hold—typically they do not generalize sufficiently to license the types of inferences about gene functions that

---

[12] Nor does Ho present her argument as counting against the external validity of experiments per se, rather than as against excessive extrapolation from the data and currently "tolerated" release of transgenic materials from experiments into the environment.

genetic engineers are seeking. That is to say, roughly, that the occurrence of the gene in contexts B, C, and D may not make the characteristics associated with the gene in A more likely to be expressed in any predictable way.

According to Ho's argument, holism can be experimentally established. But in the case of laboratory genetics the investigator is always operating with a multidimensionally rich subject matter. In contrast, economics experiments typically involve simple environments with relatively reduced outcome spaces. This may make it far less likely for holism to be established experimentally in economics labs, especially if introducing the requisite richness would involve somehow recreating extensive aspects of the naturally occurring society or economy. It also, therefore, introduces the unappealing prospect of a standoff between critics who assert holism and experimentalists who deny it, with forays into philosophical argument failing to decide the issue either way. However, as Guala (2001, 2002) points out, there is a second empirical strategy for checking external validity. If there is a body of data from the field, tracking a variety of features of some phenomenon of interest, and lab studies yield data that exhibit all of these regularities, with no evidence of different processes behind them, it would be a remarkable coincidence, a miracle even, if there were not a common process at work. Call this the "no miracle" argument; since miracles are so unlikely, a common process must be responsible.

Guala's key example of an argument for external validity by these means is Plott's (1997) trials of an auction mechanism designed for the sale of wireless telecommunications bandwiths. Data from a real auction on price and total revenues were compared with those from "design experiments" on which the former were based, and the properties of which had been extensively explored. (A design experiment is one that serves as the basis for an external application rather than exploring the properties of that which already exists. An example is the exploration of the aerodynamics of prototype cars in a wind tunnel, until a shape with the desired properties is obtained.) On the grounds that the price and revenue trajectories were similar across the two cases, it was argued, albeit tentatively, that there was evidence that the real auctions shared the efficiency properties of the design experiments.[13]

The testbed auction experiments are unusual in that the real environment is based on that developed in the lab. In these cases, there is special

---

[13] This is not so easy to judge as the diagrams presented in Plott (1997, figures 5 and 7) and reproduced in Guala (2001) suggest, since one graph shows revenue per laboratory period and the other shows total revenue in real time. However, the rights and wrongs of the case are of less interest here than the general strategy.

reason to believe that the experimental environment might be a very good working model of its target. This is favorable, for the strength of a no miracle argument depends on how "miraculous" the relevant findings would be in the absence of a shared process. Guala (2001) attributes rather strict premises to this argument, including control of or similarity between all observable features of target and experimental systems. It therefore sets a rather high standard for experimenters to meet both in designing realistic environments and in reproducing field data experimentally. The argument is methodologically significant, though, since it seems to show that there is no a priori barrier to external validity imposed by omission or contamination criticisms. For it is possible that the criticism will be met empirically. The extent of omission or contamination problems in any given case is therefore ultimately an empirical matter.

The more usual and problematic case is where we use the lab to try to learn about what exists independently. Hence as Guala (2005a, chapter 9) argues, there is a third strategy to external-validity inferences: namely, empirical cross-checking between the lab and the field.[14] Again, Guala considers cases from auctions studies. Similar evidence has been observed of effects indicative of the winner's curse (see box 5.4) in laboratory and field auctions.

Box 5.4. The winner's curse.

The winner's curse is an adverse selection problem arising in the context of auctions, in particular "common value" auctions, in which the value of what is sold is unknown ex ante but identical ex post for each bidder. Suppose that each bidder's valuation of a lot is unbiased: that is, it is drawn from a random variable centered on the true value of the lot. Then even if bidders are risk averse, bidders with higher valuations will be more likely to win the auction. It is therefore likely that the winner of the auction will have paid too much for the good. This effect depends on bounded rationality; full rationality models can be produced in which bidders effectively take this mechanism into account in their computation of an optimal bid, negating the adverse selection problem.

The notion of the winner's curse seems originally to have been mooted by engineers working for oil companies (Capen et al. 1971). Many authors have since provided experimental evidence of the winner's curse.

---

[14] One might ask whether the lab is adding anything if one needs to check its results against the field. However, what one needs to know to investigate a hypothesis without the lab data is not the same as what one needs to know with it. This is argued forcefully by Guala (2002) in his discussion of the "experimenter's regress."

For example, Bazerman and Samuelson (1983) demonstrated the phenomenon using, among other lots, jars of coins in a sealed bid auction in which the winner paid the amount bid (a "first-price" auction). The data from the coin lots showed that winners had bid on average 25% more than the true value, despite the fact that separately elicited valuations of the jars were on average only 64% of the true value.

In Kagel and Levin's (1986) study that also used first-price auctions, a model of bidders' valuations was implemented by having subjects bid on the basis of a private signal of the common value of a lot. Subjects were told the distribution of this private signal around the true value. Experimental variables manipulated included group size and public versus private information. Results included that in groups with three to four bidders, winners tended to make profits but only at around two-thirds of those predicted by risk-neutral Nash equilibrium modeling. In these groups public information raised prices. In groups with six to seven bidders, negative profits tended to be realized and public information reduced bids. The data are consistent with a winner's curse effect and reject the risk-neutral Nash equilibrium model.

In cross-checking between the lab and the field, it would seem that one is going to be lucky if natural experiments present themselves that would allow external validity checking *of a similar force* to that which is possible in the case of design experiments. Firstly, it is unreasonable to expect experimenters to *demonstrate* external validity conclusively, given the well-known problems of working with field data. And secondly, checking for broader external validity requires that the conditions are different between the lab and the field. For example, the winner's curse seems to be most easily demonstrated in the lab for examples in which the value of the object to a subject ex post is known precisely. In the field, the value of, say, an oil lease ex post may depend on factors such as changes in the regulatory environment that are impossible for bidders to anticipate. So firms might make better than anticipated profits even if they pay "too much" for a lease. Firms might also know the probability of such regulatory reform better than the researcher. Therefore, presumably, a more involved comparison has to be made to show that it would be remarkable if the same process were not behind lab and field results. Further, nowadays companies may hire auction consultants who might advise them how much to revise their bids to counteract winner's curse effects. If the winner's curse is not observed, it may still be operative in a sense, since this may be what causes the consultants to be hired.

Guala's (2005a, chapter 9) account of empirical cross-checking centers on Kagel and Levin (1986), who give an extended discussion of the external validity of their design with reference to oil lease auctions. According to Guala this is a case in which the experimenters mimicked a specific real-world auction context, by sticking closely to a formal model of it— a design feature that enables an external-validity argument to be given in terms of discounting alternative mechanisms that would produce the same result. Our earlier discussion of model-implementation counsels caution here; sticking closely to a formal model may actually *decrease* correspondence between the lab and the field. In the example outlined in box 5.4 a model was implemented of bidders' individual value signals. In the oil lease auctions, although companies bid on the basis of estimates of lease values, it is debatable whether these have probability distributions associated with them comparable to those implemented: namely, uniformity distributions within known upper and lower bounds. The relevance of the lab auction to the field data seems to depend on its counting as a comparable auction rather than the fact that it implements a model of one.

A context-mimicking experiment may be one means of making a strong inductive argument but does not seem to be a requirement, and does not on its own seem to take us beyond a local external-validity claim. It would be indicative of broader external validity if cases were investigated that depart significantly from laboratory conditions and still returned evidence of similar effects. There is an argument, then, that comparison between auctions of the kind used by Bazerman and Samuelson (1983) and field data (box 5.4) are more telling if successful. Also, one would like to discount any explanations for similar result patterns that might be lab-specific. In the winner's curse case, for example, one would like to discount the explanation of winners' losses that winning subjects were those willing to incur losses in order to win, which could arise from viewing the exercise as a competitive game. This would not necessarily be achieved by running new lab experiments with more field-like parameters.

It is notable that the example of auctions recurs as one in which researchers have found encouraging similarities between laboratory and field data. Smith (1982a), for example, also refers to supportive investigations that conducted laboratory and field studies in tandem, and even the otherwise-critical Siakantaris (2000) views auctions as a relatively unproblematic area of experimental investigation. We offer one possible reason for this plausibility in section 5.6. Assuming that auction designs do score relatively highly on external validity, the significance of the example is that society does not appear to be so entirely holistic as to preclude any experimental investigation in pursuit of transferable generalizations. There appear to be, that is, at least some regions of relative invariance with respect to a wider social and economic context. The more field evidence coheres with laboratory evidence in a given subject area, the more confident we can be, it seems, of the broader external validity of an experimental result there prior to specific checking. Further reflections on field experiments are given in section 5.7.

5.4.3   The Artificiality of Alteration

The existing literature on artificiality in experimental economics has concentrated primarily on the issues of omission and contamination. We have seen that although there may be problems with specific cases or research programs, these considerations do not seem to furnish general concerns undermining external validity a priori. There is a third sense in which experiments might be artificial, though, in the sense of altering the target phenomena. This criticism has been made by Greenwood (1982) in particular. Related skeptical arguments appear in Dilman (1996) and Harré and Secord (1972). The arguments have historically been directed against psychology and social psychology rather than economics experiments, presumably because this is the older and better-known literature. In contrast to the considerations of subsections 5.4.1 and 5.4.2 though, the notion of "artificiality of alteration" does raise issues that are very general in scope. The issues are different in character since they do not essentially concern causal complexity. Whereas a criticism of isolation, omission, or contamination questions the influences the laboratory exerts over target phenomena, the alteration charge questions whether they are actually observed.

The argument can be stated as follows. The basic premise is that social psychological phenomena (SPP) are *relational*. This means that they are defined partly by their relation to other phenomena and partly by people's perceptions that those relationships are satisfied. For example, for two people to be married, in many cultures it is necessary that a certain ceremony has taken place in which vows were exchanged. Moreover, it tends to be necessary that the event be witnessed as having taken place in accordance with various rules. The person conducting the ceremony must hold a specific office for example. Further, although it is possible to believe that one is not married when one actually is married, as with amnesiacs, a social scientist studying the behavior of married persons would usually wish to exclude such cases. For the marital amnesiac would not be acting qua married person in the domestic realm. In addition, their general behavior would be much less influenced than most by being married. To take a more economic example, a person cannot normally become a manager of a firm unless she has been appointed by the right people in the firm's hierarchy. And her choices will not fully count as managerial decisions unless she has been informed of that appointment. Relational phenomena refer to other entities in a pattern of part–whole relationships that are contrasted with purely causal relationships.

Such a relationality premise has been argued by many philosophers. Arguments supporting it appear, for example, in Taylor (1971), Searle (1995), and Hollis (1998), and it is expounded upon in Greenwood (1990). It forms part of the common thesis that *social* reality is partly constructed: that is, dependent on participants' beliefs about it. That thesis seems less controversial than the more radical idea, which most analytical philosophers would regard as inconsistent, that *all* facts are somehow socially constructed. Economic theory usually makes little explicit reference to any belief dependence of the social world, but an exception occurs, arguably, in monetary economics. Money is defined relative to its functions, meaning that anything that is accepted as a means of payment, unit of account, or store of value counts as money. This implies that whether a good counts as money depends on whether people generally regard it as fulfilling those definitive functions for others, which in turn refer to other relational phenomena such as exchange.

Greenwood (1982) argues from the relationality premise that SPP cannot be created unchanged in a laboratory experiment without deception, since subjects are necessarily aware of the additional, generative activity of the experimenter: that is, in setting up and controlling the event. The conclusion is drawn that the experiment creates its own, different, SPP. A corollary of this line of argument is that experimenters should pay attention to subjects' interpretations of the experiment in order to interpret the results. For this critique to be relevant to experimental economics it is sufficient that it sometimes investigates SPP. This appears to be common. For experimental economists have targeted, inter alia, social status, employment relations, managerial decisions, and social norms, all of which appear to be relational phenomena in the sense required. Since the artificiality of alteration concept has received relatively little attention, we consider examples where it might be applied to contrast it with considerations of contamination and omission.

5.5   Alteration Contrasted with Omission and Contamination

5.5.1   Alteration versus Omission

Consider first Ball et al.'s (2001) investigation of the effects of social status in markets (see illustration 8 of chapter 1). It illustrates well the issues arising with the alteration critique. For status is clearly a paradigmatic case of SPP. According to the authors' own definition, status is "a ranking in a hierarchy that is socially recognized," which implies that it is a relational property in the sense already outlined. The authors have a claim to implement a kind of status on this definition, since subjects who perform well in the quiz are publicly applauded in the experiment. What is debatable is whether the status implemented in the design is the same kind as that targeted: namely, socioeconomic status in the sense involved in the examples drawn from the field. An argument against this equivalence is that the hierarchy studied is a creation of the experiment, not something recognized outside of it. Because the experimenters' interpretation is contestable, the critic may come up with alternative readings of the results, such as "demand effects" or subjects' disaffection at being given low status. Bardsley (2005) argues that what is implemented is akin to "teacher's pet" status, given that the awarding of stars and orchestrated applause closely resemble a classroom context.

The objection, therefore, concerns the identification of the status used with that targeted, not the conditions copresent with the treatment variable. If this identity does not hold, this is not necessarily fatal to the study. Labs often use substitute objects of investigation, as the testing on animals of medical interventions intended for humans readily shows, and we have argued that experiments may serve as models of target systems. Vivisectionists may recognize that laboratory and target systems differ, for example, and that consequently the knowledge acquired for humans is conjectural. In contrast, Ball et al. (2001, pp. 169, 181) appear keen to deny such a difference. Their argument is that the status induced is real status because it satisfies the relational definition. This seems an insufficient defense, though, since real status in the lab can be dissimilar to real status in the field.

If, alternatively, one accepts that the experiment uses an *analogue* of socioeconomic status, the problem becomes one of judging the quality of this analogue. In the absence of evidence about this, protagonists in a debate over external validity are likely to deploy general reason and argument, incorporating casual empiricism. Bardsley (2005) argues that a link between classroom status and socioeconomic status such as nobility is tenuous, giving the reason that the former has few imaginable direct

market consequences. The authors' justification of their status manipulation also points to a potentially relevant difference, though. Prior status
characteristics, including subjects' socioeconomic status, were not used
on the grounds that some subjects would regard these as positive and
some as negative attributes, while attitudes toward stars and applause
were expected to be more uniform (Ball et al. 2001, p. 167). If so, such
heterogeneity in the field could conceivably reduce, negate, or reverse
the observed status premium.

Another relevant example is the tax evasion experiment, exemplified
in box 5.2. In tax evasion experiments subjects are given an endowment
and are later asked to report how much they received. Subjects earn some
fraction of their reported values, plus any difference between the two figures. With a certain probability, answers are checked and if subjects have
reported less than the full amount they lose earnings proportionally to
the amount unreported. In these designs, the experimental environment
clearly mirrors the way taxation is modeled in theoretical literature, for
example by Allingham and Sandmo (1972). There is a payoff from underreporting income tempered by a small risk of costly punishment, and
revenue collected funds public goods. For a review of tax experiments
see Torgler (2002).

The alteration critic argues that the actions carried out in the experiment are quite different to tax compliance and tax evasion (Bardsley
2005). The premise is again about relational matters: tax, in contrast, for
example, to theft, is revenue collected by a government, which stands
in a political authority relationship to a group of citizens. It may have
a democratic mandate to govern, for example. To qualify as tax evasion, the line goes, underreporting would have to be carried out with the
intention of paying less tax than the system requires. It can therefore be
argued that tax evasion involves a reference to tax in the agents' intentions that is missing in the experiment. For, transparently, no payment
is made to the government in the latter. The difference from an agent's
point of view between paying tax and contributing to an experimental
public good might invoke different moral attitudes. For example, any
perceived duties of citizenship would be relevant to the former case but
not to the latter.

On these grounds Bardsley (2005) argues that the results might be
more straightforwardly reported as discoveries about public-good games
incorporating a risk of costly punishment for free-riding, with conjectural conclusions about taxation. On this view it is not entirely clear what
the experiment's added value is, since there is evidence both that subjects "overweight" low probabilities relative to expected utility, and that
contributions to public goods are sensitive to the marginal per capita

return, from decision-theoretic designs. Much would then appear to rest on whether the parameter values and perhaps the extensive form of the game, such as a possible audit after each act of reporting, are representative of tax evasion scenarios. Bardsley (2005) takes exception to the conclusion that people do not comply out of moral beliefs, which Alm et al. (1992) deduce from their result that using tax-specific language did not increase honesty. If taxation has not been observed, he contends, this argument is invalid since relevant moral attitudes such as recognition of civic duties are excluded by design. If those factors are important, they may undermine the experimental model of taxation as a risky free-riding decision to fund a monetary public good. Following Titmuss (1970), for example, it is often argued that pecuniary incentives crowd out social motivations such as civic virtue. In which case overweighting of audit probabilities might also crowd out civic virtue in the field, in a manner absent from the experiment. For experimental evidence of motivational crowding out see Frey and Oberholzer-Gee (1997) and Gneezy and Rustichini (2000a,b), and for further discussion see chapter 6.

Next consider the voting experiment of box 5.3. In this case it seems that both omission criticisms and alteration arguments might be predictably raised by a critic. The omission criticisms would concern more complex causal mechanisms giving rise to different voting behavior than that observed. For example, if a party is behind in the polls it might react by intensifying its own campaign, depending on its financial resources. So a party's initial poor poll performance could set off events causing voters to eventually coordinate on it. There will also typically be a time series of polls from different sources, considerably complicating the message that voters have to react to. Also, the experiment concentrates on the simple but highly unlikely event of an exactly equal race between second- and third-placed parties in terms of the electorate's underlying preferences. The likelihood of such an event decreases exponentially with the size of an electorate. This raises the question of whether the results generalize to the normal case in which even an approximately equal split is consistent with practical certainty that an individual vote will not affect the outcome.

An alteration skeptic would argue, in contrast, that elections have not been observed. The environment chosen implements a particular game between players of types O and G, reminiscent of "battle of the sexes," who face a conflict of interest with type Bs. Inferences to politics should therefore be explicitly conjectural on this line. The argument might proceed as follows. To vote in a political election is to do more than merely to participate in a voting game with a majority scoring rule; it is to participate in a political system. Voting to elect candidates for political posts may therefore involve motivational factors such as civic duties and party loyalties. Because of this, relevant phenomena may be omitted from the design, such as "expressive voting." Expressive voting can be defined as voting stemming from individuals' political and value commitments, rather than the prospect of achieving any particular result.

If expressive voting is widespread, this could undermine external validity, since it might lower the probability that a poll changes the outcome of an election because of tactical voting. The absence of expressive voting in this setting, a critic might argue, is one reason it is necessary to use the unrealistic equal-split scenario. This shows that omission criticisms are predictably interwoven with alteration concerns; the relata of the target phenomena, such as parties and associated values that candidates represent, tend to be omitted and insofar as they are included they are altered, the argument alleges, because they are creations of the experiment.

5.5.2 Alteration versus Contamination

The examples above concern AE experiments. The alteration critique purports to more general significance though. This stems from its claim that a laboratory experiment implements its own SPP. If so, it is possible that the special situation of being in an experiment affects subjects' reactions to the stimuli deployed. The alleged artifacts are variously known as "Hawthorne effects," "demand effects," and "effects of demand characteristics." Relevant evidence is reviewed by Adair (1984). The original evidence for the Hawthorne effect is disputed (Jones 1992) and the psychological literature reveals a proliferation of experimenter–effect concepts. Despite this untidy overall picture, one theme recurs throughout, expressed most clearly, perhaps, in the work of Martin Orne (1962, 1973). According to Orne's (1973) account, any social science laboratory study consists of two potentially distinct experiments. There is the one designed by the experimenter and there is that experienced by the subjects. Since it is the latter that determines behavior, drawing the right inferences requires that these perspectives converge. Call this the "two experiments problem": there is no guarantee that the subjects' experiment can be anticipated by the designer. By extension, subjects' perceptions of each treatment might be crucial in interpreting a treatment effect.

A comparison with drug trials is useful here. There, "placebo" groups are used to control for any effects of the reactivity of the person to participation in a trial.[15] This makes sense because there is a pharmacological factor operating independently of subjects' awareness of it. If subjects' perceptions are equalized by having ineffective pills that are, to the user, indiscernible from the drugs, the trial will show only the pharmacological effects of the drug. The same control cannot be achieved in social science experiments. For different sensory stimuli are, necessarily, given in the different treatments. If in treatment 1 variable A takes value q and in treatment 2 it takes value r, subjects in 1 have to be aware that the variable takes q and those in 2 that the variable takes r. In other words, it is not possible to have a true "double-blind" in social science labs. In a true double-blind design, both the experimenter and subjects are blind to who receives which treatment at the time of the trial. Since subjects cannot be blind to the treatment they are receiving if there are informationally distinct treatments, a double-blind in this sense is not possible.

Economics experiments in which experimenters only observe the overall pattern of events, not individuals' behavior, *do* incorporate a control for being personally observed by the experimenter, though. Where subjects are blind to each other's behavior too, this seems better described as a "double-anonymous" design to avoid confusion with double-blindness to treatment. Berg et al. (1995) and Hoffman et al. (1996) offer good examples of double-anonymous designs that are not double-blind in the sense just outlined. Unintended aspects of subjects' experiences might still be affected by the differential in information across treatments in double-anonymous designs, however, alongside those aspects that are intended. Conscious experience cannot therefore be equalized across treatments with the certainty that is afforded by a placebo trial. It therefore cannot be ruled out ex ante, for example, that the different treatments give off different "demand characteristics." The phrase refers, roughly, to the set of cues the environment gives off about the behavior appropriate to it. Since volunteer subjects can be expected to approach a design in a cooperative frame of mind this may, conceivably, cause a spurious treatment effect.

It is worth noting that the argument just given is a priori in character. In contrast to psychologists' "experimenter effects," which we would include under the heading of contamination, the possibility of demand characteristics confounds cannot be entirely avoided by a competent

---

[15] As with the original Hawthorne effect, the evidence for placebo effects from clinical trials is actually a matter of some controversy, stemming from criticism by Kienle and Kiene (1997) and Hrobjartsson and Gotzsche (2004). However, neurological experiments focusing specifically on placebo effects have returned positive results, for example in Wager et al. (2004).

administration of a technically perfect design, or even the replacement of the experimenter in an entirely computerized design. For according to this line, the social situation of being in an experiment changes the actions under observation. Greenwood (1982) uses the example of handshakes to argue this point: a handshake is a different action in the context of a greeting and in the context of making a bet. In similar vein Bardsley (2005) argues that subjects' actions in experiments are acts of compliance with an experimenter, in the sense of being cooperative with the running of it if not consciously seeking to confirm or refute a hypothesis.

5.6 Evaluating Alteration Criticisms

First, consider how the arguments available to counter omission or contamination concerns fare against the alteration critique. These defenses treat artificiality as an empirical matter. However, it is natural to read the alteration critique as conceptual. The first argument was the empirical strategy of implementing alleged omissions to see if they make any difference. This would miss the point. For if the critic alleges that what is implemented differs relationally from x, then adding new features to the environment will not provide an answer. For example, in the tax evasion experiment, if we introduced an agent in the role of a government, even one elected by subjects, we still would not have an environment in which people stand in a relationship to an institution as opposed to another person. It might be possible to use real taxes in some cases, but presumably one could only do so if taxes were actually owing on experimental earnings, and the tax rate would not be under the experimenter's control.

If the critic is right to argue for relational difference as a conceptual truth though, it does not follow that behavior is altered by this difference. That remains an empirical question. It therefore seems that the strategies to explore external validity based on cross-validation between lab and field are still available, though they assume a different character from their previous incarnations. For correspondence between the lab and the field would suggest not that lab taxes, social status, and elections *are* the target phenomena, but that the social nature of the targets does not have much economic significance. This fits, arguably, with a charitable reading of economists' treatment of sociality in the tradition of Adam Smith. The approach is not so much to deny that people are social beings as to claim that we do not need to refer to this sociality in order to predict and explain the most significant features of economic behavior (see Bardsley and Sugden 2006).

The requirements of a no-miracle argument to *establish* external valid-ity are as tough here as when omission or contamination are the sup-posed problem. However, there are, again, more limited claims that can be made along similar lines. For example, Alm et al. (1992) found that compliance increased dramatically enough, with an increase in detection probability from 0 to 0.02, for this to be inexplicable by known degrees of risk aversion. They could conclude from this that there is a suggestion that overweighting of probabilities plays a role in tax compliance, even if the critic is right that taxation has not been observed. In other words, there are probably causes of compliance other than social motivations such as citizenship duties. This is an Ockham's razor argument premised on similarities in the prospects involved and the *absence* of the social motivations in question in the lab. Where no civic duties are involved, the argument goes, one observes compliance in tasks with similar mone-tary prospects to tax decisions, through overweighting. We observe high compliance in real taxation, so why would overweighting not be a factor there too? The strength of such an argument depends on how strong the claim is that the monetary incentives are similar in the lab and in real taxation.[16]

On the other hand, the "same conditions, same effect" argument for local external validity seems inappropriate in response to the alteration criticism. It may still be argued soundly that if the same conditions imple-mented in the lab obtained in the world, we should expect the same effect. However, the if-clause would then be satisfied in circumstances describing another experiment, rather than a situation "external" to an experiment. For according to the alteration critique, unlike the physics or biology lab, the social science lab is a social context. "The same" cir-cumstances obtaining would therefore include a reference to the total social interaction in which the data were observed, which comprises the experimenter–subject relationship.

The challenge of the alteration critique is partly that it argues on con-ceptual grounds that there are certain phenomena that cannot be recre-ated in the lab. If this is correct, the experiments implement analogues of them. Guala (2005a, chapter 9) suggests that external-validity assertions are analogical quite generally. Whether or not this is the case, the relevant problem if the target of a laboratory economics experiment is problem-atically relational does appear to be that of establishing the quality of an analogy. Both relevant similarity between objects of study and tar-gets, *and* relative invariance of target behavior across lablike and other

---

[16] For reflections relevant to this matter see Hogarth (2005).

conditions are apparently then required for the broader external validity of results.

Some good news, however, is that it appears that certain social events and institutions *can* be implemented straightforwardly, since they do not require specific relations or institutional involvement beyond that satisfied by a university lab experiment. For example, in many societies an auction can be held between any group of willing participants. This may presuppose a certain institutional background, including, say, private property rights and money. However, with these in place almost anyone can hold an auction. Universities can and do, for example, to divest themselves of obsolete computer equipment. So, it would seem, experimentalists can too. Siakantaris (2000) suggests that this may be because auctions are relatively self-contained, though it is not clear if he interprets self-containment as negating causal holism, alteration, or both. Thinking relationally, however, the relata involved in auctions, such as bidder–auctioneer–seller–lot, seem to be relatively confined to the auction. Arguably this contrasts with the cases considered in subsection 5.5.1. The relata involved in the status–hierarchy–social role of hierarchy, in tax–revenue–government–electorate, and in voter–poll–candidate–electorate–government, in contrast, take one well beyond the situation and actors of immediate interest to others that impose on their autonomy. Other examples of relatively self-contained situations, which also seem to be relatively untouched by the alteration argument, include everyday informal votes, competitions, lotteries, and so on.

It is arguable that there are clear examples of institutions that cannot be implemented by university labs though. A jury trial seems to be a good example, since judges and juries have to be appropriately implemented by the legal system for their decisions to count in law. We note that there is an experimental method that has been advocated to implement relational phenomena. This is active role-play, using nonincentivized scenarios, in which subjects adopt roles. The logic behind this method is that if subjects have to represent to themselves certain relational criteria for some social phenomenon to exist, one might achieve greater realism by asking them to do this. For economics examples see Webley et al. (2001) and Green (2002), and for a discussion of external validity see Bornstein (1999) on jury experiments. Hertwig and Ortmann (2001) also provide some relevant discussion of, and references to, role-play in their comparison of methods in economics and psychology.

The other part of the challenge is the alteration argument's contention on conceptual grounds that there are phenomena that are not the subject of investigation that cannot be rigorously excluded from the lab.

A predictable objection is that it is unreasonable to single out any particular experiment, absent specific reasons that could be tested for, to dismiss the evidence because of the possibility of demand characteristics confounds. Various considerations are pertinent here. If a skeptical dismissal of a particular set of results is unreasonable, this does not tell us how confident we can be that no significant confound has arisen. A difference here to the contamination case is that, unlike interpersonal experimenter effects, the alteration argument alleges that one cannot avoid the possibility of demand characteristics confounds by competent administration. However, if so, that implies generality of scope for a potential problem, but does not bear directly on the actual frequency of such confounds. Also, although it seems a reasonable request to critics to produce hypotheses about demand characteristics that might be tested, a possible reply is that such a hypothesis already exists: namely, Orne's (1962, 1973) view that subjects aim at appropriate behavior, which he coupled with testing suggestions, one of which we consider below.

One important issue to resolve, then, is how frequently the relevant effects arise, and for which types of designs. These are empirical questions. For it would be an empirical question at the level of individual experiments whether demand characteristics differed across treatments in any given case, and empirical again as to whether people respond to them sufficiently to cause a problem. For this reason Bardsley (2005) concludes that radical skeptical conclusions cannot be drawn from the alteration critique in abstraction from evidence. All that could be established a priori is the possibility of misleading results.[17]

This brings us to part of the possible future research agenda regarding external validity: namely, the extent of demand characteristics artifacts and how to test them. Officially, many experimental economists believe that with adequate incentives the "subjective" factors just discussed will not be significant confounds. However the interaction of incentives with demand characteristics does not appear to have been specifically investigated thus far. Hertwig and Ortmann (2001) do provide an overview of some relevant literature that provides a mixed picture of the effectiveness of incentives generally. Orne's work offers suggestions regarding how to study demand characteristics empirically by combining the experiment with various explorations of perceptions. A common theme

---

[17] Bardsley (2008) examines dictator games introducing taking options, finding evidence that most dictator-game givers can be induced to take. This is consistent with a demand-characteristics explanation of giving in the usual cases where only giving is possible, and of taking in the taking-game treatment. The design incorporated both the anonymity and the between-subject controls for conventional contamination effects mentioned in subsection 5.5.2.

in these suggestions is the idea of running the design protocol without the treatment variable, and comparing this exercise with the regular experiment. For example, one might ask the extra subjects to guess what the experimenter wants. If the answers do not match the experimental data, it seems unlikely that demand characteristics are behind the results. This would appear to be useful where the hypothesis is relatively difficult for the subjects to guess, as it might be if it is derived from relatively technical theory.

Bardsley (2005) suggests that versions of this strategy might be particularly suitable for designs that do not rely on monetary incentives, giving the example of Knetsch's (1989) endowment effect. The idea is to check this result by substituting vouchers for the original sweets and crockery. Subjects are not told which voucher buys which good. If the endowment effect obtains, it is likely to be an artifact since no endowment was implemented but the protocol is the same. It seems hard to think of good reasons not to conduct such investigations, and it seems clear that there is scope for future debate and empirical work in this area. For example, in addition to the incentives hypothesis, one might conjecture that strategic experiments are less at risk of artifacts, since subjects' attention is directed toward the thinking of other subjects and therefore, perhaps, away from the experimenter–subject relationship.

5.7 Field Experiments

By a field experiment, we have in mind principally an intervention in a naturally occurring environment in conditions of covert observation. We briefly discussed one example, Bryan and Test (1967), as illustration 2 of chapter 1. Field experiments in this sense are epistemologically significant since, where available, they correct for the artificiality concerns in much of the preceding discussion. (Though the problem of broader external validity may still arise, as we discuss below and in the concluding section of this chapter.) There is now a burgeoning literature on field experiments and related designs in economics, some perspectives on which are provided by Glenn Harrison and John List (2004) in particular, but see also Duflo (2006) and DellaVigna (2007). It is therefore important to consider what is emerging from these studies about the external validity of laboratory experiments.

It is difficult to discern many general lessons about external validity, partly because relatively few studies examine comparable lab and field experiments in this sense. One suggestive literature, however, is that arising from labor market experiments. The field experiments contrast strongly with the laboratory data of, for example, Fehr et al. (1993). This experiment found evidence of a strong positive relationship between "wage rates" and "effort" in markets that essentially implemented a model by George Akerlof (1982) of the labor market as a gift exchange scenario. In the model, firms find it in their interests to pay above-market clearing wages because of a negative effect of low wages on productivity, interpreted in terms of reciprocity.

Akerlof's model addresses the "puzzle" that real wages do not fall to clear unemployment in a recession. However, field experiments interested to replicate this lab result via higher-than-advertised wages treatments for temporary jobs have not done so (Gneezy and List 2006; Hennig-Schmidt et al. 2005). On the other hand, negative reciprocity has been reported in the field by Kube et al. (2007), using lower-than-advertised wages. One point worth emphasizing here is that the field experiments, like the original puzzle, concern changes in wages, while the model and lab experiment have static pay rates. One might therefore read the findings as endorsing Bewley's (2004) criticism, stemming from survey evidence, that the model works via a different mechanism than the labor market context of interest, because of this dynamic aspect. In any case, by conducting these experiments in the field, researchers inevitably incorporated factors that are abstracted from the model. The results, arguably, serve as a warning that mimicking formal models in experiments may produce results that fail to generalize to the target environment.

Field experiments do not offer a panacea to researchers for boosting external validity, though, partly for the reason that they are not always available. As we have already argued, if one wishes to test theories, it may be unclear whether a natural environment is really picked out by the theory in question. Parallel considerations apply to inductions to theoretically defined contexts. There are, however, ways in which laboratory designs can incorporate features of naturally occurring settings to reap some of the benefits of field experiments. We have already touched on this theme in our discussion of tests of AE theories. Now we consider in more detail the attempts that have been made to more closely align the lab with the target environments, and what has been learned from such exercises.

Elements of naturalism that are often incorporated include, firstly, nonstudent subject pools, and secondly, an experimental setup that incorporates some features of a naturally occurring target environment. Many experimentalists retain a restrictive environment in terms of rules governing interaction, though, for example by imposing a particular move order, restrictions on strategies, communication rules, and so on. These manipulations correspond, roughly, to the "artifactual field experiment" and "framed field experiment" categories in a taxonomy of designs proposed by Harrison and List (2004). Their taxonomy defines a conventional lab experiment as having a convenience sample (that is, students), abstract framing, and imposed rules. Artifactual field experiments are defined as lab experiments with a nonstandard sample, for example, businessmen or representative samples of the national population. Framed field experiments are defined as artifactual field experiments plus less abstract or real goods, or a more realistic task or information set. (A fourth category, "natural field experiments," is effectively equivalent to field experiments in the sense we have defined in the opening paragraph of this section.)

One question motivating such manipulations is whether results, particularly the findings of theory violation, generalize beyond student populations. For example, Smith et al. (1988) find strong "bubbling" behavior in experimental asset markets even when using professionals and businessmen. This contradicts rational expectations equilibrium predictions interpreted as unconditional claims, in the sense discussed in chapter 2. The markets *did* tend to close at the theoretical equilibrium prices, though the one case in which they did not involved the treatment with nonstudent subjects.

Other examples include Tversky and Kahneman's (1981) lab result that the relative desirability of medical programs depends on whether they are framed in terms of lives lost or lives saved. Essentially the same result was reproduced by McNeil et al. (1982) using both samples of physicians and student subjects. However, Bornstein and Emler (2001) review more recent studies finding only qualified support for this result. That is, there is evidence that acting in the role of physician attenuates such framing effects for medics, though there is also evidence that this attenuation does not transfer to medics' judgments in other roles or about other types of problems. In general the evidence seems mixed as to whether behavior adapted to one setting "travels" to others. Penny Burns (1985), for example, reports evidence that lab auctions with experienced wool traders exhibited a declining price pattern that the traders attributed to their using the same heuristics as normal. As a consequence, the experienced agents departed more from profit-maximizing strategies than did students.

A related research idea that may motivate the "framed field experiment" category is to take designs that have generated evidence against economic theory and to run them with agents who perform similar tasks in their daily lives, using familiar goods. An instructive example is the experiment of Harrison and List (2008), who find that, contrary to the usual lab results, professional sports card dealers did not exhibit a winner's curse in induced-value Vickrey auctions. Dealers also bid less than nondealers in sports card auctions with the same auction rules, which the experimenters interpret as evidence that the dealers avoid the curse there too via the same heuristics. While we find both the general research idea and the particular results interesting, one comment is in order. The use of a nonconvenience sample does not make the sample representative of the population of interest. In this case, professional sports card dealers are *un*representative of sports card auction participants as a whole, because of the usual widespread presence of nondealers and the presumably vast gulf in experience between the two groups.[18] Thus, the external-validity inference drawn (albeit tentatively) from this experiment by Harrison and List (2004, pp. 1,027–28, 2008, pp. 823–24) that certain lab anomalies might be absent in the wild, and that corresponding naturally occurring markets efficient, seems not to follow. We reiterate here our insistence from chapter 2 that a high degree of agent experience is not representative of markets generally. It is by itself, therefore, not an indicator of external validity, though it may be for some specific market situations.

Another issue researchers have sought to address using nonstudent samples is that of cultural differences. It is possible that convenience sampling suppresses such differences because one may be effectively sampling from a single globalized student culture. Henrich et al. (2001) took a familiar set of behavioral games into tribal settings, apparently finding evidence of marked cultural differences. Similar evidence of stark behavioral differences between student populations appears to be scarce. However, it is not possible at present to distinguish these effects from those of locality, as Oosterbeek et al. (2004) show in their meta-analysis. The data are ultimatum-game experiments, including both the Henrich et al. (2001) data and some studies that did find differences between student populations. Unless one samples multiple locations within the same culture one cannot distinguish between variance within and between cultures. The meta-analysis groups experiments by region since there are insufficient observations to group by country. Only one significant regional effect is found, that responders in the United States accept lower offers than those in Asia after controlling for other study characteristics, but this does not correlate with available indicators of intercultural difference.

Although they may currently be less common, there are many further cases of worthwhile naturalistic designs, which differ in important

---

[18] Harrison and List's (2008) study does contain auctions mixing dealers and nondealers, but these treatments did not eliminate the winner's curse.

ways from the two categories just considered. We have in mind principally designs that allow greater freedom of action for subjects than these categories, and that may (or may not) be conducted using convenience samples. Examples include Orbell et al. (1988), who investigated the effects of free communication before play of a social dilemma game, and Bolton et al.'s (2003) bargaining experiment. The latter also used a variant of freeform communication. Who could communicate with whom was controlled for theory-testing reasons, apart from one unconstrained treatment, but subjects could put whatever content they wished in the (e-mail) messages and no extensive form was imposed. The aim was to see whether a noncooperative extensive form model predicted for naturalistic communications settings. Interestingly, the noncooperative model did better for most settings than cooperative models, despite the fact that key features of the model, including the extensive form and discount rates, were not imposed.

Our final example of a less structured design is Chamberlin's classic market experiment in which buyers and sellers are brought together in a room and allowed to circulate freely, negotiating bilaterally with one another in whatever ways they choose (see box 4.1 (p. 152)). Later investigations of markets have usually imposed much more structure on subjects' interactions, for example by requiring them to interact through interlinked computers according to predetermined procedures.

It may be very significant that these later, less naturalistic designs are much more like formal models. (In making a model of an interaction, the first step is often to specify explicitly the order in which individuals make their "moves," and the sets of alternative moves available for each individual. This is also the first step in programming a computerized market. In contrast, Chamberlin's design is easy for participants to understand, but it would be quite impractical to produce an exhaustive specification of all the moves it allows.) But if the aim is to test hypotheses about price determination in real markets, the fact that Chamberlin's experiment does not implement a model does not make it less valid or less controlled. Indeed, arguably, it may have greater external validity to the extent that there is freedom of communication and action in naturally occurring markets. We detect a dubious tendency within experimental economics to assume that principles of good practice in modeling can be transferred straightforwardly to experimental design.

To summarize, this section has found that field experiments, in the paradigmatic sense of covertly studied interventions in naturally occurring settings, offer significant external-validity benefits, but do not offer a panacea for external-validity concerns. There are several ways to incorporate naturalism into lab designs, though, which seem likely to offer value-added along this dimension. We suspect that current practice here may be concentrating unduly on particular designs, however. This seems to be reflected in Harrison and List's (2004) widely cited typology, which has significant omissions since it restricts naturalistic lab designs to those with nonstudent samples, and retains tight model-like restrictions on interaction as the basic norm. There are important external-validity issues, especially those surrounding the adequacy of formal modeling approaches, which seem to require a less model-constrained approach but do allow convenience sampling. For example, the critique of the laboratory labor markets considered in this section seems primarily to call for wage cuts, departing from the model, rather than real effort and workers. And in some contexts, one may strengthen prospective external validity more by allowing subjects—whether students or not—to interact with each other in an unstructured and naturalistic way than one would by using naturally occurring goods or tasks. We have suggested that this design strategy is currently underutilized. We would therefore encourage those interested to address external-validity concerns to think outside the rather limited "box" of currently standard designs.

5.8 Conclusions

We find the traditional theory-testing defense against external-validity concerns to be more problematic for certain AE experiments than for tests of decision-theoretic and game-theoretic hypotheses. Many such designs that closely implement formal models may be interpreted as disguised decision-theoretic exercises. To inform us about the applied domain in question requires that the experiments function as good models in the general sense of resembling representatives, an external-validity requirement. We find that it is neither necessary nor sufficient to implement a formal model to test the associated theory. What counts for testing is rather the use of an environment for which the theory predicts. This may involve deliberate nonimplementation of several assumptions, in particular where more than a single component of a theory is to be tested.

In accounts of experimental methods in social science it is common to refer to a trade-off between external and internal validity. However, a reasonably high degree of internal validity seems to be logically prior to external validity. A certain kind of trade-off is consistent with our analysis, though. Comparing laboratory with nonlaboratory methods, the higher internal validity of the lab is secured at the expense of lower certainty about whether what is observed there has the same properties as what one is ultimately interested in. Regarding alteration, it seems that we can either opt to investigate causality on analogues of target phenomena using the lab, or we can study "the real thing" using other methods. Regarding holism, one may often be able to observe something in interaction with the rest of a system, for practical reasons, only by going beyond the lab, at a cost of internal validity. Field experiments use target phenomena with some loss of control, obeying, if easing, this trade-off. That is, going outside the lab makes internal validity more difficult to achieve. Conditional on achieving it though, the probability of achieving external validity is higher.

For genuine field experiments, there is already external validity in one way because one is observing a target system, meaning that many of the concerns discussed in this chapter do not arise, at least in the forms discussed in sections 5.4 and 5.5. In particular, contamination and alteration do not arise if data collection is covert, nor could problems arise because of factors deliberately held constant or omitted for control purposes, at least for the setting for which data are collected. That context might still be very unrepresentative of other settings of interest though. Seen in this way, the problem of the external validity of the lab is an instance, albeit one with significant idiosyncrasies, of the more general problem of achieving transferable empirical results.

This kind of trade-off has a parallel within the lab too. For example, allowing freedom of communication and association in labs would make it more difficult to achieve definitive results on causes, but having achieved them we might be more confident about generalizing to naturally occurring situations.

We have highlighted the notion of artificiality of alteration, which may be new to many readers, with the aim of generating some debate on this topic. The authors are in fact divided over whether it is likely to pose a general problem for experimentalists. Irrespective of this, if there are doubts about specific results, it seems sensible to consider the empirical investigation of demand characteristics. In general, external validity can be addressed by various comparisons between lab and field data. However, the *establishment* of broader external validity may be a lot to ask for in many cases. There are weaker claims to pursue, based both on specific correspondences and the "checking by exhaustion" strategy against omission critiques. The depth to which this is worth pursing will depend on the details of the case. For example, and here we concur with Guala (2005a), it would appear to be more important to conduct detailed checks if the experiments in question were intended to serve as a guide to policy. Currently the time seems ripe to be focusing more on external-validity claims, especially as experimenters continue to broaden their enquiries beyond theory testing.

6

Incentives in Experiments

6.1 Preliminaries

Monetary incentives lie at the heart of controversies in experimental economics and, even more markedly, between it and other disciplines such as psychology. The latter point is graphically illustrated by the practices of the different disciplines. Surveys by Colin Camerer and Robert Hogarth (1999) and Ralph Hertwig and Andreas Ortmann (2001, 2003) indicate that, while the vast majority of experiments appearing in the economics literature use task-related incentives (a concept that we define below), the majority of those appearing in the psychology literature do not. The statistical evidence is quite striking: *every* experimental study published in the *American Economic Review* between 1970 and 1997 used task-related incentives (Camerer and Hogarth 1999), while only 26% of papers published in the *Journal of Behavioral Decision Making*—a leading outlet for experimental psychologists—between 1988 and 1997 did so (Hertwig and Ortmann 2001). The differences are not only between economists and psychologists. Even among economists there are important differences of opinion about the required levels and role of incentives, as illustrated by our discussion of choice experiments in chapter 2.

In this chapter, we extend our analysis of incentives by considering in more detail the effects they may have and why they are an important experimental design issue, in order to provide a framework for adjudicating between conflicting views on their role, level, and structure. These are the main objectives of this chapter, but before pursuing them directly we consider how conventions regarding the use of incentives have developed. In our view, such conventions should not be followed unquestioningly. It remains important to ask: What are incentives in an experiment for? Are they always beneficial or could they be detrimental to the investigation? Are they useful in some settings and unnecessary in others? And, if so, what separates the two?

We begin by specifying the boundaries of the subject matter covered in this chapter more precisely.

An important ground-clearing point is a distinction between *incentives in experiments* and *experiments on incentives.* Some experimental papers (see, for example, Fehr and Falk 2002) test economic theories of incentives or are intended, subject to external-validity claims, to license conclusions about the optimal use of incentives in organizations outside the laboratory. There is a large literature on the economic theory of incentives,[1] and the structure of incentives in organizations is an area in which the views of economists (and other researchers) are sought and have important practical implications. These points motivate experiments on how incentives might operate in organizations, but they are not the main concern of this chapter. Instead, that concern is with the role of incentives in experimental research itself. Experiments on incentives in organizations are relevant only where they illuminate that issue.

The two most common types of payments from experimenters to subjects are flat-rate turn-up fees and task-related payments. Turn-up fees are rewards for *participation.* They are intended to persuade subjects to attend the experimental session but do not vary with what happens there and so are not usually intended or expected to impact on subjects' behavior in the laboratory.[2] In contrast, *task-related* incentives do depend on what happens during the experiment, such as choices made by subjects, interventions by the experimenter, resolution of gambles, and so on. Consequently, they may well affect subjects' behavior during sessions, as we will discuss.

Although both types of payments are widely used, we focus on task-related incentives.[3] Inducing subjects to participate is an important practical matter for experimenters; and use of task-related incentives, either

---

[1] See Laffont and Martimort (2002) for a textbook treatment.

[2] Turn-up fees sometimes have a different function, which is to cover losses that subjects might make in the experiment, avoiding the need to extract cash from participants unwilling to give it up. The reliability of the hypothesis that turn-up fees do not affect behavior can be questioned, for example in the light of "house money" effects (Thaler and Johnson 1990). These points are linked if protection from losses affects behavior. However, even if turn-up fees do influence behavior, it does not follow that they confound the conclusions that can be drawn, for example, from differences in behavior between treatments. The latter is the object of investigation in many experiments.

[3] Although task-related incentives in experimental economics are usually monetary payments, this is not always the case. For example, if one wishes to discover subjects' preferences over distinct bundles of goods, this can be attempted either with task-related incentives (i.e., subjects actually receive bundles of goods determined by their task-responses) or hypothetically (i.e., subjects are simply asked which bundles they prefer, or which they would choose if the choice was real); and the relative merits of the two practices turn on essentially the same issues as the relative merits of using real or hypothetical monetary payments. Although, for brevity below, we will sometimes assume that task-related incentives are monetary, this is not usually intrinsic to the argument.

instead of or as a supplement to turn-up fees, may help to achieve it (notwithstanding psychologists' success in attracting participants by other means). However, task-related incentives raise more interesting conceptual issues than participation incentives. Widespread insistence on their use, not merely *despite* but actually *because of* the fact that they may affect what happens in the experiment, and therefore the results of the research, is one of the most distinctive features of experimental economics. As we concentrate on this aspect, we have little to say about certain types of popular recommendations, for example, that subjects should be compensated for giving up their time at some particular multiple[4] of locally available wage rates.[5]

In the first part of this chapter we consider the role and effects of task-related incentives in general, taking it as given that the tasks to be studied can be incentivized if the experimenter so desires. In the later part of the chapter we turn to questions that arise when one considers how to give incentives for particular types of tasks. While it is straightforward to incentivize certain tasks, such as choices between items that the experimenter can supply, there are other tasks, such as valuing items, where it is harder to see how to elicit truthful responses. A feature of the conventional wisdom of experimental economics, in such cases, is that tasks should be *incentive compatible*. We consider the nature and implications of this concept.

6.2   Incentives, Design, and Control

A distinction between *incentives* and *motivations* underpins the argument of this chapter. Motivations are features of the subjects that determine their behavior under given conditions. Incentives are features of the experiment that form a key part of the "conditions" referred to in the definition of motivations. It is the interaction of motivations and incentives that determines behavior.

As motivations are features of the subject, they are not controllable by the experimenter—witness, for example, chapter 3's discussion of

---

[4] For example, twice the minimum wage is recommended by Rydval and Ortmann (2004, footnote 4).

[5] Incentives cannot guarantee all subjects a given level of remuneration, if they are to depend nontrivially on task-outcomes. A proposal for a guarantee might be motivated by participation considerations, but what those who call for experimental rewards to compare favorably with local wages typically have in mind is not any such guarantee, but rather that attentive subjects can expect a particular level of reward on average. Such a proposal is consistent with rewards being task-related and falls within the subject matter of this chapter, but we will focus more on the task-relatedness than the incidental participation incentive.

the difficulty of knowing whether subjects' preferences conform to the structure of the monetary payoffs in an experimental game. However, as incentives are features of the experiment, they *are* controllable by the experimenter. Decisions about whether to use incentives, at what level to set them, and how to structure their task-relatedness are therefore *design decisions.* Like all such decisions, they should be made in the light of the objectives of the experiment.

Although this last point may seem elementary, it is very important— not least because, as previous chapters have documented, there is con- siderable diversity of objectives between experimental investigations. This cautions against the adoption of very specific blanket prescriptions on task-related incentives. Rather, good practice in setting incentives, as for other important design decisions, is a matter of making considered judgments *in view of the aims of the research.*[6]

Section 6.3 briefly reviews some aspects of the convention among experimental economists in favor of the use of task-related incentives. It illustrates how the convention emerged in part because of design deci- sions that made good sense for particular early and influential branches of experimental economics. However, it also argues that there may be mechanisms that reinforce continued adherence to the convention (and an implicit view that the higher the incentives the better) even when the substantive research objectives no longer call for it.

Section 6.4 discusses why task-related incentives may affect behav- ior. An understanding of this is very important when making informed design choices, and just as disagreements about incentives may flow from differences in research objectives, so they may also flow from dif- ferent accounts of why incentives impact on behavior. We distinguish three quite different perspectives on the nature of that impact.

Section 6.5 defines the notion of incentive compatibility, arguing that its pursuit raises issues connected with the Duhem–Quine problem, introduced in chapter 3. It considers the nature of the appropriate goal of incentive compatibility for given research questions, and discusses whether the feasibility of that goal provides a suitable criterion for choosing among research questions.

The position that we adopt in sections 6.4 and 6.5 is similar to that advocated by Daniel Read (2005) in several respects, including, at

---

[6] Later in this chapter we consider a case where, because of a possible externality between researchers, the objectives of the research undertaken are not the only impor- tant issue. This case is that of deception of subjects (box 6.4). We set this issue aside for the moment by assuming that, whatever incentives are used, subjects will be told them truthfully.

the most general level, our stress on the importance of conditioning decisions about incentives on the aims of the research.

6.3   Incentives in Experimental Economics: Convention in Action

Section 6.1 illustrated the overwhelming tendency for experimental papers published in top economics journals to use incentives. The requirements of these journals provide an obvious proximate explanation of why individual experimental economists do in fact use task-related incentives in their designs. They are simply adhering to norms that have emerged, conformity to which is necessary if they are to publish their work in what they see as the most prestigious outlets. It is hardly surprising that experimental economists use incentives as a matter of routine, if not doing so provides a hostile referee with cheap ammunition.

It is more interesting to consider *why* these norms have emerged. The widespread acceptance of the usefulness of incentives in the experimental economics community is in part a legacy of the status that incentives held in early experimental work, as an essential controlling device. In earlier chapters, we have described some of the key components of that legacy.

Chapter 4 described how theory testing formed a bridgehead through which experimental methods could enter economics. Many early experiments were market games, designed to test predictions of competitive equilibrium price theory. As knowledge of the conditions of demand and supply is required for precise predictions, it was crucial to control these conditions, as explained in chapter 3. The induced-value methodology (see box 3.1 (p. 99)), which seeks to induce a particular preference structure over the objects traded in a market experiment, provided a means of doing so. To implement it, while satisfying Smith's precepts, required task-related incentives.

Chapter 2 considered other types of experiments in which incentives are also used as a means of control, but over the objects of choice rather than over preferences. In public-goods experiments, the voluntary-contributions mechanism (box 2.3 (p. 58)) is commonly used to create the public goods and private goods over which subjects allocate their endowments. Here, again, the incentives are an integral part of the experimental design and it is hard to question their importance, provided the goal of testing the theory of public goods within its base domain is accepted. A similar point applies to the use of monetary rewards to create close correlates of prospects in order to test theories of choice under uncertainty.

The investigation of individual choice behavior provides perhaps the sharpest illustration of the difference between norms of research in experimental economics and psychology in relation to incentives. Economists have been interested in certain decision anomalies (including some of the "exhibits" of chapter 4) first observed by psychologists but typically without task-related incentives. One example is provided by the various theories used to explain the preference reversal phenomenon (box 3.4 (p. 131)). David Grether and Charles Plott (1979) test for preference reversals using experiments with task-related incentives, asserting that this sets their approach apart from that of psychologists such as Lichtenstein and Slovic (see Lichtenstein and Slovic 1971; Slovic 1975), who used hypothetical payments in most of their experiments. On the latter two studies, Grether and Plott (1979, p. 624) remark that these experiments "can be disregarded as applying to economics even though they may be very enlightening for psychology." Grether and Plott's stance is that incentives are the bedrock of the theories under test, and results from experiments to test those theories cannot be taken seriously in the absence of nonnegligible task-related incentives. Someone holding such a view may hypothesize that if nothing is at stake subjects behave in a casual and unpredictable manner, and that behavioral data from the experiment would not be useful for testing the theory. As discussed in chapter 2, this position, especially when used as a reason for insisting on very substantial incentives, derives from a particular, possible though contestable, view of the domain of the theory. Given that view, emphasis on large incentives is justified; but there are other possible views of the theory's domain that do not carry such an implication.

Although Grether and Plott (1979) make it clear that their stance is founded on the belief that experimental data are useful to economists only if they are generated from decisions that "matter," other economists expressing similar views might be seen as using incentives as a marketing device in order to distance themselves from psychologists. Incentives may thus be seen as a form of product differentiation in the research market. Note that, in its purest form, this motive for using incentives has nothing to do with their supposed impact on subjects' behavior but stems merely from an attempt to "sell" the research to a different market.

There is another, equally cynical, interpretation that could be put on too dogged an insistence on the use of incentives. A reason often given for psychologists' opposition to them is that incentives present an obstacle to less-experienced researchers who find it harder to secure research funding. It may be that economists are less concerned by the presence of such obstacles, or even that some actively promote the use of incentives as a barrier to entry. Such a barrier could be enforced by using the absence of incentives as a ground for rejection of papers for publication; and the absence of published papers as grounds for denial of research funds. Like any barrier to entry, this could act to insulate the particular views on the role of incentives held by existing research participants from the "competition" of alternative views. It is not necessary to attribute base motives to established researchers to be concerned about this possibility. Whatever the motives of individuals, it is hard to deny that insistence on substantial task-related incentives does in fact act as a barrier to entry.

Even when conventions about experimental design originate from decisions that made good sense for important early research programs, the self-reinforcing property of conventions together with the strategic advantages that they might confer on established researchers provide a general reason for thinking that there *might* be a tendency for particular practices to become entrenched as universal codes and applied even when no longer justified by the research objectives. To see how far this potential danger is an actual one, it is necessary to investigate the role of incentives without preconceptions in their favor, by considering what effects they may have and what role they may play for research of different types.

6.4   Three Perspectives on the Effect of Incentives on Behavior

In this section we consider how task-related incentives may affect subjects' behavior in the laboratory. This is important because task-related incentives have a resource cost, both in terms of the direct cost of payments made to subjects and (see below) the time and effort required to make some otherwise-simple tasks incentive compatible. As there would almost certainly be easier and less-costly ways to induce subjects to participate, it is hard to see what the virtues of task-related incentives could be *unless* they affect subjects' behavior in the laboratory in some desirable way.

For researchers to make considered judgments about the presence, level, and structure of task-related incentives, it is important to assess how far, and why, they may affect behavior. It is not our objective to catalog all empirical studies on the effects of incentives.[7] Instead, the main goal of this section is to distinguish three different perspectives on this issue, paying particular attention to how they might inform researchers'

---

[7] A wide-ranging study of this issue is Camerer and Hogarth (1999).

decisions. For each perspective, we distinguish the questions of whether and why incentives affect behavior from the quite different question of whether, if there is an effect, this militates for or against higher incentives.[8] The first perspective is the "capital–labor–production" framework of Camerer and Hogarth (1999), an economic–theoretic framework in which it is assumed that cognitive effort is costly, and is used in conjunction with the subject's knowledge and experience in order to perform to a sufficient standard to achieve a desirable outcome. The second perspective is the distinction between intrinsic and extrinsic motivation, which recognizes that subjects may have many different motivations for applying effort, many of which may not be financial. The third perspective flows from the possible role of "affect," that is, raw emotions that may govern decisions. The key issue here is whether incentives are necessary to stir such emotions or whether well-meaning subjects can anticipate them even when decisions are hypothetical.

6.4.1 The Capital–Labor–Production Framework

This perspective is founded on the idea that cognitive effort is a scarce resource that is allocated strategically by the agents in possession of it. In the absence of task-related incentives, agents may see no benefit from allocating effort to the tasks, and the frequency of errors is likely to be high. This leads to one prediction that has been documented in the literature: that the presence of task-related incentives has the effect of reducing performance variability, at least in situations where there exists a sensible measure of performance (see Camerer and Hogarth (1999), and the references therein).

Possibly the earliest contribution to the economic theory of cognitive effort allocation is Smith and Walker's (1993) "labor theory," in which the greater cognitive effort expended as a result of an increase in incentives brings about a reduction in the variance of responses. Camerer and Hogarth (1999) extended the framework by introducing the concept of "cognitive capital," that is, the natural ability, knowledge, and experience possessed by the subject at the time of facing the task. This extension led to the "capital–labor–production" (CLP) framework. Note that the experimental subject is assumed to take the role of an owner-managed "firm" that simultaneously makes decisions on how much effort to supply ("labor") and how much of their natural ability or previous experience

---

[8] The distinction we make between three perspectives is similar to one made by Read (2005). He discusses three reasons why incentives may affect behavior—"cognitive exertion," "motivational focus," and "emotional triggers."

to draw upon ("capital") in order to meet an objective ("production"— usually, but not necessarily, a form of financial reward) for a given task.

Many interesting empirical questions arise immediately in the CLP framework. Is capital variable? If so, are labor and capital substitutable? That is, if a particular task is highly complex, can a lack of experience in solving similar tasks be compensated by simply applying more effort to the current task? Given that they are substitutable, which of capital and labor is the subject more willing to supply? That is, do subjects try to recall past experience of similar tasks so that they can reuse previously successful thought processes or instead apply fresh cognitive effort to each new task? And do their responses vary according to which of those is the case? More generally, how does the supply of each of labor and capital vary with experimental incentives? And what is the effect on behavior of changes in their level?

While the CLP framework is very suggestive conceptually, it is not always straightforward to subject it to empirical analysis. One reason for this is that some of the quantities appearing in the framework (particularly "performance" in the task) are notoriously hard to measure. For many economics experiments, it is not clear what an appropriate measure of subjects' performance would be. However, it is useful to begin with some cases where researchers have tried to assess the impact of incentives (and other factors) on performance in tasks in which it is measurable.

A step in this direction is taken by Uri Gneezy and Aldo Rustichini (2000a), who invite subjects to carry out a psychometric test. The subjects are assigned randomly to four "incentive treatments": no pay, very low pay, modest pay, high pay. Those with modest and high pay appear to perform the best, although there is not a significant difference between these two treatments. The apparent implication is that effort rises with incentives, but performance reaches a "ceiling" when further increases in effort become unproductive. Gneezy and Rustichini's (2000a) data were scrutinized further by Rydval and Ortmann (2004), who apply nonparametric methods to the subject-level data in order to investigate the interaction between intrinsic ability and incentives. They report the result that ability differentials between individuals account for considerably more of the variation in performance than do the levels of incentives. This finding is a useful reminder of the importance of cognitive capital in the CLP framework.

In settings in which subjects are paid for engaging in some real task, such as typing (Cappelen et al. 2005), performance is often easy to measure: it is simply the volume (and possibly quality) of the tasks they complete. An interesting finding in this sort of experiment is that subjects appear to work hard whatever the payment per task, provided it is not insultingly low.[9] Libby and Lipe (1992) present evidence of a step change in performance (through greater investment of effort) when the wage rate rises from zero to some positive value. They found that the time allocated to accounting tasks is around 20% higher for subjects paid a (task-related) wage than for subjects paid a turn-up fee. There are other examples like this in Camerer and Hogarth (1999, table 1). The message seems to be that in terms of the impact on cognitive effort allocation the presence of task-related incentives matters more than their level.

Although one can think of other cases in which an observable measure of performance would be available—for example, if subjects were asked to perform arithmetic calculations[10]—there are many economics experiments for which this is not so. Often there is no clearly "correct" course of action for a subject. Even if economic theory makes a definite prediction based on the assumptions of rationality and self-interest, such as a zero contribution in a public-goods game, we cannot describe the performance of a zero contributor as necessarily "better" than the performance of a generous contributor. It could be that each is performing equally well, relative to their own preferences, which are unknown.

More generally, for cases where the objective of the experiment is to test a theory, it does not seem appropriate to interpret conformity of behavior with the theory as "good performance" and to see the role of incentives as being to increase this. Rather, in this case, the purpose of the experiment is to assess the performance of the *theory* (not the subjects) in terms of its ability to account for the behavior of subjects in situations of interest. The role of the task-related incentives is then to create the situations of interest. Depending on one's view of the domain in which the theory should be tested, this might require higher or lower incentives, as discussed in chapter 2.

In fact, several of the views discussed in section 2.6 of chapter 2 fit very naturally within the CLP framework. Plott (1996) and Binmore (1999) see strong enough incentives to deliberate as required if the laboratory is to fall within the domain in which economic theory can legitimately be

---

[9] At a certain level this is not very surprising. People are happy to apply themselves to a task for a relatively short time. If people are asked to key in data for an hour, and this task differs sufficiently from their usual activities, we might expect them to rise to the task. However, if an individual is, in real life, embedded in a lackluster career of data entry, they may look for shirking opportunities in order to increase their utility. Here we have a potential problem with external validity (see chapter 5), if the inferences drawn from the experiment fail to take this into account.

[10] Dohmen and Falk (2006) report an experiment in which subjects' productivity is measured by their success in multiplication tasks.

tested. The CLP framework takes no particular position on the domain of the theory, but still sees higher incentives as having the effect—desirable or otherwise—of inducing greater supply of cognitive capital and effort.

Glenn Harrison's flat maximum critique (Harrison 1989, 1992, 1994) can also be interpreted in terms of the framework. One way to do this is to see the experiment's reward structure as providing the outcome of "production." If the reward structure is too insensitive in the neighborhood of the optimum, then production will also be a relatively "flat" function of inputs in the neighborhood of the production-maximizing choices. Then, given a nontrivial marginal cost of effort, the supply of effort will tend to be too low to induce optimal (i.e., production-maximizing) behavior.

We have argued that, even within the CLP framework, it is often more helpful to see the role of incentives as being to induce the effort and deliberation that, according to some views of the domain of the theory, are prerequisites for its applicability, than it is to see the role of incentives as being to stimulate "performance"; and that this is especially so when the concept of "performance" is unclear. However, there may be some correlates of "good performance" that are observable, even when subjects' preferences are not. As noted above, one possibility is to focus on the absence of error; and to postulate that the frequency of errors is negatively related to some measure of variability of behavior. Smith and Walker's (1993) emphasis on the variance of responses fits with this approach. We return to a fuller discussion of the stochastic component of behavior in chapter 7.

Another way of addressing the problem is to shift the emphasis from performance to effort, and to measure effort using some observable variable such as decision times, as done by Wilcox (1994), Hey (1995), Moffatt (2005), and Rubinstein (2007). It may sometimes be reasonable to treat effort and performance as equivalent in the sense that a high allocation of effort tends to result in a strong performance, as in the study of Libby and Lipe (1992). However, this equivalence may not always hold. If an individual has low cognitive ability, their performance in certain tasks may not be improved by greater effort. In view of such concerns, if decision times are used to represent performance (rather than just effort), it is important to control for confounding effects of subject-specific factors and task complexity.

Nevertheless, effort is of interest in its own right within the CLP framework. Peter Moffatt (2005) uses decision times as a measure of effort allocation in risky choice problems. Financial incentives, represented by a summary measure of the money amounts appearing in the choice problem, turn out to have only a small positive effect on effort allocation in the cases he considers. The "incentive elasticity of effort" is estimated to be just 0.028. In contrast, task complexity turns out to be more important: complex tasks induce greater effort. Another important determinant of effort is experience, represented by the number of tasks solved previously, which affects decision times negatively. All of these results are interpretable in the CLP framework: firstly, subjects invest quantities of cognitive effort and cognitive capital that are appropriate to the complexity of the task; secondly, in the course of an experiment consisting of a sequence of risky choice problems, subjects gradually accumulate capital and thereby bring about a gradual fall in the amount of effort that is required to perform each task. However, as with the findings of Gneezy and Rustichini (2000a), the results seem more supportive of the conceptual role that the CLP framework can play in organizing ideas than they do of any supposition that there is a strong and simple positive relationship between effort and incentives.

In fact, a particularly striking finding of Moffatt (2005) is that the key determinant of effort, measured by decision time, is closeness to indifference: if a subject is indifferent between two lotteries, they apply roughly twice the amount of effort as they would if there were a clear preference. This result is hard to reconcile with Harrison (1989, 1992, 1994), who is insistent that "payoff dominance" is essential for subjects to take a task seriously. Payoff dominance is unlikely to be satisfied in a case of near-indifference between lotteries, and yet this is the situation in which Moffatt (2005) finds subjects working hardest. One possible explanation, which connects with the idea of intrinsic motivation introduced in the next subsection, is that subjects who have been asked to select the lottery they prefer take pride in performing this task well, regardless of the perceived benefit from making the correct choice. The harder it is to decide, the more effort they put into doing so. The finding can also be rationalized by our discussion of the flat maximum critique in chapter 2. When the lotteries between which the subject must choose are quite different from each other, nearness to indifference is not a datum to which the subject has ready access, even if it holds. A subject may have to commit time and effort even to discover that, all things considered, she is nearly indifferent.

Finally, note that even in a situation where a measure of performance is readily available, and where there is reason to believe that incentives do improve performance, it is not necessarily the case that increased incentives are desirable. A straightforward example is John Castellan's (1969) probability matching experiment. Subjects bet on which of two lights (red or green) are going to light up. They are told that red lights up

60% of the time, and green the other 40%. To maximize the expected frequency of winning bets, the subject should bet on red on every occasion. In this sort of experiment, incentives are seen to move subjects closer to this profit-maximizing prediction, causing them to choose red more often. However, whether this militates for or against higher incentives in the experimental design depends on the purpose of the investigation. If it is to investigate instinctive judgments, the presence of incentives may conflict with this objective; whereas it might not do so if the purpose is to investigate highly considered judgments. This consideration applies quite generally to judgment tasks. We conjecture that it has played a major part in psychologists' reluctance to use task-related incentives, as instinctive judgments are of great interest to them. Whether instinctive judgments should be of interest to economists, or whether they should only be interested in highly considered judgments, are questions that turn, once again, on the domain of the subject.

6.4.2   Intrinsic and Extrinsic Motivation

The theme of this subsection is the recognition that it is not only financial incentives that motivate experimental subjects. In much of the literature that explores the various possible nonmonetary motivations, discussion centers on the concept of "intrinsic motivation" (see, for example, Frey 1997; Ryan and Deci 2000; Deci et al. 1999).

Intrinsic motivation is said to be present when an agent is pursuing an activity for the inherent satisfaction of the activity itself. This is particularly important in the present context because, since experimental subjects are usually volunteers, there may be a tendency for there to be some degree of self-selection of subjects with high intrinsic motivation. The opposite, extrinsic motivation, is said to be present when an agent is performing an activity with the objective of attaining some separable outcome, usually financial gain.

As an opening example, consider a commonly performed everyday task. A cryptic crossword amounts to a cognitively demanding task that many intelligent, high value-of-time people choose to engage in on a daily basis, for no financial gain. This straightforward observation provides clear evidence of strong intrinsic motivation to perform this particular task. Now let us imagine that these people are suddenly provided with a financial reward for each clue solved correctly. There may well be some solvers who perform less well as a result of this intervention, for the following reasons. Firstly, they become aware that there is an expectation to perform well, and this awareness amounts to a distraction. This is one example of "motivational crowding out" (Frey and Stutzer 2006). An extrinsic motivation has taken over the role previously played by the intrinsic motivation, and if the former is less effective, the net effect on performance is negative. Secondly, if the amount being offered for engaging the task is low in comparison with the normal hourly earnings of the individual, they may feel insulted by the offer and reduce their effort as a form of protest; or simply find that the presence of a trivial financial reward reduces their enjoyment, with a corresponding loss of concentration.[11]

Motivational crowding out is usually attributed to two factors. Firstly, the introduction of extrinsic motivation brings about a reduction in self-determination: the individual no longer feels responsible for their own behavior, and allows the outside intervention to take over. Secondly, in cases in which effort is applied as a result of a system of reciprocity between individuals, it is possible that such a system would break down as a consequence of the introduction of extrinsic motivators. Some indicative evidence relating to these factors can be found in research by Gneezy and Rustichini.

Some of the results of Gneezy and Rustichini (2000a) were summarized in the previous subsection. However, the most striking feature of their data is that subjects in the "very low pay" treatment perform worse than those in the "no pay" treatment. This could be interpreted as subjects feeling insulted by very low rates of pay, with the effect of completely eliminating the intrinsic motivation that induces unpaid subjects to apply effort. Presumably it was this finding that prompted the title of the paper: "Pay enough or don't pay at all."

Another manifestation of motivational crowding out has been documented by Gneezy and Rustichini (2000b). They consider the effect of introducing fines for arriving late to collect children from daycare centers. Their reported finding that the introduction of fines increased lateness suggests that, rather than feeling incentivized to collect early, parents took the view that their payment of a charge legitimized their lateness. On this account, the intrinsic motive not to be late to avoid inconveniencing staff was crowded out by the introduction of a financial incentive.[12]

Another way of explaining how rewards may reduce performance is in terms of "cognitive dissonance" (Leon Festinger and James Carlsmith 1959). This is a theory of human motivation that asserts that it

---

[11] In the United Kingdom, there are cryptic crossword puzzles in many daily newspapers and there are often prizes for the first few all-correct completed puzzles. But these are frequently items that appear to have more symbolic than monetary value, such as small tokens or publication of one's name in the newspaper.

[12] Viewed in this way, the finding parallels the classic argument of Titmuss (1970) that payment for blood donations crowds out the intrinsic motivation to donate.

is psychologically uncomfortable to hold contradictory cognitions. For example, if a subject has just completed a task that is undeniably tedious, they may be more willing to admit that the task was indeed tedious if they are paid more generously. Those who are paid low amounts are more likely to rate the task as interesting or challenging, thus removing the dissonance between the recognition that the task is uninteresting and pointless, and the knowledge that they are performing the task. This theory could be extended to offer an explanation of why those who are offered weaker incentives might apply greater effort *during* the task, as a way of convincing themselves, and perhaps others, that the task is actually worthwhile. Self-attribution theory (Bern 1972) goes a step further. According to this theory, agents do not have complete knowledge of the motivations driving their own behavior, and hence use their current behavior to make inferences (not necessarily correct ones) about their motivations. For example, agents may only realize that they are intrinsically motivated when the extrinsic motivators (i.e., money payments) are removed.

From the perspective of the intrinsic/extrinsic motivation trade-off, the introduction of incentives exerts positive stimulus on the motivation to earn money, but at the same time may "crowd out" other important types of motivations. It is obvious that, from this angle, the decision on whether to use incentives rests on what sort of motivation the experimenter intends to investigate. For example, the experimenter may actively seek to crowd out certain types of intrinsic motivations. Smith's precept of "dominance," discussed in chapter 3, can be seen as the result of a desire to exclude certain motivations seen as economically irrelevant or secondary (for example, those arising from treating the experiment as a competition between subjects to get the highest score, instead of as a market in which mutually beneficial trades can be made).[13] However, in other cases, the experimenter may intend to investigate a form of behavior that arises precisely from intrinsic motivation; and, in such a case, it would be important not to crowd out the relevant intrinsic motivation with financial considerations.

6.4.3   Affect and Prediction Failure

"Affect" is a term used by behavioral economists, and borrowed from psychologists, to represent an experienced emotion that impacts on

---

[13] This is not to say that experimenters should always seek to drive out all motivations that are not narrowly "economic," but merely that incentives can play the role of driving out intrinsic motivations that, in the context of particular research objectives, are a distraction. Even seeing an experimental market as a competition for top score may have an analogue in some real-world markets, as may altruistic motives.

behavior. Some of the most obvious examples are hope, thrill, regret, or disappointment in the context of risk; and fear or guilt in the context of interaction between agents.

These are undoubtedly emotions that are experienced in the real world. So it is sometimes logical to wish to induce such emotions in experimental subjects or at least to expose them to incentives sufficiently large to give rise to the affects. Without this, there would be potential concerns about external validity, that is, in this context, about the ability of experiments to inform about behavior in nonlaboratory situations that do give rise to powerful affects. This is a further reason why, for some purposes, task-related incentives might be considered not only desirable but also necessary. If an experimenter is interested in decision making in the presence of affects, it would seem far from ideal to start an experiment by asking subjects to "imagine the fear that you would experience if the money amounts in the following tasks were real." Such a procedure, or the more common one of simply facing subjects with hypothetical tasks, would be particularly problematic if subjects were unable to predict the affects to which they would be prone if the tasks were for real.[14]

Prediction failure is the problem that arises when subjects are given hypothetical tasks to perform, but are unable to anticipate the affective responses that would arise if the tasks were real. As an example, recall one of the "exhibits" of chapter 4: the endowment effect. This is a tendency for people to become more attached to an object in their possession than their prior desire to possess the object would suggest. An obvious question is whether people are aware of the endowment effect: that is, whether they realize that they will place a higher value on the object once it is in their possession. Loewenstein and Adler (1995) conducted experiments to address this question. They found that subjects without an object underestimated how much they would value the object on receiving it. A natural interpretation is that the finding results from failure to predict affective responses, such as pain of giving up the object. Cubitt et al. (1998b) also report experimental findings that can be seen as suggesting that subjects were unable to predict an affective response to "survival" of a risk.[15]

---

[14] A similar point applies to the random-lottery incentive system discussed below, if it dilutes subjects' affective responses to tasks involving risk. See Cubitt and Sugden (2001a) for further discussion of this point and of the implications of the notion of affect for the design of risky choice experiments.

[15] This is one of two explanations of their findings countenanced by Cubitt et al. (1998b, section 5). Nonlaboratory evidence of agents being unable to predict how their attitudes will change in the face of experience is discussed by Loewenstein et al. (2003).

Further evidence interpretable as prediction failure in risky choice settings can be found in a prominent paper by Charles Holt and Susan Laury (2002). It reports an experiment principally intended to assess the effect of incentives on behavior under risk.[16] The design consists of a set of ten choice problems each consisting of a pair of lotteries, of which one is safer than the other. The ten problems are ordered: problem 1 is such that nearly everyone chooses the "safe" alternative; problem 10 is such that nearly everyone chooses the "risky" one (in fact, for problem 10 the "risky" lottery first-order stochastically dominates). Each subject is asked to make a choice for each of the ten problems.[17] It is expected that each subject will switch at some stage in the sequence from the safe option to the risky option; under the assumption of expected utility (EU) maximization, the point at which they do switch sets a lower and an upper bound on their risk aversion. Their experiment had a low payoff treatment and a high-payoff treatment, the nominal payoffs in the latter being a high multiple (either twenty, fifty, or ninety) of those in the former. The high-payoff treatment was administered with both hypothetical and real payoffs. A key feature of the findings was that when the payoffs are real, the scaling-up of prize amounts causes sharp increases in risk aversion; whereas when payoffs are hypothetical, scaling-up does not significantly alter levels of risk aversion.[18] The observation that revealed risk aversion increases when real payoffs are raised but not when hypothetical payoffs are raised casts doubt on the generality of Kahneman and Tversky's (1979, p. 265) assertion that "people often know how they would behave in actual situations of choice." It is natural to conjecture that the finding may have arisen because large real payoffs generated affects that large hypothetical payoffs did not; and that, notwithstanding any intrinsic motivation

---

[16] There is evidence (see, for example, Loomes et al. 2002) that subjects become less willing to take risks as they gain experience by performing multiple tasks. Consonant with this, Harrison et al. (2005) claim that the strong incentive effects reported by Holt and Laury (2002) are in fact exaggerated by the effect of task order. See Holt and Laury (2005) for a response.

[17] The random-lottery incentive system, discussed below, is used as the means of incentivizing a set of decision problems.

[18] Beattie and Loomes (1997) also perform an experiment containing both hypothetical and real tasks. Unlike Holt and Laury (2002), they found no significant difference in responses between hypothetical tasks and real tasks when the real tasks were single-stage lotteries. However, when the real task is presented as an accumulator gamble, responses become more risk averse. An interpretation of this result suggested by Cubitt and Sugden (2001a) is that, when played for real, accumulators have a particular propensity to induce risk-related affective experiences such as fear and regret.

to respond truthfully, subjects facing hypothetical payoffs did not have access to those affects.[19]

If subjects cannot predict their affective responses when faced with a particular problem, this may provide a reason for experimenters to avoid hypothetical tasks, since even well-intentioned subjects may not be able to respond as they would if the tasks were for real. Obviously, use of task-related incentives stands more chance of generating affects that determine the latter responses. This role for task-related incentives is stressed by Cubitt and Sugden (2001a). However, even here, it is important to note that the argument is contingent on the objectives. The affect and prediction failure perspective militates for strong, real, task-related incentives, *provided* that "hot" affective decision making, rather than "cold" deliberation, is the intended object of study. This highlights why the affect and prediction failure perspective is very different from the CLP framework. It sees the role of incentives not as being to induce careful rational deliberation but rather as being to induce affective, and so possibly nonrational, gut reactions.

6.4.4   Parallels and Differences

Each of the perspectives described in subsections 6.4.1–6.4.3 gives a different account of why task-related incentives might affect subjects' behavior. According to the CLP framework, this is because they stimulate effort and the deployment of cognitive resources by subjects. According to the extrinsic–intrinsic motivation view, it is because they crowd out intrinsic motivation. According to the affect and prediction failure view, it is because they induce affects the strength of which subjects would be unable to anticipate if they were merely faced with hypothetical tasks.

However, despite the differences between these mechanisms, the three perspectives have the following in common. Each suggests a range of factors for experimenters to consider when deciding on the incentive structures to use in their designs. Each suggests that there will be some occasions or research purposes for which substantial task-related incentives *would* be called for and others for which they would be either unimportant or harmful.

6.4.5   The Perspectives in Action: Game Shows

A recent development in research on individual decision making has been the analysis of the behavior of contestants on television game

---

[19] An alternative possible argument is that risk aversion is increasing in cognitive effort; and that greater effort is supplied when nominal payoffs are scaled up for real, but not when they are scaled up hypothetically.

shows (see, for example, Post et al. (2008), Conte et al. (2008), and, as a survey, Andersen et al. (2007)). Such sources of data are often seen as "natural experiments." However, in this case, the term "natural" should be interpreted with care. Although game shows are "natural" in the sense of arising independently of the research process, there are other respects, such as the nature of the decision problems and the presence of a presenter and studio audience, in which they seem quite untypical of normal life. Questions can therefore be posed about their broader external validity, in the sense of chapter 5.

However, these points notwithstanding, a striking feature of game show data, compared with most conventional experimental data, is the very high (sometimes life-changing) stakes. Consider, for example, the game show *Deal or No Deal*, which is played in many different countries under different names. The format is always roughly the same. There is a set of around twenty boxes each containing a different amount of money from a given list. There is one contestant, who knows the list of amounts, but not which amount is in which box. The amounts vary across boxes from very small (one penny in the U.K. version) to very large (£250,000).[20] The contestant is randomly given one of the boxes and then asked to select boxes other than his own one to be opened one at a time, so revealing the amounts inside them. Through this process, the possibilities for what may be in the contestant's own box are gradually reduced, because it must be one of the sums that has not yet been revealed. At different stages of the game, an anonymous *banker* makes offers to the contestant. Each offer is of a sure amount of money that is between the highest and lowest sums that could still be in the contestant's own box. The contestant can either accept the banker's offer ("deal") or reject it and carry on playing ("no deal"). If the contestant accepts, he takes home the banker's offer and the game stops. If the contestant rejects, he opens more boxes until either the banker makes another offer or his own box is the only one remaining. In the latter case, i.e., if the contestant rejects all of the banker's offers, he takes home the amount that ultimately proves to be in his own box.

It is obvious why data from this show has interested economists, and it has even been suggested (Post et al. 2008, p. 39) that *Deal or No Deal* "has such desirable features that it almost appears to be designed to be an economics experiment rather than a TV show." Some of the money amounts are very high and others trivially small; the choice problems are for real, clearly presented, and seemingly simple in structure; and

---

[20] For reference, the 2007 Annual Survey of Hours and Earnings shows median full-time weekly earnings in the U.K. to be £457, which makes £250,000 comparable to a decade's earnings at this rate.

each offer from the banker faces the contestant with a choice between a sure amount (i.e., the offer) and a risk (i.e., staying in the game).[21] A number of researchers (Andersen et al. 2006a,b, 2007; Conte et al. 2008) have applied models and econometric techniques to these types of data that are similar to those that have traditionally been used to analyze data from risky choice experiments. Nevertheless, in order to consider how useful it is to researchers that the stakes are so high in game show settings, we return to our three perspectives.

From the CLP perspective, there is little doubt that the high stakes should be expected to induce very high effort and application of cognitive capital. Thus, to the extent that researchers are interested in decisions made when there are strong incentives to deliberate, and to the extent that the show allows such deliberation, game show data seem attractive from a CLP perspective.[22]

From the perspective of intrinsic/extrinsic motivation, we need to consider what sort of nonmonetary motivations could conceivably be driving behavior. Straightforward application of the "crowding out" idea from section 6.4.2 would suggest that high financial stakes would override many forms of intrinsic motivation. However, especially in view of the selection of game show contestants, the game show environment may actually reinforce some intrinsic motivations. For example, the motivation to impress, or to entertain an audience, might be strengthened by the size of the audience and publicity surrounding particularly striking game show outcomes—and, therefore, perhaps also by the high stakes. This is not necessarily helpful if the purpose of the study is to make inferences about real-world behavior under risk: keeping an audience on the edge of their seats is a motivation that, though perhaps not unique

---

[21] The apparent simplicity of the game masks some rather complex considerations. When a contestant is faced with a given offer by the banker, the choice would be a straightforward one between a certainty and an equiprobable gamble defined on a known set of remaining possible amounts, *but for the following considerations.* A forward-looking contestant should take into account the fact that if he rejects the current bank offer (and it is not the last one), then he will receive further offers; what they are will depend, possibly among other things, on intervening chances (i.e., other boxes opened); and the contestant may, or may not, wish to accept them. Andersen et al. (2006a) provides a detailed analysis of the resulting "option value" of declining an offer; and Conte et al. (2008) analyze the rationality of contestants' beliefs about offers.

[22] Both provisos are important. First, as noted in chapter 2, many decisions in normal life involve quite small stakes, certainly compared with those in some game shows. Second, although there may be strong incentives to deliberate in a game show, careful calculation is not always feasible. Calculation aids (such as calculators or pencil and paper) are not usually provided; and the time constraints are often severe. When faced with a potentially life-changing decision in normal life, one usually has more than a few minutes to think about it.

to game show settings, nevertheless seems likely to be more important there than in most economic contexts.

From the perspective of affect, there is little doubt that the prizes available in some game shows are large enough to induce real fear of loss and real thrill at the prospect of winning or taking a gamble. The role of affective response appears particularly prominent in the case of an example described in detail by Post et al. (2008, pp. 47–48). A contestant named Frank was seen on the Dutch show to make a sequence of "unlucky" selections of boxes to be opened (i.e., he selected boxes that turned out to contain the larger sums), and appeared to become more and more risk-seeking by rejecting ever more generous bank offers. In the final round, the two remaining amounts were €10 and €10,000. The banker's offer was an unusually generous €6,000. Presumably, nearly everyone when confronted with this choice problem in isolation would choose €6,000 with certainty over the 50:50 gamble whose possible outcomes are €10 and €10,000. Frank chose the gamble. His box contained €10. It may be surmised that Frank's response to the bank's final offer was not a fully reflective one, but rather an irrational response to his anger at the results of previous rounds going against him.[23] If so, this would be unhelpful to researchers if cold and considered decisions are what they are interested in, but not necessarily so if affective response to risky outcomes is either the object of study or important to it.

6.5   Incentive Mechanisms

There is a widely held methodological presumption that economics experiments should feature reward mechanisms that are "incentive compatible." Roughly speaking, engineering incentive compatibility amounts to designing experiments so that subjects are motivated to give *truthful* responses to the *specific* questions that the experimenter wants to observe responses to. The presence of financial (or other) incentives, related to task performance, is clearly no guarantee of incentive compatibility; indeed, inappropriately structured task-related incentives could be a source of bias in responses. For instance, suppose that an experimenter would like to know an individual's willingness to accept for giving up a particular good that they are endowed with. That is, they seek a sincere answer to the question, What is the minimum price at which

---

[23] Other possible explanations for Frank's behavior are, for example, a fallacious belief that his luck must turn or a devil-may-care playing to the crowd. But these share the feature that they would not necessarily be at work if Frank had to make the same choice in considered, sober isolation.

you are just indifferent between keeping the good and selling it? Now imagine a naive design in which subjects are paid an amount equivalent to the value they state. This payment procedure provides incentives for a payoff-maximizing subject to deliver the answer to a different question: that is, What is the maximum amount that I think I could extract from this experimenter?[24]

The pursuit of incentive compatibility raises some intriguing methodological issues. One arises from the fact that an experimental design can only be judged incentive compatible (or not) *relative* to some theory of behavior (i.e., hypotheses about preferences and/or decision processes). This leads to interesting problems given the empirical challenges confronting traditional models of choice behavior: to what extent can we base experimental design on theories challenged by experimental evidence? One overarching message of our discussion in this section will be that the development of useful incentive mechanisms cannot flow solely from a priori theoretical analysis but can and should be informed by empirical evidence about how individuals actually behave and which mechanisms "work" in practice. Hence we are led to support a distinction between *theoretical incentive compatibility*, which grounds the design of incentive mechanisms on a priori theoretical assumptions about rationality, and *behavioral incentive compatibility* (Kaas and Ruprecht 2006), which appeals to empirical evidence relating to how people actually choose to justify practically useful incentive schemes.

To motivate this discussion we first consider one of the most widely used incentive mechanisms in experimental economics: the random-lottery incentive scheme (or RLI for short).[25] The key feature of RLI is that it facilitates observation of multiple task responses per subject. There are valid reasons why experimenters may wish to obtain multiple observations per subject: this allows within-subject comparisons of behavior that may be interesting for many purposes; also, given the fixed costs of recruiting subjects, increasing the number of tasks is more cost-effective than increasing the number of subjects. However, from the point of view

---

[24] A further example is tournament payoffs. Here, subjects accumulate points during the experiment, depending on the outcomes of the various tasks, but the only financial payment is a prize to the person with most points at the end. This system can seriously distort incentives, for example, if the tasks are games. If it is intended that subjects play a non-zero-sum game and the payoffs in points implement this game, then using a tournament payoff structure will totally change the strategic structure of the situation, by turning it into a zero-sum game.

[25] This system is discussed by Cubitt et al. (1998a). It is very often used in individual choice experiments, but perhaps less commonly so in game and market experiments. Nevertheless, in principle, most of the arguments for and against it apply equally to all three contexts.

of data interpretation, it may often be important to assume that subjects have responded to each task as if it were the only decision that they faced: the RLI is intended to encourage subjects to treat each task in isolation. In box 6.1 we describe the standard RLI and some variants of it.

Box 6.1. The random-lottery incentive scheme and its variants.

Under the standard RLI scheme, each subject completes a number of distinct decision tasks. These tasks might be anything that an experimenter is interested to observe, such as choices between consumption bundles, valuations, choices of strategy in a game, and so on. Each task typically has a well-defined reward structure where the payoff to an individual may be a function of what they choose, and/or the moves of other players (in games of strategy), and/or the moves of nature (in games of chance). At the beginning of the experiment, the subject is made aware that when the sequence of tasks is completed, *one* of the tasks will be selected at random, and the payoff to the individual will be the outcome of the selected task. This random selection of a task is the "random lottery." The reward resulting from the selected task is then the subject's only task-related payoff for the entire experiment (though this might be combined with a turn-up fee).[26]

Since only one task will be for real, the RLI may encourage subjects to think about each task as if it were for real and as if it were the only task faced. If subjects do think of RLI tasks in this way, then the mechanism will have the often desirable consequence of eliminating wealth effects that could arise if payments received from tasks influence subsequent decisions. On the other hand, if the number of tasks is too large then the probability of a particular task being real may be too small to engage subjects to exert attention and effort.

A variant of the RLI scheme allows a subject's responses to determine features of subsequent tasks. So for instance, parameters of later tasks can be "tailored" interactively, to individual subjects, using data from earlier decisions about individual level characteristics such as risk attitude.[27] Johnson et al. (2007) discuss a version of the RLI with this feature. Using this approach effectively means that aspects of the design become endogenous to the experiment. This runs counter to philosophies of

---

[26] One variant of the system has all subjects complete some task; and then a random lottery selects a subgroup of subjects to be paid.

[27] Camerer (2003, p. 42) promotes this approach enthusiastically: "Because of increases in computing power, for the first time in human history we can alter the experimental design in real time—while subjects are waiting, for seconds rather than days—to optimize the amount of information collected in the experiment."

"optimal design" (see, for example, Moffatt 2007) that favor determining all relevant design features in advance of running any experimental sessions. Indeed, once design features become endogenous, this has the potential to undermine incentive compatibility if subjects may manipulate the experiment by deliberately making false responses in an effort to "steer" the task sequence toward more desirable task parameters. Harrison (1986) has found evidence of this. One way to address this problem is via a modified version of RLI in which a universal set of choice problems is determined at the outset. Then a nonrandom sequence of problems is drawn from the universal set, with each one chosen in the light of previous responses in order to locate indifference. But it is made clear at the outset that the problem that is played for real is drawn randomly from the universal set, and not just from the subset of problems solved. If one of the solved problems is drawn, the chosen lottery is played; if one of the unsolved problems is drawn, the subject is asked to solve that problem as an additional task, and then it is immediately played for real. The crucial feature of this modified RLI system is that the choices made by the subject have no effect on the set of problems over which the randomization is performed, or on the probabilities of each problem being drawn. It is this feature that guarantees incentive compatibility, given the assumption of expected utility theory.

Another variant is the conditional information lottery (CIL) due to Nicholas Bardsley (2000). The original application was to a public-goods experiment where Bardsley wanted to observe how subjects would play conditional on specific histories of past contributions by other subjects. The issue here was how to engineer those past histories. One possibility was to run many games and wait for the histories to emerge, but that would have been very costly and time consuming. Another possibility would be to falsify evidence of past history, but that runs foul of the conventional prohibition of deception, which we discuss later in the chapter. The CIL provides another solution. Subjects play multiple games. Each game has a specified history. Subjects are told in advance that only one of these histories is real—the others are fictitious. They are also told that, at the end of the experiment, the game with the true history will be revealed and that they will be paid according to the outcome of just this one game.

The CIL is similar to the RLI, in the sense that only one from a set of tasks is for real and subjects do not know which is the real task until the end of the experiment. Unlike the RLI, however, the experimenter knows which task is for real from the start, and since the subjects are aware of this fact too, they might form expectations about which task is real and possibly take some tasks more seriously than others. However, Bardsley and Moffatt (2007) find consistency between "dummy" and real tasks in a CIL experiment allaying, to some extent, such concerns.

The RLI provides a good vehicle for illustrating the point that claims about the incentive compatibility of particular incentive mechanisms are theory laden. Consider an RLI experiment in which there are n tasks labeled t_i $(i = 1, \ldots, n)$. Suppose that each task has at least two possible responses and, as is standard, each task has an equal probability $(1/n)$ of being for real. We will say that any such RLI experiment is *unbiased* if, for every task, each subject gives exactly the response that they would have given had that task been for real and the only task they had faced.

A sufficient condition for unbiasedness of the RLI is that individuals are expected utility maximizers. To see why, assume for simplicity that the terminal payoff to a participant at the end of the experiment will be a single money payment and that each possible response in any task generates a specific probability distribution (or prospect) over this reward. We use $\boldsymbol{q}_{ij}$ to represent the prospect generated by response j to task t_i in the event that t_i is selected for real. Given these assumptions, each task, if considered in isolation, can be viewed as a choice among prospects.[28] Now consider an individual making their final decision in task t_n of some RLI experiment. Viewed at the level of the experiment as a whole, that individual is selecting the final element $\boldsymbol{q}_{nj}$ of a compound lottery $C = (1/n)\{\boldsymbol{q}_{nj}\} + \boldsymbol{q}^*$ where $\boldsymbol{q}^*$ is the compound lottery $(1/n)\{\boldsymbol{q}_{1j} + \cdots + \boldsymbol{q}_{(n-1)j}\}$ determined by their $n - 1$ earlier responses. If the Independence axiom of expected utility theory holds (see box 2.5 (p. 72) for its definition), then the response to task t_n will be independent of $\boldsymbol{q}^*$ and so responses to that task will be unbiased. Since a parallel argument can be made for any task within the experiment, it follows that the RLI is unbiased assuming expected utility preferences.

Since there is considerable evidence that expected utility theory fails descriptively, and that the source of many of these violations is a failure of its Independence axiom, simply assuming expected utility preferences cannot provide a satisfactory rationale for using the RLI in practice. This concern also provides a possible reason to reconsider some of the evidence generated using RLI procedures.[29] Indeed, as Charles Holt (1986)

---

[28] This assumption is mild in the context of experiments involving risky choices where each task may be precisely a choice among well-defined prospects, but it may be more demanding in other contexts.

[29] Though notice that violations of expected utility theory observed in an RLI experiment count against that theory regardless of whether the RLI is biased because the presence of a bias is itself evidence of a failure of expected utility theory.

has shown, when subjects have nonexpected utility preferences, the RLI might be a biased procedure, as discussed in chapter 4. That conclusion rests on two sorts of assumption: assumptions about individual preferences over simple lotteries and assumptions about the way in which subjects think about, or mentally process, the set of tasks involved in an RLI experiment. Holt examines the case of experiments involving choices among simple risks and assumes that individuals treat the whole experiment as a *single* choice among a set of compound risks. He also assumes that individuals convert compound risks to simple risks by multiplying probabilities. Holt then shows that responses to an RLI experiment may be biased in the presence of nonexpected utility preferences.

It is easy to see, however, that the RLI could be unbiased in the presence of any form of non-EU preferences given different assumptions about how agents mentally process tasks. For instance, individuals might respond to the complexity of an RLI experiment by approaching each task as if it were an isolated decision. If agents did process tasks in this way, it immediately follows that the RLI would be unbiased regardless of whether or not agents have expected utility preferences.

Whether or not the RLI is biased is ultimately an empirical question and existing research on this topic suggests a number of conclusions. First, tests conducted by Starmer and Sugden (1991) show that individuals do not process risks in precisely the way that Holt's hypothesis assumes. However, rejecting the model assumed in Holt's original hypothesis does not establish that the RLI is generally unbiased. Holt's conjecture is a particular model of how behavior in one task could be influenced by the presence of other tasks in an RLI experiment when agents have non-EU preferences; and while Starmer and Sugden reject the specific model that Holt proposed, their tests do not rule out the possibility that responses to specific tasks within an RLI experiment may be biased in some way by the presence of other tasks. Several subsequent studies including Cubitt et al. (1998a), Beattie and Loomes (1997), Wilcox (1993), Hey and Lee (2005a,b), and Laury (2006) shed further light on the reliability of RLI. Based on this research there seems little evidence that the use of RLI biases decisions. While the failure to have identified significant biases does not guarantee that RLI is unbiased in every application, in the absence of contrary evidence, it does provide a relatively solid empirical foundation for application of the method, in spite of the fact that its most obvious economic–theoretic justification (in terms of expected utility theory) seems empirically unsound.

So, from a practical viewpoint, the RLI scheme can be justified even given the knowledge that subjects violate Independence. We conjecture that this may be because treating tasks in isolation is a very natural and cognitively undemanding approach for subjects to take when engaging in an RLI scheme. On this interpretation, it may simply be a happy coincidence that the RLI works, by engaging a particular mental heuristic that promotes unbiased task responses.[30] That conjecture seems all the more plausible set against evidence that another incentive scheme that would also be valid under expected utility theory apparently fails in practice. This is the *binary lottery incentive* (BLI) scheme, already described in chapter 1 (see illustration 3). This procedure is designed with the aim of inducing risk-neutral preferences in experimental subjects. In standard implementations of the mechanism, subjects complete tasks that result in "rewards" but these rewards are not given in money; they are instead given as lottery tickets that determine the probability that the subject wins a fixed money prize in a "grand lottery." If subjects are expected utility maximizers, they should have linear utility over tickets (because they are just units of probability in the grand lottery), and subjects should therefore respond to task-level rewards as if they are risk neutral. Unfortunately, there is little evidence that the scheme works as planned, and some evidence (i.e., the research of Selten et al. (1999), as discussed in illustration 3) that it has the opposite effect to that intended: it causes subjects to become more risk averse. Notice that for the BLI to work, subjects must take account of the fact that each task forms part of a larger reward scheme. Consequently, if our conjecture about why the RLI works is correct, that same conjecture could explain why the BLI fails. That is, if in multitask experiments, subjects tend to treat each task in isolation ignoring the fact that each task forms part of a larger incentive scheme, then it follows that the RLI will work and the BLI will fail.

This discussion of RLI and BLI leads us to emphasize two significant points. First, these cases illustrate that claims to incentive compatibility depend on assumptions about behavior. That fact draws us back to an issue discussed at length in chapter 3 because such assumptions can be interpreted as auxiliary hypotheses that form part of the bundle that experimenters confront with evidence in experimental tests. Second, while in the past experimental economists have tended to promote mechanisms that are incentive compatible given the truth of expected utility theory, it is now abundantly clear that expected utility theory fails empirically in many laboratory tasks. So, if experimental procedures are to be reliable, they must build on other foundations that respect the empirical realities of human behavior. The latter point is reinforced by evidence that shows that the effects of incentive mechanisms can depend on features of their implementation which are irrelevant from a conventional

---

[30] Such a heuristic is similar to those considered by Kahneman and Tversky (1979). See Cubitt et al. (1998a, section 1) for application of this point to the RLI scheme.

choice-theoretic point of view. We illustrate this in the context of two mechanisms in common use for the extraction of money valuations: the Becker–DeGroot–Marschak mechanism and the Vickrey auction.

Box 6.2. Mechanisms for incentivizing valuation tasks.

The Becker–DeGroot–Marschak mechanism (henceforth BDM) due to Gary Becker et al. (1964) may be used to elicit either willingness to pay (WTP) to obtain, or willingness to accept (WTA) to give up, a given object. In the case of selling (a parallel analysis applies for buying), a subject endowed with a particular good is asked to state a reservation price knowing that when they have reported their valuation, a random price will be drawn.[31] If the random price is less than the subject's reported valuation, the subject will not sell. If the random price is at least as high as the valuation, the subject receives that price and gives up the good. It is well-known that an expected utility maximizer should report their true WTA valuation. It is also well-known that the mechanism may induce biased responses for agents with non-expected utility preferences (Karni and Safra 1987). The BDM has been widely used in a range of experimental applications including experiments investigating the preference reversal phenomenon introduced in box 3.4 (p. 131).

A second class of mechanism that has been widely employed for eliciting valuations in experiments is the Vickrey auction (due to William Vickrey 1961). In generic form, the Vickrey mechanism works as follows for the case of selling: two or more agents are each endowed with a single unit of a good to sell; each agent submits a (sealed) bid and the $n - 1$ agents submitting the lowest bids sell at a uniform price equal to the nth lowest bid. For the case where agents have independent private values for the good, it is a weakly dominant strategy for them each to bid their own true value. The most widely employed variant of the Vickrey mechanism is the so-called second-price auction in which $n = 2$. From a theoretical point of view, the BDM is closely related to the Vickrey auction mechanism because the BDM can be interpreted as a special case of the second-price auction in which there are just two bidders and one of them bids at random.

Echoing our discussion of RLI and BLI, and the discussion of the Duhem–Quine issue in chapter 3, the claim that these value elicitation

---

[31] The choice of distribution from which the random price is drawn should have no impact on subjects' reported valuations, as long as these are in the support. However, a natural choice of distribution would often be uniform with a maximum chosen to place an appropriate upper limit on the payout.

schemes are incentive compatible requires some background assumption about the behavior of agents. Once again, if we were entitled to assume expected utility maximization, this would provide a rationale for both the BDM and Vickrey mechanisms. However, as we have already discussed, expected utility theory does not provide an empirically satisfactory foundation for implementing these mechanisms. Consequently, the relevant question to ask is whether these mechanisms are behaviorally incentive compatible. That is, do they work in the sense of encouraging subjects to give honest and considered answers to the questions that the experimenter seeks the answers to? The answer to this may depend, in part, on the details of how the mechanisms are implemented.

As an illustration of this, consider the BDM. In the case of a selling task, the BDM has traditionally been implemented by asking a subject to state an open-ended reservation price that they know will subsequently be compared against a random number from a specified distribution. Experiments using this general setup have found that even relatively minor variations around it can have significant impacts upon the revealed valuations. For instance, Bohm et al. (1997) report that elicited values are positively correlated with the upper bound from which the random bid is drawn. This type of evidence suggests that the BDM is not generally incentive compatible, though there are grounds for thinking that some versions of it may be more reliable than others. An alternative way of implementing a BDM is to present the subject with an ascending (or descending) sequence of discrete price offers for each of which they must report whether or not they would trade at that price. In this version of the BDM, the subject knows that when they have completed the set of tasks, one of the prices will be chosen at random and their decision for that price will be implemented. There is some evidence that this binary choice format for implementing the BDM is a more reliable way of eliciting valuations (see Braga and Starmer 2005).

One possible reason why details of implementation can matter is because they may change the way in which subjects understand, and mentally process, tasks. Notice that, from a subject's point of view, the two tasks might seem quite different: in the first version of the BDM, the subject must produce a single open-ended valuation, the consequences of which will be different, contingent on the draw of a random number. Considering what it is best to do in the task so construed might appear quite a complicated problem from a subject's point of view. In the second formulation, the subject is encouraged to think about a set of discrete pairwise comparisons. Each of these tasks considered in isolation simply requires the individual to report their ranking over a pair of simple alternatives. Since this second, binary choice, version of the BDM is essentially an RLI experiment featuring a series of pairwise choices, there are reasons to suppose that an individual might well approach it in this way. Consequently, whatever explains the apparent success of the RLI mechanisms may also favor this second form of presenting the BDM.

The idea that subjects find some implementations of these procedures hard to understand is consonant with evidence showing that behavior in both the BDM and Vickrey mechanisms tends to change as subjects gain experience in them. For instance, in the context of second-price Vickrey auctions there is considerable evidence that WTA valuations for at least some types of goods (e.g., low-probability/high-payoff bets) tend to fall markedly as agents gather experience of the trading institution (see, for example, Braga et al. 2009). One interpretation of this evidence is that early valuations represent overstatements of underlying WTA values that are corrected as a consequence of experience. There is some evidence to support this interpretation. Perhaps the clearest comes from experiments that apply the mechanisms in the context of induced-value markets where individuals value "tokens" with a fixed cash redemption value. In this case, each individual's valuation ought to correspond with their own redemption value, yet some studies using this approach find significant deviations. For example, Noussair et al. (2004) elicit WTP valuations for induced-value tokens using both the BDM mechanism and the second-price Vickrey mechanism. They report that both produce a substantial bias toward underbidding in early periods, but with repetition bids converge to true values. However, the Vickrey mechanism emerges as a significantly more effective elicitation device: initial bids are closer to values and convergence between bids and values is faster and goes further in the Vickrey auction.

This evidence clearly suggests that, for both mechanisms, inexperienced valuations may be unreliable, and that experience within the mechanisms can improve precision of valuations in some contexts. However, it would be a mistake to jump to the conclusion that changes in observed valuations over time, within these mechanisms, are always evidence of increased accuracy in their measurement. Indeed a variety of evidence counts against this general presumption. For instance, Knetsch et al. (2001) and Braga et al. (2009) find that valuations in different variants of the Vickrey auction gravitate toward systematically different average valuations even though the variants are strategically equivalent. Loomes et al. (2003) report that individuals' valuations in median-price auctions are systematically influenced, or "shaped," by previously observed market prices even in an environment where individuals' valuations should be completely independent of one another. Such findings suggest that changes in observed values within these mechanisms cannot always be interpreted simply as noise reduction. They may instead be evidence that individuals' reported values are, to some extent, shaped by features of the environment in which they are elicited.

These examples reinforce the conclusion that the reliability of incentive mechanisms cannot be inferred from purely theoretical considerations that presume conventional models of rationality. In practice, it is important to adopt procedures that subjects can understand, given the way they are naturally able and inclined to think about decisions presented to them. And if the procedures adopted for some scientific purpose are not simple enough, or familiar enough, for subjects to immediately understand them, then some form of practice or training may be called for. However, this is not to say that all experiments should feature practice and training: if, for a given experimental objective, there is a choice between a simple task that requires no practice or training and a more complex one that requires training, the former may be preferable since it removes an unnecessary layer of complexity and eliminates the possibility that practice and training themselves produce shaping-type biases.

From what has been said so far in this section, the reader may have the impression that some mechanisms "work" (at least given appropriate practice and training) while others do not. However, it is important to refine this position by stressing that the efficacy of particular elicitation mechanisms can vary across different types of tasks. Indeed, whether an elicitation mechanism works may depend upon the kind of research question that motivates its use. A good illustration of this is provided by the so-called *strategy method*: a technique which has been quite widely applied in the context of research on experimental games.

Box 6.3. The strategy method.

The strategy method is a particular procedure for eliciting subjects' responses in games. The procedure is most easily explained via a simple illustration. Consider the ultimatum game introduced in box 3.3 (p. 116) in which two players "bargain" over a fixed pie. In standard implementations of it which do not use the strategy method the data generated consists of *observed decisions*; that is, we record the first-mover offers and the responders' reactions to them. We will call this standard procedure the "direct decision approach." Notice that a limitation of this standard approach is that it reveals only part of the responder's *strategy*: for each game we observe the second mover's response to the actual offer made, but we do not observe how they would have responded to different offers that could have been made.

The basic idea behind the strategy method is to ask each player to reveal their whole *strategy*: that is, the decisions that they would make at each point at which they could be called upon to move in the game. In the case of the ultimatum game, this requires the responder to give a conditional response for each offer that could be made before knowing what offer actually has been made. In the context of sequential games such as the ultimatum game, once strategies have been elicited for all players, the game can be played out by implementing these strategies. Urs Fischbacher et al. (2001) implement a variant of the strategy method that can be used in the context of simultaneous-move games. Their experiment features a standard voluntary-contributions mechanism (see box 2.3 (p. 58)). A novel feature of this design, however, is that each subject, in addition to making their usual (unconditional) decision about how much to contribute to the common pool, also provides a schedule stating their preferred contribution conditional on the average contribution of all other players. They do this knowing that, after they have made both types of decisions, the game will be played out by implementing the unconditional decisions of all but one of the players and the conditional decision of one randomly selected player. Hence this variant of the strategy methods provides a clever procedure for eliciting strategies in a simultaneous-move game.

In general, an attractive feature of the strategy method is that richer data are obtained because they contain information about how agents would play at information sets that might not arise in the actual course of play. This is particularly relevant in situations where certain information sets of interest are rarely observed in actual play. For example, using the direct decision approach, we rarely observe how agents respond to very low offers in ultimatum games since very low offers are themselves rare.

This procedure was originally suggested by Selten (1967) and is discussed in more detail in Roth (1995b). It has been widely applied in experimental studies including Axelrod (1984), Mitzkewitz and Nagel (1993), Selten et al. (1997), Bolton et al. (1998), Keser and Gardner (1999), Charness and Rabin (2002), and Falk et al. (2008).

From the viewpoint of standard game theory, the direct decision approach and the strategy method are both valid procedures for eliciting decisions in games and we should expect consistency comparing across observed responses gathered via the two procedures. While relatively little research has been carried out to compare responses across the methods, a variety of studies shed some light on the issue. The current pattern of findings appears somewhat mixed. Some studies show

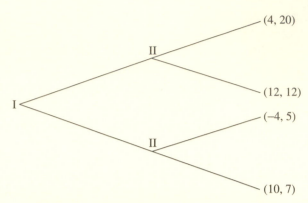

Figure 6.1. Brosig et al's punishment game.

little, if any, evidence of discrepancy between the methods (Brandts and Charness 2000; Oxoby and McLeish 2004; Muller et al. 2008; Fischbacher and Gächter, forthcoming; Solnick 2007). Other studies, however, reveal marked differences between them (Güth et al. 2001; Blount and Bazerman 1996; Brosig et al. 2003). For example, Jeanette Brosig et al. conduct a controlled test of the difference between games played under the direct decision and strategy methods. In their setup, subjects play two-person sequential games in which each player has one move. An example of one of their games is presented in figure 6.1.

This game has a unique subgame-perfect equilibrium in which both players choose "down" resulting in a payoff of 10 and 7 respectively for players I and II. But the equilibrium is not efficient: both players could achieve payoffs of 12 if player I played up and player II played down; and a first mover who plays down (in line with their equilibrium strategy) condemns the second mover to a relatively low payoff compared with the upper branch. An interesting feature of this game is that a second mover at the lower of their two choice nodes has the opportunity of "punishing" the first mover: that is, by playing up they can take a slightly lower payoff for themselves (5 versus 7) but significantly damage the first mover's payoff.

Brosig et al. find that, in play of this game under the direct decision method, a significant proportion of subjects in the role of player II who find themselves at the lower decision node do in fact exploit the punishment opportunity. This may be no great surprise given what we know about play in other games such as the ultimatum game. A novel finding of this study, however, is that when responses are elicited via the strategy method, subjects in the role of player II are much less likely to punish—contingent on arriving at the lower node.

What might account for this difference? Brosig et al. speculate that it may be due to differences in the extent to which the two procedures provoke affective (or "visceral") responses, in second movers, to the play of down by first movers. The thought is a very simple one: under the direct method second movers at the lower node may feel anger about the fact that the first player has just condemned them both to lower payoffs than they could have had, and that this feeling of anger might prompt them to punish. By comparison, under the strategy method, second movers have to *imagine* how it would feel to arrive at the lower node. The observed difference between treatments would then follow from assuming that imagining one's feelings fails to produce the same level of affective response: that is, "you have to be there" to feel, and hence to be motivated to act upon, the anger. This explanation seems consistent with the growing evidence (mentioned above in section 6.4) that human beings find it difficult to anticipate aspects of their own future emotions.

Supposing that this is the right explanation, would that undermine use of the strategy method? We think the answer is no—at least not in all potential applications. If affective reactions to decision settings are significant factors in some strategic interactions, and on the assumption that the strategy method systematically fails to provoke them, there would be a case against using the method in applications where it could be expected that affective reactions are an important determinant, relative to the phenomenon of interest. On the other hand, the strategy method could still be defended as a practical research tool in application to decisions where there were grounds for thinking that the role of affect was sufficiently small. Furthermore, the strategy method may be the ideal approach if the research question in hand requires the researcher to control out, as far as possible, the affective components in decisions.[32]

In general, however, this illustration reinforces our argument that it is a mistake to think of elicitation procedures as incentive compatible (or not) per se. Whether or not a mechanism is appropriate in a particular research context will depend on what the investigator is aiming to find out. Given a research question, judging whether a particular mechanism is appropriate for its investigation ultimately rests on some theory of what will determine subjects' behavior in the relevant arena of investigation. Since investigators are often trying to find out more about how

---

[32] For example, there may be contexts in which subjects can foresee some affective responses, yet do not regard them as guides to rational behavior. Such subjects might use the precommitment facility offered by the strategy method to reveal their considered views as to appropriate responses. If so, this would provide a reason to use the strategy method when one wishes to investigate those views.

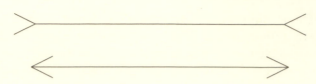

Figure 6.2. A bias in visual judgments.

agents make decisions, such judgments are bound to rest on assumptions about which we cannot be completely confident. But while our understanding of these things is necessarily imperfect, it seems reasonable to think that better decisions regarding research design are likely to follow from taking account of the multiple perspectives on human motivation that current research provides.

If the pursuit of incentive compatibility requires subtle and perhaps contentious judgments, this suggests it would be a mistake to think that any satisfactory task payment system *must* feature incentive compatible rewards. In our view, judgments about appropriate rewards should be subordinate to the research question in hand. Moreover, there may be interesting research questions, worthy of investigation, which may be difficult, and in some cases perhaps even impossible, to incentivize.

As an illustration of something that seems difficult to imagine incentivizing, consider tasks in which snap judgments can produce biases. A well-known example is a task that involves the following visual illusion. A subject is asked which of the two horizontal lines illustrated in figure 6.2 is the longer one.

People approaching this task for the first time often think that the top line is longer even though it is slightly shorter. Now suppose that an investigator is interested to know whether subjects are prone to this illusion when they make a reasonably quick assessment of the length of the two lines.[33] In this case, the introduction of a financial incentive for picking the longer line would likely be counterproductive, relative to the research objective, since if the subject knows they will receive a payoff for correctly identifying the longer line, and zero otherwise, they may be prompted to discount their initial impression and apply more effort in order to find out which line is truly longer. Moreover, in this case, the higher the incentive, the less likely it becomes that the investigator observes the genuine snap judgment that is the object of their enquiry.

---

[33] Investigating biases from snap decisions can be interesting for any number of reasons, not least because they can have serious consequences. For instance, it is well-known that, when making unreflective judgments, humans are prone to overestimate distance in fog—a tendency that can have very serious consequences on the roads.

While the relevance of this example to economics might be questioned, it is not hard to think of other judgment errors that may be of considerable relevance in a wide range of economic contexts. For example, there is widely cited evidence (e.g., Bar-Hillel 1980) that human beings make systematic errors in probability judgments in cases where the correct response requires application of Bayes's rule (the well-known formula giving the conditional probability of an event in terms of other conditional and marginal probabilities). This may be because applying Bayes's rule is a nontrivial mathematical exercise that most ordinary people are not practiced in and also because the results obtained from correct application can be counterintuitive. For instance, suppose you are told that drunk drivers are ten times more likely to cause accidents than sober drivers; and that between the hours of midnight and 2 a.m., one in twenty drivers are drunk. Now, if you observe an accident during this time, should you think it highly likely that the driver who caused it is drunk? Many people may be inclined to think so, but the correct answer is "no." Despite drunk drivers being ten times as dangerous, the conditional probability of the driver in the accident being drunk is only 0.34. An experimenter who wants to study the impact of such biases on real decisions may wish to create laboratory conditions that stimulate the types of reasoning that ordinary people bring to bear on such tasks in the wild environments that motivate their study. Notice that this might or might not suggest tasks with incentives, depending upon which class of wild environment has motivated the experiment.

We have argued that where snap judgments are the object of study it may be counterproductive to incentivize the tasks with which these judgments are elicited. It is possible to think of other phenomena that experimental economists might wish to study, but where incentivized elicitation is inherently problematic.

One example, which we will explore further in chapter 7, is confidence in choices. Butler and Loomes (2007) show how eliciting agents' confidence can illuminate the study of a model of imprecise preferences that, they argue, is a candidate explanation of phenomena such as preference reversals (see box 3.4 (p. 131)).

A further example is provided by agents' plans in the context of sequential decision making.[34] An important question in the study of

---

[34] For a survey of recent research on sequential decision making, see Cubitt et al. (2004b). Plans are considered, for example, by Barkan and Busemeyer (1999), Bone et al. (2003, 2009), Hey (2002, 2005b), and Hey and Knoll (2007).

sequential decision making is whether agents are *dynamically consistent*: that is, whether their subsequent behavior conforms to their initial plans. While it is fairly straightforward to set up a sequential decision problem in the laboratory and to observe subjects' behavior in it, it is not clear how to elicit their initial plans in order to assess whether their behavior conforms to them. Experimenters have found ways of sidestepping[35] this problem, but not of solving it directly using task-related incentives. It seems almost, perhaps completely, impossible to provide a financial incentive for truthful revelation of plans, while retaining the original research objective of checking dynamic consistency. In particular, it would not work to try to incentivize subjects to state a carefully considered, truthful plan by rewarding them if their stated plan turns out to describe how they subsequently behave, since this would provide an incentive to modify subsequent behavior in the direction of the plan, so biasing the test of dynamic consistency. Nor would it work to try to give an incentive for formulating the plan by requiring subjects to follow their stated plan through, as this would amount to providing subjects with a binding precommitment device.[36] Dynamic consistency is likely to be at issue in contexts of potential intrapersonal conflict; and, in these contexts, what the agent would commit to may differ from what she would plan when precommitment is impossible.

For example, sophisticated planners take into account that they can reconsider their plan and that, in the absence of binding precommitment, they will act on any reconsideration. In contrast, with binding precommitment, acting on any reconsideration will not be an option. As an everyday example, consider someone who, after one alcoholic drink, is

---

[35] Cubitt et al. (1998b) show that a condition they call "timing independence" may be tested, using only data on behavior. Timing independence is similar to dynamic consistency, but not identical to the latter because it makes no reference to plans. Related research is also reported by Busemeyer et al. (2000) and Johnson and Busemeyer (2001). Bone et al. (2003, 2009) and Hey and Knoll (2007) show how, *provided one makes certain assumptions about preferences*, it is possible to draw conclusions from behavior about whether, and how far, agents plan ahead.

[36] There are several variants on this technique. One is to impose a small penalty for deviating from the stated plan (Hey 2005b). But this also acts as a precommitment device, albeit not a fully binding one. Another technique is to require subjects both to state a plan and then to play out the decision problem sequentially, with a random device then determining whether it is the plan or the sequential play that is used to determine payoffs (Barkan and Busemeyer 1999). Although ingenious in allowing a within-subject comparison of planned and sequential play, this method introduces a chance node. In principle, a subject could use the incentive mechanism to construct a gamble not attainable in the original problem. Another variant involves asking subjects to make a commitment, believing it to be binding, and then allowing them a surprise opportunity to deviate (Camerer 1989). But this elicits what the subject would do when they think precommitment is available, not what they would plan in the original problem.

tempted to have another. If sophisticated, he might both plan and actually stick to mineral water all evening. But, if offered a facility that allows him to commit to have no more than one alcoholic drink, he might take it and have one beer. If so, his behavior when he can precommit is different from what he would plan when commitment is not available. This is not to say that choices among alternative commitments are uninformative, but merely that they are not the same thing as plans made when commitment devices are unavailable. By attempting to incentivize the elicitation of plans for some decision problem, one risks eliciting behavior in another decision problem instead.

If, as we have argued, there are certain types of tasks that it is inherently difficult, if not impossible, to incentivize, then insistence on task-related incentives for all tasks puts certain research topics off-limits. We think that would unnecessarily narrow the scope of experimental investigation. Moreover, such a narrowing of focus would be out of line with conventions that appear to govern research in other spheres of economic enquiry. For instance, there is considerable contemporary interest in understanding the determinants of human "happiness."[37] Standard econometric investigations of this phenomenon use measures of happiness derived from various surveys. Despite the fact that these measures of happiness come from nonincentivized subjective self-reports, the results of such research are reported in leading journals and are widely discussed in academic and policy circles. They seem to correlate with other people's judgments of how happy a person is and with other indicators of well-being. The more such correlations are found, the more credible it is to suppose that constructs based on these survey responses provide meaningful proxies for what they are supposed to measure. In view of this, we suggest that a more permissive attitude to the role that incentives should play in experiments would be both defensible from a scientific point of view and consonant with more general attitudes to data that prevail in the broader academic community of economists.

This last point goes with the general thrust of this chapter by telling against simple blanket prescriptions and prohibitions that purport to delineate what count as good incentive mechanisms. Before concluding, however, we note an important qualification to this position.

---

[37] See, for example, Oswald (1997), Di Tella et al. (2001), Clark et al. (2008), and, for overviews, Frey and Stutzer (2002), Layard (2005), Frey et al. (2008), and symposia in the winter 2006 issue of the *Journal of Economic Perspectives* and the August 2008 issue of *Journal of Public Economics*.

So far, we have argued that the key criterion in judging whether an experimental design is appropriate in its use (or nonuse) of task-related incentives is whether its incentive system serves the scientific objectives of the research being conducted in the experiment. However, there may be cases where the use of some design feature by one group of experimental researchers could harm the ability of other experimenters to achieve their objectives. If there are significant negative externalities flowing from particular types of designs, this might suggest a case for constraints on design choice beyond those dictated by the immediate objectives of the research. In fact, we can think of just one obvious category of design feature where significant negative externalities of this kind might arise. This relates to the use of deception as an experimental tool.

Box 6.4. Deception: a case of negative externality.

The proposition that experimenters should not actively mislead experimental subjects is probably the most widely endorsed methodological principle of experimental economics: the prohibition of deceptive practices is almost universally accepted by experimental economists (in contrast to psychologists). Those who are perceived to have violated it may find the work in which they do so severely criticized and very hard, if not impossible, to publish in peer-reviewed economics journals.

Absent externality concerns, deceiving subjects could be a convenient way of achieving certain experimental objectives (see Bonetti 1998).[38] For instance, deceptive methods could provide a tool for making subjects believe that they are in situations of research interest that would be difficult to bring about by other means (perhaps because engineering them would be prohibitively costly or ethically questionable). But, while there may sometimes seem to be attractions to deception, most commentators in economics argue for its prohibition (see Hey 1998; McDaniel and Starmer 1998; Hertwig and Ortmann 2001, 2003).

To a large extent, the prohibitionist case rests on the argument that trust between subjects and experimenters is a valuable public good in research, which might be seriously eroded by even limited use of deception. To appreciate this case, it is necessary to understand the

---

[38] That said, critics of deception sometimes argue that it can undermine even the objectives of the current research if subjects begin to see through it. Others, such as Bardsley (2000), have argued that the goals that seem to call for deception can often be achieved in nondeceptive ways.

role that trust plays in establishing control over an experimental set-ting. Consider, for example, a design where the experimenter wants to use task-related incentives to create a particular decision environment (e.g., a certain game, or a market with certain demand and supply schedules). The experimenter aims to create, and to put subjects in, the intended setting in order to see how they behave in it. But subjects actually act on their *beliefs* about the setting they face. So even if the experimenter has in fact provided a complete and truthful description of the setting that is understood by subjects, the interpretation of the experimental outcomes as features of behavior in the intended setting still requires a further assumption, namely that subjects believed the experimenter's description. If there is reason to doubt this assumption, this would undermine the inferences that the experimenter wishes to draw.

Obviously, no experimenter can (with current technology) achieve complete control over all beliefs that subjects hold. The most she can aim for is the partial control that would flow from subjects believing what the experimenter tells them about the decision environment. But, crucially, an individual researcher could not be sure of achieving this control merely by her own actions if there was a widespread perception among subjects that experimental instructions are not trustworthy. If deceptive practices are used by other researchers, knowledge of that fact might spread among a local subject pool (e.g., by word of mouth). More worryingly, it could spread more widely as knowledge of experimental method is disseminated, for example through journals, and teaching in which experimental research is discussed. The importance of this trans-mission route should not be underestimated, given that experimental subjects tend to be drawn from among university students. The concern is obviously particularly acute where subjects are drawn from among students of the researchers' own discipline, since in this case they are more likely to know something of the conventions governing research in that discipline.

For reasons discussed in box 6.4, there is a case for thinking that the internal validity of experimental research (see box 2.1 (p. 52)) usually depends on subjects trusting the experimenters enough to believe what the experimental instructions say about the decision environment. To the extent that this trust depends on the actions of all experimental researchers, not just on those conducting a particular experiment, this grounds a departure, in the case of deception, from the broadly plural-istic conclusions about incentives that we argue for elsewhere in this chapter. In fact, we agree with those who argue that deception should be avoided in laboratory experiments.[39]

The externality argument for a blanket rule only applies when there is the potential for the inferences drawn from one experiment to be undermined by the conduct of others. Apart from the no deception rule, we think few, if any, other blanket prescriptions related to incentives are licensed by the externality argument. So we set it aside when summing up the main conclusions of this chapter in the next section. These relate to the use of task-related incentives, conditional on a background assumption that, whatever incentives are used, subjects will be told them truthfully before they undertake the tasks to which they relate.

6.6 Conclusion

At the start of this chapter we documented the overwhelming predominance in the economics literature of experiments that do use task-related incentives. Our discussion suggests that matters are more complicated than routine conformity with this convention might indicate.

There are several reasons why incentives may affect subjects' behavior. Although inducing subjects to exert more cognitive effort is a possible

---

[39] By deception, we have in mind telling subjects things about the experimental environment they face and the possible consequences of their actions that are not true. We do not mean that subjects should always be told "everything" about the experiment; nor that experimenters should never permit a subject to hold a false belief. (It is uncontroversial among economists that there are many experiments where it would be counterproductive to tell subjects what treatments *other* subjects are being exposed to. Equally, it would be silly to see it as essential to prevent subjects from forming any false belief in an experiment, such as one on game-theoretic equilibrium concepts, part of whose goal is to see if subjects can form correct beliefs, in this case about each other's behavior.) In the laboratory, it is usually fairly clear what is lying and what is merely permitting a subject to entertain a belief that may prove false; and it is lying in the laboratory that seems most likely to undermine the trust on which future experiments depend. However, there can sometimes be a grey area between lying and other forms of nondisclosure; and there may occasionally be ethical concerns that do not arise from externalities between experiments. As an example that raises both issues, consider field experiments where the experimenter conceals from subjects their involvement in an experiment. If subjects are members of the public whose behavior is covertly observed in a situation that seems quite normal to them, the likelihood of future lab or field experimental control being undermined seems remote. But have subjects nevertheless been misled in an ethically concerning way? This may turn on the specifics of the case. It is interesting to compare the two experiments reported in Bryan and Test (1967): see illustration 2 of chapter 1. If all money donated by the public and the stooges was given to the Salvation Army in the charitable donations case, but the supposedly lone female driver was not really unsupported in the car tyre experiment, then it could be argued that the latter experiment is ethically more concerning because some subjects are induced to give up time and effort when there was no real need. But if this is an ethical concern, it has nothing to do with undermining future experiments.

effect of stronger incentives that springs naturally to mind, it is not necessarily the only one, nor is it always the most important. Incentives may
also drive out intrinsic motivations or stimulate emotions that subjects
could not fully anticipate if faced with hypothetical tasks. Each of these
effects suggests a different, and sometimes useful, role for task-related
incentives.

However, whether it is actually useful to have subjects straining with
mental effort, drained of their intrinsic motivation, or at the mercy of
affective experiences, depends on the purpose of the investigation. The
question turns on many factors, including the view one takes of the
domain of any theory under test, the nature of the intrinsic motivations
that might be crowded out, the types of tasks involved, and so on. Good
experimental design in this situation is not a matter of applying inflexible
rules of thumb, but rather of thinking through the function of incentives
in relation to the research questions that the experiment is intended to
answer. There are objectives for which very high task-related incentives
would be important; others for which quite modest ones would be adequate; and others still for which task-related incentives might actually
be harmful.

Our discussion of incentive compatibility leads us to similarly plural-
istic conclusions. While traditionally experimentalists have looked for
incentive mechanisms that can be justified relative to standard theoretical models of rational behavior, sound foundations for incentive mechanisms require understanding of the psychology of choice that may go
beyond, or perhaps even conflict with, the standard approach. There may
be trade-offs between the pursuit of theoretical incentive compatibility
and intelligibility of incentive mechanisms that should enter as considerations in experimental design. Finally, we caution against a presumption
that all tasks in worthwhile economics experiments must feature material rewards. There may be occasions where it is productive to set aside
the conventions that have developed about task-related incentives, no
matter how well-founded their use is on other occasions.

7

Noise and Variability in Experimental Data

7.1 "Noise" in Economics and in Experimental Economics

While much of this book has been concerned with broad issues of methodological principle, this chapter addresses what might seem to be a more specific and practical question associated with the analysis and interpretation of experimental data.

Proponents of experimental economics often claim that experiments are particularly well suited to testing economic theory, since they give a much greater degree of control than can generally be found in the "natural" economic environment. While that may be true, this chapter will suggest that insufficient consideration has so far been given to the question of which tests are suitable for different kinds of experimental data and under what conditions particular null hypotheses are appropriate. There seems to be a widespread assumption that statistical and econometric techniques developed for use with nonexperimental data can be applied quite straightforwardly to the data generated by experiments. But is this a safe assumption? This chapter will suggest that it is not, and will show that this apparently practical problem of statistical analysis connects back to some of the broader methodological issues raised earlier in the book.

Consider first the general approach underlying much econometric work. Economic theory has traditionally developed models where one variable—say the quantity demanded of good X—is a function of other variables (such as the price of X, consumers' incomes, the prices of complements and substitutes for X, and so on). As presented by theorists in standard mathematical forms, these are for the most part deterministic models: that is to say, the model is written as if the dependent variable is completely and precisely determined by the values of the independent variables. Econometricians then take whatever data are available about those different variables in order to examine how well particular models work and to obtain numerical estimates of the coefficients that express the impacts of the different independent variables upon the dependent variable.

When undertaking this task, they typically face a number of problems. First, the ways in which variables interact may not be fully specified by the model—or if they are, the specification may not correspond exactly with the ways in which those variables actually do interact. Second, there may be many variables that actually have *some* effect on the value of the dependent variable, but many of these effects may be relatively small and/or there may be little or no available data about some of them. Third, the data for the most significant variables may be imperfect: they may be liable to measurement error, and, if they are derived from some sampling procedure, they will also be subject to sampling error. Fourth (although this may be regarded by some as a subset of the second category), there may be heterogeneity in the preferences and motivations of different actors in the economy that is difficult to observe directly. Fifth, there may be some "within-subject" variability, so that even when presented with what might appear to be exactly the same conditions, agents may act differently on different occasions. All of these may be sources of "noise" and "error" that make it difficult to identify and quantify the underlying core relationships with total precision.

Many econometric studies therefore focus on a manageable set of what theory suggests are the most important independent variables and then model all other influences as if their collective impact upon the dependent variable operates much like random error. Within this framework, tests may be conducted to see whether particular variables are significantly influential and how different models, or different specifications of those models, compare. As part of this process, the robustness of the assumptions about the error term may also be investigated, and tests (or the conclusions drawn from them) may be modified in the light of the results of those investigations.

However, there are differences between experimental and nonexperimental data that may mean, at the very least, that careful thought should be given to the ways in which statistical and econometric techniques developed for nonexperimental data are applied to experimental results. In particular, the fifth source of noise listed above—within-subject variability in expressed or revealed preferences—does not feature very prominently as a separate consideration in most econometric applications; and even the fourth source—variability of tastes/goals *between* agents—may be swamped by the first three categories. But precisely because experiments are designed to control many of the other sources of noise in nonexperimental data, variability within and between actors' beliefs, preferences, and judgments may play a larger and more central role in the generation of experimental data; and this may have significant implications for the analysis and interpretation of those data.

In the nonexperimental world of decision making under risk, people operate on the basis of their own perceptions and evaluations of consequences and their own subjective estimates of the risks, which may vary widely in ways that are hard to observe. By contrast, individual decision experiments typically involve a small number of clearly specified payoffs and use probabilities that correspond with some explicit random mechanism, as explained in chapter 2. In the nonexperimental world of strategic interaction, requirements of game theory (such as common knowledge) are rarely satisfied and it is hard to say what different players know or believe about the strategies and payoffs available to other players. By contrast, in the laboratory, experimenters often go to considerable lengths to try to make it common knowledge among the players what the strategies available to each player are and how payoffs depend upon them, at least in monetary terms.[1] In nonexperimental markets, it is often the case that little is known about the cost functions of suppliers or the true willingness to buy of purchasers across a wide range of prices; and even when some knowledge of these things can be obtained, it is rare to find two or more market institutions operating under comparable demand and supply conditions. By contrast, market experiments may induce the same underlying demand and supply functions and then study how different institutions perform under those conditions (see chapter 3 for details of inducing values in markets).

In short, in classic theory-testing experiments, the conventional experimental wisdom is to aim for as much control as possible over the experimental environment and then to introduce human actors into that environment and observe their behavior. Under such circumstances, the noise from other sources is greatly reduced: the principal—or at least, a major—element in any stochastic component in the data is likely to derive from the participants themselves.[2] Thus, modeling the stochastic component in the data, and deciding upon the appropriate tests to conduct, requires us to model the sources and nature of noise and error in human judgment and decision making. And it turns out that

---

[1] Strictly speaking, the standard game-theoretic assumption is that payoffs are common knowledge *in utility form*. The methods by which monetary payoffs and other features of the game are made common knowledge—for example, publicly announcing a set of instructions in which these matters are described—cannot actually make payoffs in utility terms common knowledge. As will be discussed in section 7.3, not having control over *these* features is liable to be a source of "noise."

[2] Since any underlying population of economic actors is liable to be heterogeneous, sampling error is also likely to be an element.

different "error stories" can have quite different implications for the hypotheses we consider and for the validity of the statistical tests used to discriminate between them.

The next section will discuss three different forms of error story that have been proposed in the context of individual decision making under risk. Section 7.3 will consider some issues and implications for experiments examining game theory. The final section will reflect upon some possible strategies for adding to our understanding in this challenging and underdeveloped area of experimental methodology.

In what follows, we deliberately restrict attention to what might be thought of as individuals' inherent uncertainty/imprecision/propensity to error when considering their own preferences and/or weighting of probabilities. There is also a substantial literature concerned with the ways in which people may learn about the experimental environment they are placed in and/or the behavior of others whose actions affect them—for example, how they may adapt to the strategies of other players in the course of a repeated experimental game. Camerer (2003, chapter 6) provides a very useful review of learning models, many of which take a stochastic form. Our focus, however, is upon variability in response that cannot very easily be attributed to feedback and the acquisition of new information, but that seems intrinsic to the human judgmental apparatus.

7.2 "Noise" in Individual Decision Experiments

The focus in this section will be upon individual decision making under risk. In fact, the scope of individual decision experiments is a good deal wider than that (see Camerer 1995) but decision making under risk is a convenient place to start because, as discussed in chapters 2–4, there is a wealth of material from studies investigating seemingly systematic departures from standard theory and/or trying to compare the performance of one decision theory against another.

One particularly pertinent feature of *some* of these studies is that they provide evidence about what happens when the same individuals are asked to undertake exactly the same decision task on two or more occasions within a short space of time—i.e., either within the same experimental session or in repeated sessions a day or two apart. The bulk of this evidence relates to pairwise choices. For example, Graham Loomes and Robert Sugden (1998) reported a study where, in the first part of each experimental session, they asked respondents to make a series of forty-five choices between pairs of simple lotteries involving no more than three payoffs. They then gave the respondents a short "distractor" task before presenting them a few minutes later with the same forty-five pairwise choices again. The only difference between the two series was the order in which the questions were presented, which was randomized on both occasions; but all other features—not least the particular way in which each pair was set out—were kept exactly the same in both series, in order to minimize any noise due to presentational or "framing" effects. In order to control for income effects, the random-lottery incentive system, discussed in chapter 6 and defined in box 6.1 (p. 266), was used.

Despite these efforts to keep the tasks as similar as possible across stages, there were many instances where an individual chose one alternative on the first occasion that they were asked to make a decision and chose the other alternative when they were presented with exactly the same pair of lotteries for a second time. In fact, out of a total of 3,680 comparisons (ninety-two respondents each making forty choices[3] on two occasions), there were 676 cases (18.4%) where the choice on the second occasion was different from that on the first.[4] To what extent might such behavior be regarded as white noise or random error? And to the extent that it is, how should it be understood and modeled?

One possibility is that what is being observed here is not error, but rather some kind of learning. Could it be that, in facing the decision tasks the first time round, the respondents gradually learned how to deal with them more rationally, or gradually discovered their "true" preferences, and that their choices the second time round revealed the benefits of this experience? (Such an interpretation would be consistent with the discovered preference hypothesis, discussed in chapter 2 and defined in box 2.7 (p. 77).)

In fact, there is *some* evidence that behavior changed systematically over the course of the experiment. In each of the forty pairs, one lottery could be regarded as the "safer" (*S*) option while the other was the "riskier" (*R*) option, with the latter usually offering a higher expected value than the former. If there were only purely random disturbances in respondents' choices in the first series and a corresponding pattern of random disturbance in the second series, we might expect as many

---

[3] We focus here on the forty choices that did not involve dominance and exclude the five choices where one option strictly dominated the other. More will be said about those choices later.

[4] These rates of reversal are by no means untypical: for some time it has been accepted that in similar circumstances, when neither lottery is obviously inferior to the other, as many as 30% of respondents may choose differently when presented with the same pair on two occasions a few minutes apart (see, for example, Camerer 1989; Starmer and Sugden 1989; Hey and Orme 1994).

cases where S was chosen in the first series and R in the second series (denoted by SR) as cases where R was chosen first time round and S on the second occasion (denoted by RS). But this was not so. From the total of 676 instances where S was chosen on one occasion and R on the other, 407 were RS as opposed to 269 SR. If the null hypothesis were that all reversals of choice between the first and second occasions were due *only* to random error such that SR was just as likely to be observed as RS, a standard binomial test would reject that null hypothesis with a very high degree of confidence. Rather, there appears to have been some trend toward making safer choices on the second occasion than the first—a trend that also turned out to be present in the data reported by Hey and Orme (1994) and by Ballinger and Wilcox (1997). However, even if the excess of RS over SR reversals is attributed to learning, more than 14% of the observations remain to be accounted for. This suggests that there is a considerable degree of purely stochastic variation in these data.[5]

To try to capture such variability, three sorts of stochastic model have been most prominent in experimental economics in recent years. We shall refer to these as the *Tremble model*, the *Fechner model*, and the *Random Preference (RP) model*. These are described in the following subsections, together with a discussion of their strengths and limitations, and some of their respective implications for the interpretation of different patterns of data from experiments examining individual decision making under risk.[6]

7.2.1   The Tremble Model

Perhaps the simplest notion of error is that people have some "true" preferences, but occasionally make mistakes in reporting them, due possibly to momentary inattention or some similar lapse—in short, due to a slip or a "trembling hand." For pairwise choices, this could be formalized by supposing that an individual truly prefers one option but that there is some probability ω that she will make a slip in the course of translating preference into choice and will be observed to choose the truly less-preferred option. Intuitively, it seems implausible that ω is totally

---

[5] Loomes et al. (2002) use econometric methods to try to disentangle the effects of stochastic variation and learning in the data reported by Loomes and Sugden (1998). In detail, their conclusions depend on the way stochastic variation is modeled, but the broad picture is clear: there is a significant learning effect, but even at the end of the ninety decision tasks, individual responses show a high degree of stochastic variation.

[6] Our discussion draws on Loomes (2005) and reflects a line of research going back to Loomes and Sugden (1995). A different, and very useful, review of the approaches we consider here has recently been provided by Wilcox (2008).

independent of the characteristics of the pair of alternatives being considered. However, when this specification was used by David Harless and Colin Camerer (1994) to facilitate a meta-analysis of studies of violations of Independence, they had insufficient detailed information about patterns of choice at the level of individual respondents, so that the rather crude assumption of the same ω being applied to all choices was convenient for processing the data in the aggregated form available to them.

A somewhat more refined approach was used by Barry Sopher and Gary Gigliotti (1993) when investigating the extent to which nontransitive choice cycles might be attributable to error. In their study they had data at the level of individual respondents and were able to allow ω to vary from one choice problem to another, and they found some evidence that there was such variability. Later, Loomes and Sugden (1998) used the data referred to in the previous subsection to test the very restrictive assumption that ω was the same across all problems and strongly rejected it.[7]

So while there may be circumstances where the data do not allow anything more sophisticated, the Tremble model has limited intuitive or empirical appeal. It is also difficult to see how it might be used for some other kinds of decision problems, such as those involving certainty equivalent valuations. Suppose it is truly the case that an individual's certainty equivalent for a particular lottery is $5. What would/could the Tremble model say about the chances that other values will be reported? How *many* other values might be reported as a result of slips? And would each of those slips be equally likely to occur?

However, since there is already good evidence that this model performs poorly even in relation to pairwise choice tasks, there seems little point in investing time and effort into generalizing it to a broader set of tasks. That is not to say that slips and momentary inattention play *no part at all* in decision data. When respondents are being asked to make a large number of choices of a somewhat unfamiliar kind in a relatively short period of time, it would be surprising if there were no such trembles; and indeed, Loomes et al. (2002) argued that a "tremble term" is a useful adjunct to other ways of specifying the stochastic element in choice. But it is not viable as the principal model.

---

[7] The proposition was clearly rejected on the basis of the forty pairs that did not involve dominance. Had the tests also considered the five pairs where one lottery dominated the other, the result would have been even stronger: by contrast with the 18.4% average reversal rate across the forty "no dominance" pairs, the average rate for the five pairs involving dominance was just 2.4%.

7.2.2 The Fechner Model

Gustav Fechner (1860) was one of the founding fathers of psychophysics. The particular focus of psychophysics is the way human subjects judge the magnitudes of physical stimuli: in particular, how subjective judgments of magnitude map to "objective" measures.[8] For example, is a sound that involves twice as much energy perceived by human subjects to be twice as loud? Is one weight that is actually twice as heavy as another perceived to be so?

One of the things that emerged very early in the course of such research was the imperfection of human judgment. Take the case of judging weight and imagine the following experiment. The respondent is blindfolded and seated at a table. Two objects are placed on the table, each with a cord attached. The respondent is told to lift each object in turn by the cord (so that any differences in shape or texture are neutralized) and then is asked to judge which of the two is heavier.

Suppose that one object weighs 500 grams and the other weighs 510 grams: how likely is it that the subject will correctly judge the 510 gram object to be heavier? The evidence is that when the difference between two stimuli is relatively small, there is a significant probability (though less than 0.5) of making a mistaken judgment—in this case, judging the 500 gram object to be heavier. In addition, the evidence shows two other patterns. First, if one stimulus is held constant while the other is changed so that the difference between them becomes greater, the chance of making a mistake reduces: for example, if the heavier weight were increased to 550 grams, the frequency of mistaken judgments would be considerably lower. Second, if the difference between the two stimuli is then held constant at 50 grams but their magnitudes are both increased, the chance of making a mistake increases: that is, if we add 1.5 kilograms to both weights so that they become 2 kilograms and 2.05 kilograms respectively, we should expect many more errors than in the case where 500 grams is being compared with 550 grams.

In other words, although one object *actually* weighs more than the other, the imperfections of human perception/judgment mean that on some occasions, so long as the difference is not too great, the lighter object may be *perceived/judged* as being at least as heavy as the heavier object.

This can be modeled as follows. Denote the actual weights of the two objects by W_1 and W_2. The individual lifts the first object and mentally

---

[8] Fechner built on the work of E. H. Weber, and some of the relevant literature refers to the "Weber–Fechner law" as an attempt to formalize the relationship between objective and subjective measures.

registers its weight as $W_1 + \varepsilon_1$, with ε_1 being a random variable representing the degree to which the individual's perception of weight is labile. Then the second object is lifted and its weight is mentally registered as $W_2 + \varepsilon_2$. The judgment about which object is heavier is then made on the basis of whether $W_1 + \varepsilon_1$ is greater than, equal to, or less than $W_2 + \varepsilon_2$.

As long as ε_1 and ε_2 are independent random errors, the probability of identifying the first object as the heavier can be expressed as $\mathrm{pr}[(W_1 - W_2 + \varepsilon) > 0]$, where ε is a symmetrically distributed random variable with a mean of zero. One interpretation of this is as follows. The true "core" difference is $W_1 - W_2$, and if human perception were perfect, judgment would always correspond with that true difference. But in a world of imperfect judgment it is as if some additional random amount is either added to, or subtracted from, the true difference. If this additional noise happens to operate in the same direction as the true difference or else only partially offsets it, the truly heavier object is correctly identified; but if the random element happens to be a large enough disturbance in the opposite direction, it outweighs the true difference and results in a mistaken judgment.

If the variance of ε is some increasing function of the magnitude of the smaller stimulus, the two main patterns in the data can be accommodated, that is, if we hold the smaller stimulus constant and increase the larger stimulus, the probability of making a mistake will fall; and if we hold the absolute difference between stimuli constant but increase the magnitude of both by the same amount, the probability of making a mistake will increase.

A model of this kind may seem to many economists the obvious one to apply to the data from individual decision experiments: it fits with the econometric convention of a deterministic core combined with a well-behaved disturbance term; and it also appears to be justified by a substantial body of psychophysical research into judgment. So it is not surprising that this form of error model has been popular as the basis for the statistical/econometric analysis of data from individual decision experiments.

For example, John Hey and Chris Orme (1994) used a version of the Fechner model to estimate the parameters of various competing core decision theories and to assess which provided the best fit to their data. For each theory in turn, they supposed an individual's true preferences to be determined according to that theory. On that basis, the *true net advantage* of any option f over any other option g can be expressed as $V(f, g)$. For example, taking standard expected utility (EU) theory as the core, $V(f, g)$ is the difference between the expected utilities of f and g computed according to the individual's true von Neumann–Morgenstern utility function, $u(\cdot)$. Alternative theories generate their own values of $V(f, g)$ according to their particular functional forms.

To this core value, Hey and Orme added a Fechnerian noise term, assuming that the actual choice on any particular occasion is made according to the net advantage of f over g, as *perceived* at the moment when the choice is made and given by $V(f, g) + \varepsilon$. In their version of the model, Hey and Orme supposed that the variance of ε was constant across all (f, g) pairs. On that basis, they used standard econometric techniques to compare the relative performance of a number of different core theories.

However, the assumption of constant variance of ε is only one of a number of ways that a Fechnerian error term might be implemented. An obvious alternative, consonant with the psychophysical evidence, might be to model the variance of ε as an increasing function of the magnitude of the stimuli (in this case, that magnitude being the core EU of each option). And there are more elaborate possibilities: the variance might (also) be a function of the complexity of a prospect, and/or may be distributed asymmetrically around the core EU, and so on. We shall discuss some of these possibilities in subsection 7.2.4, after we have outlined the other main candidate model to have emerged from the literature so far.

7.2.3 The Random Preference Model

Instead of supposing an individual to have a single true preference function to which white noise is added, the random preference (RP) approach (see Becker et al. 1963; Loomes and Sugden 1995) supposes it is as if an individual's preferences consist of a *set* of such functions. The intuition here is that any individual's perceptions and judgments are liable to vary to some extent from one moment to another along some spectrum of "states of mind." If we think of each state of mind as being represented by a slightly different preference function, the probability of any one of these functions being applied to the decision in hand is given by the probability of the individual being in the corresponding state of mind at the time when that decision is made. So to say that a particular individual behaves according to a certain "core" theory is to say (i) that the individual's preferences can be represented by some set of functions, all of which are consistent with that theory; and (ii) that for any particular decision task, the individual acts as if she picks one of those functions at random from the set and applies it to the task in question; then (iii) "puts back" that function into the set before picking again at random when tackling another decision (even if it is the identical task encountered another time).

When applied to EU, the RP model supposes an individual's preferences to be represented by some set of von Neumann–Morgenstern utility functions $u(\cdot)$, any one of which may be chosen at random to be applied to a particular decision task. To illustrate, imagine some set of concave increasing functions all calibrated so that the utility of a zero gain is set at zero. For any three payoffs $x_1 > x_2 > x_3 \geqslant 0$, each function entails $u(x_1) > u(x_2) > u(x_3) \geqslant 0$, but different functions are liable to entail different subjective judgments about the extent to which x_1 is better than x_2, x_2 better than x_3, and so on.

Consider two binary lotteries, as follows. Lottery A offers payoff x_1 with probability p and x_3 with probability $1 - p$, while lottery B offers x_2 with probability q (where $q > p$) and x_3 with probability $1 - q$. Under EU theory, A will be preferred to (less preferred than) B according to whether $[u(x_1) - u(x_2)]/[u(x_2) - u(x_3)]$ is greater than (less than) $[q - p]/p$. Representing the variability of an EU maximizer's judgment in terms of a set of $u(\cdot)$ functions amounts to allowing for that individual's perceptions of how $[u(x_1) - u(x_2)]$ compares with $[u(x_2) - u(x_3)]$ to vary from one state of mind to another. On those occasions where his state of mind is such that he judges $[u(x_1) - u(x_2)]/[u(x_2) - u(x_3)]$ to be greater than $[q - p]/p$—that is, where it is as if he has selected at random a function $u(\cdot)$ for which that is true—he chooses A; alternatively, on other occasions where it is as if he has picked at random a $u(\cdot)$ for which $[u(x_1) - u(x_2)]/[u(x_2) - u(x_3)] < [q - p]/p$, he chooses B.

This way of modeling the stochastic nature of preferences is easily extended to tasks such as judging equivalences. Suppose he is asked to state a sure payoff x_C such that he is indifferent between the certainty of that payoff and playing out lottery A. Under the RP version of EU, it is as if he picks some $u(\cdot)$ at random and then identifies the payoff x_C such that $[u(x_1) - u(x_C)]/[u(x_C) - u(x_3)] = [1 - p]/p$. Since the value of x_C that satisfies this equation is liable to vary from one $u(\cdot)$ to another, the RP model entails some distribution of x_C derived from the distribution of $u(\cdot)$ that constitutes the individual's stochastic preferences.

7.2.4 Comparing the Fechner and RP Approaches

Chapter 3 discussed the Duhem–Quine thesis (DQT) in some detail. The DQT asserts that it is impossible to test any particular target hypothesis in isolation from (a possibly large number of) auxiliary assumptions. The corollary of this is that the seeming failure of the target hypothesis might in fact be attributable to a failure of one or more of the auxiliary assumptions. Put another way, the implications or predictions of a particular theory may to some extent depend upon, and perhaps vary with, the nature of the auxiliary assumptions being made.

In this sense, the nature of the stochastic component in people's individual or interactive decision making might be seen as the subject matter of a set of auxiliary assumptions. Thus, what is being tested by any particular experiment or program of experiments is not just one or more "core" theories, but one or more combinations of a core theory with a stochastic specification; and the difficulty raised by the DQT is the problem of knowing exactly what is being rejected if the results of an experiment contradict some implication of a particular "core-plus-error" combination. Is it the core theory that is wrong? Is it the wrong stochastic specification? Or is it both?

The rest of this subsection takes its cue from those questions and considers examples where combining the same core theory either with some form of Fechner model or else with some version of the RP approach may lead to radically different implications. For each case, we discuss what to infer from the available evidence.

We start with what is generally taken to be the most widely and reliably replicated violation of the Independence axiom of EU theory: namely, the form of the Allais paradox now known as the "common ratio effect" (CRE). This effect was introduced in box 2.6 (p. 74), but it will be helpful here to restate its key features. Consider two pairwise choices of the following form:

Choice 1 $R_1 : (x_1, p; x_3, 1 - p)$ versus $S_1 : (x_2, q; x_3, 1 - q)$;

Choice 2 $R_2 : (x_1, \lambda p; x_3, 1 - \lambda p)$ versus $S_2 : (x_2, \lambda q; x_3, 1 - \lambda q)$;

where $x_1 > x_2 > x_3 \geqslant 0$, $p < q = 1$, and $0 < \lambda < 1$.

The Independence axiom of deterministic EU theory requires that if an EU maximizer prefers the riskier lottery R_1 in Choice 1, she should also prefer the riskier lottery R_2 in Choice 2; or alternatively, if she prefers the safer lottery S_1 in Choice 1, she should also prefer S_2 in Choice 2. Yet it has very often been found that a substantial proportion of any sample either choose R_1 in Choice 1 and S_2 in Choice 2, or else choose S_1 in Choice 1 and R_2 in Choice 2. Moreover, the combination of S_1 and R_2 is much more frequently observed than the opposite "violation" in the form of choosing both R_1 and S_2. Any such violations are incompatible with the deterministic form of EU theory; but what if we consider some stochastic form of the theory? Might that be capable of accommodating the existence and asymmetric pattern of violations?

Let us start with an RP version of EU. In this case, the answer is straightforward and requires no particular restrictions on the distribution of the

$u(\cdot)$ functions. Setting $u(x_3) = 0$, all that needs to be said is that whatever proportion of an individual's $u(\cdot)$ functions entail $u(x_1)/u(x_2) > q/p$ gives, for that individual, the probability that she will choose R_1 in Choice 1; and exactly the same proportion of that individual's $u(\cdot)$ functions will entail $u(x_1)/u(x_2) > \lambda q/\lambda p$, for all λ, which means the probability that she chooses R_2 in Choice 2 is exactly the same as the probability of choosing R_1 in Choice 1. Let that probability be denoted by α, which may vary from one individual to another. So for any individual, the probability of choosing R_1 and also R_2 is α^2, while the probability of choosing S_1 and S_2 is $(1 - \alpha)^2$. Of course, if $0 < \alpha < 1$, there are also probabilities of making choices that violate deterministic EU theory: the individual will choose R_1 and S_2 with probability $\alpha(1-\alpha)$ and will choose S_1 and R_2 with the same probability. So even without placing any restrictions on the distributions of individuals' $u(\cdot)$ functions, the RP version of EU produces a clear null hypothesis: namely, that there should be no significant asymmetry in the frequencies with which the combinations $R_1 \,\&\, S_2$ and $S_1 \,\&\, R_2$ are observed.

However, there are now many experimental datasets that reject these implications with a high degree of confidence: as noted above, the common ratio effect has typically involved frequencies of $S_1 \,\&\, R_2$ so much greater than frequencies of $R_1 \,\&\, S_2$ that the asymmetry is extremely unlikely to have occurred by chance if both combinations are truly equally probable. Thus, if the RP approach is the appropriate way to model the stochastic nature of preferences, then EU is the wrong core theory, and an alternative core is needed. Alternatively, if EU is to be defended as the core, some other stochastic specification must be invoked. Can some form(s) of the Fechner model accommodate these data?

It turns out that combining EU with one relatively simple form of the Fechner model *can* accommodate these asymmetries—although only up to a point. To see this, consider the Fechner model with the assumption made by Hey and Orme (1994) that ε is symmetrical around zero and has constant variance across all pairwise choice problems.

In most reported cases of CRE, the (great) majority of respondents choose the safer lottery S_1 in Choice 1 (especially when S_1 offers the *certainty* of x_2). Under the Fechner model, this implies that for most individuals, $qu(x_2) - pu(x_1) + \varepsilon > 0$: that is, the typical difference between expected utilities is sufficiently large and positive that it is only overturned by a negative ε in a (small) minority of cases.[9]

---

[9] Of course, there may also be respondents who are risk seeking to the extent that $qu(x_2) - pu(x_1) < 0$; and so long as this difference is not overturned by a sufficiently large positive ε, they will choose their truly preferred option, R_1.

But now consider the choice between R_2 and S_2. Here, the difference between expected utilities is $\lambda[qu(x_2) - pu(x_1)]$, so that with λ often taking values as small as or smaller than 0.25, the "true" difference in expected utilities in Choice 2 is only a small fraction of that in Choice 1. With the variance of ε held constant, this means that the true difference is more likely to be overturned in Choice 2: that is, a bigger proportion of the majority who truly prefer S_1 to R_1 will now choose R_2 rather than S_2, thereby generating S_1 & R_2 observations. And although there will also be a greater likelihood that someone in the minority group who truly prefer R_2 will actually pick S_2 (thereby generating R_1 & S_2 observations), it is easy to imagine that these will be considerably outnumbered by the S_1 & R_2 observations, producing just the kind of asymmetry that has been found in so many studies.

On this account, then, it might seem that the asymmetry is not a violation of EU theory: on the contrary, the CRE data might be no more than a manifestation of what we should expect from a specification of EU theory that allows for a Fechnerian stochastic element in people's preferences. Could it be that the data have simply been misinterpreted and that this formulation of the theory should be rehabilitated as the core model of decision making under risk? It turns out that it would be premature to jump to that conclusion, for several reasons.

First, although *much* of the existing CRE evidence might be accommodated by this story, not all of it can be. To see why, consider what happens as λ tends toward zero. Under these circumstances, any true difference between expected utilities would also tend toward zero, so that the actual choice made would depend increasingly on the realization of ε. But since ε is symmetrical around zero, this means that in the limit we should expect choices to split 50:50. What we should *not* expect is that the modal preference should actually cross the 50:50 line. And yet there are at least some cases where we observe a substantial majority preferring the safer lottery in Choice 1 but a substantial majority preferring the riskier option in Choice 2, and this switch of modal preference is *not* explicable in terms of this version of the Fechner model. Another result that certainly cannot be accommodated by that model is the case where the majority choose the riskier lottery even in Choice 1 and an even bigger majority choose the riskier option in Choice 2, in contrast to the implication of the model that the Choice 2 split should be closer to 50:50. Such a result is not often reported—mainly, one supposes, because most experimenters set the parameters so as to induce a majority preference for the safer option in Choice 1—but an example can be found in Bateman et al. (2006).

So even within the realm of CRE data, adding on a Fechner noise term with constant variance does not rescue EU theory. In addition, such an add-on cannot accommodate the "other" version of the Allais paradox now known as the "common consequence effect" (CCE).

An example of the CCE scenario was given in footnote 13 of chapter 4, but it may help to summarize it in more general terms. Here, the two pairwise choices are as follows:

Choice 1 $R_1 : (x_1, p; x_2, r; x_3, 1 - p - r)$ versus $S_1 : (x_2, 1)$,

Choice 2 $R_2 : (x_1, p; x_3, 1 - p)$ versus $S_2 : (x_2, 1 - r; x_3, r)$,

where $x_1 > x_2 > x_3 \geqslant 0$.

In this case, each of options R_2 and S_2 is produced by taking, respectively, R_1 and S_1 and replacing the r probability of x_2 with an r probability of x_3. Under EU theory, therefore, the expected utilities of R_2 and S_2 are, respectively, lower than those of R_1 and S_1 by $r[u(x_2) - u(x_3)]$. Thus those EU maximizers who truly prefer R_1 to S_1 also truly prefer R_2 to S_2; and vice versa. So once again there are two ways of violating EU theory: either by choosing R_1 in Choice 1 and S_2 in Choice 2; or else by choosing S_1 in Choice 1 and R_2 in Choice 2. Just as with CRE, what has been observed in experiments is that the numbers of people departing from EU theory by choosing $S_1 \& R_2$ are substantially greater than the numbers choosing $R_1 \& S_2$.

The reason why this pattern cannot be accommodated, even in part, by adding a Fechner term with constant variance is that since the expected utilities of R_2 and S_2 are, respectively, lower than those of R_1 and S_1 by $r[u(x_2) - u(x_3)]$, the true difference between the alternatives is exactly the same for each choice. If ε has the same distribution in both cases, the chance of a true R_1-preferer actually picking S_1 as a result of noise is exactly the same as the chance of a true R_2-preferer picking S_2; and conversely. Thus under this model the appropriate null hypothesis for the CCE is that both forms of violation are equally likely to occur— a null that would clearly be rejected by the bulk of the experimental evidence.

Of course, the assumption that ε has constant variance is only one possible auxiliary assumption. Might some other specification do better?

As noted at the end of subsection 7.2.2, it might be more in keeping with the psychophysical origins of the Fechner model to suppose that the variance of ε is positively correlated with the magnitude of the stimuli, which in this case might mean that the variance increases as the magnitude of expected utility increases. But such a model does even less well in accommodating the CRE and CCE data. In both cases, it would entail the variance of ε being smaller in Choice 2 than in Choice 1. For the CRE, this would be liable to ameliorate any tendency to switch as the probabilities of the positive payoffs are scaled down.[10] For the CCE, it would tend to produce the *opposite* patterns to the ones observed: with the variance of ε greater in Choice 1 but the true difference between expected utilities the same for both pairwise choices, the implication is that the split would be driven more by noise—and hence would be closer to 50:50—in Choice 1 than in Choice 2, which is quite contrary to the evidence.

Another possibility mentioned in subsection 7.2.2 is that the variance of ε is some function of complexity: options involving several payoffs may make heavier cognitive demands and be more prone to noise than those involving just two payoffs; and/or options involving one positive and one negative payoff, with respective probabilities related to a roulette wheel and therefore expressed in multiples of 1/36, may be more taxing to evaluate than ones that involve just a positive and a zero payoff, with probabilities expressed as multiples of 0.05. However, as yet there does not seem to be any well-developed theory of complexity that enables us to make the variance of ε a function of some set of measurable independent variables.[11]

A somewhat different way of trying to accommodate CRE and CCE patterns within a stochastic form of EU has been proposed by Blavatskyy (2007). The key idea here is to take an initially symmetric distribution of ε around the true EU of a lottery but then truncate and redistribute it so that all realizations of EU $+\varepsilon$ lie within bounds set by the highest and lowest payoffs. In conjunction with some rather particular assumptions— that the true EU of R_1 is a little higher than the true EU of S_1 and that the true EU of R_1 is sufficiently close to $u(x_1)$—Blavatskyy shows how both the CRE and the CCE might be compatible with this model. However, as we shall see below, this model is unable to account for other well-attested phenomena; and since it fails in ways that could be regarded as direct

---

[10] Much would depend on the particular relationship between the magnitude of the stimuli and the variance of ε, but if, for example, the reduction in the variance were such that the true expected utility difference accounted for a constant proportion of the distribution of ε, there would be no systematic tendency whatsoever to switch from safer to riskier, or vice versa.

[11] Even in the absence of such a theory, there have been some attempts to explore other factors that might be influential. Buschena and Zilberman (2000), for example, considered three different variables that might affect the variance of ε. One specification made the variance a function of the "true" difference between the values of the alternatives (as estimated according to whichever core theory was being examined); the second specification allowed the variance to increase with the average number of outcomes for which the two lotteries had positive probabilities; the third allowed the variance to be affected by the area between the lotteries' cumulative distribution functions over the range of outcomes.

tests of its basic premises, its potential as a general model of stochastic EU would appear to be limited.

Of course, there are many other variants of a Fechnerian error model that we might consider in conjunction with different implications of an EU core—or indeed, different implications of any one of the many non-EU alternative core theories that have been proposed during the past three decades. But at every turn we are liable to run up against the DQT difficulty of trying to decide how far any divergence between model and data might be attributable to one assumption or another. So if our primary concern is to distinguish between one stochastic specification and another, a more efficient approach might be to take some principle or axiom that is common to many core theories and that commands very wide, if not universal, acceptance and then use data about that principle to try to discriminate between different stochastic specifications.

One such principle—indeed, possibly the only such principle—is respect for First-Order Stochastic Dominance (FOSD), as described earlier in box 2.5 (p. 72). What has become apparent in the course of hundreds of experiments examining individual decision making under risk is that although almost every *other* axiom or basic postulate about rational choice is liable to be violated in seemingly systematic ways, *transparent* FOSD appears to be the exception: so long as the dominance relation is transparent, it is respected by the overwhelming majority of participants in experiments.[12]

However, such respect for all forms of transparent FOSD is at odds with the Fechner model. To see this, recall the evidence from Loomes and Sugden (1998), cited earlier, where forty choices *not* involving dominance were each presented to respondents on two occasions within the same experimental session, and where the choice on the second occasion was different from that on the first in 18.4% of cases. Scattered among those forty choices were another five pairs where one lottery dominated the other. In each of these pairs, the lotteries were really quite similar to each other, mostly with one offering a 0.05 higher chance of £20 or £30 than the other and a corresponding 0.05 lower chance of 0. Thus each of these five pairs involved differences between expected values in the region of £1 or £1.50: that is, considerably smaller differences than in most of the other forty choices. So although differences in expected values may only be a rough proxy for $V(f, g)$, any variant of the Fechner model discussed above can reasonably be expected to entail error rates

---

[12] However, when dominance is disguised, it is possible to induce substantial rates of violation (see, for example, Tversky and Kahneman 1986 and Charness et al. 2007).

at least as high as observed in the majority of the other forty choices.[13]
But this was not the case at all: in fact, out of a total of 920 observations
(ninety-two respondents each making five choices on two occasions),
FOSD was violated in just thirteen cases—a rate of less than 1.5%.

This suggests that the Fechner model, which works well in the context
of simple physical stimuli, is liable to greatly overpredict violations of
FOSD if transplanted into the context of decision making under risk,
provided that dominance is relatively easy to detect. Arguably, this is
because the two contexts are crucially different, in the following way.

When a respondent is judging the relative heaviness of objects, what
matters is the "resultant weight" of each object: that is, the overall force
exerted by gravity on each of them. The variability in judgment comes
solely from the respondent's perception of the muscular force he has to
exert to counteract gravity. For this model to carry through to choices
between lotteries, it would have to be the case that the respondent processes the task by evaluating each lottery as if in isolation, so that only
the "resultant weight" of each lottery, taken individually, matters.

This *might* be the case when a certainty equivalent is elicited for each
lottery separately: under those conditions, it would not be too surprising to find some of the certainty equivalents elicited for the dominated
lottery on some occasions being higher than some of the certainty equivalents elicited for the dominating lottery on other occasions. For example, Cubitt et al. (2004a) reported an experiment where respondents were
asked to value a number of lotteries, one of which offered a 0.36 chance
of £7 and a 0.64 chance of zero, while another offered a 0.41 chance of
£7 and a 0.59 chance of zero. When these were valued separately, 36 out
of 230 respondents (15.7%) gave a higher value to the dominated alternative. But when those same respondents were asked to make a straight
choice between those two lotteries, only 7 (3%) of them chose the dominated alternative. That is, when the two lotteries were compared *directly*,
so that the superiority of one over the other was quite transparent, the
error rate was greatly reduced. This is contrary to the idea that it is only
the "resultant weight" of each lottery that matters, since those resultant weights were the same for both valuation and choice. That in turn
casts doubt upon any error story that supposes that a choice between

---

[13] This is clearly true for the Hey and Orme (1994) constant-variance version; and a
model that allows the variance of ε to vary with the magnitudes of f and g would give
much the same prediction, since the difference in their magnitudes is small. By the standards of the Buschena and Zilberman (2000) model, f and g were roughly equally complex, and no less complex than other lotteries in the experiment. And since f and g had
the same upper and lower bounds and their EUs were close to each other but often not
close to either bound, Blavatskyy's (2007) model would also predict violations of FOSD
by a substantial minority of respondents.

two alternatives can be modeled as if each is evaluated separately and subject to independent error prior to a decision being made.[14]

But is RP a better alternative? Consider first how RP fares in relation to the kind of behavior observed by Cubitt et al. (2004a) and cited above. As seen in subsection 7.2.3, RP entails that an individual has a distribution of certainty equivalents for a lottery offering a 0.36 chance of £7 and also has a distribution of certainty equivalents for a lottery offering a 0.41 chance of £7. For any set of $u(\cdot)$, the distribution of certainty equivalents will be shifted to the right as the probability of the positive payoff increases, but there is liable to be some overlap of the two distributions—at least so long as the probabilities are not *too* different. So if we model the certainty equivalent stated on one particular occasion for $(£7, 0.36)$ as a value drawn at random from one distribution, and the certainty equivalent elicited on another occasion for $(£7, 0.41)$ as a value drawn at random from another distribution somewhat to the right but overlapping with the first, we can accommodate cases where a nontrivial minority (in the case in question, 15.7%) give a higher value to the dominated lottery.

By contrast, RP does not allow *any* violation of FOSD in a direct choice between the two lotteries. Let the dominant lottery be labeled D and call the dominated lottery E. For E to be chosen over D would require $[u(7) - u(7)]/[u(7) - u(0)]$ to be greater than $[q - p]/p$; but for every $u(\cdot)$, $[u(7) - u(7)]/[u(7) - u(0)]$ must be zero while $[q - p]/p$ is strictly positive, so that there is a zero probability of picking the dominated lottery in a straight choice between the two,[15] except as a result of some

---

[14] In fact, this is precisely the supposition that Blavatskyy (2007) makes. His model amounts to saying that for any nondegenerate monetary lottery, the distribution of EU $+\varepsilon$ will map directly to a distribution over the sure sums of money between the highest and lowest payoffs offered by the lottery. Thus, making a choice between two nondegenerate lotteries is supposed by this model to be exactly the same as drawing a sure value independently from each lottery's distribution, then comparing the two and choosing whichever lottery happens on that occasion to be associated with the higher value. It is therefore a fundamental implication of the Blavatskyy model that the pattern of preference inferred from comparing the two valuations should be no different from the pattern observed via direct choice. However, this implication is clearly rejected by the case reported by Cubitt et al. (2004a). More generally, it is rejected by the very large number of "preference reversal" datasets (about which more later) showing pronounced and systematic differences between preferences inferred from valuations and those revealed by straight choices.

[15] Although the notation here is most readily associated with EU theory, the argument carries through much more generally. Instead of a von Neumann–Morgenstern $u(\cdot)$ function, we might consider any subjective value function $v(\cdot)$, requiring only that it is a nondecreasing function of wealth; and instead of using the "objective" probabilities p and q as weights, we might allow any transformation so long as it does not entail assigning negative weights to positive probability differences.

"tremble" due to occasional lapse of attention, misreading, etc. However, as noted earlier, the RP model does not exclude the possibility of some additional source of noise/error of the kind captured by trembles, so RP plus a small tremble term may be a plausible way of accounting for the low but positive rate of violations of transparent FOSD actually observed in many experiments—including the one conducted by Cubitt et al. (2004a). But according to RP, any such rate can be expected to be considerably lower than the propensity to give a higher certainty equivalent to **E** than to **D** when those certainty equivalents are elicited on different occasions; and this, too, accords with the evidence.

Thus—at least when considered in the context of one particular principle that is common to many core theories—it would appear that the RP framework is superior to the Fechner approach for modeling noise/error in decisions involving risky prospects. Of course, we should be wary of jumping too confidently to the conclusion that RP is *the* right model on the strength of the current rather limited evidence base. But *if* RP is a more appropriate way of allowing for the stochastic component in people's decision making, the implication is clear, since applying RP to EU generates null hypotheses that are strongly rejected in large numbers of experiments. On *this* reading, then, we would have to conclude that it is the EU core rather than the auxiliary assumptions that fails.

This raises a number of questions for future research, including:

(1) *If* RP is the appropriate model and EU is the wrong core, how should RP be applied to alternative core theories in order to test them and to discriminate between their respective claims? In particular, different restrictions on the distributions of parameters central to the various core theories may well have different implications for which patterns of behavior are consistent with the core theory, so which restrictions should be adopted? In the discussion above, about how RP might be applied to EU, it was supposed that the variability of judgment from one decision to another is exclusively about the relative subjective values of the payoffs, that is, about how $[u(x_1) - u(x_2)]/[u(x_2) - u(x_3)]$ varies from one judgment to another; and it was supposed that choice involved comparing the realization of $[u(x_1) - u(x_2)]/[u(x_2) - u(x_3)]$ with the ratio $[q - p]/p$, which was taken as given and as always perceived as taking its "objective" value. However, a number of alternative core theories involve some transformation of "objective" probabilities into subjective decision weights. Should an RP version of such theories require not only that $[u(x_1) - u(x_2)]/[u(x_2) - u(x_3)]$—or its

counterpart in the alternative theory—is determined on any particular occasion as if on the basis of a random draw from some set of $u(\cdot)$, but also that $[q - p]/p$ is determined as if on the basis of some independent random draw from some set of probability transformation functions?

(2) If both the EU core and the essence of the Fechner approach are inconsistent with the data from individual decision experiments, can they provide a credible basis for explaining other experimental data—for example, those generated in experimental games and markets? And if not, could an RP specification of some alternative core theory be used to analyze and organize those data?

(3) Or is there some other way of modeling the nature of people's preferences and beliefs that is different—and perhaps radically so—from any of those discussed so far?

To have some chance of answering the first of these questions, experimenters would need to undertake a substantial program of research. However, before discussing what such a program of research might entail, we turn to the second question and, in the next section, consider the additional issues raised by data from experimental games.

7.3 "Noise" in Experimental Games

As discussed in chapter 3, in standard presentations of (complete information) game theory, players are assumed to know their own and others' payoffs contingent upon all possible combinations of their own and others' strategies. Moreover, it is conventionally assumed that they know all those payoffs in (von Neumann–Morgenstern) utility terms. The usual assumption is that any player is only interested in others' utilities to the extent that they inform him about the probabilities of the strategies that the other player(s) might select—information that he can then take into account when formulating his own strategy.

When games are implemented experimentally, payoffs are typically expressed in the form of sums of money. This may be easier for participants to understand and it provides straightforward incentives, but in the light of the discussion above, it also means that participants may not know the precise utility of each payoff to each potential recipient, which is what standard theory assumes. Indeed, the lesson from individual decision experiments is that most individuals do not know their *own* utilities with precision, in which case it seems plausible to suppose that

Table 7.1. A normal form representation.

	Left	Right
Up	$4, w$	$0, x$
Down	$0, y$	$1, z$

Table 7.2. A mixed strategy game.

	Left	Right
Up	$4, 2$	$0, 3$
Down	$0, 4$	$1, 1$

they have even less precise ideas about how payoffs map to utilities for other players.

Consider a normal form representation of a 2×2 game where the row player (Row) has to decide between U(p) and D(own) and the column player (Col) chooses between L(eft) and R(ight), with all payoffs in some money currency. In the example shown in table 7.1, Row's payoffs are given as specific numbers, while Col's are, for the moment, left unspecified as w, x, y, and z.

If payoffs were utilities and both players knew each other to be EU maximizers, Row would still need to figure out the probability that Col will play L or R. In some games, that might be supposed to be quite easy. For example, if $w > x$ and $y > z$, Col would be expected to see that L dominates R,[16] and she would therefore be expected to play L for sure; and realizing this, Row would play U. Similarly, if $w < x$ and $y < z$, Col would identify R as her dominant strategy and play it for sure; and knowing that, Row would choose D.

But there are many patterns of w, x, y, and z that do not lead to such straightforward conclusions, even if payoffs are utilities and players are both EU maximizers. For example, consider the case shown in table 7.2 where neither L nor R dominates the other.

There is no pure strategy Nash equilibrium in this game: if Row were to play U, Col's best response would be R, to which Row's best response would be D, to which Col's best response would be L, to which Row's best response would be U, and so on. The unique Nash equilibrium is in mixed strategies, with each player playing their pure strategies with

---

[16] Notice that we are here using the game-theoretic notion of dominance. To avoid possible confusion and to distinguish this usage from First-Order Stochastic Dominance in cases where probabilities are known, the latter will be referred to in terms of *stochastic dominance* and/or *FOSD*.

probabilities that make the other player indifferent, so that in equilibrium each player is willing to randomize in whatever way satisfies the "mutual indifference" requirement. While not all game theorists would agree that such Nash equilibria are appropriate as predictions of play, they are often taken to constitute the maintained hypothesis in experimental tests of standard game theory, when there is no Nash equilibrium in pure strategies.

In the example shown in table 7.2, Col's Nash equilibrium mixed strategy is to play L with 0.2 probability and R with 0.8 probability so that Row gets the same expected utility of 0.8 from both U and D. Row therefore does not mind which mix he adopts and is willing to play U with probability 0.75 and D with probability 0.25, which makes Col indifferent between L and R (both yielding an EU of 2.5) so that she remains content with her own mixed strategy.

However, when such games are being implemented experimentally, noise may arise from several sources.

First, as noted above, in the great majority of experimental games, payoffs are sums of money. Such cases are liable to entail the kind of noise discussed in section 7.2: namely, the noisy translation of money payoffs into utilities. Even if Row were told the probabilities with which Col would play L and R—let us call them p and $1 - p$ respectively—and if Row were a stochastic EU maximizer, he would have to judge whether $p[u(4) - u(0)]$ was greater or less than $(1 - p)[u(1) - u(0)]$, and for some (range of) $p < 0.5$, his stochastic preferences might mean that there were some moments when he would perceive U to have a higher expected utility than D and other moments when he would perceive D to be the better option. Moreover, the proportions of U choices and D choices would be liable to vary with p: when p is close to 0.5, U would very likely be judged better than D, but progressively lower values of p diminish the perceived value of U and raise the perceived value of D so that U becomes less and less likely to be judged preferable to D.

Much the same is also true for Col's decisions, of course: even if she knew the chances of Row playing U and D—call these q and $1 - q$ respectively—there are liable to be values of q such that Col sometimes perceives $qu(2) + (1-q)u(4)$ to be greater than $qu(3) + (1-q)u(1)$, and sometimes makes the opposite judgment. And the proportion of times L is judged better than R could be expected to fall as q rises.

So just allowing for the kind of noise suggested by individual decision experiments has the effect of greatly complicating experimental game behavior. Even under the assumption that players have EU preferences, the probability that each player will play a particular strategy itself has a stochastic element. In the next two subsections we shall consider two

Table 7.3. Asymmetric Matching Pennies payoffs.

	Left	Right
Up	4, 0	0, 1
Down	0, 1	1, 0

possible ways of incorporating stochastic judgment into the modeling of strategic behavior.

7.3.1 Quantal Response Equilibrium

A technically neat way of modeling this seemingly untidy problem is Richard McKelvey and Thomas Palfrey's (1995, 1998) notion of a *quantal response equilibrium* (QRE). To illustrate how the QRE idea works, and examine its strengths and possible limitations, consider a case where the money values of w, x, y, and z in table 7.1 are set so as to produce an "asymmetric matching pennies" game, as in table 7.3.

Again, there is no Nash equilibrium in pure strategies in this game. Rather, the conventional approach is to suppose that players' utilities are proportional to their money payoffs and to identify the mixed strategy equilibrium. It entails Row playing U and D with equal probability while Col plays L and R with probabilities 0.2 and 0.8 respectively.[17] If a sample of participants behave as if they are implementing such mixed strategies, we should expect to observe those strategies being played with the corresponding frequencies.

However, there is evidence from experiments that under such circumstances, Row players choose U significantly more than 50% of the time (see Ochs 1995; Goeree et al. 2003). QRE attempts to provide an account for such data by adding a Fechnerian stochastic element to players' behavior.

Consider Row's decision. If Row's behavior has a stochastic component of the Fechnerian kind, the probability of choosing U from the pair (U, D) is given by $\mathrm{pr}[V(U, D) + \varepsilon > 0]$. Thus Row's probability of choosing U or D depends on an interaction between her belief about Col's strategy and the distribution of ε.

---

[17] The assumption that utilities are strictly proportional to money payoffs could be relaxed by assuming instead that players operate according to some nonlinear utility function. If we set $u(0) = 0$ and if players are risk averse, so that $u(4) < 0.25u(1)$, Col would need to play L with probability greater than 0.2 in order to make Row indifferent between U and D; however, since Col's payoffs are 0 or 1 whichever strategy she plays, Row would still need to play both U and D with equal probability in order to make Col indifferent between L and R.

A parallel story applies to Col. If she believes that there is a better than 0.5 chance that Row will play U, the standard deterministic model entails her playing R with probability 1. But if the probability of playing R is given by $\text{pr}[V(\text{R}, \text{L}) + \varepsilon > 0]$, then there is some chance that she could play L.

On this basis, an equilibrium occurs when players' beliefs and behavior are mutually compatible, so that there exists some pair of probabilities (p^*, q^*) such that Row's choice satisfies $\text{pr}(\text{U}) = q^*$ when Row believes that $\text{pr}(\text{L}) = p^*$, and Col's choice satisfies $\text{pr}(\text{L}) = p^*$ when Col believes that Row's $\text{pr}(\text{U}) = q^*$.

Logit equilibrium is a particular case of QRE where the probabilities of choosing the different pure strategies are proportional to exponential functions of their expected utilities. Goeree et al. (2003) have analyzed a number of datasets on the basis of assuming that the probability of playing strategy i when there are two strategies i and j, denoted by P_{ij}, can be expressed as

$$P_{ij} = \exp(\text{EU}_i / \mu) / [\exp(\text{EU}_i / \mu) + \exp(\text{EU}_j / \mu)],$$

where μ may be thought of as an "error variance" parameter, with higher values of μ giving greater weight to the stochastic component at the expense of the true EU difference.[18] Even under the restrictive assumption of risk neutrality, it appears that the logit equilibrium approach can accommodate many experimental datasets much better than deterministic Nash equilibrium.[19]

However, although it achieves a better fit to the data from a number of experiments, there is still a question about whether this is a plausible equilibrium concept. The main difficulty, as with the Fechner model when it is applied to individual decisions, is that, given the equilibrium probabilities, it appears to entail high rates of violation of FOSD.

For example, consider the game in table 7.3 with $\mu = 1$ and risk-neutral players. Here, the logit equilibrium is where $q^* \approx 0.722$ and $p^* \approx 0.391$. But is this a credible equilibrium? For this equilibrium to hold, it requires that if faced with the choice between choosing L and getting a 0.278 chance of 1 or choosing R and getting a 0.722 chance of 1, Col will choose L on nearly 40% of occasions. Yet when seen in this way, L is clearly stochastically dominated by R, and as seen earlier, when the positive payoff is the same and when one lottery offers a better chance of that payoff than another, the stochastically dominated alternative is rarely

---

[18] In the limit, as μ goes to infinity, the choice of pure strategy becomes entirely random, with each one likely to be chosen with equal probability.

[19] With the additional degree of freedom provided by allowing for subjects' risk aversion, even better fits of even more datasets can be achieved (see Goeree et al. 2003).

chosen, even when the probability difference is *much* smaller (0.05) than in the present example.

How is it, then, that QRE can entail the stochastically dominated strategy being chosen nearly 40% of the time? The answer is that the QRE approach, like the Fechner model in individual decision making, assumes that each strategy is evaluated separately, and that each evaluation involves an independent draw of ε from the noise distribution. Setting $u(x) = x$, the QRE approach supposes that L is evaluated in utility terms as $0.278 + \varepsilon_L$, where ε_L denotes a random draw from the distribution of ε when L is being evaluated; meanwhile, R is evaluated separately as $0.722 + \varepsilon_R$. When $\mu = 1$, $\varepsilon_L - \varepsilon_R > 0.722 - 0.278$ on nearly 40% of the occasions when both evaluations are undertaken independently, so that on these occasions $0.278 + \varepsilon_L > 0.722 + \varepsilon_R$, and thus L is chosen even though when the two are considered together L is clearly stochastically dominated by R, given the equilibrium probabilities of Row's play.

In short, QRE achieves a better fit than Nash equilibrium to some of the data from experimental games, but it does so by making the same contestable assumption that the Fechner model makes when applied to individual decisions under uncertainty: namely, that players behave as if they evaluate the EU of each strategy separately with an independent ε, and are thereby liable to choose stochastically dominated strategies to an extent that seems implausible.[20] How different would things be if we used RP rather than the Fechnerian model?

7.3.2 Random Preference in Experimental Games

Consider first the game shown in table 7.2, starting with the view from Row's perspective. If the probability of Col playing L is p, then Row is facing the choice between $U = pu(4) + (1-p)u(0)$ and $D = pu(0) + (1-p)u(1)$. The probability of Row choosing U depends on the probability that she picks a $u(\cdot)$ from her notional set of functions such that $[u(4) - u(0)]/[u(1) - u(0)] > (1-p)/p$.

Of course, by contrast with individual risky choice problems, Row is not told what value p will take: that is determined by Col. However, for

---

[20] Another possible concern relates to the evidence that the value of μ varies a good deal from one type of game to another and, even within the same game type, from one particular experiment to another, even after controlling for scale effects. When commenting on this in relation to different "matching pennies" datasets, Goeree et al. (2003) conjecture that other things that could account for such differences might include factors such as different subject pools and procedures. However, it is not obvious why different subject pools should exhibit different values of μ while their estimated risk aversion parameters are very similar. On the other hand, it might be argued that (scale effects aside) variations in μ across different game types/procedures may to some extent be explicable in terms of some measure(s) of the difficulty or complexity of the different games.

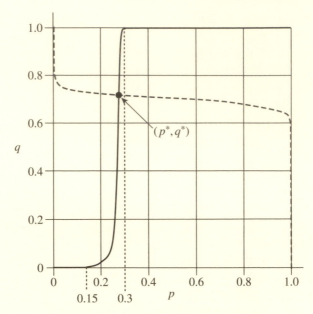

Figure 7.1.   An RP equilibrium analysis.

each possible value that p *might* take there will be some corresponding probability q that Row will choose U. For all increasing functions $u(\cdot)$, it must be the case that $[u(4)-u(0)]/[u(1)-u(0)] > 1$, so we can be sure that U will be chosen for all $p \geqslant 0.5$; but for at least some $0.5 > p > 0$, we may expect q to fall as p falls.

To illustrate, consider a Row player whose most concave $u(\cdot)$ is such that $[u(4) - u(0)] = 2\frac{1}{3}x[u(1) - u(0)]$, while at the other end of the set his most convex $u(\cdot)$ entails $[u(4) - u(0)] = 5\frac{2}{3}x[u(1) - u(0)]$. For any $p > 0.3$, even his most concave $u(\cdot)$ gives a strict preference for U, so $q = 1$ for all $p > 0.3$. However, once p falls below the 0.3 threshold (where Row is indifferent between U and D when his most concave $u(\cdot)$ is applied), there will be more and more $u(\cdot)$ that entail choosing D, so that q falls. However, once p drops below 0.15, Row will choose D even when his most convex $u(\cdot)$ is applied—which means that for all $p < 0.15$, $q = 0$. Thus for any set of $u(\cdot)$, there will exist some function showing q contingent on p. In figure 7.1, a function of this kind is shown by the solid line.

Correspondingly, from Col's perspective the probability of choosing L represents the proportion of Col's $u(\cdot)$ functions such that $[u(4) - u(1)]/[u(3)-u(2)] > q/(1-q)$. Suppose Col's most concave $u(\cdot)$ entails $[u(4) - u(1)] = 1\frac{1}{2}x[u(3) - u(2)]$, while her most convex $u(\cdot)$ function gives $[u(4) - u(1)] = 4x[u(3) - u(2)]$. It follows from this that for all

$q < 0.6$, L will certainly be chosen (i.e., $p = 1$). As q rises above 0.6, there will be more and more $u(\cdot)$ for which $[u(4) - u(1)]/[u(3) - u(2)]$ falls short of $q/(1 - q)$, so that R is chosen rather than L and p falls; and once q exceeds 0.8, L will never be chosen, so that $p = 0$ over this range. This relationship between p and q is represented by the dashed line in figure 7.1.

On the assumption that both functions are continuous and weakly monotonic, there will be a unique point at which the two functions will intersect: this point is the pair of probabilities (p^*, q^*) such that Row's $\mathrm{pr}(U) = q^*$ when Row believes Col's $\mathrm{pr}(L) = p^*$, and Col's $\mathrm{pr}(L) = p^*$ when Col believes Row's $\mathrm{pr}(U) = q^*$. This is the RP analogue to QRE for this game.

What makes the RP analysis different from the Fechnerian QRE, however, is that RP builds in respect for stochastic dominance. In the example above, RP entails that Col will *never* choose R when $q \leqslant 0.5$, whereas QRE permits the possibility that the perceived EU of R (i.e., $qu(3) + (1 - q)u(1) + \varepsilon_R$) may be greater than the perceived EU of L (i.e., $(1 - q)u(4) + qu(2) + \varepsilon_L$) even when $q \leqslant 0.5$, since there is some probability that $\varepsilon_R - \varepsilon_L$ may be positive enough to outweigh the "true EU" difference between L and R.

This difference becomes especially important in cases such as the matching pennies game in table 7.3. Here, RP entails that Col will choose R or L according to whether $q[u(1) - u(0)]$ is greater than or less than $(1 - q)[u(1) - u(0)]$. In other words, under RP the relationship showing p as a function of q is that $p = 0$ for all $q > 0.5$ and $p = 1$ for all $q < 0.5$, while p can take any value (Col is indifferent between all probability mixes of L and R) when $q = 0.5$. This rules out an equilibrium of the kind permitted by QRE where q^* deviates from 0.5. Thus, RP does not allow any violation of stochastic dominance to arise from the equilibrium concept. So *if* RP is the appropriate way of modeling noise in decision making, the data from matching pennies experiments would reject conventional core theory, represented by the requirement that beliefs and behavior conform probabilistically. As with individual choice, the conclusions one should draw from the data about core theory seem to depend on assumptions about stochastic specification.

In the case of games, conventional core theory may be "saved" by QRE—but only if we are prepared to accept an equilibrium concept that allows substantial violations of stochastic dominance, entailing a model of individual decision making that is not well supported by individual choice data. It remains to be established whether more direct tests of QRE will identify other grounds for concern—for example, values of μ varying inexplicably or implausibly under controlled conditions. As in the case of individual decision experiments, there is still much work to be done to explore the possible ways in which noise/error/imprecision might be modeled and to examine how far data that appear to violate core principles may or may not be accommodated by particular "auxiliary" assumptions—if that is what stochastic models are.[21]

Moreover, if it appears that no plausible stochastic specification of conventional core theory can be reconciled with the data, we shall have to turn our attention to ways in which alternative core theories might be specified stochastically and investigated experimentally. The next subsection indicates some of the issues arising from certain recent developments in modeling behavior in experimental games that take a rather different approach.

7.3.3 Alternative Models of Strategic Behavior

In the previous two subsections, QRE and RP were discussed in conjunction with "standard" core assumptions: in particular, that players are EU maximizers (albeit noisy ones) who believe all other players to be essentially the same as they are. Different players may have differing attitudes to risk and perhaps different degrees of noisiness, but in key respects they are assumed to conform with the standard view of rational players: that is, their judged utility comes only from their own payoffs, and they are interested in others' payoffs only to the extent that this allows them to form correct beliefs about the probabilities with which the other player(s) will choose their strategies.

However, these core assumptions might be modified in various, more or less radical, ways, and such modifications may be offered as explanations for many of the seemingly robust and systematic deviations from standard predictions. For example, it may be that when respondents are presented with information not only about their own monetary payoffs but also about the other players' monetary payoffs, they reinterpret their true payoffs to include an additional element due to "social" or "interpersonal" considerations—some attitude to fairness, perhaps, or a degree of envy. Thus, a payoff structure that appears to entail a dominant strategy when analyzed from the perspective of unmodified self-interest may not be seen as such by some players inclined to bring interpersonal considerations to bear (Rabin 1993).

The issue of how such interpersonal considerations might complicate the implementation of experimental games was discussed in chapter 3.

---

[21] If some degree of variability/imprecision/noise is *intrinsic* to human information processing, judgment, and decision processes, it is not obvious that we can so easily distinguish between what are "core" and what are "auxiliary" assumptions; so such a distinction is made subject to that caveat.

Table 7.4.   A dominance-solvable game.

	Left	Right
Up	3, 10	2, 2
Down	2, 1	0, 0

Such considerations may make it much harder for each player to judge the utility value placed by other players on the money payoffs and therefore make it difficult to judge the chances of other players selecting particular strategies—or, indeed, to know exactly what game is "really" being played.

To illustrate, consider the game shown in table 7.4, where the figure gives monetary payoffs from the different strategy combinations.

Viewed conventionally, this game is straightforward: for Row, U dominates D; for Col, L dominates R; and so the equilibrium involves Row playing U and Col playing L and the two players receiving payoffs of 3 and 10 respectively.

But suppose Row is averse to the payoff inequality this outcome entails: so much so, in fact, that the subjective value of a nominal payoff of 3 under these circumstances is perceived by him to be lower than receiving a payoff of 2 when Col gets a payoff of 1. That is to say, if Row anticipates that Col will play her conventionally dominant strategy L, Row would prefer the joint outcome $(2, 1)$ to the joint outcome $(3, 10)$ and will therefore play D. Such a result, were it to account for $x\%$ of all observations, might therefore not be due to Fechnerian noise large enough to overwhelm the true value difference between U and D on $x\%$ of occasions but could reflect $x\%$ of the sample population having more than the relevant threshold level of aversion to being on the wrong end of an unequal outcome.

And then what if column players were alert to the existence and prevalence of such people? If Col were only interested in her own payoffs, she would continue to play her conventionally dominant strategy L, since even just 1 is better than 0. But if she were to feel resentful of Row deliberately trying to deprive her of the 10 she might have had, she might feel a desire to retaliate: rather than allow Row to reduce her payoff to 1 while still getting 2 himself, she might prefer that they both end up with 0; in which case, her best response to D (when she perceives D to have been deliberately chosen for the motives described) would be R. On this basis, L would not be regarded by Col as dominating R.

What this example illustrates is that if players' values are not simply functions of their own nominal payoffs but also take account of *relative* payoffs and/or the interpersonal motivations of other players, each player's computation of the expected utility of each strategy may involve (a) modifications of their own payoffs and (b) judgments about the probabilities attached to the other player's strategies that depend in part on some estimate of the likelihood that the other player has motivations beyond maximizing the expected value of nominal payoffs and on some assessment of what those other motivations might be.

Under these conditions, even if there is no "noise" of the Fechnerian or RP kind, there would still be patterns of play that would depart from conventional predictions and that *might appear* to be due to noise of some sort. Moreover, there may now be additional sources of "genuine" (Fechnerian or RP) noise. First, not only may an individual's judgment about the relative utility differences between payoffs vary from one occasion to another, but also her judgment about the utility of receiving x_i when the other player is receiving x_j may vary from one occasion to another. So too might her judgment about the proportion of other players who are purely interested in their own payoffs, as opposed to those who take account of relativities and other interpersonal motivations—a source of variability somewhat analogous to the possibility that in "games against nature," objective probabilities may be transformed differently into subjective decision weights on different occasions.

Allowing the possibility that different players may have different propensities to modify nominal payoffs to take account of comparisons with opponents' payoffs and motivations may seem to be complicated enough. But thus far we have continued to suppose that all players, whatever their personal and interpersonal attitudes might be, are capable of the sort of sophisticated reasoning that is characteristic of conventional game theory.

However, when trying to interpret data from experimental games, a further complicating factor is the possibility that many participants in such experiments either themselves have limited capacities for reasoning according to standard game-theoretic logic and/or may believe that other players have such limitations. For example, although participants in individual decision experiments rarely fail to respect transparent FOSD, solutions involving some element of successive elimination of dominated strategies may require several steps of reasoning combined with a belief that the other player can be relied upon to reason similarly and act accordingly. But, in practice, players may not (all) reason in that way and/or may not be totally confident that others do.

Thus, instead of assuming that all players have equal powers of reasoning about each others' strategic choices, an alternative strategy for trying to accommodate the experimental data involves allowing for different "types" of players, characterized by different degrees of sophistication. The last decade has seen considerable interest in modeling this heterogeneity and fitting such models to the data (see, for example, Stahl and Wilson 1995; Costa-Gomez et al. 2001; Camerer et al. 2004a). Essentially, the modeling strategy adopted by these and other authors involves positing different "levels" or "steps" of sophistication, with step 0 being the most basic and least "reasoned," with players on higher steps able to take account of the existence and behavior of others on lower levels.

For example, Camerer et al. (2004a, p. 863) propose the idea of a *cognitive hierarchy* (CH) in which "step k" players

> assume that their opponents are distributed, according to a normalized Poisson distribution, from step 0 to step $k - 1$: that is, they accurately predict the relative frequencies of players doing fewer steps of thinking, but ignore the possibility that some players may be doing as much or more.
>
> Camerer et al. (2004a)

Essentially, step 0 (hereafter, S0) players are modeled as behaving at random and thus are assumed to play each available strategy with equal probability; step 1 (S1) players are assumed to act so as to maximize their expected payoff on the supposition that all other players are S0; step 2 (S2) players maximize their expected payoffs on the assumption that the rest of the population is some mix of S0 and S1; and so on. Camerer et al. find such a model to be a parsimonious way of organizing a large amount of data, with the mean and variance of the fitted Poisson distribution[22] often taking a value in the region of 1.5 (meaning that the "central tendency" in many games is for the bulk of players to operate as if at S1 or else at S2).

To illustrate how the model might work, consider again the asymmetric matching pennies game from table 7.3. To keep the example simple, suppose that in a particular sample of 200 participants—100 assigned to play Row, 100 to play Col—there are four levels of players, distributed in the same way within each role: twenty S0 players; forty S1 players; thirty S2 players; and ten S3 players.

S0 players choose at random: so half of the twenty Row players choose U, the other half choose D; likewise, half of the twenty Col players choose L, half choose R.

---

[22] The intuition suggested for using the Poisson distribution is as follows. Higher levels of reasoning require more intelligence/time/effort/working memory, so that out of any set of players who can reason at least at level k, the percentage who can also reason at level $k + 1$ falls as k rises—this is well captured by Poisson distributions.

S1 players suppose all other players are S0—which means that they expect each of their opponent's strategies to be chosen with probability 0.5. On this basis, Col players are indifferent between L and R, so that, on average, twenty of the forty play L while the other twenty play R. Meanwhile, as all S1 Row players expect L and R to be played with equal frequency by S0 Col players, all forty S1 Row players will choose U.

S2 players suppose all other players are either S0 or S1 and it is assumed that they judge the relative numbers of S0 and S1 correctly: i.e., one-third S0 and two-thirds S1. In this example, the proportions of S0 and S1 among Col players are not important for S2 Row players, since both S0 and S1 Col players are equally likely to play L or R. On this basis, all thirty S2 Row players will opt to play U. And actually, the exact proportion of S0 and S1 among Row players is not crucial for S2 Col players: as long as there are at least *some* S1 Row players, all of whom will choose U, the probability of U being played is greater than 0.5, in which case all thirty S2 Col players will choose R.

Finally, consider the S3 players. Since the payoffs for L and R are the same, Col players are only concerned with the probabilities associated with U and D; and as long as there is at least one S1 or S2 player, the probability of U being played will be greater than 0.5, in which case all ten S3 Col players will choose R. Meanwhile, for S3 Row players, the proportions of Col players *might* matter: for U to be strictly preferred, S3 Row players must expect the probability of L to be greater than 0.2—which in turn requires S3 Row players to judge that at least 40% of Col players are either S0 or S1 (since both of these types play L and R with equal probability). In fact, since two-thirds of the non-S3 Col players are S0 or S1, and since S3 Row players are assumed to judge that proportion correctly, this condition is easily satisfied, and all ten S3 Row players choose U.

On this basis, what would the experimenter observe? Half of the S0 and S1 Col players opt for each strategy, while all S2 and S3 Col players choose R; the overall pattern is therefore that L is played by thirty players and R by seventy players. Meanwhile, half of the S0 Row players opt for D but all the rest choose U, so that D is played by ten players and U by ninety players.

Of course, the precise numbers in this example depend on the initial distribution of types, here chosen so that it broadly resembles a truncated Poisson distribution, but rounded for simplicity of exposition. Simplified though it is, it serves to illustrate a number of points.

First, this CH approach can accommodate substantial departures from the Nash equilibrium prediction—and here in the direction observed by Ochs (1995) and also accommodated by QRE: namely, greater frequency of U and L than the 0.5 and 0.2, respectively, given by the mixed strategy equilibrium.

However, there is a sense in which such a CH model is not a thorough-going stochastic model. Apart from S0 players, who pick a strategy at random, all other types may be supposed to behave deterministically, acting in order to maximize expected payoffs on the basis of their beliefs about the other players.[23] These beliefs are a hybrid of the correct and the mistaken: players at each level are assumed to judge correctly the relative frequencies of all players at lower levels than themselves; but since they wrongly assume that there are no other players at the same or higher levels than themselves, they are liable to misjudge the actual probability with which any strategy is played. Thus, play is replete with errors but not, except in the case of S0 players, of the kind modeled by QRE or RP.

The example also shows that the CH model—in contrast with both Nash and QRE—is liable to be insensitive to changes in payoffs that do not alter the optimal strategy for any particular type of player. Suppose the payoff to Row from (U, L) was 9 rather than 4. The Nash mixed strategy equilibrium (somewhat counterintuitively) entails no change in the probability that Row plays U, but requires Col to reduce the probability of playing L to 0.1. Intuition, QRE, and the evidence (see, for example, McKelvey et al. 2000; Goeree et al. 2003) all suggest that Row will be more likely to play U as that payoff increases. But in the example above (and for many near-Poisson distributions with a mean in the same vicinity) there is no such implication in the CH model. Indeed, in this example, that payoff would have to fall below 2 before S3 Row players would switch to D.[24]

So the CH approach has a number of appealing features—not least that it taps into the intuitively plausible idea that there are limits to the extent to which people are able (or at least willing) to think through the many levels of reasoning that some games might entail. On the other hand, in its current form—which might be characterized as a deterministic super-structure resting on a stochastic base—it has certain counterintuitive features and implications that are contrary to the evidence. But might

---

[23] This statement is arguably too sweeping: a generalization of CH, as we have presented it, might relax the assumption of deterministic play by higher-level players to allow some uncertainty among players at level 2 or above about the exact mix of lower-level players.

[24] On the basis of the figures in the example, S3 Row players believe that all S2 Col players will choose R but that half of all S0 and S1 Col players will choose L. Since S3 Row players believe that two-thirds of Col players are either S0 or S1, the probability of L being played is one-third: S3 Row players will therefore be indifferent between U and D when the payoff in the {U, L} cell is 2 and will strictly prefer U for all payoffs greater than 2.

there be scope for developing the model to allow for noise and imprecision that might complement the basic idea in a manner compatible with the data from experimental games?

It is beyond the scope of this chapter to do more here than indicate one or two broad lines of possible development. The most obvious candidate, given our earlier discussion, may be some modification to the deterministic superstructure of the model. As it stands, the model assumes that S1 players operate deterministically, given their assumption about their opponent *certainly* being S0. In turn, S2 players operate deterministically on the basis that they accurately predict the relative frequencies of players doing fewer steps of thinking and on this basis work out without noise or imprecision which strategy is optimal. This is a strong assumption; especially in a one-shot game where a player has had no opportunity to learn about the type or types of other players, one might expect that judgments about the likely proportions of other types might be a source of noise in the choice of strategy.

Something similar might be said for one further assumption: namely, that players sophisticated enough to do all that S2 or S3 players are supposed to do nevertheless disregard the possibility that any players operate at the same or higher levels as they themselves do. Camerer et al. (2004a) defend this assumption by appealing to some of the literature about "overconfidence" in judgment. But, against that, there is the possibility that players can conceive of some other players being at least as proficient at reasoning as they are. Indeed, much of the success displayed by participants in coordination games rests on the capacity of players to judge what others will choose when both players are required to play the same strategy. However, having players try to take account of the frequency of others with the same or higher powers of reasoning would present considerable analytical difficulties within a deterministic framework and for that reason this possibility is ruled out by assumption in existing models. Yet there may be scope for incorporating this possibility if uncertainties and variability in players' judgements about the probabilities with which their opponents will play the strategies available to them are considered.

7.3.4 Summary Remarks

In the previous three subsections we have seen two rather different ways of responding to the challenge of accommodating experimental data that appear to depart systematically from the predictions of standard game theory.

The first way is to take the standard theory but reformulate it in some stochastic form. As discussed in section 7.3.1, QRE does this by adding an essentially Fechnerian error term to try to account for the observed departures—thereby achieving some improvement in fit, but relying on an equilibrium concept that entails substantial violation of stochastic dominance in order to get this improvement. Section 7.3.2 showed how an RP specification might share some of the broad characteristics of QRE but would not allow the same violations of stochastic dominance— thereby suggesting that if RP were the appropriate way of modeling noise and imprecision, the conventional core could *not* be reconciled with the experimental data. These conclusions run parallel with those drawn in section 7.2, where it was argued that although the Fechner model might appear to be able to reconcile *some* anomalies with the core provided by conventional theory, no such reconciliation was possible if the RP specification were used.

The second way of accommodating the experimental data is to modify various of the core assumptions. One version of this approach involves allowing for interactions between payoffs and modifying the nominal form of those payoffs to take account of comparative and/or interpersonal considerations. This may be seen as analogous to the various alternative individual decision theories such as regret theory (Bell 1982; Fishburn 1982; Loomes and Sugden 1982, 1987; and box 3.5 (p. 135)) and disappointment theory (Bell 1985; Loomes and Sugden 1986) that allowed interactions between consequences as a means of accommodating violations of Independence and Transitivity. A rather different kind of modification of core assumptions is to take payoffs more or less as stated but to suppose that players' reasoning is bounded to different degrees—which might be regarded as broadly analogous to the explanations of individual decision anomalies in terms of simplifying heuristics. As things currently stand, the different ways of modifying various core assumptions do not build in noise and imprecision (except, in the case of CH, for SO players). Considering how to specify such models stochastically will be a necessary part of testing them.

These points suggest that the construction and development of stochastic game-theoretic models, whether based on core game-theoretic assumptions or not, remains a crucial avenue for further research. Such research may run in parallel with, and draw on, research on the stochastic component of individual decision making. However, as games will also involve additional complexities, we shall, in the next section, focus mainly upon individual decision making in order to make some further points about possible forms of research on this topic.

7.4   Exploring Different Stochastic Specifications

The discussion in section 7.2 raised serious doubts about the appropriateness of a Fechnerian model of the stochastic component in individual decision making under risk and uncertainty. The suggestion made there was that, of the models currently available in this area, the RP model is a rather stronger candidate. However, that would imply that EU is the wrong core; and that in turn poses the question of how to apply RP to alternative core theories.

For example, consider how to apply RP to (some member of) the family of rank-dependent expected utility models. Such models usually entail some function $v(\cdot)$ that maps payoffs to subjective values and another function $\pi(\cdot)$ that transforms probabilities into decision weights according to a procedure that ensures FOSD.[25] The question then is, How much freedom should we allow to the set of value functions $v(\cdot)$ and to the set of probability weighting functions $\pi(\cdot)$? Taking cumulative prospect theory (Tversky and Kahneman 1992), for instance, the restrictions placed by the theory on the shape of $v(\cdot)$ are quite modest: the function is expected to be concave in the domain of gains, convex in the domain of losses, and steeper for losses than for corresponding gains, with a kink at zero. An RP form of such a core may require us to consider how we model the distributions of $v(\cdot)$ and $\pi(\cdot)$ and whether we require/disallow any particular relationships between the two. To date, so little attention has been paid to the question of the different candidate stochastic specifications that such questions take us into largely uncharted territory.[26]

Moreover, when we move into the arena of experimental games, the issues appear to be even more wide open. As discussed in section 7.3, there are at least two plausible sources of noise: first, the same kind of noise manifested in individual decision experiments, relating to the translation of money payoffs into subjective utilities/values—this being even further complicated by possible considerations of interpersonal utility interactions not present in "games against nature"; second, the uncertainty about what other "types" of player one might interact with,

---

[25] An early form of this type of model was Quiggin's (1982) "anticipated utility" theory. Subsequently, Starmer and Sugden (1989) proposed a form that incorporated a reference point and allowed losses to be treated differently from gains. Essentially the same idea is at the heart of Tversky and Kahneman's (1992) cumulative prospect theory. Numerous other variants have also been proposed.

[26] A recent foray into part of this territory is reported by Stott (2006), who considers a number of combinations of different "core" specifications with various error models. However, he explicitly avoids the RP approach, confining attention to models that take an essentially Fechnerian approach.

and what the likelihoods are of encountering any particular type. Given the multiplicity of ways in which one could "not unreasonably" model how players translate the payoffs into utilities and how they could imagine other players to be likely to think and act, one might ask whether there are *any* patterns of behavior for which it would be impossible to construct a "not unreasonable" account.

One possible response to this is to recall the Lakatosian distinction, discussed in chapter 3, between progressive and degenerating research programs. On this account, merely mopping up anomalies with "not unreasonable" adjustments to protective belt assumptions is insufficient for progress; novel predictions and expanding empirical success are also required.

An alternative response is to try to investigate "noise" directly. How it operates in individual and/or interactive decision environments is essentially an empirical question. But the existing stock of evidence designed to address this issue is limited. Thus, a pressing task is to gather data about the nature and structure of the stochastic component of behavior. The question then—and this is the question that the rest of this section will address, albeit in an indicative rather than a comprehensive manner—is how that might be done.

7.4.1   Other Potentially Useful Forms of Data

The bulk of the existing relevant evidence from individual decision experiments takes the form of repeated pairwise choice data. As described earlier, such experiments have usually involved asking respondents to make large numbers of choices between pairs of lotteries, with particular pairs being presented on more than one occasion and with no feedback about the resolution of any choices until all decisions have been made. Then, typically, one pair will be selected at random from all those that have been presented and the respondent will be paid according to her choice in that case.

Arguably, this is about as close as one can get to taking random sample observations of a respondent's preferences. Even so, as noted in section 7.2, there is some evidence of systematic change in the course of a session, with choices tending to become somewhat more risk averse in later responses. Quite what causes this is not known, but the patterns suggest that experience/familiarity has some impact even when there is only rather minimal feedback.

However, one drawback with discrete choice data of this kind is that they provide only rather limited information. All we observe on each occasion is which alternative was chosen, and the only visible "action" occurs in cases where the choice changes from one occasion to another. In most cases, when no switch of choice occurs, we gain very little insight; and for any one individual it would require a great many repeated choices targeted in the vicinity of her switch-points to build up a picture of how the noise/error component of her preferences is configured.

It might seem that a much more efficient way of eliciting the information would be by means of a series of "equivalence" tasks in one of two forms: certainty equivalence and probability equivalence. For any lottery, the certainty equivalence task requires the respondent to state the sure sum of money she regards as exactly equally preferable to that lottery. Probability equivalence tasks require respondents to construct some other lottery that she regards as exactly equally preferable to the lottery being evaluated. One simple way of formulating this task is in terms of a "standard" or "reference" lottery with two payoffs, one of which is zero while the other is a sum greater than any of the payoffs in the lottery being evaluated.

Probability equivalence tasks have not been much used in economics experiments,[27] but there are many experiments that have involved certainty equivalents. Unfortunately, most of these do not provide data that can be used for our present purpose. Many individual decision experiments only ask respondents for a single valuation of each lottery. And although there are also some "repeated market" experiments that ask respondents to value the same lottery on a number of occasions in successive trading rounds, these generally provide considerable feedback between each round—feedback that is liable to exert substantial systematic influences upon later responses. Thus even though the repeated discrete choice data are not completely "pure," the valuation datasets from repeated market experiments are even less like sets of random sample observations of respondents' preferences.[28]

In order to obtain equivalence data comparable to the kind of repeated choice data discussed earlier, it would be necessary to ask respondents to state a number of equivalences, with particular lotteries presented

---

[27] One area in which they *have* been more widely used is in the context of health state elicitation: in the simplest form of "standard gamble," respondents are asked to set the probabilities of two outcomes of a health treatment—full health if the treatment succeeds and death if the treatment fails—such that they are indifferent between that risky prospect and the certainty of some intermediate health state. For further details, see Gafni (2005).

[28] Even when lotteries are not actually played out at the end of each round of trading, information about market prices (and sometimes about the distribution of bids and asks of other traders) is usually available to respondents and is liable to "shape" their subsequent responses. In addition, early bids/asks may be "contaminated" by strategic behavior, which may be modified to some extent by experience during subsequent rounds. For some evidence and discussion, see Loomes et al. (2003).

to them on more than one occasion within each session, and play out a randomly selected task only at the end of the session. However, we know of no substantial datasets that satisfy these requirements. In the absence of such datasets, we consider some data from an experiment that does not exactly fit this design but that may nevertheless provide some insights—as well as indicating some of the potential problems and pitfalls involved in collecting and analyzing equivalence data.

In a recent paper, Butler and Loomes (2007) (henceforth B&L) explored the role of imprecision in people's preferences as a possible (part of the) explanation of the preference reversal phenomenon (see box 4.3 (p. 157)). Their design revolved around two lotteries: a *P*-bet offering a 0.70 chance of $24 (and a 0.30 chance of zero), and a $-bet offering a 0.25 chance of $80 (and a 0.75 chance of zero).[29] The experiment sought, among other things, to elicit from each respondent a certainty equivalent and a probability equivalent for each lottery. The elicitation of those equivalences was implemented as follows. The bet in question—say, the $-bet—was fixed and labeled A, while the other option (a sure sum of money in the case of the certainty equivalence task, or some chance of a $160 payoff in the case of the probability equivalence task) was labeled B and was initially set at some "extreme" value.[30] Both alternatives were displayed on a computer screen, and the individual was then asked to respond in one of four ways: if they "definitely preferred" option A, this was coded as a 1; if they "probably preferred" A, this was recorded as a 2; "probably preferring" B was recorded as a 3; and a "definite preference" for B was coded as a 4. Then the value in B was altered—progressively increasing if it initially started at the bottom extreme, progressively falling if it initially started high. Thus the typical respondent began by being sure they preferred one alternative and ended up being sure they preferred the other, and in half of the cases this entailed a transition from A to B while in the other half the movement was from B to A. In this way, each respondent not only effectively stated a certainty and probability equivalent for the target bet (the point at which they switched from probably preferring one to probably preferring the other, that is, the 2 ↔ 3 switch-point), but also indicated the interval (between 1 ↔ 2 and 3 ↔ 4) over which they considered themselves to be less than sure about their equivalence. We shall refer to these latter intervals as "imprecision intervals."

---

[29] These payoffs were in Australian dollars.

[30] In the certainty equivalence task for the $-bet, for example, for half the sample the alternative was initially set as a sure payoff of $1, while for the other half it started at $80; in the probability equivalence task, the initial alternative was either a 0.01 chance of $160 or else a 0.25 chance of $160.

Someone who was totally sure of their preference could go straight from recording a definite preference for one option to a definite preference for the other, in which case indifference for them would be represented by the 1 ↔ 4 switch-point. In the event, however, all but a handful of respondents recorded at least some 2s and also some 3s in each exercise. This is consistent with most people not only exhibiting variability in their decisions but also being aware of the possibility that they might reach different decisions on different occasions. And although it is not known exactly what individuals were thinking when they changed from recording a "definite" preference to a "probable" one, and vice versa, these responses may still provide useful data for evaluating competing ways of modeling the stochastic component in decision behavior.

The main patterns that emerged were as follows. In the case of the certainty equivalence task, the mean imprecision interval for the P-bet was less than one-third of the corresponding interval for the $-bet (approximately $6 compared with $20). In the probability equivalence task, the mirror-image pattern was observed: for the $-bet, the average interval between the 1 ↔ 2 and 3 ↔ 4 switching points was roughly 0.07, compared with a figure of 0.20 for the P-bet.[31]

Could these results be reconciled with a Fechnerian specification of EU—even one that allows the variance of ε to be some function of the characteristics of a lottery and therefore to vary from one lottery to another? To see that the answer is probably "No," consider the following.

One way of thinking about imprecision intervals in Fechnerian terms is as confidence intervals. Under Fechnerian assumptions, in any choice between two lotteries there is some probability that the individual will choose the alternative whose "true EU" is lower, with this probability becoming smaller as the difference between the true EUs of the two lotteries becomes larger. It seems reasonable to suppose that individuals' expressions of confidence in their choice should become stronger as the chance of picking the "wrong" alternative becomes smaller, and so we might think of the statement that they "definitely prefer" one lottery as indicating that they consider the chance of being mistaken lying below some threshold, while "probably preferring" might signify that they think the chance of being mistaken is greater than that threshold. It would be in keeping with the spirit of Fechner to suppose that a given

---

[31] Those aggregate patterns were also evident at the level of the individual: for seventy-three of the eighty-nine individuals, the imprecision intervals for their certainty equivalents of the $-bet were strictly greater than the corresponding intervals for the P-bet; while in the probability equivalence task, seventy-one of the eighty-nine exhibited strictly wider intervals for the P-bet than for the $-bet.

individual applies the same threshold to all choices.[32] Thus an impreci-sion interval can be thought of, in Fechnerian terms, as an individual's confidence interval over the joint distribution of the noise associated with a choice between any two alternatives.

Now consider the case of an EU-maximizing individual who is truly indifferent between two lotteries, F and G: the same true EU therefore maps to the same true certainty, denoted by C^*, and the same true prob-ability equivalent, denoted by p^* (where this is the probability of receiv-ing the high payoff in a reference lottery R, with that payoff high enough to guarantee $p^* < 1$). In addition, suppose that for some reason the vari-ance of ε is greater for F than for G (with both distributions symmetrical around the same true EU).

Consider first the B&L method of eliciting probability equivalences for the two lotteries, starting with (say) a high value of p that is progressively reduced from a level where the individual definitely prefers R to a level where she definitely prefers either F or G. At every level of p, the joint distribution of the error terms in the $\{R, F\}$ choice will be higher than the corresponding joint distribution for $\{R, G\}$, with the result that for any individual applying the same threshold "level of significance" to both, the confidence interval/imprecision interval will be wider for F than for G.

Now consider the B&L method of eliciting certainty equivalences, start-ing with (say) a sure sum large enough for it to be definitely preferred to the lottery and then progressively reduced until it is low enough for the lottery to be definitely preferred. Whether or not we assume some noise associated with the perceived utility of the sure sum,[33] at any level of C the joint distribution of the error terms in the $\{C, F\}$ choice will be higher than the corresponding joint distribution for $\{C, G\}$. Thus, just as with the probability equivalent elicitation, each individual's confidence inter-val/imprecision interval expressed in certainty equivalent terms will be wider for F than for G.

In short, under the assumptions of the Fechner model, if the ε asso-ciated with lottery F has greater variance than that for the ε associated with lottery G, this would tend to be reflected in broader confidence/imprecision intervals, whether measured via the probability of some reference payoff or via sure sums of money.

So if the intervals identified by B&L are proxies for such confidence intervals, the patterns in the experimental data are incompatible with

---

[32] We can, of course, allow that the degree of confidence separating a "definite" from a "probable" preference might vary from one individual to another.

[33] In the case of Blavatskyy's (2007) variant, the utilities of sure sums are always per-ceived without any error at all. But this assumption is not necessary to derive the results presented here.

the Fechner model: instead of one lottery being associated with a wider interval whichever way the interval is measured, the average imprecision interval for the $-bet was more than three times wider than the interval for the P-bet when elicited by certainty equivalence, while the $-bet interval was barely one-third of the width of the P-bet interval when these were elicited via the probability equivalence procedure.

By contrast, the ways in which the relative sizes of intervals varied in that experiment is much more easily accommodated by the RP framework. To illustrate this, consider an example of a risk-averse EU maximizer whose set of $u(\cdot)$ functions all take the form $u(x) = x^\beta$, where β is distributed over some range. Suppose that a particular individual acts as if sure that her β is not less than 0.6 and not more than 0.8, but reports herself as only having a "probable" preference in cases that fall within that range. Applying those two values of β to give the ends of her imprecision intervals, her interval for the probability equivalent of B&L's P-bet would lie between 0.154 and 0.224—that is, an interval of 0.070—while her interval for the $-bet would lie between 0.144 and 0.165—that is, an interval of 0.021, which is less than one-third of the P-bet interval. Applying those same two "end" values of β to the certainty equivalence task would give an interval of $2.12 for the P-bet and $6.21 for the $-bet, so that in this case the $-bet interval is almost three times as wide as its P-bet counterpart. Stylized though this example may be, it serves to show how the pattern of the imprecision intervals reported by B&L is much more easily reconciled with the RP model than with any reasonably straightforward version of the Fechner specification.[34]

Although it would be rash to draw strong conclusions from a single exploratory study, the approach developed by B&L may provide insights into the imprecise and/or stochastic nature of people's preferences—in which case, extensions of the approach might enable us to build a more complete picture of the nature of noise/imprecision in the behavior of experimental subjects.

On the other hand, the type of procedure used by B&L is not uncontroversial, for (at least) two reasons. First, it relies upon introspection about confidence in a decision, which is a difficult notion to pin down and interpret. Second, there is no obvious way of linking the $1 \leftrightarrow 2$ and $3 \leftrightarrow 4$ switch-points to standard monetary incentives. As chapter 6 explained,

---

[34] In the light of what was said earlier about the rejection of EU as the core theory, conditional on RP being the appropriate model of the stochastic component, the use of EU in the example here is not meant to suggest that EU can be rehabilitated; rather, an EU core is deployed to keep things simple and make it clear that the result does not depend on invoking some more complicated core theory involving nonlinear probability transformations and/or more complex value functions.

we do not take the view that information obtained via a procedure that cannot be made incentive compatible in the eyes of orthodox theory should necessarily be ruled inadmissible. But there is a strong presumption among some experimental economists in favor of incentives. In view of this, a possible task for future research is to explore whether the possibilities suggested by the B&L procedure can be substantiated by experimental designs that *can* employ more standard incentive-compatible mechanisms.

7.5 Concluding Remarks

Even when making choices between pairs of the most basic and well-defined lotteries, many participants in experiments display variability that may be modeled as stochastic. If this is true for individual choices under risk, it is likely to be at least as significant in the behavior observed in experimental games where there is additional uncertainty and room for variable judgment about the likelihood of different strategies being played.

To date, this issue has received less attention than we believe it deserves. Often, statistical tests are applied that implicitly assume some error structure, but these are taken "off the shelf," perhaps with too little thought about the appropriateness of the assumptions that underlie them. And to the extent that the issue has been more explicitly addressed, the usual approach has been to model noise as an "add-on" in the Fechnerian tradition.

We have argued that such specifications, while they may seem quite "natural" to economists and econometricians, are not neutral or uncontroversial. Indeed, there are grounds for thinking that, at least in the context of individual choice and experimental games, the Fechner specification is conceptually flawed and empirically inadequate. In particular, such a specification is liable to (greatly) overestimate the frequency of violations of *transparent* dominance (which are actually quite rare in individual risky choice experiments) and, in conjunction with standard core theories, entails a number of patterns that do not cohere with the evidence.

To demonstrate that the Fechnerian approach is not the only possible way to model the stochastic component in people's preferences, we have discussed the potential of the RP approach as an alternative. Whether RP can provide an entirely satisfactory—or even a less unsatisfactory—account is still open to debate. But what the comparisons between RP

and Fechner have shown beyond doubt is that different stochastic specifications of the same core theory can produce radically different implications, and the message is clear: the choice of stochastic specification
is not an "optional extra" but is absolutely central to the analysis and
interpretation of experimental data in key areas of economic behavior
and theory testing.

While this chapter has given most prominence to the Fechner and RP
approaches, we have not intended to suggest that they are the only ways
of modeling the stochastic nature of preferences. Other formulations—
for example, Busemeyer and Townsend's (1993) "decision field theory"—
may offer additional and perhaps rather different insights. The main
purpose of the chapter has been to draw attention to how little has
yet been done in this important area of enquiry and to stimulate further debate and research. While we might stop a *little* short of Chairman
Mao's invocation to "let a hundred flowers bloom; let a hundred schools
of thought contend," it is right in spirit. There is an important sym-
biotic relationship to be explored here: experimental economists must
understand the stochastic elements of behavior better if we are to analyze and interpret our data appropriately; and yet it is hard to see how
to advance our understanding of those elements without further experimentation, including the development and use of methods that may
reach beyond some of the orthodoxies that we have examined in the
course of this book.

8
Conclusion

Over the preceding chapters we have reviewed a wide range of experiments, all carried out with the intention of contributing in some way or other to the understanding of economic behavior. We have considered an equally wide range of arguments—sometimes very general, sometimes specific to particular experimental designs—about how experiments in economics do or do not achieve these intentions. We now draw these threads together to offer an assessment of how well experimental economics is doing and where it is heading. To avoid repetition, our assessment will be stated rather than argued for; the supporting arguments are to be found in the preceding chapters.

We will pose the question, How well is experimental economics doing? in three different ways. The first, which follows most naturally from the subject matter of this book, is, How successful has experimental economics been in developing a sound methodology? To pose the question in this way is to ask whether, when experimental economists set out with the intention of increasing our understanding of economic behavior, their methods are appropriate for that task.

The second question will perhaps come to mind more immediately for most economists: How successful has experimental economics *in fact* been in increasing our understanding of economic behavior? These first two questions are logically independent, and focus attention on different aspects of experimental economics; but one might expect some relationship between their answers. It would be difficult to argue convincingly that a scientific research program had been using sound methods for a protracted period of time without actually achieving anything. Conversely, if such a program had repeatedly made significant discoveries about its subject matter, it would be odd to claim that its methods were completely unsound. However, it could be that some of the methods that experimentalists treat as valid are sound and some are not, and that practical success in experimental economics is attributable to the sound ones. Or it could be that progress is being held back by mistaken beliefs about the *in*validity of methods that would in fact be productive. And there might be mismatches between the practice of experimental economists and the precepts that they endorse when they think in methodological terms: a sound "official" methodology might coexist with practical failure, or an unsound one with practical success.

The third question adopts a rather different perspective. It is this: Has the development of experimental methods had a positive impact on economics in general? In the abstract, it is easy to conceive of the possibility that, in a broad-ranging discipline such as economics, a subdiscipline might develop its own methodology and its own agenda of problems, gradually taking on a separate identity. Such a subdiscipline might be successful in its own terms while its influence on its parent discipline declined. Arguably, this has been the case for economic history. Most present-day economists, we guess, think of economic history as a branch of history that can make use of some of the methods of economics. The view that historical enquiry might be a core research method for economics as a whole would not occur to them. But there was a time when such a view was widely held by economists. Similarly, it is at least imaginable that experimental economics could develop into a self-contained subdiscipline, while the rest of economics continued on as before. Alternatively, experimental methods might slowly permeate the discipline as a whole, in the way that those of econometrics have already done. And, of course, that might be assessed positively or negatively.

8.1   How Successful Has Experimental Economics Been in Developing a Sound Methodology?

As we said at the beginning of chapter 1, and as we have documented throughout the book, there are ongoing controversies within experimental economics about what its methodology should be. And there are controversies among practitioners of experimental economics, and between practitioners and outsiders, about what can be learned from experiments. We have tried to contribute toward resolving these controversies. On some issues, in contrast, there is a folk wisdom about the proper methodology of experimental economics that is widely accepted by practitioners. Elements of this have emerged at various points in this book. We have probed these consensus positions and sometimes found them to be much more open to question than is generally thought.

As illustrations, we list ten methodological claims, each of which has either been made explicitly by at least one prominent experimental economist or is part of the folk wisdom of experimental economics—or, as is often the case, both. Each of these claims has been discussed in one or more of the previous chapters. We have argued that all of them are at least contestable, and that none of them should be accepted uncritically as part of "the" methodology of experimental economics.

Claim 1. *An experiment should not be criticized for being "unrealistic" if it is being used to test a theory and if the unrealistic features of the experimental environment are also properties of that theory.*

This "blame-the-theory" argument was advanced by several of the pioneers of experimental economics, and remains a common defense of experiments. We have argued that it presupposes that a theory can legitimately be tested throughout its "base domain." That is, it can be tested with respect to any of the possible phenomena to which, on a normal interpretation of its language, it refers. (For example, a theory that refers without qualification to "markets" is held to apply to *all* markets, including "unrealistic" markets implemented in experimental laboratories; a theory that refers without qualification to "choice under uncertainty" is held to apply to *all* choice under uncertainty; and so on.) However, theories that have failed experimental tests in their base domains are often defended on the grounds that the relevant experiments did not satisfy implicit conditions on those theories' applicability (for example, that agents must have adequate experience of the decision environment). Although such arguments can be misused to insulate theories from disconfirming evidence, it would be naive to expect the statement of a theory to include a complete specification of the conditions of its applicability. Thus, external-validity concerns may have force even when a theory is tested in its base domain. We have presented criteria for assessing these concerns in such a case and, by implication, how convincing the blame-the-theory defense is of particular experimental findings (chapter 2).

Claim 2. *For tests of economic theory, experimental designs that use markets are more valid than those that do not.*

We have raised both theoretical and empirical doubts about this often-stated position. From a theoretical point of view, it is simply not the case that economic theory is intended to apply only to markets; thus, there can be no *general* presumption that market experiments are closer to the intended domain of economic theory than are other experimental designs. Claim 2 is often presented along with the supposed fact that behavior in market experiments tends to confirm the predictions of traditional economic theory, while disconfirmations that occur in non-market designs are discounted as being less relevant for testing the theory. We have argued that when like is compared with like—that is, when one compares the success of *given* theoretical hypotheses in market and nonmarket experiments—the evidence base for that "fact" is rather weak (chapter 2).

Claim 3. *Game theory can be tested experimentally, but only if the experimenter "gets the payoffs right first."*

This is often asserted, both by game theorists and by experimentalists. The idea is that game theory is not committed to any substantive interpretation of "payoff": a player's payoff is just a generic representation of whatever he is trying to achieve. Thus (it is said), a valid test of the theory must include some empirical verification that the payoffs assumed for the test correspond with the players' objectives. We have argued that if game theory is to be interpreted as having predictive or explanatory content, some substantive assumptions must be made about how payoffs relate to observable properties of the real-world situations to which the theory is applied. These assumptions must be sufficiently fixed that payoffs can be defined before the behavior implied by the theory is observed. In other words, getting the payoffs right is part of what game theory has to do if it is to be a predictive or explanatory enterprise. Only then can experimenters test the success of the resulting theory (chapter 3).

Claim 4. *If an "anomaly" has been found in many experiments but does not occur in an experiment that implements all known controls for subjects' misperceptions, we should infer that the anomaly is an artifact of inadequately controlled experimental procedures.*

This claim treats the idea of "correct" perception of experimental procedures as unproblematic, with the implication that if all misperceptions are removed, subjects' true preferences will be revealed. It also assumes that procedures that control for misperception are well-defined and separable, so that adding any such procedure to a given design leads to an unambiguous increase in the overall degree of control. We have questioned both features of the claim. Some significant psychologically based theories of choice propose that individuals' preferences are influenced by subjective perceptions (for example, about reference points) for which there are no clearly correct objective correlates. For many experimental procedures, it is a matter of judgment whether, on balance, they increase or decrease subjects' understanding of tasks. The existence of such procedures makes the idea of implementing all known controls ambiguous (chapter 4).

Claim 5. *All theories are false, so we can learn very little from observations of small anomalies in experimental tests of received theories.*

The maxim that all theories are false expresses a significant truth. Theoretical hypotheses in economics must be interpreted as qualified by what methodologists call "vague ceteris paribus clauses"; if stated without such qualifications and read literally, economic theories are indeed false. Thus, if a theoretical hypothesis is stated in an unqualified form, we should expect it to be disconfirmed in at least some empirical tests; since all theories have this property, such disconfirmation cannot be a sufficient reason for rejecting a theory. However, we have resisted the suggestion that "small" anomalies are uninformative. Any systematic deviation between a theory's predictions and the evidence is an indicator that some causal mechanism, not included in the theory, is at work. Experience shows that searching for such mechanisms can lead to valuable new knowledge and to the creation of theories with an expanded domain of explanatory success (chapter 4).

Claim 6. *Hypotheses should be derived from theory, prior to the experiments that test them; they should not be induced ex post to organize experimentally observed regularities.*

This claim reflects the view, held by many economists, that scientific method is or should be hypothetico-deductive. We have argued that scientific progress can also be achieved by inductive methods, and that such methods are gradually gaining ground in experimental economics. Successful research programs can start from the discovery of surprising empirical regularities for which, at the time, there are no adequate theoretical explanations. Such regularities may first come to light as unexpected features of experimental data. However, advocates of claim 6 are right to distinguish between prior and ex post hypotheses. The discovery of *some* pattern in the results of an experiment is not as surprising as the discovery of a *specific* pattern that was predicted in advance. A general hypothesis that is induced ex post to organize a given body of data cannot be said to have been *tested* against those data; but it can be useful in recording a hunch and in suggesting directions for further enquiry (chapter 4).

Claim 7. *When an economic theory is based on a formal model, the theory should be tested by implementing the assumptions of the model as closely as possible in the laboratory and finding out whether behavior in the experimental environment conforms with behavior in the model.*

This claim is presupposed by many experimental designs that are used to investigate issues in applied economics, as well as more fundamental economic theory. The kind of experiment we have in mind, in the former case, purports to assess a theory that makes assertions about real economic situations based on a stylized formal model of such situations. The experiment configures the laboratory environment to reproduce the assumptions of the model, except that the abstract agents of the model are replaced by human subjects; the payoffs of these subjects are structured so as to "induce" the objectives attributed to agents in the model. This environment may depart substantially from the real situations about which the theory makes its assertions. We have argued that such an experiment can play only a limited role in testing an applied economic theory. The theory uses a model to make claims about situations in the (real) world, supported by alleged similarities between the world and the model. If the experiment is to be judged informative about the world, there must be a corresponding appeal to similarities between the experiment *and the world*; to support such an appeal, it is not enough to show that the experiment mimics the model (chapter 5).

Claim 8. *For maximum control, interactive experiments should be designed so that subjects are anonymous to one another and interactive moves are prescripted.*

Some such claim seems to be implicit in the practice of many experimental economists. In general (though there are significant exceptions), experimenters are reluctant to use designs that allow subjects to interact with one another in an unstructured and naturalistic way. This attitude can be seen as part of a more general tendency, also revealed in claim 7, to favor experimental designs that resemble formal models; for a design to include features of the real world (such as spontaneous speech) that would be difficult to include in a formal model is seen as a lack of control. But if, as we have argued, theory testing requires similarity between the experiment and the world, naturalistic designs can sometimes have significant advantages (chapter 5).

Claim 9. *Economics experiments should always be incentive compatible.*

This is one of the most widely held methodological precepts in experimental economics—so much so that experiments without task-related incentives are hardly ever reported in economics journals. We have argued that this precept, if stated unconditionally, is ambiguous. Incentive compatibility can be defined only in relation to a given theory of decision making: a design may be incentive compatible for subjects who act according to one theory but not for subjects who act according to another. It is not self-evident that task-related incentives always increase the validity of experimental results: the balance of advantages and disadvantages depends on the nature of the investigation. We have pointed to some significant problems in economics that appear to be capable of experimental investigation only in nonincentivized designs (chapter 6).

Claim 10. *When analyzing experimental data, one should choose the error model according to considerations of econometric tractability alone.*

This claim seems to be implicit in the data analysis reported in many experimental studies. We have argued that the interpretation of a given set of experimental data can be very different depending on the error model used. For example, data that appear to show a systematic failure of a received theory when analyzed in relation to one error specification may be compatible with that theory when analyzed in relation to another. Thus, experimental economics needs to investigate the *actual* sources of stochastic variation in individual behavior, rather than treating error modeling as a technical problem for econometricians (chapter 7).

It will be obvious by now that we do not see experimental economic research as governed by a unified, uncontroversial, and clearly defensible methodology that needs only to be codified, taught to aspiring experimental economists, and explained to outsiders. Indeed, it would be unrealistic to expect any scientific research program to have a *completely* unified and uncontroversial methodology; and the existence of some degree of methodological disagreement is perhaps a sign of vitality rather than failure. But our sense is not that there is too much methodological diversity and reflection in experimental economics, but rather that there is too little. There is a danger that the practices of the discipline may ossify prematurely in unhelpfully restrictive forms.

In many cases, we suggest, these overly restrictive methodological principles are the residue of the particular history of experimental economics. Over a short period of time, experimental methods have been introduced into a science that had a long history of favoring other research tools, particularly those of model building and of deductive reasoning from "reasonable" or "self-evident" postulates about rational economic agents. It would not be surprising if many experimental economists have continued to think in ways that reflect the nonexperimental history of their discipline. Another factor to consider is that in the early years, work in experimental economics was concentrated in a narrow range of research programs. The practices of these programs, and in some cases the self-conscious reflections of their leading exponents, formed the methodological conventions that later experimental economists then followed. Ideas that are properly applicable only to particular experimental objectives or to particular types of experiments, or that reflect the idiosyncratic beliefs of particular pioneers, may have been imprinted too firmly on the folk wisdom. For example, Vernon

Smith's influential "precepts" of experimental methodology (examined in chapter 2) provide a useful code for cases in which the experimenter wishes to induce particular preferences, but can be misapplied to experiments in which the content of subjects' actual preferences is the object of enquiry.

Some research programs seem to be premised on a search for experimental designs that will yield decisive answers where, because of the Duhem–Quine problem, such answers are unattainable. Examples include the search for a method of testing "pure" game theory without making any substantive assumptions about payoffs (claim 3), and the idea that it is possible to design an experiment that incorporates all known controls for misperception (claim 4). Some types of designs tend to be used inappropriately. In particular, designs that implement formal models are often presented as tests of theoretical hypotheses about the real world (claim 7). Conversely, there are other types of designs that are potentially useful, but that experimental economists are reluctant to use. Examples include naturalistic designs (claim 8) and nonincentivized designs (claim 9). We suggest that the thinking behind claims 7 and 8 reflects a misplaced tendency within experimental economics to assume that principles of good practice in theoretical modeling can be transferred straightforwardly to experimental design.

8.2 How Successful Has Experimental Economics Been in Increasing Understanding of Economic Behavior?

Despite our reservations about some aspects of the current methodology of experimental economics, we have no hesitation in asserting that it *has* made significant contributions to the understanding of economic behavior. Over the course of the book, we have given many examples, drawn from a wide range of research programs, of discoveries that have been made by using the methods of experimental economics. Regularities (to use empiricist language: a realist would prefer to say "causal mechanisms") have been found that economists were previously unaware of, and that might never have come to light if economics had continued to use a nonexperimental methodology.

We feel particularly confident in making claims for the internal validity of experiments. That is, we are particularly confident in claiming that experimental economics has generated reliable knowledge about causal mechanisms that operate in economics experiments. We have described many experimental results that have proved to be highly robust and replicable. The ability of experimental economics to establish such results is in part due to the standardization of methods among practitioners. In many aspects of experimental design, there has been convergence to "industry standards"—for example, about incentive mechanisms, anonymity controls, randomization of subgroups, and counterbalancing of treatments. Whether or not these particular conventions are optimal, standardization in itself makes results more comparable across research groups, and so promotes replicability.

Of course, knowledge about causal mechanisms that operate in economics experiments is not of much use *in itself*. But even so, there is no prior guarantee that a program of experimental research will discover previously unsuspected regularities in behavior, and that those results will prove to be robust and replicable. Nor is there any prior guarantee that if regularities are found, they will be capable of being organized or explained by more general theories. To achieve these things is a genuine success. Having achieved them, experimental economists are entitled to feel some confidence that their experiments are tapping into fundamental systems of causal mechanisms that previous theories have not taken into account. To the extent that the experimental settings in which these discoveries have been made are judged similar to situations "in the field," one can at least hope that the same causal mechanisms will be at work in both.

Because this book is about experimental methodology, we have said much more about the results of experiments than about the theories that have been developed to explain those results, and still less about how those theories have performed in predicting and explaining behavior in nonexperimental environments. For this reason, the previous chapters do not provide as much evidence of the external validity of experimental results as they do of their internal validity. And, as has emerged repeatedly in the book, doubt about the external validity of experimental results is a major theme in the arguments of commentators who are skeptical about experimental economics. Nevertheless, it is increasingly clear that experimental research has led to discoveries that *do* apply, and *do* have significant implications, beyond the lab.

In particular, many recent developments in economics have followed from a growing recognition that important aspects of economic behavior can be explained using empirically based principles of psychology, rather than a priori principles of rationality. This "behavioral" approach to economics entered the discipline largely as a result of experimental research. Many psychologically explained phenomena, first documented in economics as experimental exhibits, have since been found to impact on the behavior of economic agents in the field. New branches of applied economics, such as "behavioral finance" and "behavioral industrial organization," have developed from these ideas.[1]

While behavioral economics can be interpreted as a challenge to previously received ideas, it would be a mistake to think that experiments have contributed to economics only by overturning orthodox theories. In particular, experimental research into the properties of different market institutions has tended to be complementary with developments in mainstream theory. Vernon Smith's early finding that, even with surprisingly small numbers of traders, repeated oral double auctions tend to converge to Walrasian equilibrium is a famous example (box 3.1 (p. 99)). A more recent example is the use of experiments to assist in the design of the auction which, in 2000, raised £22.5 billion from the sale of telecom licenses for third-generation mobile phone networks in the United Kingdom.[2]

In claiming that experimental economics has made a significant contribution to the understanding of economic behavior in the field, we do not mean to imply that the behavioral theories created in response to experimental findings are invariably superior to their more traditional counterparts. As we argued in chapter 4, there are reasons for thinking that the most famous exhibits of anomalies may overstate the degree to which, across its domain as a whole, conventional theory fails to predict correctly. There has been a tendency for experimental investigation to focus on narrow ranges of phenomena, clustered around famous exhibits. For example, investigation of choice under uncertainty has been heavily concentrated on binary choices between pairs of lotteries that can be defined in Marschak–Machina triangles—a device whose popularity stems from its ability to represent the common ratio effect and related anomalies. Similarly, investigation of social preferences has clustered around the Prisoners' Dilemma, the ultimatum game, the trust game, and voluntary contributions to public goods. A critic might reasonably ask how far these particular areas of investigation are representative of the much wider domain to which economic theories are expected to apply.[3] Thus,

---

[1] For surveys of behavioral finance and behavioral industrial organization, see Barberis and Thaler (2003) and Ellison (2008), respectively.

[2] The design process is described by Binmore and Klemperer (2002). As this account makes clear, the final auction design drew on insights from auction theory, industrial organization theory, and what economists of almost all persuasions would recognize as the common sense of their discipline. It appears that experimental research played a significant but supporting role.

[3] This question is raised by Schram (2005), who argues that "the 'mutual internal validity' of theory and experiment has the danger of creating its own world." Schram's concern is that if theory comes to be used to explain laboratory behavior while laboratory experiments are structured in accordance with theory, "the connection between these two on the one hand and the outside-the-laboratory world on the other may be lost."

even if a new theory of choice under uncertainty or of social preferences is highly successful in organizing experimental findings, it is not
necessarily the best buy for general-purpose use.

Nor do we mean to dismiss the arguments of economists who have
questioned whether particular experimental results apply in particular
field settings. For example, as we explained in chapter 2, there is an ongoing controversy about whether anomalies in individual choice behavior,
such as those exhibited in the Allais paradox (box 2.6 (p. 74)) and the
endowment effect (box 4.3 (p. 157)), tend to become less prevalent, or
even to disappear altogether, if individuals make decisions in repeated
markets. Our view is that this is an issue that can be resolved only by further experimental research; progress is being made, but it is too early to
draw firm conclusions. However, even if it turns out that repeated market experience *does* eliminate these anomalies, it will remain true that
the experiments in which the anomalies were first exhibited had external
validity in relation to significant areas of economic behavior.

Commentators who argue that repeated and/or market experiments
are the only valid tests of conventional economic theory are defending that theory by restricting its domain in a way that few economists
imagined to be necessary before experimental research impinged on economics. The discovery that systematic anomalies occur in nonrepeated
and nonmarket choices was surprising when it was first made. And that
is the time that matters: it is easy to be unsurprised after the event. It
is surely undeniable that economics needs to be able to explain choice
behavior in many nonrepeated and nonmarket situations.

As an example of the latter, consider the problem of discovering people's preferences for environmental public goods, to be used as data for
cost–benefit analysis. This is a practical problem that would normally
be thought to be within the professional competence of economists.
A standard method of proceeding is to use questionnaire studies to
elicit individuals' self-reported preferences. Normally, the survey questions are nonrepeated, nonmarket (and hypothetical) choices. The first
economists to use this "stated preference" methodology to provide guidance for public policy were surprised to find systematic divergences
between their data and the theoretical models they wanted to use. Initially, most economists were so confident of the reliability of the received
theory of rational choice that they attributed all these problems to inadequate survey methods; these methods, it was assumed, were failing to
elicit "true" preferences. We now know that anomalies found in stated
preference data often have the same form as experimental exhibits such
as the endowment effect, and that the same anomalies appear in at least
some economic behavior in the field. These similarities between survey,

experiment, and field have allowed experimental methods to be used to understand the causes of anomalies in stated preference data and to assist in survey design.[4] That this is possible is further evidence of the external validity of economics experiments.

8.3   Has Experimental Economics Had a Positive Impact on Wider Economics?

Our short answer to this third question is "Yes." We have no doubt that, on balance, the growth of experimental economics has been a good thing for economics as a whole.

Current trends strongly suggest that experimental economics is gradually becoming an accepted and even conventional tool of mainstream economics, as econometrics has long been. So far, at least, it shows few signs of becoming a distinct subdiscipline in the sense that economic history is now. One piece of evidence that supports this claim is the fact that, although there has been an explosion of journal articles using experimental methods, only one significant specialist journal, *Experimental Economics*, has been launched. Instead, reports of experimental research have become standard fare in the leading general journals, and in the journals of many topic-related branches of economics, such as public economics, environmental economics, financial economics, and industrial economics.

In the preceding section we argued that experimental research has made significant contributions to the understanding of economic behavior. Having said that, and now having said that experimental economics is developing as an integral part of economics rather than as a subdiscipline, we have effectively declared our judgment that experimental methods have been good for economics. But we want to end by making the less tangible claim that developments in experimental economics are part of what may turn out to be a fundamental—and, for us, welcome—shift in the way economists think about the world.

To see the nature of this shift, one has to look back to the way economics was done in the 1970s and early 1980s—the period just before experimental methods began to be widely used. Obviously, any simple characterization of a whole discipline will be a caricature; but we suggest that the following description captures core features of the methodology of economics, and of the self-perceptions of economists, in that era. As

---

[4] Sugden (1999) reviews the anomalies that have been found in the data generated by stated preference surveys, and relates these to experimentally observed regularities in decision-making behavior.

we pointed out in chapter 4, economic theorists of that time had the aspiration of creating a unified theory of rational choice. Many of the most highly regarded achievements of economics took the form of extensions of the domain of rational-choice theorizing to new fields (uncertainty, macroeconomic expectations, information, collective choice, the refinement of Nash equilibrium, and so on). Theories were prized for the mathematical elegance with which general implications were derived from formally simple axioms. Questions about the credibility of those axioms as representations of the motivations and reasoning of real human beings were brushed aside. These features of economics cohered with two perceptions of scientific hierarchy. The first was the idea of a separation between "pure" and "applied" science, with the underlying (and usually unspoken) thought that a pure science of economics could be constructed by a priori analysis from self-evident axioms. Configuring the pure theory to fit empirical data was one of the tasks of applied economics, but it was not expected that applied economics might discover anything that might require the pure theory to be changed. The second perceived hierarchy (of course, as perceived by economists) was between economics and the other social sciences. There was an expectation—often called "imperialism" by noneconomists—that the domain of economic theory would gradually expand to include the former subject matter of other disciplines. The thought that there might be transfers of ideas in the opposite direction—that the explanatory principles of other disciplines might be put to use in economics—was not one to be taken seriously.

These ways of thinking in economics have certainly not died out. For example, the common idea (expressed in claim 3) that one has to "get the payoffs right" before claiming to test game theory illustrates the continuing allure of the idea that pure and applied theory stand in a hierarchical relationship, so that questions about how the concept of "payoff" is to be interpreted in concrete situations are not the concern of game theory in its pure form. But we think we detect a broadening out of economics, of which the development of experimental economics is both a symptom and a cause.

Experimental economics has focused attention on questions that needed to be asked but that economists previously felt able to ignore. Most obviously, it has opened up questions about the status of rationality assumptions. Why do economists define "rationality" in terms of the particular axioms they do, rather than others? Having found, for example, experimental evidence that individuals' choices systematically contravene the Independence and Transitivity axioms, can we still be confident in asserting that those axioms are principles of rationality? If we had a better understanding of the psychological motivation that lies behind this initially surprising behavior, might we have to question our a priori account of rationality? Or suppose we accept that some part of the conventional model of rationality is indeed normatively valid, and that experimentally observed deviations are the result of errors. What grounds do we have for assuming that similar errors will not be made by individuals in the situations that economic theory purports to explain? What mechanisms lead to the correction of error? Do they operate with equal force throughout the traditional domain of economic theory? Do they also operate in the domains of those other disciplines that economists might hope to colonize? And so on. Crucially, these kinds of questions cannot be answered by purely a priori methods: they require empirical investigation. And they raise issues that lie within the domain of competence of other disciplines, such as psychology.

Experimental economics has forced economists to take serious account of empirical evidence about behavior at the level of the individual and the small group. It has provided a methodology for investigating, testing hypotheses about, and identifying regularities within such behavior. In doing so, it has undercut many of the methodological and rhetorical strategies by which economists were previously able to brush aside charges of "unrealism."[5] Recall Ariel Rubinstein's suggestion (discussed in chapter 1) that, when appraising a putative "consideration" that might impact on choice behavior, a good theorist can test its significance by intuition—by "feeling" it to be true or false. Experimental research has exposed the limitations of this methodology by repeatedly discovering that the firmly held intuitions of theorists are mistaken. And that should not be surprising. What we call "scientific intuition" is surely the product of experience of dealing with the subject matter of one's science. If you want a sound judgment about the likely truth or falsity of an as-yet-unproved theorem, or about what approach to proving a particular result is most likely to work, it is a good idea to ask an experienced mathematical theorist for his intuitions. But if the question is about the psychology of actual human decision makers, the intuitions of someone who spends her time conducting psychological experiments are likely to be more reliable.

Our sense is that in economics, the idea of a distinction between a priori "pure" theory and empirically based "application" is in retreat. Economists are becoming more broad-minded and enterprising about

---

[5] The increasing availability of individual-level field data, and of the computing power to make their econometric analysis feasible, is having a parallel effect. These developments in econometrics have been roughly contemporary with the growth of experimental economics.

the kinds of assumptions they are willing to entertain, and are taking more account of empirical evidence when they judge the credibility and usefulness of alternative assumptions. Perhaps they are still too conservative. For example, as we suggested in chapter 3, the agenda of decision theory may still be influenced too much by a hard core of presuppositions that reflect a priori ideas about rationality. Or is economics now *too* adventurous? More cautious members of the economics profession often express unease about some of the radical approaches to theorizing that are now associated with experimental economics. For example, there is much controversy about the developing field of *neuroeconomics*— the application to economics of the theoretical ideas and experimental research methods of neuroscience. For its proponents, neuroeconomics is a natural extension of behavioral economics, drawing on one of the most exciting and rapidly developing branches of psychology. For its critics, it is the *reductio ad absurdum* of the behavioral approach and evidence (if more were needed) of the lengths to which economists will go to promote their self-image as "real" scientists.[6] Another example: some economists are proposing wide-ranging hypotheses about the effects of natural selection on human psychology, using observations of nonselfish behavior in economics experiments as a significant part of their supporting evidence. Is this a sign that experimental economics is capable of discovering previously unknown principles of psychology that played a significant role in the evolutionary history of mankind? Or is it another instance of overreaching imperialism on the part of economics?[7] We do not take any collective view about the substantive merits or demerits of these particular developments. But we do welcome the changes in the discipline that have made it legitimate for economists to propose such radical hypotheses, to support them by appeal to experimental evidence, and to subject them to experimental test.

We hope that what we are seeing is the evolution of economics in the direction of a more genuinely empirical science. Such a science is likely to be less monolithic than the economics of the middle years of the last century. Because its theories will have been adapted to be compatible with

---

[6] For reviews of developments in neuroeconomics, written by practitioners, see Camerer et al. (2004b, 2005). Gul and Pesendorfer (2008) is probably the best-known critique. For further references, see footnote 1 on page 46.

[7] Gintis et al. (2005) explore the hypothesis that "strong reciprocity" (defined to include a motivation to engage in costly punishment of individuals who violate norms) is a hardwired property of human psychology that plays a fundamental role in social organization. Strong reciprocity was first proposed as an explanation of experimental observations of costly punishment. (Illustration 5 in chapter 1 of this book is an example.) Bacharach (2006) proposes an analogous hypothesis, but with "team reasoning" as the fundamental property of human psychology. The supporting evidence cited by Bacharach includes evidence from experimental games.

observed regularities in human behavior, rather than by deduction from a priori principles, we should expect less theoretical unity across the discipline as a whole and greater openness to ideas from other disciplines. For the same reason, we should expect a less hierarchical approach to theory building. The overall shape of the theory will be determined less by the inclinations and intuitions of practitioners of pure theory and more by the combined efforts of researchers investigating specific problems. Our sense is that this is the direction in which economics is moving. Is this progress? We think so.

References

Abraham, K. G., and J. C. Haltiwanger. 1995. Real wages and the business cycle. *Journal of Economic Literature* 33:1215-65.

Adair, J. G. 1984. The Hawthorne effect: a reconsideration of the methodological artefact. *Journal of Applied Psychology* 69:334-45.

Akerlof, G. A. 1982. Labour contracts as partial gift exchange. *Quarterly Journal of Economics* 97:543-69.

Akerlof, G. A., and J. L. Yellen. 1985a. A near-rational model of the business cycle with wage and price inertia. *Quarterly Journal of Economics* 100:823-38.

——. 1985b. Can small deviations from rationality make significant differences to economic equilibria? *American Economic Review* 75:708-20.

Allais, M. 1953. Le comportement de l'homme rationnel devant le risque: critique des postulats et axiomes de l'école américaine. *Econometrica* 21:503-46.

——. 1979. The foundations of a positive theory of choice involving risk and a criticism of the postulates and axioms of the American school. In *Expected Utility Hypotheses and the Allais Paradox* (ed. M. Allais and O. Hagen), pp. 27-145. Dordrecht: Reidl. (Paper first published in 1953 as "Fondements d'une théorie positive des choix comportant un risque et critique des postulats et axiomes de l'école américaine." In *Econometrie* pp. 257-332. Colloques Internationaux du Centre National de la Recherche Scientifique, volume 40. Paris: Centre National de la Recherche Scientifique.)

Allingham, M. G., and A. Sandmo. 1972. Income tax evasion: a theoretical analysis. *Journal of Public Economics* 1:323-38.

Alm, J., G. H. McClelland, and W. D. Schulze. 1992. Why do people pay taxes? *Journal of Public Economics* 48:21-38.

Andersen, S., G. W. Harrison, M. I. Lau, and E. E. Rutström. 2006a. Dynamic choice behavior in a natural experiment. Working Paper 06-10, College of Business Administration, University of Central Florida.

——. 2006b. Dual criteria decisions. Working Paper 06-11, College of Business Administration, University of Central Florida.

——. 2007. Risk aversion in game shows. In *Risk Aversion in Experiments* (ed. J. C. Cox and G. W. Harrison). Research in Experimental Economics, volume 12. Greenwich, CT: JAI Press.

Andreoni, J. 1988. Why free ride? Strategies and learning in public goods experiments. *Journal of Public Economics* 37:291-304.

——. 1995. Cooperation in public-goods experiments: kindness or confusion? *American Economic Review* 85:891-905.

Apesteguia, J., S. Huck, and J. Oechssler. 2007. Imitation—theory and experimental evidence. *Journal of Economic Theory* 136:217-35.

Ariely, D., G. Loewenstein, and D. Prelec. 2003. "Coherent arbitrariness": stable demand curves without stable preferences. *Quarterly Journal of Economics* 118:73-105.

Axelrod, R. 1984. *The Evolution of Cooperation.* New York: Basic Books.

Bacharach, M. O. L. 1993. Variable universe games. In *Frontiers of Game Theory* (ed. K. G. Binmore, A. Kirman, and P. Tani). Cambridge, MA: MIT Press.

———. 2006. *Beyond Individual Choice: Teams and Frames in Game Theory* (ed. N. Gold and R. Sugden). Princeton University Press.

Ball, S., C. Eckel, P. J. Grossman, and W. Zame. 2001. Status in markets. *Quarterly Journal of Economics* 116:161–88.

Ballinger, T. P., and N. T. Wilcox. 1997. Decisions, error and heterogeneity. *Economic Journal* 107: 1090–105.

Barberis, N., and R. H. Thaler. 2003. A survey of behavioral finance. In *Handbook of the Economics of Finance* (ed. G. Constantinides, M. Harris, and R. M. Stulz), pp. 1053–128, Elsevier.

Bardsley, N. 2000. Control without deception: individual behaviour in free-riding experiments revisited. *Experimental Economics* 3:215–40.

———. 2005. Experimental economics and the artificiality of alteration. *Journal of Economic Methodology* 12:239–53.

———. 2008. Dictator game giving: altruism or artefact? *Experimental Economics* 11:122–33.

Bardsley, N., and P. G. Moffatt. 2007. The experimetrics of public goods: inferring motivations from contributions. *Theory and Decision* 62:161–93.

Bardsley, N., and R. Sugden. 2006. Human nature and sociality. In *Handbook of Altruism, Gift Giving and Reciprocity* (ed. S. Kolm and J. M. Ythier), volume 1, pp. 731–68. Elsevier.

Bar-Hillel, M. 1980. The base-rate fallacy in probability judgments. *Acta Psychologica* 44:211–33.

Barkan, R., and J. R. Busemeyer. 1999. Changing plans: dynamic inconsistency and the effect of experience on the reference point. *Psychonomic Bulletin and Review* 6:547–54.

Basu, K. 1994. The traveller's dilemma: paradoxes of rationality in game theory. *American Economic Review* 84:391–95.

Bateman, I., A. Munro, B. Rhodes, C. Starmer, and R. Sugden. 1997. A test of the theory of reference-dependent preferences. *Quarterly Journal of Economics* 112:479–505.

Bateman, I., B. Day, G. Loomes, and R. Sugden. 2006. Ranking versus choice in the elicitation of preferences. Working Paper, University of East Anglia.

Bateman, I., S. Dent, E. Peters, P. Slovic, and C. Starmer. 2007. The affect heuristic and the attractiveness of simple gambles. *Journal of Behavioral Decision Making* 20:365–80.

Battalio, R. C., J. H. Kagel, H. Rachlin, and L. Green. 1981. Commodity-choice behavior with pigeons as subjects. *Journal of Political Economy* 89:67–91.

Bazerman, M. H., and W. F. Samuelson. 1983. I won the auction, but don't want the prize. *Journal of Conflict Resolution* 27:618–34.

Beattie, J., and G. Loomes. 1997. The impact of incentives upon risky choice experiments. *Journal of Risk and Uncertainty* 14:149–62.

Becker, G., M. DeGroot, and J. Marschak. 1963. Stochastic models of choice behaviour. *Behavioral Science* 8:41–55.

———. 1964. Measuring utility by a single-response sequential method. *Behavioral Science* 9:226–32.

Bell, D. 1982. Regret in decision making under uncertainty. *Operations Research* 30:961–81.

Bell, D. 1985. Disappointment in decision making under uncertainty. *Operations Research* 33:1–27.

Bellomo, N., M. Delitala, and V. Coscia. 2002. On the mathematical theory of vehicular traffic flow. I. Fluid dynamic and kinetic modelling. *Mathematical Models and Methods in Applied Sciences* 12:1801–43.

Berg, J. E., J. W. Dickhaut, and J. R. O'Brien. 1985. Preference reversal and arbitrage. In *Research in Experimental Economics* (ed. V. L. Smith), volume 3, pp. 31–72. Greenwich, CT: JAI Press.

Berg, J. E., J. W. Dickhaut, and K. McCabe. 1995. Trust, reciprocity, and social history. *Games and Economic Behavior* 10:122–42.

Bern, D. J. 1972. Self-perception theory. In *Advances in Experimental Social Psychology* (ed. L. Berkowitz), volume 6. Academic Press.

Bernheim, B. D. 2008. Neuroeconomics: a sober (but hopeful) assessment. Working Paper 13954, National Bureau of Economic Research.

Bernoulli, D. 1738. Specimen theoriae novae de mensura sortis. *Proceedings of the St. Petersburg Imperial Academy of Sciences* 5:175–92. (See the 1954 translation, Exposition of a new theory on the measurement of risk (transl. from Latin by L. Sommer), *Econometrica* 22:23–36.)

Bewley, T. 2004. Fairness, reciprocity and gift exchange. Discussion Paper 1137, Institute for the Study of Labour (IZA), Bonn.

Binmore, K. G. 1994. *Game Theory and the Social Contract. Volume I: Playing Fair.* Cambridge, MA: MIT Press.

——. 1999. Why experiment in economics? *Economic Journal* 109:F16–24.

——. 2007. *Does Game Theory Work? The Bargaining Challenge.* Cambridge, MA: MIT Press.

Binmore, K. G., and P. Klemperer. 2002. The biggest auction ever: the sale of the British 3G telecom licences. *Economic Journal* 112:C74–96.

Binmore, K. G., and A. Shaked. 2007. Experimental economics: science or what? Working Paper 263, Centre for Economic Learning and Social Evolution, University College London. (Available at http://else.econ.ucl.ac.uk/papers/uploaded/263.pdf, posted June 18, 2007.)

Binmore, K. G., A. Shaked, and J. Sutton. 1985. Testing noncooperative bargaining theory: a preliminary study. *American Economic Review* 75:1178–80.

Binmore, K. G., J. Swierzbinski, and C. Proulx. 2001. Does minimax work? An experimental study. *Economic Journal* 111:445–65.

Binmore, K. G., J. McCarthy, G. Ponti, L. Samuelson, and A. Shaked. 2002. A backward induction experiment. *Journal of Economic Theory* 87:48–88.

Bird, A. 1998. *Philosophy of Science.* Abingdon, U.K.: Routledge.

Birnbaum, M. H., and L. A. Thompson. 1996. Violations of monotonicity in choices between gambles and certain cash. *American Journal of Psychology* 109:501–23.

Blaug, M. 1992. *The Methodology of Economics: Or How Economists Explain*, 2nd edn. Cambridge University Press.

——. 1994. Why I am not a constructivist, or confessions of an unrepentant Popperian. In *New Directions in Economic Methodology* (ed. R. E. Backhouse). London: Routledge.

Blavatskyy, P. R. 2007. Stochastic expected utility theory. *Journal of Risk and Uncertainty* 34:259–86.

Blount, S., and M. H. Bazerman. 1996. The inconsistent evaluation of absolute versus comparative payoffs in labor supply and bargaining. *Journal of Economic Behavior and Organization* 30:227–40.

Bohm, P., J. Linden, and J. Sonnegard. 1997. Eliciting reservation prices: Becker-De Groot-Marschak mechanisms versus markets. *Economic Journal* 107:1079-89.

Bolton, G. E. 1998. Bargaining and dilemma games: from laboratory data towards theoretical synthesis. *Experimental Economics* 1:257-81.

Bolton, G. E., and A. Ockenfels. 2000. ERC: A theory of equity, reciprocity and competition. *American Economic Review* 90:166-93.

Bolton, G. E., and R. Zwick. 1995. Anonymity versus punishment in ultimatum bargaining. *Games and Economic Behavior* 10:95-121.

Bolton, G. E., J. Brandts, and A. Ockenfels. 1998. Measuring motivations for the reciprocal responses observed in a simple dilemma game. *Experimental Economics* 1:207-19.

Bolton, G. E., K. Chatterjee, and K. L. McGinn. 2003. How communication links influence coalition bargaining: a laboratory investigation. *Management Science* 49:583-98.

Bone, J. D., J. D. Hey, and J. R. Suckling. 1999. Are groups more consistent than individuals? *Journal of Risk and Uncertainty* 8:63-81.

——. 2003. Do people plan ahead? *Applied Economics Letters* 10:277-80.

——. 2009. Do people plan? *Experimental Economics* 12:12-25.

Bonetti, S. 1998. Experimental economics and deception. *Journal of Economic Psychology.* 19:377-95.

Bornstein, B. H. 1999. The ecological validity of jury simulations: Is the jury still out? *Law and Human Behavior* 23:1, 75-91.

Bornstein, B. H., and A. C. Emler. 2001. Rationality in medical decision making: a review of the literature on doctors' decision-making biases. *Journal of Evaluation in Clinical Practice* 7:97-107.

Boumans, M. 2003. How to design Galilean fall experiments in economics. *Philosophy of Science* 70:308-29.

Boyd, R. 1983. On the current status of the issue of scientific realism. *Erkenntnis* 19:45-90.

Braga, J., and C. Starmer. 2005. Preference anomalies, preference elicitation and the discovered preference hypothesis. *Environmental & Resource Economics* 32:55-89.

Braga, J., S. J. Humphrey, and C. Starmer. 2009. Market experience eliminates some anomalies—and creates new ones. *European Economic Review* 53:410-16.

Brandts, J., and G. Charness. 2000. Hot vs. cold: Sequential responses in simple experimental games. *Experimental Economics* 2:227-38.

Brandts, J., and A. Schram. 2001. Cooperation and noise in public goods experiments: applying the contribution function approach. *Journal of Public Economics* 79:399-427.

Bresnahan, T. 1981. Duopoly models with consistent conjectures. *American Economic Review* 71:934-45.

Brosig, J., J. Weimann, and Y. Chun-Lei. 2003. The hot versus cold effect in a simple bargaining experiment. *Experimental Economics* 6:75-90.

Bruni, L., and R. Sugden. 2007. The road not taken: how psychology was removed from economics, and how it might be brought back. *Economic Journal* 117:146-73.

Bryan, J. H., and M. A. Test. 1967. Models and helping: naturalistic studies in aiding. *Journal of Personality and Social Psychology* 6:400-407.

Buchan, N., R. Croson, and R. Dawes. 2002. Swift neighbours and persistent strangers: a cross-cultural investigation of trust and reciprocity in social exchange. *American Journal of Sociology* 108:168–206.

Burlando, R., and F. Guala. 2005. Heterogeneous agents in public good experiments. *Experimental Economics* 8:35–54.

Burns, P. 1985. Experience and decision making: a comparison of students and businessmen in a simulated progressive auction. In *Research in Experimental Economics* (ed. V. L. Smith), volume 3, pp. 139–57. London: JAI Press.

Buschena, D., and D. Zilberman. 2000. Generalized expected utility, heteroscedastic error, and path dependence in risky choice. *Journal of Risk and Uncertainty* 20:67–88.

Busemeyer, J. R., and J. T. Townsend. 1993. Decision field theory: a dynamic-cognitive approach to decision making. *Psychological Review,* 100:432–59.

Busemeyer, J. R., E. Weg, R. Barkan, X. Li, and Z. Ma. 2000. Dynamic consequential consistency of choices between paths of decision trees. *Journal of Experimental Psychology: General* 129:530–45.

Butler, D., and G. Loomes. 2007. Imprecision as an account of the preference reversal phenomenon. *American Economic Review* 97:277–98.

Caldwell, B. 1984. *Beyond Positivism: Economic Methodology in the Twentieth Century,* 2nd edn. London: George Allen & Unwin.

Camerer, C. F. 1989. An experimental test of several generalized utility theories. *Journal of Risk and Uncertainty* 2:61–104.

——. 1995. Individual decision-making. In *The Handbook of Experimental Economics* (ed. J. Kagel and A. Roth). Princeton University Press.

——. 2000. Prospect theory in the wild: evidence from the field. In *Choices, Values and Frames* (ed. D. Kahneman and A. Tversky). Cambridge University Press and Russell Sage Foundation.

——. 2003. *Behavioral Game Theory: Experiments in Strategic Interaction.* Princeton University Press.

——. 2007. Neuroeconomics: using neuroscience to make economic predictions. *Economic Journal* 117:C26–42.

Camerer, C. F., and T. H. Ho. 1999. Experience-weighted attraction learning in normal form games. *Econometrica* 67:827–74.

Camerer, C. F., and R. M. Hogarth. 1999. The effects of financial incentives in experiments: a review and capital–labor–production framework. *Journal of Risk and Uncertainty* 19:7–42.

Camerer, C. F., and R. H. Thaler. 1995. Anomalies: ultimatums, dictators and manners. *Journal of Economic Perspectives* 9:209–20.

Camerer, C. F., T. H. Ho, and J. K. Chong. 2004a. A cognitive hierarchy model of one-shot games. *Quarterly Journal of Economics* 119:861–98.

Camerer, C. F., G. Loewenstein, and D. Prelec. 2004b. Neuroeconomics: why economics needs brains. *Scandinavian Journal of Economics* 106:555–79.

Camerer, C. F., G. Loewenstein, and M. Rabin (eds). 2004c. *Advances in Behavioral Economics.* Princeton University Press.

Camerer, C. F., G. Loewenstein, and D. Prelec. 2005. Neuroeconomics: how neuroscience can inform economics. *Journal of Economic Literature* 43:9–64.

Capen, E. C., R. V. Clapp, and W. M. Campbell. 1971. Competitive bidding in high-risk situations. *Journal of Petroleum Technology* 23:641–53.

Caplin, A., and A. Schotter (eds). 2008. *The Foundations of Positive and Normative Economics: a Handbook.* Oxford University Press.

Cappelen, A., E. Sorensen, and B. Tungodden. 2005. Responsible for what? An experimental approach to fairness and responsibility. Working Paper, Norwegian School of Economics and Business Administration.

Carlton, D. W., and J. M. Perloff. 2005. *Modern Industrial Organization*, 4th edn. Pearson Addison Wesley.

Cartwright, N. 1983. *How the Laws of Physics Lie.* Oxford University Press.

———. 1989. *Nature's Capacities and their Measurement.* Oxford University Press.

———. 2007. The vanity of rigour in economics: theoretical models and Galilean experiments. In *Hunting Causes and Using Them: Approaches in Philosophy and Economics* (ed. N. Cartwright). Cambridge University Press.

Castellan, N. J. 1969. Effect of change of payoff in probability learning. *Journal of Experimental Psychology* 79:178-82.

Chalmers, A. F. 1993. So the laws of physics needn't lie. *Australasian Journal of Philosophy* 71:196-205.

———. 1999. *What Is This Thing Called Science?* Maidenhead and New York: Open University Press.

Chamberlin, E. 1948. An experimental imperfect market. *Journal of Political Economy* 56:95-108.

Charness, G., and M. Rabin. 2002. Understanding social preferences with simple tests. *Quarterly Journal of Economics* 117:817-69.

Charness, G., E. Karni, and D. Levin. 2007. Individual and group decision making under risk: an experimental study of Bayesian updating and violations of first-order stochastic dominance. *Journal of Risk and Uncertainty* 35:129-48.

Chu, Y.-P., and R.-L. Chu. 1990. The subsidence of preference reversals in simplified and marketlike experimental settings: a note. *American Economic Review* 80:902-11.

Clark, A. E., P. Frijters, and M. A. Shields. 2008. Relative income, happiness, and utility: an explanation for the Easterlin paradox and other puzzles. *Journal of Economic Literature* 46:95-144.

Clarke, S. 1995. The lies remain the same. A reply to Chalmers. *Australasian Journal of Philosophy* 73:152-55.

Conte, A., P. G. Moffatt, F. Botti, D. T. Di Cagno, and C. D'Ippoliti. 2008. A test of the rational expectations hypothesis using data from a natural experiment. Working Paper, Quaderni DPTEA no. 146, Department of Economics, LUISS Guido Carli, Rome.

Cookson, R. 2000. Framing effects in public goods experiments. *Experimental Economics* 3:55-79.

Costa-Gomez, M., V. P. Crawford, and B. Broseta. 2001. Cognition and behavior in normal-form games: an experimental study. *Econometrica* 69:1193-235.

Cox, J. C. 2004. How to identify trust and reciprocity. *Games and Economic Behavior* 46:260-81.

Cox, J. C., and D. M. Grether. 1996. The preference reversal phenomenon: response mode, markets and incentives. *Economic Theory* 7:381-405.

Crawford, V. P. 2008. Lookups as the windows of the strategic soul. In *The Foundations of Positive and Normative Economics: A Handbook* (ed. A. Caplin and A. Schotter). Oxford University Press.

Cross, J. G. 1980. Some comments on the papers by Kagel and Battalio and by Smith. In *Evaluation of Econometric Models* (ed. J. Kmenta and J. Ramsey). New York University Press.

Cubitt, R. P. 2005. Experiments and the domain of economic theory. *Journal of Economic Methodology* 12:197–210.

Cubitt, R. P., and R. Sugden. 2001a. Dynamic decision-making under uncertainty: an experimental investigation of choices between accumulator gambles. *Journal of Risk and Uncertainty* 22:103–28.

——. 2001b. On money pumps. *Games and Economic Behavior* 37:121–60.

Cubitt, R. P., C. Starmer, and R. Sugden. 1998a. On the validity of the random lottery incentive system. *Experimental Economics* 1:115–31.

——. 1998b. Dynamic choice and the common ratio effect: an experimental investigation. *Economic Journal* 108:1362–80.

——. 2001. Discovered preferences and the experimental evidence of violations of expected utility theory. *Journal of Economic Methodology* 8:385–414.

Cubitt, R. P., A. Munro, and C. Starmer. 2004a. Testing explanations of preference reversal. *Economic Journal* 114:709–26.

Cubitt, R. P., C. Starmer, and R. Sugden. 2004b. Dynamic decisions under uncertainty: some recent evidence from economics and psychology. In *The Psychology of Economic Decisions. Volume II: Reasons and Choices* (ed. I. Brocas and J. D. Carrillo). Oxford University Press/CEPR.

Davidson, D., and J. Marschak. 1959. Experimental tests of a stochastic decision theory. In *Measurement: Definitions and Theories* (ed. C. West Churchman and P. Ratoosh), pp. 233–69. New York: Wiley.

Davidson, D., P. Suppes, and S. Siegel. 1957. *Decision Making: An Experimental Approach.* Stanford, CA: Stanford University Press.

Davis, D. D., and C. A. Holt. 1993. *Experimental Economics.* Princeton University Press.

Deci, E. L., R. Koestner, and R. M. Ryan. 1999. A meta-analytic review of experiments examining the effects of extrinsic rewards on intrinsic motivation. *Psychological Bulletin* 125:627–68.

DellaVigna, S. 2007. Psychology and economics: evidence from the field. Working Paper 13420, National Bureau of Economic Research.

De Marchi, N. 1991. Introduction: rethinking Lakatos. In *Appraising Economic Theories: Studies in the Methodology of Research Programmes* (ed. N. De Marchi and M. Blaug). Cheltenham, U.K.: Edward Elgar.

De Marchi, N., and M. Blaug (eds). 1991. *Appraising Economic Theories: Studies in the Methodology of Research Programmes.* Cheltenham, U.K.: Edward Elgar.

Diamond, P., and H. Vartiainen (eds). 2007. *Behavioral Economics and Its Applications.* Princeton University Press.

Dilman, I. 1996. Science and psychology. In *Verstehen and Human Understanding* (ed. A. O'Hear). Cambridge University Press.

Di Tella, R., R. MacCulloch, and A. J. Oswald. 2001. Preferences over inflation and unemployment: evidence from surveys of happiness. *American Economic Review* 91:335–41.

Dohmen, T., and A. Falk. 2006. Performance pay and multi-dimensional sorting: productivity, preferences and gender. Discussion Paper 2001, Institute for the Study of Labour (IZA), Bonn.

Duflo, E. 2006. Field experiments in development economics. Working Paper, Massachusetts Institute of Technology.

Dufwenberg, M., and G. Kirchsteiger. 2004. A theory of sequential reciprocity. *Games and Economic Behavior* 47:268–98.

Duhem, P. 1954. *The Aim and Structure of Physical Theory* (transl. P. P. Wiener). Princeton University Press. (Originally published in French by Chevalier et Rivière in 1906.)

Edgeworth, F. Y. 1881. *Mathematical Psychics.* (See the 1967 Kelley edition.)

Ellison, G. 2008. Bounded rationality in industrial organisation. In *Advances in Economics and Econometrics: Theory and Applications, Ninth World Congress of the Econometric Society* (ed. R. Blundell, W. Newey, and T. Persson), volume 2. Cambridge University Press.

Ellsberg, D. 1961. Risk, ambiguity, and the Savage axioms. *Quarterly Journal of Economics* 75:643–69.

Erev, I., and A. E. Roth. 1998. Predicting how people play games: reinforcement learning in experimental games with unique mixed strategy equilibria. *American Economic Review* 88:848–81.

Evans, D. A. 1997. The role of markets in reducing expected utility violations. *Journal of Political Economy* 105:622–36.

Falk, A., E. Fehr, and U. Fischbacher. 2003. On the nature of fair behavior. *Economic Enquiry* 41:20–26.

———. 2008. Testing theories of fairness—intentions matter. *Games and Economic Behavior* 62:287–303.

Farquhar, P. H. 1984. Utility assessment methods. *Management Science* 30:1283–300.

Fechner, G. T. 1860. *Elemente de Pyschophysik.* Amsterdam: Bonset. (Reprinted in 1966 by Holt, Rinehart and Winston, New York.)

Fehr, E., and A. Falk. 2002. Psychological foundations of incentives. *European Economic Review* 46:687–724.

Fehr, E., and U. Fischbacher. 2002. Why social preferences matter—the impact of non-selfish motives on competition, cooperation and incentives. *Economic Journal* 112:C1–33.

Fehr, E., and S. Gächter. 2000. Cooperation and punishment in public goods experiments. *American Economic Review* 90:980–94.

Fehr, E., and K. M. Schmidt. 1999. A theory of fairness, competition and cooperation. *Quarterly Journal of Economics* 114:817–68.

———. 2003. Theories of fairness and reciprocity: evidence and economic applications. In *Advances in Economics and Econometrics: Theory and Applications; Eighth World Congress of the Econometric Society* (ed. M. Dewatripont, L. P. Hansen and S. J. Turnovsky), volume 1. Cambridge University Press.

Fehr, E., and J. R. Tyran. 2005. Individual learning and aggregate outcomes. *Journal of Economic Perspectives* 19:43–67.

Fehr, E., G. Kirchsteiger, and A. Riedl. 1993. Does fairness prevent market clearing? An experimental investigation. *Quarterly Journal of Economics* 108:437–59.

Festinger, L., and J. M. Carlsmith. 1959. Cognitive consequences of forced compliance. *Journal of Abnormal and Social Psychology* 58:203–11.

Feyerabend, P. 1975. *Against Method: Outline of an Anarchistic Theory of Knowledge.* London: New Left Books.

Fischbacher, U. 2007. Z-tree: Zurich toolbox for ready-made economic experiments. *Experimental Economics* 10:171–78.

Fischbacher, U., and S. Gächter. 2006. Heterogeneous social preferences and the dynamics of free riding in public goods. CeDEx Discussion Paper 2006-1, University of Nottingham.

Fischbacher, U., and S. Gächter. Forthcoming. Social preferences, beliefs, and the dynamics of free riding in public good experiments. *American Economic Review*, in press.

Fischbacher, U., S. Gächter, and E. Fehr. 2001. Are people conditionally cooperative? Evidence from a public goods experiment. *Economics Letters* 71: 397–404.

Fishburn, P. C. 1978. On Handa's "New theory of cardinal utility" and the maximization of expected return. *Journal of Political Economy* 86:321–24.

——. 1982. Nontransitive measurable utility. *Journal of Mathematical Psychology* 26:31–67.

Forsythe, R., R. B. Myerson, T. A. Rietz, and R. J. Weber. 1993. An experiment on coordination in multi-candidate elections: the importance of polls and election histories. *Social Choice and Welfare* 10:223–47.

Forsythe, R., J. Horowitz, N. E. Savin, and M. Sefton. 1994. Fairness in simple bargaining experiments. *Games and Economic Behavior* 6:347–69.

Frey, B. S. 1997. *Not Just for the Money: An Economic Theory of Personal Motivation.* Cheltenham, U.K.: Edward Elgar.

Frey, B. S., and F. Oberholzer-Gee. 1997. The cost of price incentives: an empirical analysis of motivation crowding-out. *American Economic Review* 87:746–55.

Frey, B. S., and A. Stutzer. 2002. *Happiness & Economics: How the Economy and Institutions Affect Human Well-Being.* Princeton University Press.

——. 2006. Environmental morale and motivation. Working Paper 288, Institute for Empirical Research in Economics, University of Zurich.

Frey, B. S., A. Stutzer, M. Benz, S. Meier, S. Luechinger, and C. Benesch. 2008. *Happiness: A Revolution in Economics.* Cambridge, MA: MIT Press.

Friedman, M. 1953. The methodology of positive economics. In *Essays in Positive Economics*, pp. 3–43. Chicago University Press.

Gafni, A. 2005. The standard gamble technique. In *Encyclopaedia of Biostatistics.* New York: Wiley.

Garber, P. M. 2000. *Famous First Bubbles: The Fundamentals of Early Manias.* Cambridge, MA: MIT Press.

Garnweidner, E. 1994. *Mushrooms and Toadstools of Britain and Europe* (transl. M. Shaffer-Fehre). London: HarperCollins.

Gibbard, A., and H. Varian. 1978. Economic models. *Journal of Philosophy* 75: 664–77.

Gintis, H., S. Bowles, R. Boyd, and E. Fehr (eds). 2005. *Moral Sentiments and Material Interests.* Cambridge, MA: MIT Press.

Gjerstad, S., and J. M. Shachat. 2007. Individual rationality and market efficiency. Working Paper 1204, Krannert Graduate School of Management, Purdue University.

Gneezy, U., and J. A. List. 2006. Putting behavioral economics to work: testing for gift exchange in labor markets using field experiments. *Econometrica* 74: 1365–84.

Gneezy, U., and A. Rustichini. 2000a. Pay enough or don't pay at all. *Quarterly Journal of Economics* 115:791–810.

——. 2000b. A fine is a price. *Journal of Legal Studies* 29:1–17.

Gode, D. K., and S. Sunder. 1993. Allocative efficiency of markets with zero-intelligence traders: markets as a partial substitute for individual rationality. *Journal of Political Economy* 101:119–37.

Goeree, J., and C. A. Holt. 2001. Ten little treasures of game theory and ten intuitive contradictions. *American Economic Review* 91:1402-23.

Goeree, J., C. A. Holt, and T. Palfrey. 2003. Risk averse behavior in generalized matching pennies games. *Games and Economic Behavior* 45:97-113.

Green, K. C. 2002. Forecasting decisions in conflict situations: a comparison of game theory, role-playing and unaided judgement. *International Journal of Forecasting* 18:321-44.

Greenwood, J. D. 1982. On the relation between laboratory experiments and social behaviour: causal explanation and generalisation. *Journal of the Theory of Social Behaviour* 12:225-49.

———. 1990. The social constitution of action: objectivity and explanation. *Philosophy of the Social Sciences* 20:195-207.

Grether, D. M., and C. R. Plott. 1979. Economic theory of choice and the preference reversal phenomenon. *American Economic Review* 69:623-38.

Grüne-Yanoff, T., and P. Schweinzer. 2008. The roles of stories in applying game theory. *Journal of Economic Methodology* 15:131-46.

Guala, F. 1998. Experiments as mediators in the non-laboratory sciences. *Philosophica* 62:57-75.

———. 2001. Building economic machines: the FCC auctions. *Studies in the History and Philosophy of Science* 32:453-77.

———. 2002. On the scope of experiments in economics: comments on Siakantaris. *Cambridge Journal of Economics* 26:261-67.

———. 2005a. *The Methodology of Experimental Economics*. Cambridge University Press.

———. 2005b. Economics in the laboratory: completeness versus testability. *Journal of Economic Methodology* 12:185-97.

———. 2006. Has game theory been refuted? *Journal of Philosophy* 103:239-63.

Gul, F., and W. Pesendorfer. 2008. The case for mindless economics. In *The Foundations of Positive and Normative Economics: A Handbook* (ed. A. Caplin and A. Schotter). Oxford University Press.

Güth, W., and R. Tietz. 1990. Ultimatum bargaining behavior: a survey and comparison of experimental results. *Journal of Economic Psychology* 11:417-49.

Güth, W., R. Schmittberger, and B. Schwarze. 1982. An experimental analysis of ultimatum bargaining. *Journal of Economic Behavior and Organization* 3:367-88.

Güth, W., S. Huck, and W. Mueller. 2001. The relevance of equal splits in ultimatum games. *Games and Economic Behavior* 37:161-69.

Hagen, E. H., and P. Hammerstein. 2006. Game theory and human evolution: a critique of some recent interpretations of experimental games. *Theoretical Population Biology* 69:339-48.

Haltiwanger, J. C., and M. Waldman. 1984. Rational expectations and the limits of rationality: an analysis of heterogeneity. *American Economic Review* 75:326-40.

Hammond, P. J. 1998. Objective expected utility. In *Handbook of Utility Theory* (ed. S. Barbera, P. J. Hammond, and C. Seidl). Dordrecht: Kluwer.

Hands, D. W. 2001. *Reflection without Rules: Economic Methodology and Contemporary Science Theory*. Cambridge University Press.

Harbaugh, W. T., K. Krause, and T. R. Berry. 2001a. GARP for kids: on the development of rational choice behavior. *American Economic Review* 91:1539-45.

Harbaugh, W. T., K. Krause, and L. Vesterlund. 2001b. Are adults better behaved than children? Age, experience and the endowment effect. *Economics Letters* 70:175–81.

Harless, D. W., and C. F. Camerer. 1994. The predictive utility of generalized expected utility theories. *Econometrica* 62:1251–89.

Harré, R., and P. Secord. 1972. *The Explanation of Social Behaviour.* Oxford: Basil Blackwell.

Harrigan, J. 2003. Specialisation and the volume of trade: do the data obey the laws? In *The Handbook of International Trade* (ed. J. Harrigan and K. Choi). Oxford: Basil Blackwell.

Harrison, G. W. 1986. An experimental test for risk aversion. *Economics Letters* 21:7–11.

———. 1989. Theory and misbehavior of first price auctions. *American Economic Review* 79:749–63.

———. 1992. Theory and misbehavior of first price auctions: reply. *American Economic Review* 82:1426–43.

———. 1994. Expected utility theory and the experimentalists. *Empirical Economics* 19:223–53.

Harrison, G. W., and J. A. List. 2004. Field experiments. *Journal of Economic Literature* 62:1009–55.

———. 2008. Naturally occurring markets and exogenous laboratory experiments: a case study of the winner's curse. *Economic Journal* 118:822–43.

Harrison, G. W., E. Johnson, M. M. McInnes, and E. E. Rutström. 2005. Risk aversion and incentive effects: comment. *American Economic Review* 95: 897–901.

Harsanyi, J., and R. Selten. 1988. *A General Theory of Equilibrium Selection in Games.* Cambridge, MA: MIT Press.

Hartley, J. E., K. D. Hoover, and K. D. Salyer. 1997. The limits of business cycle research: assessing the real business cycle model. *Oxford Review of Economic Policy* 13:34–54.

Hausman, D. M. 1992. *The Inexact and Separate Science of Economics.* Cambridge University Press.

———. 2005. Testing game theory. *Journal of Economic Methodology* 12:211–23.

Hayek, F. A. 1945. The use of knowledge in society. *American Economic Review* 35:519–30.

Hennig-Schmidt, H., B. Rockenbach, and A. Sadrieh. 2005. In search of workers' real effort reciprocity—a field and a laboratory experiment. GESY Discussion Paper 55, University of Mannheim.

Henrich, J., R. Boyd, S. Bowles, C. F. Camerer, E. Fehr, H. Gintis, and R. McElreath. 2001. In search of homo economicus: behavioral experiments in 15 small-scale societies. *American Economic Review* (Papers and Proceedings) 91:73–78.

Hertwig, R., and A. Ortmann. 2001. Experimental practices in economics: a methodological challenge for psychologists. *Behavioral and Brain Sciences* 24: 383–403.

———. 2003. Economists' and psychologists' experimental practices: how they differ, why they differ, and how they could converge. In *The Psychology of Economic Decisions* (ed. I. Brocas and J. Carrillo), volume 1, pp. 253–72. Oxford University Press.

Hesse, M. B. 1970. Quine and a new empiricism. In *Knowledge and Necessity* (foreword by G. N. A. Vesey). Royal Institute of Philosophy Lectures, volume 3, pp. 191–209. London: Macmillan.

Hey, J. D. 1995. Experimental investigations of errors in decision making under risk. *European Economic Review* 39:633-40.

——. 1998. Experimental economics and deception: a comment. *Journal of Economic Psychology* 19:397-401.

——. 2001. Does repetition improve consistency? *Experimental Economics* 4: 5-54.

——. 2002. Experimental economics and the theory of decision making under risk and uncertainty. *Geneva Papers on Risk and Insurance Theory* 27:5-21.

——. 2005a. Why we should not be silent about noise. *Experimental Economics* 8:325-45.

——. 2005b. Do people (want to) plan? *Scottish Journal of Political Economy* 52: 122-38.

Hey, J. D., and J. A. Knoll. 2007. How far ahead do people plan? *Economic Letters* 96:8-13.

Hey, J. D., and J. Lee. 2005a. Do subjects separate (or are they sophisticated)? *Experimental Economics* 8:233-65.

——. 2005b. Do subjects remember the past? *Applied Economics* 37:9-18.

Hey, J. D., and C. Orme. 1994. Investigating generalizations of expected utility theory using experimental data. *Econometrica* 62:1291-326.

Ho, M. W. 1998. *Genetic Engineering: Dream or Nightmare?* Bath, U.K.: Gateway.

Hoffman, E., K. McCabe, K. Shachat, and V. L. Smith. 1994. Preferences, property rights, and anonymity in bargaining games. *Games and Economic Behavior* 7: 346-80.

Hoffman, E., K. McCabe, and V. L. Smith. 1996. Social distance and other-regarding behavior in dictator games. *American Economic Review* 86:653-60.

——. 2000. The impact of exchange context on the activation of equity in ultimatum games. *Experimental Economics* 3:5-9.

Hogarth, R. M. 2005. The challenge of representative design in economics and psychology. *Journal of Economic Methodology* 12:253-63.

Hollis, M. 1998. *Trust Within Reason.* Cambridge University Press.

Holt, C. A. 1985. An experimental test of the consistent conjectures hypothesis. *American Economic Review* 75:314-25.

——. 1986. Preference reversals and the independence axiom. *American Economic Review* 76:508-14.

——. 1995. Industrial organization: a survey of laboratory research. In *The Handbook of Experimental Economics* (ed. J. H. Kagel and A. E. Roth). Princeton University Press.

Holt, C. A., and S. K. Laury. 2002. Risk aversion and incentive effects. *American Economic Review* 92:1644-55.

——. 2005. Risk aversion and incentive effects: new data without order effects. *American Economic Review* 95:902-4.

Horowitz, J., and K. McConnell. 2003. Willingness to accept, willingness to pay and the income effect. *Journal of Economic Behavior and Organization* 51: 537-45.

Hrobjartsson, A., and P. C. Gotzsche. 2004. Is the placebo powerless? Update of a systematic review with 52 new randomized trials comparing placebo with no treatment. *Journal of International Medicine* 256:91-100.

Hume, D. 1739-40. *A Treatise of Human Nature,* books 1-3. London: John Noon and Thomas Longman. (See the 1978 Clarendon edition for page references.)

——. 1748. *An Enquiry Concerning Human Understanding.*

Humphrey, S. J. 2001. Non-transitive choice: event-splitting effects or framing effects? *Economica* 68:77-96.

——. 2006. Does learning diminish violations of independence, coalescing and monotonicity? *Theory and Decision* 61:93-128.

Innocenti, A. 2008. How can a psychologist inform economics? The strange case of Sidney Siegel. Working Paper 8, Department of Economic Policy, Finance and Development, University of Siena.

Isoni, A., G. Loomes, and R. Sugden. 2009. The willingness to pay-willingness to accept gap, the "endowment effect," subject misconceptions, and experimental procedures for eliciting valuations: replication and reassessment. Working Paper, University of East Anglia.

Jevons, W. S. 1870. On the natural laws of muscular exertion. *Nature* 2:158-60.

——. 1871. *The Theory of Political Economy*. London: Macmillan. (See 1970 Penguin edition for page references.)

Johnson, C., J. Engle-Warnick, and C. Eckel. 2007. Adaptively eliciting risk preferences through an incentive compatible mechanism. Working Paper, University of Arizona.

Johnson, J. G., and J. R. Busemeyer. 2001. Multi-stage decision making: the effect of planning horizon length on dynamic consistency. *Theory and Decision* 51:217-46.

Jones, S. R. G. 1992. Was there a Hawthorne effect? *American Journal of Sociology* 98:451-68.

Kaas, K. P., and H. Ruprecht. 2006. Are the Vickrey auction and the BDM mechanism really incentive compatible? Empirical results and optimal bidding strategies in cases of uncertain willingness-to-pay. *Schmalenback Business Review* 58:37-55.

Kachelmeier, S. J., and M. Shehata. 1992. Examining risk preferences under high monetary incentives: experimental evidence from the People's Republic of China. *American Economic Review* 82:1120-41.

Kagel, J. H., and D. Levin. 1986. The winner's curse and public information in common value auctions. *American Economic Review* 76:894-920.

Kagel, J. H., and A. E. Roth (eds). 1995. *The Handbook of Experimental Economics*. Princeton University Press.

Kagel, J. H., R. C. Battalio, H. Rachlin, and L. Green. 1981. Demand curves for animal consumers. *Quarterly Journal of Economics* 96:1-16.

Kahneman, D., and A. Tversky. 1979. Prospect theory: an analysis of decision under risk. *Econometrica* 47:263-91.

Kahneman, D., and A. Tversky (eds). 2000. *Choice, Values and Frames*. Cambridge University Press/Russell Sage Foundation.

Kahneman, D., J. L. Knetsch, and R. H. Thaler. 1986. Fairness and the assumptions of economics. *Journal of Business* 59:S285-300.

Karni, E., and Z. Safra. 1987. Preference reversals and the observability of preferences by experimental methods. *Econometrica* 55:675-85.

Keser, C., and R. Gardner. 1999. Strategic behavior of experienced subjects in a common pool resource game. *International Journal of Game Theory* 28:241-52.

Keser, C., and F. van Winden. 2000. Conditional cooperation and voluntary contributions to public goods. *Scandinavian Journal of Economics* 102:23-39.

Kienle, G. S., and H. K. Kiene. 1997. The powerful placebo effect: fact or fiction? *Journal of Clinical Epidemiology* 50:1311-18.

Kindleberger, C. P. 1996. *Manias, Panics and Crashes: A History of Financial Crises*, 3rd edn. Basingstoke, U.K.: Macmillan.

King, R. G., and S. T. Rebelo. 1999. Resuscitating real business cycles. In *Handbook of Macroeconomics* (ed. J. B. Taylor and M. Woodford), volume 1B. Elsevier.

Knetsch, J. L. 1989. The endowment effect and evidence of nonreversible indifference curves. *American Economic Review* 79:1277-84.

Knetsch, J. L., F.-F. Tang, and R. H. Thaler. 2001. The endowment effect and repeated market trials: is the Vickrey auction demand revealing? *Experimental Economics* 4:257-69.

Kube, S., M. A. Maréchal, and C. Puppe. 2007. Wages and working morale—positive versus negative reciprocity in the field. Working Paper, University of St. Gallen, Switzerland.

Kuhn, T. 1962. *The Structure of Scientific Revolutions*. University of Chicago Press.

——. 1970. Reflections on my critics. In *Criticism and the Growth of Knowledge* (ed. I. Lakatos and A. Musgrave), pp. 231-78. Cambridge University Press.

Kydland, F. E., and E. C. Prescott. 1982. Time to build and aggregate fluctuations. *Econometrica* 50:1345-69.

Laffont, J.-J. and D. Martimort. 2002. *The Theory of Incentives: the Principal-Agent Model*. Princeton University Press.

Lakatos, I. 1970. Falsification and the methodology of scientific research programmes. In *Criticism and the Growth of Knowledge* (ed. I. Lakatos and A. Musgrave). Cambridge University Press.

——. 1973. *Lectures on Scientific Method*. (Reprinted in 1999 in *For and Against Method* (ed. M. Motterlini). University of Chicago Press.)

——. 1978. The methodology of scientific research programmes. In *Philosophical Papers* (ed. J. Worrall and G. Currie), volume 1. Cambridge University Press.

Laury, S. K. 2006. Pay one or pay all: random selection of one choice for payment. Working Paper 2006-24, Georgia State University.

Lawson, T. 1997. *Economics and Reality*. London: Routledge.

Layard, P. R. G. 2005. *Happiness: Lessons from a New Science*. London: Penguin.

Ledyard, J. O. 1995. Public goods: a survey of experimental research. In *The Handbook of Experimental Economics* (ed. J. H. Kagel and A. E. Roth). Princeton University Press.

Lei, V., C. Noussair, and C. R. Plott. 2001. Non-speculative bubbles in experimental asset markets: lack of common knowledge of rationality vs actual irrationality. *Econometrica* 69:831-59.

Levitt, S. D., and J. A. List. 2007. What do laboratory experiments measuring social preferences tell us about the real world? *Journal of Economic Perspectives* 21:153-74.

Libby, R., and M. G. Lipe. 1992. Incentives, effort, and the cognitive processes involved in accounting-related judgements. *Journal of Accounting Research* 30:249-73.

Lichtenstein, S., and P. Slovic. 1971. Reversals of preference between bids and choices in gambling decisions. *Journal of Experimental Psychology* 89:46-55.

——. 1973. Response-induced reversals of preference in gambling: an extended replication in Las Vegas. *Journal of Experimental Psychology* 101:16-20.

——. 2006. The construction of preference: an overview. In *The Construction of Preference* (ed. S. Lichtenstein and P. Slovic). Cambridge University Press.

Lindman, H. 1971. Inconsistent preferences among gambles. *Journal of Experimental Psychology* 89:390–97.

Lipsey, R. G. 1979. *An Introduction to Positive Economics*, 5th edn. London: Weidenfeld and Nicolson.

List, J. A. 2002. The more is less phenomenon: preference reversals of a different kind. *American Economic Review* 92:1636–43.

——. 2003. Does market experience eliminate market anomalies? *Quarterly Journal of Economics* 118:41–73.

——. 2004. Neoclassical theory versus prospect theory: evidence from the marketplace. *Econometrica* 72:615–26.

——. 2006. Field experiments: a bridge between lab and naturally occurring data. *Advances in Economic Analysis & Policy* 6(2):article 8. (Available at http://www.bepress.com/bejeap/advances/vol6/iss2/art8.)

Loewenstein, G. 1999. Experimental economics from the vantage-point of behavioural economics. *Economic Journal* 109:F25–34.

Loewenstein, G. and D. Adler. 1995. A bias in the prediction of tastes. *Economic Journal* 105:929–37.

Loewenstein, G., T. O'Donoghue, and M. Rabin. 2003. Projection bias in predicting future utility. *Quarterly Journal of Economics* 118:1209–48.

Loomes, G. 2005. Modelling the stochastic component of behaviour in experiments: some issues for the interpretation of data. *Experimental Economics* 8: 301–23.

Loomes, G., and R. Sugden. 1982. Regret theory: an alternative theory of rational choice under uncertainty. *Economic Journal* 92:805–24.

——. 1983. A rationale for preference reversal. *American Economic Review* 73: 428–32.

——. 1986. Disappointment and dynamic consistency in choice under uncertainty. *Review of Economic Studies* 53:271–82.

——. 1987. Some implications of a more general form of regret theory. *Journal of Economic Theory* 41:270–87.

——. 1995. Incorporating a stochastic element into decision theories. *European Economic Review* 39:641–48.

——. 1998. Testing different stochastic specifications of risky choice. *Economica* 65:581–98.

Loomes, G., C. Starmer, and R. Sugden. 1989. Preference reversals: information processing or rational non-transitive choice? *Economic Journal* (Supplement) 99:14–51.

——. 1991. Observing violations of transitivity by experimental methods. *Econometrica* 59:425–39.

——. 1992. Are preferences monotonic? Testing some predictions of regret theory. *Economica* 59:17–33.

Loomes, G., P. G. Moffatt, and R. Sugden. 2002. A microeconometric test of alternative theories of risky choice. *Journal of Risk and Uncertainty* 24:103–30.

Loomes, G., C. Starmer, and R. Sugden. 2003. Do anomalies disappear in repeated markets? *Economic Journal* 113:C153–164.

Maas, H. 2005. Jevons, Mill and the private laboratory of the mind. *The Manchester School* 73:620–49.

Machina, M. J. 1982. "Expected utility" theory without the independence axiom. *Econometrica* 50:277–323.

Maffioletti, A., and M. Santoni. 2005. Do trade union leaders violate subjective expected utility? Some insights from experimental data. *Theory and Decision* 59:207-53.

Mäki, U. 1992. On the method of isolation in economics. *Poznań Studies in the Philosophy of Science and the Humanities* 26:316-51.

———. 2002. Some non-reasons for non-realism about economics. In *Fact and Fiction in Economics: Models, Realism, and Social Construction* (ed. U. Mäki). Cambridge University Press.

———. 2003. "The methodology of positive economics" does not give us *the* methodology of positive economics. *Journal of Economic Methodology* 10: 495-506.

———. 2005. Models are experiments, experiments are models. *Journal of Economic Methodology* 12:303-15.

Mandler, M. 2005. Incomplete preferences and rational intransitivity of choice. *Games and Economic Behavior* 50:255-77.

Mankiw, N. G. 2007. *Macroeconomics*, 6th edn. New York: Worth.

Marmot, M. 2004. *Status Syndrome: How Your Social Standing Directly Affects Your Health and Life Expectancy*. London: Bloomsbury.

Mayo, D. G. 1991. Novel evidence and severe tests. *Philosophy of Science* 58: 523-52.

———. 1996. *Error and the Growth of Experimental Knowledge*. University of Chicago Press.

McCloskey, D. N. 1983. The rhetoric of economics. *Journal of Economic Literature* 21:481-517.

McDaniel, T., and C. Starmer. 1998. Experimental economics and deception: a comment. *Journal of Economic Psychology* 19:403-9.

McKelvey, R., and T. Palfrey. 1995. Quantal response equilibria for normal form games. *Games and Economic Behavior* 10:6-38.

———. 1998. Quantal response equilibria for extensive form games. *Experimental Economics* 1:9-41.

McKelvey, R., T. Palfrey, and R. Weber. 2000. The effects of payoff magnitude and heterogeneity on behavior in 2×2 games with unique mixed strategy equilibria. *Journal of Economic Behavior and Organization* 42:523-48.

McNeil, B. J., S. G. Pauker, H. C. Sox, and A. Tversky. 1982. On the elicitation of preferences for alternative treatments. *New England Journal of Medicine* 306: 1259-62.

Mehta, J., C. Starmer, and R. Sugden. 1994. The nature of salience: an experimental investigation. *American Economic Review* 84:658-73.

Mill, J. S. 1843. *A System of Logic*. (See the 1967 Longman edition for page references.)

Mitzkewitz, M., and R. Nagel. 1993. Experimental results on ultimatum games with incomplete information. *International Journal of Game Theory* 22:171-98.

Moffatt, P. G. 2005. Stochastic choice and the allocation of cognitive effort. *Experimental Economics* 8:369-88.

———. 2007. Models of decision and choice. In *Measurement in Economics: A Handbook* (ed. M. Boumans). Elsevier.

Morgan, J., H. Orzen, and M. Sefton. 2006. An experimental study of price dispersion. *Games and Economic Behavior* 54:134-58.

Morgan, M. S. 1990. *The History of Econometric Ideas.* Cambridge University Press.

———. 2005. Experiments versus models: new phenomena, inference and surprise. *Journal of Economic Methodology* 12:317–29.

Morgan, M. S., and M. M. Morrison. 1999. *Models as Mediators.* Cambridge University Press.

Mosteller, F., and P. Nogee. 1951. An experimental measure of utility. *Journal of Political Economy* 59:371–404.

Mueller, D. 2003. *Public Choice,* volume 3. Cambridge University Press.

Muller, L., M. Sefton, R. Steinberg, and L. Vesterlund. 2008. Strategic behavior and learning in repeated voluntary-contribution experiments. *Journal of Economic Behavior and Organization* 67:782–93.

Myagkov, M. and C. R. Plott. 1997. Exchange economies and loss exposure: experiments exploring prospect theory and competitive equilibria in market environments. *American Economic Review* 87:801–28.

Neurath, O. 1937. Unified science and its encyclopaedia. *Philosophy of Science* 4: 265–77.

Noussair, C. N., C. R. Plott, and R. G. Riezman. 1995. An experimental investigation of the patterns of international trade. *American Economic Review* 85: 462–91.

———. 1997. The principles of exchange rate determination in an international finance experiment. *Journal of Political Economy* 105:822–61.

Noussair, C. N., S. Robin, and B. Ruffieux. 2004. Revealing consumers' willingness-to-pay: a comparison of the BDM mechanism and the Vickrey auction. *Journal of Economic Psychology* 25:725–41.

Nozick, R. 1981. *Philosophical Explanations.* Oxford: Clarendon Press.

Ochs, J. 1995. Games with unique mixed strategy equilibria: an experimental study. *Games and Economic Behavior* 10:202–17.

Oosterbeek, H., R. Sloof, and G. van de Kuilen. 2004. Cultural differences in ultimatum game experiments: evidence from a meta-analysis. *Experimental Economics* 7:171–88.

Orbell, J., R. Dawes, and A. Van de Kragt. 1988. Explaining discussion-induced cooperation. *Journal of Personality and Social Psychology* 54:811–19.

Orne, M. T. 1962. On the social psychology of the psychological experiment: with particular reference to demand characteristics and their implications. *American Psychologist* 17:776–83. (Reprinted in 2002 in *Prevention and Treatment,* volume 5, article 35.)

———. 1973. Communication by the total experimental situation. In *Communication and Affect* (ed. P. Pliner, L. Krames, and T. Alloway), 2nd edn, pp. 157–91. London: Academic Press.

Osborne, M. J., and A. Rubinstein. 1994. *A Course in Game Theory.* Cambridge, MA: MIT Press.

Oswald, A. J. 1997. Happiness and economic performance. *Economic Journal* 107:1815–31.

Oxoby, R. J., and K. N. McLeish. 2004. Sequential decision and strategy vector methods in ultimatum bargaining: evidence on the strength of other-regarding behavior. *Economics Letters* 84:399–405.

Pareto, V. 1906. *Manuale d'economia politica con una introduzione alla scienza sociale.* (For an English translation see the Kelley 1971 *Manual of Political Economy.*)

Park, E.-S. 2000. Warm-glow versus cold-prickle: a further experimental study of framing effects on free-riding. *Journal of Economic Behavior and Organization* 43:405–21.

Pawson, R., and N. Tilley. 1997. *Realistic Evaluation*. London: Sage.

Payne, J. W., J. R. Bettman, and E. J. Johnson. 1993. *The Adaptive Decision Maker*. Cambridge University Press.

Payne, J. W., J. R. Bettman, and D. A. Schkade. 1999. Measuring constructed preferences: towards a building code. *Journal of Risk and Uncertainty* 19: 243–70.

Plosser, C. I. 1989. Understanding real business cycles. *Journal of Economic Perspectives* 3:51–78.

Plott, C. R. 1982. Industrial organisation theory and experimental economics. *Journal of Economic Literature* 20:1485–527.

——. 1991. Will economics become an experimental science? *Southern Economic Journal* 57:901–19.

——. 1996. Rational individual behaviour in markets and social choice processes: the discovered preference hypothesis. In *The Rational Foundations of Economic Behaviour* (ed. K. J. Arrow, E. Colombatto, M. Perlman, and C. Schmidt). Basingstoke, U.K.: Macmillan.

——. 1997. Laboratory experimental testbeds: application to the PCS auction. *Journal of Economics and Management Strategy* 6:605–38.

Plott, C. R., and K. Zeiler. 2005. The willingness to pay–willingness to accept gap, the "endowment effect," subject misconceptions and experimental procedures for eliciting valuations. *American Economic Review* 95:530–45.

Pommerehne, W., F. Schneider, and P. Zweifel. 1982. Economic theory of choice and the preference reversal phenomenon: a re-examination. *American Economic Review* 73:569–74.

Popper, K. 1934. *Logik der Forschung*. (See Hutchinson & Co.'s *The Logic of Scientific Discovery* (1959) for Popper's own translation of his 1934 German text.)

——. 1963. *Conjectures and Refutations: The Growth of Scientific Knowledge*. London: Routledge & Kegan Paul.

Post, T., M. J. van den Assem, G. Baltussen, and R. H. Thaler. 2008. Deal or no deal? Decision making under risk in a large-payoff game show. *American Economic Review* 98:38–71.

Quiggin, J. 1982. A theory of anticipated utility. *Journal of Economic Behavior and Organization* 3:323–43.

Quine, W. V. O. 1951. Two dogmas of empiricism. *Philosophical Review* 60:20–43.

——. 1953. *From a Logical Point of View*. New York: Harper and Rowe.

Rabin, M. 1993. Incorporating fairness into game theory and economics. *American Economic Review* 83:1281–302.

Read, D. 2005. Monetary incentives, what are they good for? *Journal of Economic Methodology* 12:265–76.

Reilly, R. J. 1982. Preference reversal: further evidence and some suggested modifications in experimental design. *American Economic Review* 73:576–84.

Robbins, L. 1935. *An Essay on the Nature and Significance of Economic Science*, 2nd edn. London: Macmillan.

Rosenthal, R. 1966. *Experimenter Effects in Behavioral Research*. New York: Appleton-Century-Crofts.

Roth, A. E. 1995a. Introduction to experimental economics. In *The Handbook of Experimental Economics* (ed. J. H. Kagel and A. E. Roth), pp. 3–109. Princeton University Press.

——. 1995b. Bargaining experiments. In *The Handbook of Experimental Economics* (ed. J. H. Kagel and A. E. Roth). Princeton University Press.

Rubinstein, A. 2001. A theorist's view of experiments. *European Economic Review* 45:615–28.

——. 2007. Instinctive and cognitive reasoning: a study of response times. *Economic Journal* 117:1243–59.

Rustichini, A. 2005. Neuroeconomics: present and future. *Games and Economic Behavior* 52:201–12.

Ryan, R. M., and E. L. Deci. 2000. Self-determination theory and the facilitation of intrinsic motivation, social development and well-being. *American Psychologist* 55:68–78.

Rydval, O., and A. Ortmann. 2004. How financial incentives and cognitive abilities affect task performance in laboratory settings: an illustration. *Economics Letters* 85:315–20.

Samuelson, L. 1997. *Evolutionary Games and Equilibrium Selection.* Cambridge, MA: MIT Press.

——. 2002. Evolution and game theory. *Journal of Economic Perspectives* 16: 47–66.

——. 2005. Economic theory and experimental economics. *Journal of Economic Literature* 43:65–107.

Sauermann, H., and R. Selten. 1959. Ein Oligopolexperiment. *Zeitschrift für die Gesamte Staatswissenschaft* 115:427–71.

Schelling, T. C. 1960. *The Strategy of Conflict.* Cambridge, MA: Harvard University Press.

Schram, A. 2005. Artificiality: the tension between internal and external validity in economics experiments. *Journal of Economic Methodology* 12:225–38.

Searle, J. R. 1995. *The Construction of Social Reality.* London: Allen Lane.

Seidl, C. 2002. Preference reversal. *Journal of Economic Surveys* 6:621–55.

Selten, R. 1967. Die Strategiemethode zur Erforschung des eigeschrankt rationalen Verhaltens im Rahmen eines Oligopolexperiments. In *Beitrage zur Experimentellen Wirtschaftsforschung* (ed. H. Sauermann), pp. 136–68. Tubingen: J. C. B. Mohr.

Selten, R., M. Mitzkewitz, and G. Uhlich. 1997. Duopoly strategies programmed by experienced players. *Econometrica* 65:517–55.

Selten, R., A. Sadrieh, and K. Abbink. 1999. Money does not induce risk neutral behavior, but binary lotteries do even worse. *Theory and Decision* 46:211–49.

Selten, R., T. Chmura, T. Pitz, S. Kube, and M. Schreckenberg. 2007. Commuters route choice behavior. *Games and Economic Behavior* 58:394–406

Siakantaris, N. 2000. Experimental economics under the microscope. *Cambridge Journal of Economics* 24:267–81.

Siegel, S., and L. Fouraker. 1960. *Bargaining and Group Decision Making: Experiments in Bilateral Monopoly.* New York: McGraw-Hill.

Slovic, P. 1975. Choice between equally-valued alternatives. *Journal of Experimental Psychology: Human Perception and Performance* 1:280–87.

——. 1995. The construction of preference. *American Psychologist* 50:364–71.

Slovic, P., and S. Lichtenstein. 1968. Relative importance of probabilities and payoffs in risk taking. *Journal of Experimental Psychology: Monograph Supplement* 78:1–18.

Slovic, P., D. Griffin, and A. Tversky. 1990. Compatibility effects in judgment and choice. In *Insights in Decision-Making* (ed. R. M. Hogarth), pp. 5–27. University of Chicago Press.

Smith, V. L. 1962. An experimental study of competitive market behavior. *Journal of Political Economy* 70:111–37.

———. 1976. Experimental economics: induced value theory. *American Economic Review* 66:274–79.

———. 1982a. Microeconomic systems as an experimental science. *American Economic Review* 72:923–55.

———. 1982b. Markets as economizers of information: experimental examination of the "Hayek hypothesis." *Economic Inquiry* 20:165–79.

———. 1994. Economics in the laboratory. *Journal of Economic Perspectives* 8: 113–33.

———. 2002. Method in experiment: rhetoric and reality. *Experimental Economics* 5:91–110.

———. 2008. *Rationality in Economics: Constructivist and Ecological Forms.* Cambridge University Press.

Smith, V. L., and J. M. Walker. 1993. Rewards, experience and decision costs in first price auctions. *Economic Inquiry* 31:237–44.

Smith, V. L., G. Suchanek, and A. Williams. 1988. Bubbles, crashes and endogenous expectations in experimental spot asset markets. *Econometrica* 56: 119–51.

Søberg, M. 2005. The Duhem-Quine thesis and experimental economics. *Journal of Economic Methodology* 12:581–97.

Solnick, S. J. 2007. Cash and alternate methods of accounting in an experimental game. *Journal of Economic Behavior and Organization* 62:316–21.

Sopher, B., and G. Gigliotti. 1993. Intransitive cycles: rational choice or random error? An answer based on estimation of error rates with experimental data. *Theory and Decision* 35:311–36.

Stadler, G. W. 1994. Real business cycles. *Journal of Economic Literature* 32: 1750–83.

Stahl, D., and P. Wilson. 1995. On players' models of other players: theory and experimental evidence. *Games and Economic Behavior* 10:218–54.

Starmer, C. 1992. Testing new theories of choice under uncertainty using the common consequence effect. *Review of Economic Studies* 59:813–30.

———. 1999a. Experiments in economics: should we trust the dismal scientists in white coats? *Journal of Economic Methodology* 6:1–30.

———. 1999b. Experimental economics: hard science or wasteful tinkering? *Economic Journal* 109:F5–15.

———. 1999c. Cycling with rules of thumb: an experimental test for a new form of non-transitive behaviour. *Theory and Decision* 46:141–58.

———. 2000. Developments in non-expected utility theory: the hunt for a descriptive theory of choice under risk. *Journal of Economic Literature* 38:332–82.

Starmer, C., and R. Sugden. 1989. Violations of the independence axiom in common ratio problems: an experimental test of some competing hypotheses. *Annals of Operations Research* 19:79–102.

———. 1991. Does the random-lottery system elicit true preferences? *American Economic Review* 81:971–78.

———. 1998. Testing alternative explanations of cyclical choices. *Economica* 65: 347–61.

Stock, J. H. 1988. A re-examination of Friedman's consumption function puzzle. *Journal of Business and Economic Statistics* 6:401–7.

Stott, H. 2006. Cumulative prospect theory's functional menagerie. *Journal of Risk and Uncertainty* 32:101–30.

Sugden, R. 1982. On the economics of philanthropy. *Economic Journal* 92:341–50.

——. 1984. Reciprocity: the supply of public goods through voluntary contributions. *Economic Journal* 94:772–87.

——. 1986. *The Economics of Rights, Cooperation and Welfare.* Oxford: Basil Blackwell. (Second edition published in 2004 by Palgrave Macmillan.)

——. 1991. Rational choice: a survey of contributions from economics and philosophy. *Economic Journal* 101:751–85.

——. 1999. Alternatives to the neoclassical theory of choice. In *Valuing Environmental Preferences: Theory and Practice of the Contingent Valuation Method in the US, EC and Developing Countries* (ed. I. Bateman and K. Willis), pp. 152–80. Oxford University Press.

——. 2000. Credible worlds: the status of theoretical models in economics. *Journal of Economic Methodology* 7:1–31.

——. 2003. Reference-dependent subjective expected utility. *Journal of Economic Theory* 111:172–91.

——. 2004a. The opportunity criterion: consumer sovereignty without the assumption of coherent preferences. *American Economic Review* 94:1014–33.

——. 2004b. Alternatives to expected utility: foundations. In *Handbook of Utility Theory. Volume 2: Extensions* (ed. S. Barbera, P. J. Hammond, and C. Seidl), pp. 685–755. Dordrecht: Kluwer.

——. 2005. Experiments as models and experiments as tests. *Journal of Economic Methodology* 12:291–302.

——. 2006. Hume's non-instrumental and non-propositional decision theory. *Economics and Philosophy* 22:365–92.

——. 2008. The changing relationship between theory and experiment in economics. *Philosophy of Science* 75:621–32.

——. Forthcoming. Neither self-interest nor self-sacrifice: the fraternal morality of market relationships. In *Games, Groups and the Global Good* (ed. S. Levin). Springer.

Sugden, R. and I. Zamarrón. 2006. Finding the key: the riddle of focal points. *Journal of Economic Psychology* 27:609–21.

Taylor, C. 1971. Interpretation and the sciences of man. *Review of Metaphysics* 25:3–51.

Taylor, M. P. 2003. Purchasing power parity. *Review of International Economics* 11:436–52.

Thaler, R. H. 1988. Anomalies: the ultimatum game. *Journal of Economic Perspectives* 2:195–206.

Thaler, R. H., and E. Johnson. 1990. Gambling with the house money and trying to break even: the effect of prior outcomes on risky choice. *Management Science* 36:643–60.

Thurstone, L. 1931. The indifference function. *Journal of Social Psychology* 2:139–67.

Tirole, J. 1988. *The Theory of Industrial Organization.* Cambridge, MA: MIT Press.

Titmuss, R. M. 1970. *The Gift Relationship.* London: Allen & Unwin.

Torgler, B. 2002. Speaking to theorists and searching for facts: tax morale and tax compliance in experiments. *Journal of Economic Surveys* 16:657–58.

Tversky, A. 1969. Intransitivity of preferences. *Psychological Review* 76:31–48.

Tversky, A., and D. Kahneman. 1981. The framing of decisions and psychology of choice. *Science* 211:453–58.

——. 1986. Rational choice and the framing of decisions. *Journal of Business* 59: S251–78.

——. 1991. Loss aversion in riskless choice: a reference-dependent model. *Quarterly Journal of Economics* 106:1039–61.

——. 1992. Advances in prospect theory: cumulative representation of uncertainty. *Journal of Risk and Uncertainty* 5:297–323.

Tversky, A., S. Sattath, and P. Slovic. 1988. Contingent weighting in judgment and choice. *Psychological Review* 95:371–84.

Tversky, A., P. Slovic, and D. Kahneman. 1990. The causes of preference reversal. *American Economic Review* 80:204–17.

van de Kuilen, G. and P. P. Wakker. 2006. Learning in the Allais paradox. *Journal of Risk and Uncertainty* 33:155–64.

van Dijk, F., J. Sonnemans, and F. van Winden. 2002. Social ties in a public good experiment. *Journal of Public Economics* 85:275–99.

Varian, H. R. 1980. A model of sales. *American Economic Review* 70:651–59.

Vickrey, W. 1961. Counter speculation, auctions and competitive sealed tenders. *Journal of Finance* 16:8–37.

Wager, T. D., J. K. Rilling, E. E. Smith, A. Sokolik, K. L. Casey, R. J. Davidson, S. M. Kosslyn, R. M. Rose, and J. D. Cohen. 2004. Placebo-induced changes in FMRI in the anticipation and experience of pain. *Science* 303:1162–67.

Wallis, W. A., and M. Friedman. 1942. The empirical derivation of indifference functions. In *Studies in Mathematical Economics and Econometrics in Memory of Henry Schultz* (ed. O. Lange, F. McIntyre, and T. O. Yntema), pp. 175–89. University of Chicago Press.

Webley, P., A. Lewis, and C. Mackenzie. 2001. Commitment among ethical investors: an experimental approach. *Journal of Economic Psychology* 22(1): 27–42.

Weibull, J. 2004, Testing game theory. In *Advances in Understanding Strategic Behavior* (ed. S. Huck). New York: Palgrave.

Wilcox, N. T. 1993. Lottery choice: incentives, complexity, and decision time. *Economic Journal* 103:1397–417.

——. 1994. On a lottery pricing anomaly: time tells the tale. *Journal of Risk and Uncertainty* 7:311–24.

——. 2008. Stochastic models for binary discrete choice under risk: a critical primer and econometric comparison. In *Research in Experimental Economics. Volume 12: Risk Aversion in Experiments* (ed. J. C. Cox and G. W. Harrison). Greenwich, CT: JAI Press.

Wilde, L. 1980. On the use of laboratory experiments in economics. In *The Philosophy of Economics* (ed. J. Pitt). Dordrecht: Reidel.

Wittgenstein, L. 1953. *Philosophical Investigations.* Oxford: Blackwell.

Zahar, E. 1983. The Popper–Lakatos controversy in the light of "Die beiden Grundprobleme der Erkenntnistheorie." *British Journal for the Philosophy of Science* 34:149–71.

Index